Taxation of Husband and Wife
The New Rules

Taxation of Husband and Wife
The New Rules

Philip Wylie LLB, FCA
Senior Lecturer in Law at Cardiff Law School

Butterworths
London, Dublin, Edinburgh
1990

United Kingdom	Butterworth & Co (Publishers) Ltd, 88 Kingsway, LONDON WC2B 6AB and 4 Hill Street, EDINBURGH EH2 3JZ
Australia	Butterworths Pty Ltd, SYDNEY, MELBOURNE, BRISBANE, ADELAIDE, PERTH, CANBERRA and HOBART
Canada	Butterworths Canada Ltd, TORONTO and VANCOUVER
Ireland	Butterworth (Ireland) Ltd, DUBLIN
Malaysia	Malayan Law Journal Sdn Bhd, KUALA LUMPUR
New Zealand	Butterworths of New Zealand Ltd, WELLINGTON and AUCKLAND
Puerto Rico	Equity de Puerto Rico, Inc, HATO REY
Singapore	Malayan Law Journal Pte Ltd, SINGAPORE
USA	Butterworth Legal Publishers, AUSTIN, Texas; BOSTON, Massachusetts; CLEARWATER, Florida (D & S Publishers); ORFORD, New Hampshire (Equity Publishing); ST PAUL, Minnesota; and SEATTLE, Washington

A CIP Catalogue record for this book is available from the British Library.

ISBN 0 406 51090 3

Typeset by Kerrypress, Luton
Printed and bound by Billings & Sons, Worcester

Preface

Recent years have seen major changes in the tax treatment of husband and wife. The main change has been the introduction of independent taxation for both income tax and capital gains tax, but there has also been fundamental reform of the tax implications of marriage breakdown and of the tax implications of cohabitation, in particular the restriction of claims for mortgage interest relief and the additional personal allowance. The introduction of the community charge, or poll tax, is the most recent tax change to affect spouses and cohabitees. This book attempts to cover in detail all these changes, and also to deal with the tax planning problems and opportunities involved in the transfer of income from parents to children. The book developed out of *Butterworths Taxation of the Family* (1983) but the changes in the law since 1983 have been so great that much of this book is completely new. Chapters 7 and 8 concentrate on the tax implications of marriage breakdown and make use of material originally contained in the Institute of Chartered Accountants Tax Digest No 64, 'Taxation on Divorce and Separation'.

The tax law discussed is that in force for 1990-91, and statutory references are to the original legislation as subsequently amended. The text of the current legislation can be obtained from *Butterworths Yellow* and *Orange Tax Handbooks 1990-91*. The table of cases contains a full list of citations of cases dealt with in the text, which may be of help in tracing a case report if the citation used in the text is not readily available. The Revenue have published a very useful booklet on independent taxation aimed at tax practitioners, 'Independent Taxation—A guide for Tax Practitioners', IR 83. It is available free of charge, but only from Inland Revenue, Room 529, New Wing, Somerset House, Strand, London WC2R 1LB.

My thanks are due to Butterworths editorial staff for their help and efficiency in transforming the manuscript to printed page, and to the indexer.

I have endeavoured to state the law as at 31 July 1990.

O P Wylie
Cardiff
August 1990

Contents

Chapter 8   Marriage breakdown — the matrimonial home and other capital provision

Chapter 9   The poll tax, foreign aspects, and future developments

Table of statutes

References in this Table to *Statutes* are to Halsbury's Statutes of England (Fourth Edition) showing the volume and page at which the annotated text of the Act may be found.

Table of cases

CHAPTER 1

Independent taxation of spouses' incomes — principles, personal allowances and administration

1.1 The background to independent taxation

Income tax was first introduced in Great Britain in 1799 and, from its inception, a married woman's income was reported as, and taxed as, the income of her husband. The Income Tax Act of 1806 directed that the profits of any married woman living with her husband 'shall be deemed to be the profits of the husband', which differs little from the codification of the rule in ICTA 1988 s 279:

> 'Subject to the provisions of this Chapter, a woman's income chargeable to income tax shall, so far as it is income for—
>
> (a)   a year of assessment; or
> (b)   any part of a year of assessment, being a part beginning with 6th April,
>
> during which she is a married woman living with her husband, be deemed for income tax purposes to be his income and not to be her income.'

The changes made between 1799 and 1989 to the principle of aggregation are conveniently summarised in Appendix 2 of the Government's Green Paper 'The Taxation of Husband and Wife'[1] published in December 1980. The more important landmarks were:

1914   The introduction of an election for separate assessment. Under this election, which could be made by either spouse, each spouse was able to file a tax return reporting their own income, and each spouse was liable to pay the tax due on their own income. But an election for separate assessment had no effect on the aggregate tax liability of the spouses. Their incomes were added together, tax due on their joint income was computed as if the joint income was the husband's, and the tax liability was then apportioned between the spouses roughly in the ratio of their incomes. A separate assessment computation was complicated, and in practice the election did not prove particularly popular with either taxpayers or the Revenue.

1918   An increased personal allowance for married men was introduced. A man who was married to, and living with, his wife qualified for a higher personal allowance than if he was single. For 1989-90, the last year of aggregate taxation, the married man's allowance was £4,375, whereas the single allowance was £2,785.

1942   Wife's earned income relief, which had existed in a limited form prior to this date, was increased to the level of the single person's

1   Cmnd 8093.

allowance. Wife's earned income relief was an allowance given to the husband, but was only deductible from his wife's earnings taxable as his income. Thus, by 1989-90, a married man whose wife had earned income was effectively entitled to two and a half personal allowances.

1971   An election for separate taxation of wife's earnings was introduced. Under this election, which had to be made jointly by the spouses, a wife's earned income was disaggregated from her husband's and taxed as if she was a single person. Her unearned income remained aggregated with her husband's. However the penalty for making the election was that the husband lost the married man's allowance, receiving the single person's allowance in its place. He also lost the wife's earned income relief, but that was compensated for by giving the wife a single person's allowance of equivalent value. For an election for separate taxation of wife's earnings to be beneficial, the saving in higher rate tax resulting from the disaggregation of the wife's earned income had to more than offset the increased tax liability resulting from a loss of personal allowances of the difference between the married and single allowances. Thus by 1989-90 the spouses had to have a minimum joint income of £30,511, of which the wife's earned income had to be at least £7,026, before the election would be beneficial.

A tax system devised in an era when married women in taxpaying families normally did not work and married men were responsible for the financial running of the family became increasingly unacceptable as more and more married women joined the labour force. Many married women resented the fact that their husbands were responsible for their tax affairs, and particularly resented the lack of privacy that the existing system produced. Pressure for reform of the system built up and, in December 1980, the Government published a Green Paper, 'The Taxation of Husband and Wife', outlining possible options for reform. The Green Paper identified the major issue for decision[1]:

> 'The fundamental question underlying any option for structural change in the taxation of the family is the choice of the unit of taxation. There are in principle three basic approaches. The first is to treat the family (husband, wife, children, perhaps also other dependants) as the unit. The second approach takes the married couple (husband and wife) as the tax unit. The third is to look at each person as a separate individual regardless of whether they are single or married.'

In reaching a decision on this issue the Government had available a number of reports on tax structures in developed western economies. In 1966 the Canadian Royal Commission on Taxation, the Carter Commission, recommended in favour of a comprehensive income tax, and further recommended that there should be two tax units, the family and single persons. The family should be treated as consisting of husband, wife, and dependent children, with the children's income being aggregated with their parents' income. There would then be separate tax rate bands for single people and families, but cohabitees would have the right to elect to be

1   Cmnd 8093 para 56.

taxed as if they were a married couple[1]. In making their recommendations the Commission commented[2]:

> 'Taxation of the individual in almost total disregard for his inevitably close financial and economic ties with other members of the basic social unit of which he is ordinarily a member, the family, is in our view another striking instance of the lack of a comprehensive and rational pattern in the present tax system .... We firmly believe that the family is to-day, as it has been for many centuries, the basic economic unit in society.'

However the Commission also recommended that the spouses should be free to file separate returns, in which case they would be taxed under the family unit rate schedule in a way which would normally involve a higher aggregate liability than if a joint return had been filed, with the income of minor children being aggregated with the income of either parent.

This reasoning and recommendation was accepted and followed in the 'First Report of the Irish Commission on Taxation', the O'Brien Commission, issued in July 1982. In contrast, the Australian Tax Review Committee, the Asprey Committee, reporting in 1975, took the opposite view[3]:

> ' ... the adoption of a compulsory family unit basis must be rejected on the grounds of general social principle. The right to be taxed as an individual has always been accorded in Australia. At a time when women are playing an ever greater role in the economic and other affairs of society, the withdrawal of this right would certainly be regarded as a retrograde step. And objections would come not only from women: men too might take exception to a universal and compulsory commingling of their tax affairs with those of their wives.'

It seemed clear from the views expressed in the Green Paper that the Government had virtually precluded a family basis of taxation and would opt for the individual as the unit of taxation, and so it eventually proved. Once this initial decision of principle was taken, certain subsidiary matters had to be decided. In particular, should there be independent taxation of both the earned and investment income of husband and wife, or should the unearned income of spouses continue to be aggregated? If each spouse were to receive only the single person's allowance, how should the extra tax revenue resulting from the abolition of the married man's allowance be reallocated? If one spouse had unused personal allowances, should the unused allowance be transferable to the other spouse? And should special arrangements remain for elderly taxpayers?

The Government allowed an unusually long gestation period for consideration of comments on the Green Paper, from 1981 to 1988, but in his March 1988 Budget Chancellor Nigel Lawson announced[4]:

> 'The time has come to take action. I therefore propose a major reform of personal taxation, with two objectives: first, to give married women the same privacy and independence in their tax affairs as everyone else; and, second, to bring to an end the ways in which the tax system can penalise marriage. I have decided to introduce, at the earliest practicable date, April 1990, a

1   Vol 3 p 142.
2   Vol 3 pp 122-123.
3   P 134, quotation taken from p 229 of the Irish report.
4   129 HC Official Report (6th series), cols 997-998, 15th March 1988.

completely new system of independent taxation. Under this new system, a husband and wife will be taxed independently, on income of all kinds. All taxpayers, male or female, married or single, will be entitled to the same personal allowance, which will be available against all income, whether from earnings, pensions or savings.'

The detailed legislation was published in the Finance Bill 1988, which subsequently became the Finance Act 1988, but the new provisions only took effect from 6th April 1990. It became clear from the legislation that, apart from choosing the individual as the unit of taxation, the Government had opted for two basic principles. First, independent taxation should operate with non-transferable personal allowances; and, second, there should be no losers as a result of the change from aggregate taxation to independent taxation. One consequence of this latter decision is that the married man's allowance has been retained in another guise, the married couple's allowance, equal to the difference between the married and single personal allowance. Further, the married couple's allowance can only be deducted from the husband's income and may not be deducted from the wife's income unless the husband has insufficient income to exhaust it, in which case the unused balance is transferable. Again, for a limited period a husband's but not a wife's, unused personal allowance may be transferred to the other spouse, and the special arrangements for elderly taxpayers continue to exist. The change to independent taxation has therefore not resulted in a married couple being equated for all tax purposes with two single people, and has produced its own anomalies. These anomalies are further discussed in chapter 9, which considers possible future developments in the taxation of the family. The intervening chapters concentrate on the nuts and bolts of the new system.

1.2 The fundamentals of the independent taxation of income

As from 1990-91 husband and wife are taxed as independent taxpayers on their separate incomes[1]. The election for separate assessment and separate taxation of wife's earnings are superfluous and are repealed[2]. A married couple who were previously entitled to a married man's allowance and a wife's earned income allowance are now entitled to two personal allowances and a married couple's allowance equivalent to the difference between the old married and single personal allowances. It might therefore appear that the change of system will make no overall difference to the tax liability of the couple. Where, prior to the change, the combined income of both spouses was not liable to higher rate tax and the wife had earned income in excess of the wife's earned income allowance, this will indeed be the case. But this is to ignore a fundamental effect of the change to independent taxation, which is that each spouse now has a basic rate tax band of £20,700 whereas previously, with a limited exception if a separate taxation of wife's earnings election had been made, the couple only had a single £20,700 basic rate band between them.

If, under the aggregation system, the couple were liable to higher rate

1   FA 1988 s 32.
2   FA 1988 Sch 14 Part VIII.

tax and the wife had taxable income which was wholly unearned, the new system will result in a reduction in the couple's overall tax burden, because the wife's income is now removed from the top part of her husband's income, she has a personal allowance to set against it which did not exist previously, and she has her own basic rate band of £20,700. There will therefore be a 40p saving for every pound of the wife's income up to her personal allowance of £3,005, and a further 15p saving for every pound of the wife's income up to the next £20,700 of her taxable income.

Example

For 1990-91 a married couple have combined incomes of £40,000, of which £30,000 is the husband's and £10,000 is unearned income of the wife. If independent taxation had not been introduced their tax liability would have been:

		£	£
	Husband's income		30,000.00
	Wife's income		10,000.00
	Total income		40,000.00
Less	Married man's allowance (£3,005 + £1,720)		(4,725.00)
	Taxable income		35,275.00
	Tax payable		
	£20,700.00 @ 25%		5,175.00
	14,575.00 @ 40%		5,830.00
	£35,275.00		11,005.00

Under independent taxation their liability is:

Husband

	Income		30,000.00
Less	Personal allowance	3,005.00	
	Married couple's allowance	1,720.00	(4,725.00)
	Taxable income		25,275.00
	Tax payable		
	£20,700.00 @ 25%		5,175.00
	4,575.00 @ 40%		1,830.00
	£25,275.00		7,005.00

Wife

	Income	10,000.00
Less	Personal allowance	(3,005.00)
	Taxable income	6,995.00
	Tax on £6,995.00 @ 25%	1,748.75

Combined tax liability

Husband	7,005.00
Wife	1,748.75
	8,753.75

6   Independent taxation of spouses' incomes

The change from a system of aggregate taxation of spouses' income to a system of independent taxation has therefore resulted in a tax saving of £2,251.25 (£11,005.00 — £8,753.75). An alternative explanation of the saving is the reduction of tax on the wife's income that has resulted from the change, ie

£ 3,005 @ 40%	1,202.00
6,995 @ 15% (40% — 25%)	1,049.25
£10,000	2,251.25

If, in the above example, the wife's income had been earned income, so that it would have been advantageous for the spouses to elect for separate taxation of wife's earnings, the new system of independent taxation will still result in a tax saving, although the saving will be less. This is because an election for separate taxation of wife's earnings caused a husband to lose the married man's allowance and receive only a single person's allowance. Under independent taxation the husband is always entitled to married couple's allowance, so this loss of allowances no longer occurs. The tax saving that results can be demonstrated by computing the tax liability of the couple in the above example assuming that aggregation of income remained in force for 1990-91, but that the wife's £10,000 was earned income and that an election for separate taxation had been made.

Husband		£
	Income	30,000.00
Less	Personal allowance	(3,005.00)
	Taxable income	26,995.00
	Tax payable	
	£20,700.00 @ 25%	5,175.00
	6,295.00 @ 40%	2,518.00
	£26,995.00	7,693.00
Wife		
	Income	10,000.00
Less	Personal allowance	(3,005.00)
	Taxable income	6,995.00
	Tax on £6,995.00 @ 25%	1,748.75
Combined tax liability		
	Husband	7,693.00
	Wife	1,748.75
		9,441.75

The tax saving from the change of system is therefore £688 (£9,441.75 — £8,753.75). An alternative way of representing this is to say that the change of system has resulted in the husband gaining additional personal allowances of £1,720 which have attracted tax relief at his top tax rate of 40% (£1,720 @ 40% = £688).

The change from a system of aggregate taxation of spouses' incomes to a system of independent taxation will only result in a higher overall tax bill for the couple in the rare case where the husband's taxable income is less than his personal allowance but his wife has taxable income in excess of her personal allowances, and even then there may be an element of transitional relief which will enable the husband to transfer some of his unused personal allowance to his wife (see **1.7** below). In all other cases the change will result either in no change to the overall tax liability, or in an overall tax reduction. Where a married couple were liable to higher rate tax in 1989-90 and the wife has significant taxable income, the reduction in their overall income tax bill is likely to be substantial.

1.3 The personal allowance — neither spouse over 65

Under independent taxation each spouse is entitled to a personal allowance, £3,005 for 1990-91[1]. Any unused personal allowance of a wife can never be transferred to her husband. Normally the same principle will apply to prevent a husband transferring his unused personal allowance to his wife. However one of the objectives in implementing the change from aggregate to independent taxation was to ensure that the total personal allowances which a couple receive in 1990-91 or a later year should not be less than the total personal allowances they received in 1989-90, the last year of aggregate taxation. If a wife has taxable income and the husband does not, such a loss of personal allowances could occur. To prevent such a loss of allowances there is a complex transitional relief, dealt with in detail in **1.7** below, which may enable a limited transfer of a husband's unused personal allowance to his wife. However this relief is only a transitional one which will eventually disappear from the system of independent taxation. It does not affect the basic principle that unused personal allowances cannot be transferred from one spouse to the other.

1.4 Married couple's allowance — neither spouse over 65

If a husband and wife are living together for the whole or any part of a year of assessment he is entitled to a married couple's allowance[2]. Following the Court of Appeal decision in *Nabi v Heaton*[3] interpreting equivalent legislation in ICTA 1970 s 8 the allowance should be available whether the marriage is monogamous or recognised by UK law as a valid polygamous marriage. However the couple must be formally married; cohabitation for a lengthy period is not sufficient[4]. Technically the allowance has to be claimed[5], and the time limit for making a claim is 6 years after the end of the year of assessment to which the claim relates[6].

Conceptually the married couple's allowance is meant to represent the difference between the old married man's allowance and the single person's allowance, and the illustrative allowance used in the original ICTA 1988

1 ICTA 1988 s 257(1).
2 ICTA 1988 s 257A(1).
3 [1983] STC 344.
4 *Rignell v Andrews* [1990] STC 410.
5 ICTA 1988 s 256.
6 TMA 1970 s 43.

s 257A[1] was the difference between the two allowances in 1988-89. For 1990-91 the married couple's allowance is £1,720. It will be noted that the allowance is the husband's allowance and not the wife's. If the husband has sufficient taxable income the allowance must be set against that income even if it would be more beneficial to set it against the income of the wife because, for example, she is a higher rate taxpayer whereas her husband is only a basic rate taxpayer. The main reason for this was to ensure that a husband did not suffer a drop in his personal allowances, and hence an increase in his tax liability, solely as a result of the change to independent taxation. For 1989-90 every husband would have been entitled to at least the married man's allowance of £4,375. For 1990-91 every husband is entitled the single allowance of £3,005 plus the married couple's allowance of £1,720, giving total allowances of £4,725, an increase on the amount available for 1989-90.

A married couple's allowance is only available if husband and wife are 'living together' at some time during the tax year. 'Living together' is defined in ICTA 1988 s 282, a revised version of which was inserted by FA 1988 Sch 3 para 11. A husband and wife are to be treated as living together unless —

> '(a)   they are separated under an order of a court of competent jurisdiction, or by deed of separation, or
> (b)   they are in fact separated in such circumstances that the separation is likely to be permanent.'

The original s 282 also treated spouses as living apart for tax purposes if one of them was, and the other was not, resident in the UK. The change to independent taxation has rendered this provision superfluous and it has therefore been repealed.

For tax purposes the phrase 'living together' is being used in the legal sense of living as husband and wife, rather than the factual sense of living in the same house. A soldier who is on a two year tour of duty in Northern Ireland and who visits his home only occasionally, but remains happily married, is living with his wife for income tax purposes[2]. Conversely, if a husband and wife have in fact separated, the mere fact that they continue to live in the same house because, for example, no other suitable accommodation is available, should not prevent them from being assessed as single people for income tax purposes. If divorce cases are followed as an analogy it will not be enough merely to show that the spouses slept in separate bedrooms, had no sexual relationship, and effectively treated the marriage as over, if they otherwise shared the living accommodation, household chores, and had their meals together[3]. However, if they lived completely separate lives[4], or the wife has effectively taken in the husband as a lodger[5], then the spouses should be treated as living apart, with the result that married couple's allowance will not be available in the year after separation. Where there is no court order or deed of separation the legislation does not attempt to define the circumstances in which a separation is likely to be permanent. It is understood that the Revenue will accept

1   Inserted by FA 1988 s 33.
2   *Nugent-Head v Jacob* (1948) 30 TC 83.
3   See *Mouncer v Mouncer* [1972] 1 All ER 289; *Hopes v Hopes* [1948] 2 All ER 920.
4   *Smith v Smith* [1940] P 29; *Naylor v Naylor* [1926] 2 All ER 129.
5   *Fuller v Fuller* [1973] 2 All ER 650.

that a separation is likely to be permanent where the spouses have voluntarily lived apart for over a year, but the issue remains a factual one and a much shorter period may suffice.

1.4:1 Transfer of married couple's allowance

If a husband's taxable income is less than his personal allowance and married couple's allowance, any unused married couple's allowance may be transferred to his wife and set against her income[1]. Again it must be emphasised that it is only an unusable married couple's allowance that can be transferred. If a husband's taxable income exceeds his personal allowance and his married couple's allowance no transfer of allowances is permitted. To determine whether there is any unused married couple's allowance one computes the husband's taxable income after deducting all tax deductible expenditure and all personal allowances other than married couple's allowance. However payments which qualify for deduction under the business expansion scheme provisions, and payments of mortgage interest made under MIRAS, are *not* to be deducted[2]. If the married couple's allowance exceeds the husband's taxable income after these deductions the excess may be transferred to his wife.

Example

For 1990-91 H has earned income of £3,500. He pays mortgage interest net under MIRAS of £1,000. His transferable married couple's allowance for 1990-91 is:

		£
	Earned income	3,500
Less	Personal allowance	(3,005)
	Taxable income before MCA	495
Less	Married couple's allowance	(1,720)
	Transferable amount	1,225

The transfer of unused married couple's allowance to the wife is not automatic. It only occurs following a written notice to the inspector by the husband[3]. The notice must be served not later than six years after the end of the year of assessment to which it relates; must be in the prescribed form (Form 575); and is irrevocable[4]. However if a notice to transfer unused married couple's allowance is given and it subsequently transpires that the husband has additional taxable income for that year, part or all of the transferred allowance will have to be clawed back. This is because under the legislation a husband is only able to transfer married couple's allowance in excess of his taxable income for the year. If a clawback becomes necessary the wife will find that her tax liability for the year in question will be increased. In their booklet IR 82 'Independent Taxation — A Guide for Husbands on Low Incomes', March 1989, the Revenue state that, where it is relevant, they are prepared to estimate the unused amount of married

1   ICTA 1988 s 257B(1).
2   ICTA 1988 s 257B(2).
3   ICTA 1988 s 257B(3).
4   ICTA 1988 s 257B(3).

couple's allowance so that a wife may receive a deduction for it in her PAYE notice of coding for the year, or in a tax assessment, for example against her Sch D Case I profits which are assessable on a preceding year basis. At the end of the year of assessment the Revenue will review their estimate, and make any appropriate adjustment to the wife's tax liability.

1.5 Elderly married couples

Higher personal allowances are available if either spouse attains 65 or 75 during the course of a year of assessment[1]. The higher allowance is given if the taxpayer is 65 or 75 at the end of the year of assessment, and a taxpayer who dies in a year of assessment in which he would have attained the age of 65 or 75 is entitled to the higher age allowance for the year in which he dies[2]. For 1990-91 the single age allowances are:

65-74	£3,670
75+	3,820

These higher personal allowances are reduced if the taxpayer's total income exceeds £12,300 by one half of the excess total income over £12,300, but the reduced allowance can never be less than the normal personal allowance of £3,005[3]. The Inland Revenue point out in their pamphlet IR 81 'Independent Taxation, Guide for Pensioners', March 1989 that it is important to remember that income received under deduction of composite rate tax, particularly building society and bank deposit interest, must be grossed up at the basic rate of income tax in computing total income. This is done by multiplying the actual interest received by 100/(100 — the basic rate of income tax for the year). For 1990-91 the multiple is therefore 100/75, so that actual building society interest received in 1990-91 of £75 gives rise to income chargeable to tax of £100 of which non-refundable basic rate tax of £25 is deemed to have been paid by withholding at source.

Example

For 1990-91 John is aged 67 and has earned income of £13,000 and received £900 building society interest. He pays mortgage interest net under MIRAS of £750, equivalent to £1,000 gross interest. The reduction in his age allowance for 1990-91 is:

		£
	Earned income	13,000
	BSI £900 x 100/75	1,200
	Gross income	14,200
Less	Mortgage interest	(1,000)
	Total income	13,200
Less	Income limit	(12,300)
	Excess income	900

---

1   ICTA 1988 s 257(2) (3).
2   ICTA 1988 s 257(4).
3   ICTA 1988 s 257(5).

The reduction in age allowance is therefore $\frac{1}{2} \times £900 = £450$, and the age allowance becomes:

	Personal allowance 65-74	3,670
Less	Income restriction	(450)
	Personal allowance	3,220

As £3,220 is higher than the normal personal allowance of £3,005 the taxpayer gains the benefit of the higher allowance.

Under independent taxation if a husband and wife are living together they are each treated completely independently in computing their personal allowance. Thus if a husband is 63 but his wife is 67 the husband will have a personal allowance for 1990-91 of £3,005 and the wife will have a personal allowance of £3,670. Only the wife's total income will be taken into account in determining whether the age allowance has to be reduced because her total income for 1990-91 exceeds £12,300.

The position is more complicated when it comes to married couple's allowance. If *either spouse* is over 65 or 75 at some time in the year of assessment *the husband* is entitled to a higher married couple's allowance computed using the age of the older spouse[1]. As for the ordinary personal allowance, the higher married couple's allowance is given if a spouse dies in a year in which he or she would have attained 65 or 75[2]. The higher married couple's allowances are:

65-74	£2,145
75+	2,185

The allowance is always the husband's allowance. As with the personal allowance, it will be restricted if *the husband's* total income exceeds £12,300[3]. The allowance is never restricted if the wife's income exceeds £12,300. Consequently if a husband aged 63 with total income of less than £12,300 is married to a wife aged 67 with total income of £15,000 each spouse will receive the ordinary personal allowance of £3,005. The reduction in the wife's age allowance is $£15,000 - £12,300 = £2,700 \times \frac{1}{2} = £1,350$, which reduces it below the normal allowance. However the husband is entitled to a married couple's allowance of £2,145 notwithstanding that he is not over 65 and that his wife's income is well above the threshold for restricting the higher allowances.

If the husband is over 65 or 75, and so entitled to higher personal allowances, the income restriction is first used to reduce the personal allowance to the normal amount of £3,005, and any excess income then reduces the married couple's allowance to a minimum of the normal allowance of £1,720[4].

Example

For 1990-91 Peter, aged 77 and a married man living with his wife, has total income of £14,600. The income restriction on his age allowance is $£14,600 - £12,300 = £2,300 \times \frac{1}{2} = £1,150$. His allowances for 1990-91 are:

---

1 ICTA 1988 s 257A(2) and (3).
2 ICTA 1988 s 257A(4).
3 ICTA 1988 s 257A(5).
4 ICTA 1988 s 257A(5).

	Higher personal allowance		3,820
Less	Income restriction		(815)
	Personal allowance		3,005
	Higher married couple's allowance		2,185
Less	Income restriction	1,150	
	less used against personal allowance	(815)	(335)
	Married couple's allowance		1,850

£1,850 is higher than the normal married couple's allowance of £1,720, and is therefore Peter's married couple's allowance for 1990-91.

If a husband's taxable income is less than his higher married couple's allowance then, as with the normal married couple's allowance, the excess allowance can be transferred to his wife[1]. A transfer is available even if the wife is under 65, and irrespective of the amount of income that she has. The rules for determining whether there is any unused married couple's allowance are the same as for the normal married couple's allowance, ie the husband's taxable income is computed after deducting all charges on income except mortgage interest paid under MIRAS and payments under the business expansion scheme, and all allowances except the married couple's allowance. Any excess of the married couple's allowance may, on a claim in writing being made by the husband, be transferred to the wife.

Example

For 1990-91 Simon, 67, who is married to and living with Mary, 60, has earned income of £3,900. The transferable married couple's allowance for 1990-91 is:

	Earned income	£3,900
Less	Personal allowance	(3,670)
		230
Less	Married couple's allowance	(2,145)
	Transferable allowance	1,915

1.5:1 Elderly married couples — transitional relief

In the absence of transitional relief it would be possible for a husband to receive less personal allowances in 1990-91 than he received in 1989-90. This anomaly will arise where the husband is younger than his wife and was entitled to married age allowance in 1989-90 on the basis of his wife's age rather than his own. Assume that Bill, aged 60 in 1989-90, was married to a wife then aged 67 and that their combined income was and remains less than the income restriction limit, £11,400 for 1989-90 and £12,300 for 1990-91. For 1989-90 Bill was entitled to the higher married age allowance of £5,385. For 1990-91 he is entitled to the ordinary personal allowance of £3,005 and the higher married couple's allowance of £2,145, giving total allowances for 1990-91 of £5,150, a reduction of £235.

To deal with the anomaly transitional relief is provided in ICTA 1988 s 257E. Section 257E applies where a husband was entitled to married age allowance for 1989-90 on the basis of his wife's age rather than his own,

1   ICTA 1988 s 257B(1).

because she was over 65 or 75 and he was under those ages, and the married allowance he was entitled to for 1989-90 exceeds the total of his personal and married couple's allowance for 1990-91[1]. In computing the allowances to which the husband was entitled in 1989-90 any election under ICTA 1988 s 283 for separate assessment is disregarded[2]. If s 257E applies then, instead of the ordinary personal allowance, the husband is entitled to the personal allowance *his wife* would have been entitled to *in 1989-90* had she been a single person, ie £3,400 if she was then under 75 and £3,540 if she was 75 or older. Thus, in the above example, Bill's allowances for 1990-91 will be a personal allowance of £3,400 plus a married couple's allowance of £2,145, giving total allowances of £5,545.

If in 1990-91 the husband's total income exceeds £12,300 and he is entitled to a higher personal allowance under s 257E the normal income restriction applies[3], so that the higher allowance will be reduced by half his excess total income over £12,300, but not below the normal personal allowance of £3,005. The transitional relief continues until the husband's allowances for a later tax year are greater than his allowances for 1989-90, or he ceases to live with his wife, whichever is the earlier.

1.6 Blind person's allowance

For 1990-91 and later years FA 1988 Sch3 para8 substitutes a new ICTA 1988 s 265 to deal with blind person's relief. Under s 265(1) if a claimant proves that he or she is a registered blind person the claimant is entitled to an additional allowance of £1,080[4]. Under independent taxation this provision initially applies separately to each spouse. Thus the allowance is deducted from the taxable income of the spouse who is blind and, if both spouses are blind, both are entitled to claim the additional allowance of £1,080. However if a spouse who is blind does not have sufficient income fully to absorb the allowance, the unused blind person's allowance can be transferred to the other spouse, even if that other spouse is not blind[5]. If the husband is blind, blind person's allowance is deducted *before* married couple's allowance but *after* the personal allowance and any other allowances to determine whether there is any unused allowance[6]. Mortgage interest payments under MIRAS or payments under the business expansion scheme are ignored in the computation[7].

Example

John, who is blind, is married to Abigail. Both are under 65 in 1990-91. For 1990-91 John's taxable income, before personal allowances, is £3,400. From this income he deducts his personal allowance of £3,005 and £395 of his £1,080 blind person's allowance. He can claim to transfer to Abigail £685 unused blind person's allowance plus £1,720 unused married couple's allowance.

1 ICTA 1988 s 257E(1).
2 ICTA 1988 s 257E(5).
3 ICTA 1988 s 257E(3).
4 Doubled from £540 by FA 1990 with effect from 1990-91.
5 ICTA 1988 s 265(2) and (4).
6 ICTA 1988 s 265(3).
7 ICTA 1988 s 265(3).

If it is the wife who is blind the blind person's allowance is deducted after all other allowances, again ignoring payments of mortgage interest under MIRAS and payments under the business expansion scheme[1].

A transfer of unused blind person's allowance does not occur automatically; it has to be claimed. The claim must be made by the person entitled to the relief by notice in writing to the inspector not more than six years after the end of the year of assessment to which it relates[2]. The notice must be in the prescribed form (Form 575) and is irrevocable[3]. A notice by a husband to transfer unused blind person's allowance automatically also operates as a notice to transfer the married couple's allowance[4]. Because of the order of set-off of the allowances, if any blind person's allowance can be transferred, the whole of the married couple's allowance will also be transferable.

1.7 Transfer of husband's personal allowance

The system of independent taxation introduced by the Finance Act 1988 is a system of non-transferable personal allowances. If either spouse does not have sufficient income to cover the personal allowance, the unused personal allowance is wasted. It cannot be transferred to the other spouse for deduction from taxable income of that other spouse. This is in contrast to unused married couple's allowance, which can be transferred from husband to wife. Where a wife has an unused personal allowance the principle of non-transferability applies without exception. But to apply the principle without exception where the husband has an unused personal allowance could result in a married couple receiving lower usable personal allowances in 1990-91 than they received in 1989-90. This is because, under the system of aggregate taxation of spouses' income in operation for that year, a husband was effectively able to deduct his personal allowances from his wife's income.

Example

For both 1989-90 and 1990-91 Bob and Jill are husband and wife living together. Bob had a total income of £300 for 1989-90 and £500 for 1990-91, and Jill had earned income of £9,000 for both years.

For *1989-90* Bob reported taxable income of £9,300 and claimed the following personal allowances:

	£
Married man's allowance	4,375
Wife's earned income relief	2,785
	7,160

---

1 ICTA 1988 s 265(4).
2 ICTA 1988 s 265(5) (a).
3 ICTA 1988 s 265(5)(b) and (c).
4 ICTA 1988 s 265(6).

For *1990-91*, if no transitional relief is given, the usable allowances claimable by Bob and Jill would be:

	£
Bob's personal allowance (restricted to his income)	500
Jill's personal allowance	3,005
Married couple's allowance	1,720
Total personal allowances	5,225

There is therefore a reduction of £1,935 in usable personal allowances.

One of the principles underlying the change from a system of aggregate taxation of spouses' income to a system of independent taxation is that, at least in the short term, no-one should be worse off simply because of the change in the system of taxation. To deal with husbands on low income ICTA 1988 s 257D therefore contains provisions which may enable, for a transitional period, some of the husband's unused personal allowance in 1990-91 or a later year to be transferred to his wife. The allowance which can be transferred under s 257D is known as the transferable amount. The provisions of s 257D are complicated, perhaps excessively complicated for the type of factual situation they are designed to deal with. The rules for 1990-91 are different from the rules for later years and, for 1990-91, there are different rules depending on whether the couple were married on or before 6th April 1989 or married during 1989-90.

Transitional relief under s 257D only applies if it is claimed by the husband. The claim must be made by notice in writing to the inspector in the prescribed form (Form 575) not more than six years after the end of the year of assessment to which it relates[1]. The notice is irrevocable, and automatically also operates as a notice to transfer unused married couple's allowance and, if it is relevant, unused blind person's allowance[2]. The relief is not available if the husband is not resident in the UK, even if he qualifies for personal allowances[3]. The relief is available if a wife is non-resident but entitled to personal allowances under ICTA 1988 s 278 because, for example, she is a Commonwealth citizen.

1.7:1 Transferable personal allowance for 1990-91 where spouses married on or before 6th April 1989

For 1990-91 the objective of the transitional provisions is to ensure that the personal allowances which a married couple can use against their incomes in 1990-91 are not less than the personal allowances to which the husband was entitled in 1989-90. Transitional provisions in ICTA 1988 s 257D(1) and (2) apply if the couple were married to, and living with, each other for the whole or part of 1989-90, including 6th April 1989, and for the whole or part of 1990-91. No election for separate taxation of wife's earnings election must have been in force for 1989-90[4]. If a separate taxation

1 ICTA 1988 s 257D(9).
2 ICTA 1988 s 257D(9).
3 ICTA 1988 s 278(2A).
4 ICTA 1988 s 257D(1) (a).

of wife's earnings election was in force there can be no transitional relief, but such an election is only likely to be relevant in very unusual circumstances, for example where a husband had high earnings for most of 1989-90, but was made redundant towards the end of the tax year, and has little or no income in 1990-91. A transferable amount will only be available for 1990-91 if the husband's taxable income for 1990-91, without deducting payments of mortgage interest under MIRAS or payments under the business expansion scheme, is less than his personal allowance for 1990-91. The transferable amount is computed as follows:

(1)   Compute the husband's personal allowances for 1989-90. In doing the computation the effect of any election for separate assessment in force for 1989-90 is to be ignored[1]. In practice the husband's allowances for 1989-90 will normally be the married man's allowance of £4,375 plus the wife's earned income allowance of £2,785 if, and to the extent that, it was claimed.

(2)   From the personal allowances for 1989-90 deduct the aggregate of the husband's total income, ignoring MIRAS and BES payments, for 1990-91 plus the wife's personal allowance for 1990-91 plus the transferred married couple's allowance. The difference is the amount transferable to the wife.

Example

The facts are as in the previous example, ie for both 1989-90 and 1990-91 Bob and Jill are husband and wife living together. Bob had total income of £300 for 1989-90 and £500 for 1990-91, and Jill had earned income of £9,000 for both years. For 1990-91 the transferable amount is:

		£	£
	Bob's personal allowances for 1989-90		
	(£4,375 + £2,785)		7,160
Less	Bob's total income for 1990-91	500	
	Jill's personal allowance for 1990-91	3,005	
	Transferred married couple's		
	allowance 1990-91	1,720	(5,225)
	Transferable amount		1,935

It will be noted that, in the above example, the total allowances for Bob and Jill for 1990-91 now become:

	£
Bob's personal allowance	500
Jill's personal allowance	3,005
Transferred married couple's	
allowance	1,720
Transferred personal allowance	1,935
Total allowances	7,160

This is identical to the personal allowances they received in 1989-90, and thus the objective of the transitional relief has been achieved. The

1   ICTA 1988 s 257D(8).

example illustrates that the transitional relief is only designed to prevent a loss of personal allowances as a result of the change to a system of independent taxation with non transferable personal allowances. Thus, if the relief applies, the couple only receive in 1990-91 the allowances they received in 1989-90, and derive no benefit from the increase in personal allowances in the March 1990 Budget.

1.7:2 Transferable personal allowance for 1990-91 where the spouses married during 1989-90

If a couple married during 1989-90 the transitional relief is computed differently under provisions contained in ICTA 1988 s 257D(3) and (4). The need for different rules arises because, under ICTA 1988 s 279, prior to 1990-91 spouses continued to be taxed separately in the year of marriage, and aggregation of income first occurred in the tax year following the year of marriage. Thus, if a couple married in 1989-90, the wife was taxed on her own income for that year and had her own personal allowance of £2,785. The husband, however, was entitled to the married man's allowance reduced by one twelfth of the difference between the married and single allowances for each complete month, working from 6th April, for which he was unmarried[1]. He was only entitled to a wife's earned income allowance in the unusual circumstances where he had separated from a wife who had earned income, divorced, and remarried, all in the same tax year, in which event he would also remain entitled to the full married man's allowance. If the husband had unused personal allowances in the year of marriage he was able to transfer the unused amount to his wife for deduction from her income[2].

Where a couple married during 1989-90 transitional relief for 1990-91 is computed as follows:

(1) Deduct the husband's taxable income (again ignoring MIRAS and BES payments) for 1990-91 from his personal allowances for 1989-90, but ignoring any wife's earned income relief in the limited circumstances in which it was available[3].

(2) If the wife's personal allowances, including transferred married couple's allowance, exceed *the lower* of
   (a) her taxable income, ignoring MIRAS and BES payments, for 1989-90, or
   (b) her personal allowances for 1989-90 ignoring additional personal allowance for single parent families, widow's bereavement allowance, and any transferred allowances from her husband, compute the excess[4].

(3) The transferable allowance is 1–2[5].

---

1 ICTA 1988 s 257(8).
2 ICTA 1988 s 280(1)(2).
3 ICTA 1988 s 257D(3)(a).
4 ICTA 1988 s 257D(4).
5 ICTA 1988 s 257D(4).

Example

Andy and Linda married on 15th September 1990. As in the previous example, Andy had a total income of £300 for 1989-90 and £500 for 1990-91, and Linda had earned income of £9,000 in both years. For 1990-91 the transferable amount is:

			£	£
(1)		Andy's personal allowances 1989-90		
		married man's allowance		4,375
		Less 5/12 x £1,590		(662)
				3,713
	Less	Andy's income for 1990-91		(500)
		Maximum transferable amount		3,213
(2)		Linda's allowances for 1990-91		
		personal allowance	3,005	
		transferred married couple's	1,720	4,725
	Less	Linda's personal allowance for 1989-90		(2,785)
		Deduction		1,940
(3)		Maximum transferable amount		3,213
	Less	Deduction		(1,940)
		Transferable amount		1,273

The addition of this transferable amount to her other allowances for 1990-91 ensures that the combined allowances of Andy and Linda remain the same as if independent taxation had not been introduced, but there had been no increase in the level of personal allowances from 1989-90, as the following computation demonstrates:

Personal allowances 1989-90

	£	£
Andy		300
Linda		
personal	2,785	
transferred from Andy (£3,713-£300)	3,413	6,198
Total allowances		6,498

Personal allowances 1990-91

	£	£
Andy		500
Linda		
personal	3,005	
transferred married couple's	1,720	
transferred personal	1,273	5,998
Total allowances		6,498

1.7:3 Transferable personal allowance in 1991-92 and later years

Different rules apply in working out whether a husband's unused personal allowance for 1991-92 or a later year can be transferred to his wife and, if so, the amount that can be transferred. The rules are the same irrespective of whether the couple married before or during 1989-90. The rules are very restrictive, but it should be remembered that the ability to transfer unused personal allowance from husband to wife is only intended to provide transitional relief to ensure that the change to independent taxation does not result in a decrease in the total personal allowances received by a married couple. The new system of independent taxation has been designed as a system of non-transferable personal allowances, and the transitional rules are intended to achieve this result as soon as possible.

For a husband's unused personal allowance to be transferable to his wife in 1991-92, or a later year, the following conditions must be satisfied[1]:

(1)   The married couple must have been living together for the whole or part of 1989-90 and all subsequent tax years up to and including the year for which transfer of allowance is sought[2].
(2)   The husband must have unused personal allowance for the current year[3].
(3)   Some or all of the husband's unused personal allowance must have been transferred to, and used by, the wife in 1990-91 and in every subsequent tax year prior to the year transfer of allowance is sought[4]. In determining whether a wife used a transferred personal allowance the amount transferred is presumed to have been deducted from her income after all other deductions except payments made under the business expansion scheme[5].
(4)   The aggregate increase in the personal allowance and the married couple's allowance for the year in respect of which a claim is being made over the same allowances in the previous year must be less than both (*a*) the transferable amount for the previous year and (*b*) the husband's unused personal allowances for the current year of claim[6].

If any one of these conditions are not satisfied no claim to transfer the husband's unused personal allowance can be made for that or any subsequent year.

If all four conditions are satisfied then the transferable amount is computed as follows[7]:

(1)   Compute the husband's unused personal allowance for the year.
(2)   From the transferable amount transferred to, and used by, the wife in the preceding year of assessment deduct any increase in both the personal and married couple's allowance since the previous tax year.

The transferable amount is the *lower of* 1 or 2.

1   ICTA 1988 s 257D(5)-(7).
2   ICTA 1988 s 257D(5)(a) and (b).
3   ICTA 1988 s 257D(5)(d).
4   ICTA 1988 s 257D(5)(b) and (c).
5   ICTA 1988 s 257D(7).
6   ICTA 1988 s 257D(5)(c),(d) and (6).
7   ICTA 1988 s 257D(6).

Example

This example continues the previous example in 1.7:1 of Bob and Jill into 1991-92. To recap on the facts, for both 1989-90 and 1990-91 Bob and Jill were husband and wife living together. Bob had total income of £300 for 1989-90 and £500 for 1990-91, and Jill had earned income of £9,000 for both years. For 1990-91 the transferable amount was computed as £1,935. For 1991-92 Jill has earned income of £12,000 and Bob has taxable earned income of £1,300. For 1991-92 the personal allowance is assumed to be £3,300 and the married couple's allowance £1,850 (the exact amounts will not be known until after the March 1991 Budget). The transferable amount is:

1   Bob's unused allowance for 1991-92

		£	£
	Income		1,300
Less	Personal allowance		(3,300)
	Unused personal allowance		2,000

2   Jill's maximum claim

		£	£
	Transferable amount 1990-91		1,935
Less	personal allowance + MCA 1991-92	5,150	
	— personal allowance + MCA 1990-91	(4,725)	(425)
	Maximum claim		1,510

The transferable amount for 1991-92 is therefore £1,510, the lower of the two figures computed in one and two.

1.7:4 Transferable personal allowance and elderly couples

The ability to transfer unused personal allowance from husband to wife for a transitional period applies to couples where one spouse is over 65 as it applies to spouses under 65, and it also applies where the husband is under 65 but his wife is over that age so that the husband is entitled to a higher personal allowance under transitional provisions in ICTA 1988 s 257E, which were discussed in 1.5:1 above.

Example

In 1989-90 Paul, aged 60 and with a taxable income of £700, was married to Mary who was aged 68 with a taxable earned income of £10,000. For 1990-91 Paul's personal allowance is £3,400, the personal allowance Mary would have been entitled to in 1989-90 had she been a single person. As Paul has insufficient income to utilise this allowance transitional relief can be claimed, and the amount transferable is computed as follows:

		£	£
	Paul's personal allowances for 1989-90 (£5,385 + £2,785)		8,170
Less	Paul's income for 1990-91	700	
	Mary's personal allowance for 1990-91	3,670	
	Transferred married couple's allowance 1990-91	2,145	(6,515)
	Transferable amount		1,655

It will be noted that, in the above example, the total allowances for Bob and Jill for 1990-91 now become:

	£
Paul's personal allowance	700
Mary's personal allowance	3,670
Transferred married couple's allowance	2,145
Transferred personal allowance	1,655
Total allowances	8,170

This is identical to the personal allowances they received in 1989-90 of £5,385 + £2,785 = £8,170. The objective of the transitional provisions, to ensure that a married couple do not receive less allowances in 1990-91 than they received in 1989-90, has therefore been achieved.

1.8 Life assurance premium relief

Life assurance relief is traditionally classified with personal allowances, although it differs from other personal allowances in two important respects. First, life assurance relief requires the payment of premiums, whereas other personal allowances are simply deductions from income. Second, tax relief on life assurance premiums is limited to 12½% of the premium irrespective of whether the taxpayer is liable to tax at the higher or basic rate. The relief is therefore worth the same in net cash terms to all taxpayers. In contrast, personal allowances are deductions from income. They eliminate the top slice of a taxpayer's income from charge to tax. Every pound of a personal allowance is therefore worth 40p to a higher rate taxpayer, but only 25p to a basic rate taxpayer.

Life assurance relief was abolished for new policies taken out, or old policies varied, after 13th March 1984. However relief continues to be available on premiums paid on policies taken out before that date. If the policy was taken out after 19th March 1968 it must also be a qualifying policy complying with provisions now contained in ICTA 1988 Sch 15[1]. To qualify for tax relief an insurance policy, whether taken out before or after 19th March 1988, must insure the life of the payer or his spouse[2], and the insurance contract must have been made by the payer or his spouse[3]. Policies on the lives of children will only qualify if written in the course of an industrial insurance or registered friendly society business within ICTA 1988 Sch 14 para 2 up to the maximum premium permitted, currently £64 per annum. Industrial assurance or registered friendly society policies may also be written on the lives of parents or grandparents without premium limit[4].

Assuming the premiums qualify, the maximum premium on which an individual is entitled to relief is £1,500 or 1/6th of his total income, whichever is the greater[5], and the rate of relief is 12½% of the premium[6]. Relief is now normally given by permitting the payer to withhold and retain 12½% of the gross premium on payment of the premium[7], but the Revenue may

1 ICTA 1988 s 266(3)(b).
2 ICTA 1988 s 266(2)(b).
3 ICTA 1988 s 266(2)(c).
4 ICTA 1988 Sch 14 para 2(3).
5 ICTA 1988 s 274(1).
6 ICTA 1988 s 274(3).
7 ICTA 1988 s 266(5).

direct that premiums be paid gross[1], and any inadequate or excessive grant of relief can be adjusted in a tax assessment[2].

Under the system of aggregate taxation of spouses' income a married couple were only entitled to one £1,500, or 1/6th total income, limit between them. Under the new system of independent taxation each spouse will be treated separately for the purposes of life assurance relief, but without changing the rule that insurance policies taken out on the life of a spouse qualify for relief. This is achieved by FA 1988 Sch 14 Part VIII, which repeals the aggregation provisions originally in ICTA 1988 Sch 14 para 1(2) and (3). Consequently each spouse can now claim tax relief on pre-13th March 1984 insurance policies of 12½% of the premium up to £1,500 or 1/6th of their total income, whichever is the greater.

1.9 Personal allowances in the year of marriage

The rules relating to the taxation of husband and wife in the year of marriage were changed as from 1976-77. As from that year husband and wife have been treated as single persons throughout the year of marriage, unless the marriage took place on 6th April. Thus their income, earned and unearned, remained disaggregated, and charges were deducted from their respective incomes. Apart from the removal of the aggregation of incomes for couples who marry on 6th April, the introduction of independent taxation has little new effect in the year of marriage, as it merely confirms statutory provisions which were already in force.

In the year of marriage both husband and wife will be entitled to a personal allowance to set against their respective incomes. The husband will also be entitled to claim married couple's allowance but, unless prior to the marriage he has been entitled to claim the allowance for that year, for example because he separated, divorced, and remarried in the same year, the married couple's allowance is liable to reduction[3]. The allowance is reduced by 1/12 for each complete month of the tax year, working from 5th April, in which the couple were unmarried to each other.[4]

Example

John married on 3rd August 1990. He is under 65. His married couple's allowance for 1990-91 is:

		£
Married couple's allowance		1,720
Less 3/12 x £1,720		(430)
		1,290

The same principle applies to reduce the higher married couple's allowance which applies if one of the spouses is over 65 or 75 at any time in the year of marriage. If a husband has insufficient income in the year of marriage fully to use his reduced married couple's allowance, the unused

---

1   ICTA 1988 Sch 14 para 4.
2   ICTA 1988 Sch 14 para 5.
3   ICTA 1988 s 257A(6).
4   ICTA 1988 s 257A(6).

amount is transferable to his wife in exactly the same way as an unused married couple's allowance of a year following the year of marriage.

If either spouse has a child resident with them prior to their marriage, entitlement to additional personal allowance in the year of marriage may be in issue. Additional personal allowance can be claimed if a qualifying child is resident with the claimant for the whole or part of the year of claim, and is commonly known as single parent family allowance. The amount of the allowance is equivalent to the married couple's allowance[1], £1,720 for 1990-91. The conditions for obtaining this allowance are set out in ICTA 1988 s 259 and are discussed in detail in chapter 5 on cohabitation (see **5.2**), where the allowance will normally be more relevant. Under ICTA 1988 s 259(1), a revised version of which has been enacted for 1990-91 and later years by FA 1988 Sch 3 para 5, the allowance can be claimed by:

(*a*) Any woman who is not throughout the year of assessment married to and living with her husband. If a claim is made by a woman who is married to and living with her husband for part of a year of assessment, a qualifying child must be resident with her during the part of the year she was not married to and living with her husband[2].

(*b*) Any man who has not been married to and living with his wife for *the whole or any part* of a year of assessment, and who is not entitled to a married couple's allowance under ICTA 1988 s 257F because a wife from whom he is separated is being wholly maintained by voluntary maintenance payments from him.

(*c*) Any man who for the whole or any part of the year is married to and living with a wife who is totally incapacitated by physical or mental infirmity throughout the year. In this case the allowance will be in addition to the married couple's allowance.

Thus in the year of marriage the wife can claim additional personal allowance provided a qualifying child was resident with her prior to her marriage. She cannot claim it if a qualifying child was only resident with her after the date of her marriage. Prima facie a husband cannot claim additional personal allowance in the year of marriage, because he was living with his wife for part of the year of claim, and so is debarred by ICTA 1988 s 259(2)(b). However, under ICTA 1988 s 261, a man may claim by notice to an inspector that his marriage should be disregarded in determining his entitlement to additional personal allowance for the year in which he marries. If such an election is made, the man ceases to be entitled to any married couple's allowance for the year of marriage. Nevertheless, if a man marries during the year and has a qualifying child, it will normally be to his advantage to make the election, as additional personal allowance will be awarded in full, whereas married couple's allowance will be subject to reduction for each complete month the man was unmarried.

It should be noted that under these provisions there is a minor difference between the ability of a man and the ability of a woman to claim additional personal allowance in the year of marriage. A woman can only claim the allowance if a qualifying child is resident with her during the part of the year she was not married to and living with her husband. A man can claim

1 ICTA 1988 s 259(2).
2 ICTA 1988 s 259(4).

the allowance if a qualifying child was resident with him for any part of the year of marriage, even if the period of residence is wholly after the date of marriage.

1.10 Tax administration under independent taxation

1.10:1 Tax returns

Under aggregate taxation a husband, if requested to do so, was obliged to make a return of both his own and his wife's income. Only the husband was required to sign the return, and this was one of the major criticisms of the system. A husband had privacy in his tax affairs, because he was under no obligation to show a tax return to his wife, but a wife had no equivalent privacy, because she was required to disclose her income and expenditure to her husband. Either spouse could elect for separate assessment under ICTA 1988 s 283, in which case either spouse could file a joint return of both spouses' income, with the Revenue having the right to demand a return from the non-filing spouse[1]. In practice, the Revenue permitted each spouse to file a return of their own incomes. An election for separate taxation of wife's earnings did not, of itself, alter the obligation of a husband to file a return of the incomes of both himself and his wife[2].

When independent taxation is fully in force each spouse will be obliged, if requested to do so by an inspector, to make a tax return of their own income. A husband will no longer have any obligation to return his wife's income, thus ensuring that, if she wishes it, a wife can have complete privacy in her tax returns. The new provisions will apply for tax returns sent out after 5th April 1991 requesting details of income and expenditure received and incurred in 1990-91, and allowances claims for 1991-92. If a husband is requested to make a return of income and expenditure for 1989-90 he must make a joint return of both his own and his wife's income[3]. This applies even if his wife has income which is assessable on a preceding year basis, for example if she is carrying on a business, so that the profits reported will be assessable income for 1990-91 and can therefore only be assessed on the wife. If a husband fails to make the return, or makes it fraudulently or negligently, in computing any penalty that may be leviable under TMA 1970 s 93(2) or s 95(2), tax chargeable on a wife's income which should have been included in the return is to be treated as if it was tax chargeable on the husband[4].

In addition to having the right to request from a husband a return of the spouses' joint incomes for 1989-90, the Revenue have said that in a limited number of cases they will also require a wife to make a return of her own income for 1989-90. Requests are likely to be made where the wife's income is assessable on a preceding year basis, so that she will be solely liable to pay the tax on it when it comes to be assessed for 1990-91[5]. However the Revenue have no legal authority to require a wife to

1   ICTA 1988 s 284(4).
2   ICTA 1988 s 287(10).
3   FA 1988 Sch 3 para 26.
4   FA 1988 Sch 3 para 27.
5   [1988] STI 178 and IR 83 para 161.

complete such a return, and no penalty will attach if she declines to do so[1].

The new provisions consequent on the introduction of independent taxation which require each spouse to file a tax return will only have practical consequences for a minority of taxpayers. As the Revenue have pointed out in a press release[2]:

> 'At present only a minority of husbands are asked to fill in tax returns each year. The operation of the PAYE system and arrangements for deduction of tax at source from many forms of income from saving mean that annual returns are not required from many taxpayers. The same will be true under independent taxation: only a minority of husbands and wives will need to complete a tax return every year.'

1.10:2 Tax assessments and the elections for separate assessment and separate taxation

Income which is assessable for 1990-91, or a later year, can only be assessed on the spouse entitled to the income. Accordingly the elections for separate assessment and separate taxation of wife's earnings have been abolished for 1990-91 and later years[3]. Income of spouses assessable for 1989-90, or an earlier year, can only be assessed on the husband unless tax has been withheld at source, as with PAYE, or an election for separate assessment or separate taxation of wife's earnings has been made. For 1989-90 the latest date for an election for separate assessment, which could be made by either spouse, was 5th July 1989. The Revenue have no statutory discretion to extend or vary this time limit[4]. However, TMA 1970 s 43A may provide an opportunity to make a late election if an assessment is raised on or after 27th July 1989; this is discussed in the next section. The latest date for an election for separate taxation of wife's earnings for 1989-90 is 5th April 1991, but the Revenue have a discretion to extend this time limit[5]. An election must be made by both spouses in the prescribed form, currently Form 14. In Statement of Practice A25 the Inland Revenue have stated that they ordinarily exercise their discretion to extend the time limit:

> '. . . in favour of cases involving the sickness or absence abroad of either spouse or other serious personal difficulties which prevented their prompt attention to tax affairs at the critical time, and also cases where, through no fault of the taxpayer or his advisers, relevant information was not available for reaching a decision within the statutory time limit.'

As an election for separate taxation involves a net loss of personal allowances of the difference between the married and single personal allowances, the election is only beneficial if sufficient earned income of the wife can be removed from the husband's higher rate tax band to offset the increased tax liability arising from the loss of personal allowances. For 1989-90 the election will not be beneficial unless the joint income of the spouses, after deducting all tax deductible expenditure such as pension

1 See Parliamentary reply by Mr Lilley [1990] STI 452.
2 [1988] STI 173.
3 FA 1988 Sch 14 Part VIII
4 *Shortt v Yallop* (1936) 20 TC 298.
5 ICTA 1988 s 288(1).

contributions and mortgage interest payments but before personal allowances, is at least £30,511 and includes wife's earned income of at least £7,026. The calculation may be affected if the couple have chargeable capital gains in excess of the exempt threshold of £5,000 as, for 1988-89 and 1989-90, chargeable gains of a married couple are taxed as if they were the top slice of the husband's income. If as a result of a separate taxation of wife's earnings election a husband's income is reduced to below the higher rate income tax threshold of £20,700, the consequent savings in capital gains tax may outweigh any increase in the aggregate income tax liabilities of the spouses. **3.4** below includes a worked example which illustrates this point.

1.10:3 No fault prior year assessments

If there has been no fault by a taxpayer the Revenue can raise an assessment for any of the six years preceding the year of assessment in which the assessment is raised[1]. Thus an assessment raised in 1990-91 can assess any year from 1984-85 to 1989-90. As aggregate taxation applied for all these years, any assessment of a wife's income must be made on her husband unless an election for separate assessment or separate taxation of wife's earnings was in force for the year in question. However relief may be available under TMA 1970 s 43A, inserted by FA 1989 s 150 with effect for assessments issued on or after 27th July 1989. Under TMA 1970 s 29(3), if an inspector discovers that profits have not been assessed, or an assessment has become insufficient, he is entitled, subject to the normal time limits, to assess the profits. If a taxpayer receives a back assessment by virtue of TMA 1970 s 29(3) charging additional tax and the assessment does not result from his fraud or neglect, he may, within one year of the end of the year of assessment in which the back assessment is raised, make any election or claim in relation to the year covered by the back assessment notwithstanding that the election or claim would otherwise be out of time[2]. Any election already made may be revoked within the same time limit except where by virtue of any enactment the election was irrevocable[3]. If a late election, or revocation of an election, affects the tax liability of another person that other person must consent in writing[4]. An election, or revocation of an election, cannot reduce tax liabilities to below what they would have been had the late assessment not been raised[5]. It therefore seems that, if a 'discovery' assessment is raised under TMA 1970 s 29(3), both spouses may elect for separate assessment or separate taxation of wife's earnings for the year to which the late assessment relates. Under ICTA 1988 s 288(3) an election for separate taxation of wife's earnings in force for any year may be revoked. Accordingly, if a back assessment is made and a separate taxation election was in force for the year to which the back assessment relates, the spouses may jointly agree to revoke the election. But an election for separate assessment can only be revoked for a year subsequent to that in respect of which it is made[6]. It therefore seems that s 43A does not authorise the

1   TMA 1970 s 34(1)
2   TMA 1970 s 43A(1),(2)(a).
3   TMA 1970 s 43A(2)(b).
4   TMA 1970 s 43B(1)
5   TMA 1970 s 43B(3)
6   ICTA 1988 s 283(3),(4); *Cowdray v IRC* (1930) 15 TC 255, CA.

revocation of a separate assessment election for an earlier year.

TMA 1970 s 43A is a recent section, and it will be some time before it becomes clear how it will be operated. Its purpose was explained in an Inland Revenue press release[1]:

'Taxpayers are allowed extra time to make claims for reliefs against default assessments. It is proposed to introduce a similar extension of time limits for claims to relief where the Revenue discover that further tax is due but there is no offence by the taxpayer — for instance as a result of an innocent error.'

The implication from the press release is that TMA 1970 s 43A is only intended to allow late elections or claims where some further assessment has to be made as a result of a discovery, and is not designed to cover the case where the Revenue are simply late in making an assessment. Yet every time an inspector reads a tax return and decides he needs to raise an assessment he has made a discovery, so, if necessary, it may be possible to argue that s 43A should be interpreted widely. The meaning of 'discover' in TMA 1970 s 29(3) has been discussed in two cases. In *Cenlon Finance Co Ltd v Ellwood*[2] the appellant company submitted trading accounts to an inspector. The company had excluded from its profits a dividend of £25,000 which it had received on the basis that it was a capital receipt. The company fully disclosed the circumstances of the receipt. The inspector took the view that the dividend was not taxable. Subsequently another inspector took the view that the dividend was taxable and assessed it. The House of Lords held that he had made a discovery and was entitled to raise the assessment. As Lord Denning put it[3]:

'Every lawyer who, in his researches in the books, finds out that he was mistaken about the law, makes a discovery. So also does an Inspector of Taxes.'

In *Jones v Mason Investments (Luton) Ltd*[4] Goff J said that all that was necessary for a discovery was for an inspector to have a bona fide change of mind. These two cases seem to support the view that something more is necessary for a discovery assessment then merely a late assessment; but in both cases on the facts there had been something more. The meaning of the word 'discover' in TMA 1970 s 29(3) should therefore not be regarded as having been finally determined.

If the Revenue raise a back assessment more than one year after the end of the year of assessment to which the back assessment relates, relief from payment of the tax assessed may be available under extra-statutory concession A19. For the concession to apply the loss of tax must be due to the failure of the Revenue to make proper and timely use of information supplied to them by the taxpayer about his income and personal circumstances. The concession is only intended to relieve hardship caused by a sudden requirement to pay a tax bill; it is not intended to be a blanket waiver and accordingly it only applies to taxpayers whose gross income for the year the arrears are notified is below certain levels. These levels have varied since the introduction of the relief in 1971. The most recent ones apply

1   [1989] STI 227, para 23.
2   (1961) 40 TC 176.
3   (1961) 40 TC 176 at 207.
4   (1966) 43 TC 570.

to arrears first notified on or after 14th March 1990. The limits are[1]:

Gross income	Fraction of arrears	
	collected	remitted
To £12,000	None	All
£12,001-14,500	¼	¾
£14,501-18,500	½	½
£18,501-22,000	¾	¼
£22,001-32,000	⁹⁄₁₀	¹⁄₁₀
£32,001 +	All	None

In the case of taxpayers who are over 65, or who are in receipt of a national retirement pension or a widow's pension, the gross income levels are all increased by £3,300. Under aggregate taxation the limits applied to the joint incomes of husband and wife living together. Under independent taxation the income scale will apply only to the spouse assessed[2]. As the income limit relates to the year the late assessment is raised, and not the year to which it relates, if a late assessment is raised after 5th April 1990 only the income of the spouse liable to pay the tax, normally the husband, will be taken into account even if the assessment relates to a year prior to 1990-91, when aggregate taxation applied.

1.10:4 Back duty assessments
If the Revenue wish to raise a back assessment for a year more than six years before the tax year in which the assessment is raised they must show fault on the part of the taxpayer. FA 1989 s 149 substituted a new TMA 1970 s 36 which greatly simplifies the conditions for making such a back assessment. The Revenue may back assess the preceding twenty years of assessment to collect tax lost through the taxpayer's fraudulent or negligent conduct, or through the fraudulent or negligent conduct of his agent. No leave is required before the back assessment is raised[3], although on an appeal against an assessment the Revenue will have to prove fraud or neglect. However the new rules do not apply to any year of assessment prior to 1983-84[4]. Viewed from 1990-91, the Revenue can back assess as of right to 1984-85. Accordingly the only year to which the new rules currently apply is 1983-84, and it will be many years before the original provisions in TMA 1970 are finally superseded.

The original provisions in TMA 1970 drew a distinction between fraud or wilful default and neglect. If tax was lost through the fraud or wilful default of the taxpayer the Revenue, subject to obtaining the permission of a single General or Special Commissioner on proof of a prima facie case, could back assess any year to 1936-37[5]. Although a husband is generally taxable on his wife's income he is not guilty of fraud, or assessable on that basis, if she fraudulently, and unknown to him, conceals income. Thus in *Wellington v Reynolds*[6] for many years the appellant's wife carried on alone the business of an inn keeper while he independently carried on

---

1 See IR Press Release, [1990] STI 203, reporting a written Parliamentary answer by Mr Peter Lilley, Financial Secretary to the Treasury. The limits were previously raised on 23rd July 1985.
2 Para b of the Parliamentary answer, [1990] STI 203.
3 FA 1989 s 149(2)
4 FA 1989 s 149(7).
5 TMA 1970 s 36 Sch 4 para 3(1).
6 (1962) 40 TC 209.

other businesses. She concealed some of her trading profits. The Inland Revenue raised out of time assessments on the husband. The High Court held that, although there was ample evidence of fraud by the wife, there was no evidence that the husband knew about it. The husband was therefore not fraudulent, and his wife's fraud could not be imputed to him. No additional assessments could therefore be made. Further it would not have been possible to assess the wife as the profits were not her income for tax purposes, so the fraudulently concealed profits escaped tax. If a back assessment for fraud is made for a year prior to 1990-91 to collect tax due on a wife's income concealed as a result of a fraud of which the husband was aware, the husband will be assessable even if the spouses have since ceased to live together.

If the Revenue seek to back assess a year prior to 1983-84 for neglect rather than fraud, they have to proceed by a complex hopping procedure set out in TMA 1970 s 37. An assessment must have been raised to collect tax lost through the fraud or neglect of the taxpayer in one of the preceding six years, the normal years[1]. This gives the Revenue the right, subject to obtaining the consent of a single General or Special Commissioner, to go back and search for neglect in the six years prior to the normal year for which the first back assessment had been made. The second six years back are known as the earlier years[2]. If neglect is found it can be assessed. If there was neglect or fraud in the earlier years, this opens up a further six years for neglect assessments, but an assessment can only be raised with the consent of at least two General or Special Commissioners[3], and the taxpayer has a right to be heard before the Commissioners[4]. If there is a consecutive six year period in which there was no fault by the taxpayer, that bars neglect assessments for prior years.

As far as back assessments on the ground of the taxpayer's fault are concerned, the system of aggregate taxation of spouses' income will remain relevant for many years, because it will be 1997-98 at the earliest before out of time assessments based on fault will be needed to assess tax for 1990-91, the first year of independent taxation. It is provided in FA 1988 Sch 3 para 29 that if an assessment has to be made on a married woman for 1990-91 or a later year to collect tax due to her fraud, wilful default or neglect, and prior to 1990-91 she was living with her husband so that her income was deemed to be his for income tax purposes, the default assessment is to be deemed to have been made on the husband to the extent that it is relevant in raising default assessments on him for any year in which he was married to and living with his wife. However the Revenue will only need to make use of this provision if they wish to assess a year prior to 1983-84 for neglect as, under the new TMA 1970 s 36, back assessments to 1983-84 for negligent conduct can now be made without the need to show fault in the intervening years.

One of the unexplained oddities about the new rules relating to negligent conduct is the repeal of the definition of neglect in TMA 1970 s 118. This definition read:

1   TMA 1970 s 37(1).
2   TMA 1970 s 37(3).
3   TMA 1970 s 37(5)
4   TMA 1970 s 37(7).

'"Neglect" means negligence, or a failure to give any notice, make any return or to produce or furnish any document or other information required by or under the Taxes Acts.'

The attraction of this definition to the Revenue was the latter part of it, which meant that the Revenue merely had to prove a failure by the taxpayer to submit relevant documents to sustain a neglect assessment, irrespective of the reason for the failure. The removal of the definition from the new offence of negligent conduct now means that the Revenue have to prove that the taxpayer's conduct was in fact negligent.

TMA 1970 s 37A, inserted by FA 1988 Sch 3 para 30 and effective for 1990-91 and later years, provides that if a back assessment is made to collect tax due to the fraudulent or negligent conduct of the taxpayer, an increased assessment is not to affect any married couple's allowance, personal allowance, or blind person's allowance which was transferred to the taxpayer's spouse when assessments for the default year were originally finalised. The taxpayer's personal allowances for the default year remain at their reduced level in computing the taxpayer's revised tax liability for the default year.

1.10:5 Penalties

After 1989-90 penalties for failure to file a tax return when requested, or for the fraudulent or negligent provision of information contained in the return, will be leviable only on the spouse liable to make the return. The main penalty provisions were revised and updated in the Finance Act 1989. Under TMA 1970 s 93(1) if a taxpayer fails to comply with a request to deliver a tax return he is initially liable to a penalty not exceeding £300 and, if the failure continues after the initial penalty has been imposed, to a further penalty of up to £60 for each day of default. If the default continues beyond the end of the year of assessment after that in which the request to make the return was served, the taxpayer is additionally liable to a penalty not exceeding the tax chargeable on the income and capital gains which should have been included in the return and which is assessed after the end of the tax year following that in which the notice to make the tax return was served[1]. If a taxpayer fraudulently or negligently omits information from his tax return he is liable to a maximum penalty, in addition to the tax and interest, of the tax under assessed as a result of the default[2].

If a tax return is made after 5th April 1990, in computing the amount of any penalty under TMA 1970 s 93(2) or s 95(2) only the income of the spouse who is liable to the penalty will normally be taken into account. However a married man may be required to file a tax return which includes details of both his own and his wife's income for 1989-90, even if that income is not assessable until 1990-91[3]. If a husband fraudulently or negligently makes a return of his or his wife's income for 1989-90, any tax payable by the wife on her income will be treated as if it was payable by her husband in computing any penalty payable by the husband under

1   TMA 1970 s 93(2).
2   TMA 1970 s 95(1) and (2), inserted by FA 1989 s 163, and effective for returns or statements made on or after 27th July 1989.
3   FA 1988 Sch 3 para 26.

TMA 1970 s 93(2) or s 95(2)[1]. If a woman is required to make a tax return covering assessable income for 1989-90 or an earlier year and becomes liable to a penalty for failing to make it, or for providing fraudulent or negligent information, tax payable by her husband on her income because it was taxable as his income under the aggregation provisions in force for years prior to 1990-91 is treated as if it had been payable by the woman in computing any penalty payable by her under TMA 1970 s 93(2) or s 95(2)[2].

1   FA 1988 Sch 3 para 27.
2   FA 1988 Sch 3 para 28.

CHAPTER 2

Income and expenditure under independent taxation

2.1 The allocation of income

Under aggregate taxation of spouses' income it was normally immaterial to determine which spouse beneficially owned the income, as it would be taxed as the husband's whoever in fact owned it. The only exception was where the spouses had elected for the wife's earned income to be taxed separately, but even then it was only important to disentangle the earned income, as the wife's unearned income remained taxable as the income of her husband. Under independent taxation all this changes, and it becomes vital for tax purposes to determine which spouse owns each item of income that is chargeable to tax. In making this determination ordinary principles of property and trust law apply, and it is beneficial ownership that is important, not legal title. For example, if a husband uses his wife's assets to purchase an income producing asset in his own name, under the law of resulting trusts the husband is treated as holding legal title to the new asset on trust for his wife, who remains beneficially entitled to both the asset and the income from it, unless there is clear evidence that the wife intended to make a gift of the asset to her husband. Consequently the income from the asset would be taxable as the wife's income rather than the husband's, despite the fact that he is the legal owner of it. In practice it is unlikely that the Revenue will make strenuous efforts to dispute the spouses' declaration of their ownership of income, but declarations in tax returns will henceforth be at least *prima facie* evidence of beneficial ownership should a dispute over ownership subsequently arise between the spouses.

Apart form anti-avoidance provisions to deal with income arising from settlements made by one spouse on the other (see **4.4** below), legislative provisions only deal with the allocation of income between spouses in one set of circumstances, namely where spouses are entitled to joint ownership of an asset. ICTA 1988 s 282A(1) provides that income derived from assets which are in the joint names of the spouses shall be deemed for tax purposes to belong to them equally, irrespective of whether it does in fact so belong. The deeming provision in s 282A(1) therefore overrides the general principle explained in the previous paragraph that it is the beneficial owner of income who is taxable on it. S 282A(1) does not apply to earned income, including income from a trade or profession, or to partnership profits assessable on the partnership under ICTA 1988 s 111, whether or not the profits are earned income[1]. It also does not apply to income to which neither spouse is beneficially entitled, for example where the spouses are holding the asset

---

1   ICTA 1988 s 282A(4).

on trust for someone else[1], or to income which is deemed to be the income of someone else under some other provision in the income tax legislation[2].

If income from an asset which is in the joint names of spouses who are living together does not in fact belong to them equally, either because one spouse is wholly beneficially entitled to it or because their entitlement is in unequal shares, the spouses may declare their beneficial entitlement and notify the Revenue of the declaration. They will then be taxed according to their beneficial entitlements[3]. A couple of points need to be emphasised. First, there is no obligation to notify the Revenue of an unequal entitlement to income from jointly owned assets. If the spouse with the greater beneficial entitlement to income is a higher rate taxpayer and the other spouse is not, there will be a tax advantage in having the income split equally. The spouses are free to adopt this approach. Second, the notification of the beneficial entitlement to income is not an election — it does not allow the spouses to elect to be taxed on jointly owned income in whichever way they choose irrespective of who actually owns the income. The declaration must specify the true beneficial ownership of both the asset and the underlying income. It will have strong evidential value should there be any subsequent dispute over ownership, for example in divorce proceedings. It is therefore not something which spouses should treat lightly.

Provisions governing the declaration of unequally owned income are contained in ICTA 1988 s 282B. The spouses must jointly make a declaration specifying their ownership both of the income and of the asset from which the income is derived[4]. For a declaration to be effective for tax purposes both the income and the asset from which it is derived must be owned in the same proportions[5]. The declaration must specify each asset to which it relates, and only applies to those assets. Thus spouses may choose to have the 50:50 rule applied to some of their assets in joint ownership, but not to others. Within 60 days of making the declaration notice of it must be given in the prescribed form (Form 17) to the inspector[6]. The notice may be sent to the inspector dealing with the tax affairs of either of the spouses[7]. It will therefore be noted that there is a two-stage procedure; first, the making of the declaration, and second, the notification of the declaration to the Revenue. However, as a matter of practice, the Revenue have somewhat subverted this process by effectively requiring the declaration of the beneficial interests to be on their prescribed Form 17, and the notification to be the transmission of that form to an inspector. This is not what the legislation requires. It allows the declaration of the beneficial interests to be in any form, but requires the notification to be in a prescribed form. The distinction has some practical significance because, as will be seen in the following paragraph, the declaration is effective from the date of the declaration and not from the date of notification, which is likely to be much later. Nevertheless it will avoid complications later if the Revenue's Form 17 is used for the actual declaration of the beneficial interests.

1 ICTA 1988 s 282A(2).
2 ICTA 1988 s 282A(5).
3 ICTA 1988 s 282A(3).
4 ICTA 1988 s 282B(1).
5 ICTA 1988 s 282B(4).
6 ICTA 1988 s 282B(3).
7 IR 83 para 86.

A declaration is effective for tax purposes for income arising on or after the day it is made, except that a declaration made on or before 6th June 1990 also covers income arising before the declaration[1]. A declaration, once made and properly notified, continues to have effect until the beneficial interests of the spouses in either the income or the asset cease to be in accordance with the declaration[2], or until the death of one of the spouses, or their separation or divorce.

2.2 Computation of wife's income

Under the system of aggregate taxation of the income of husband and wife, a wife's assessable income was computed independently of that of her spouse and then aggregated with his for assessment purposes[3]. This was of particular importance for income, such as trading or professional profits, which is normally assessable on a preceding year basis. For example, if a wife has been in business for many years and regularly makes up her accounts to 31st December, her tax adjusted profits for the year ended 31st December 1988 will be assessable under Sch D Case I for the tax year 1989-90. Under aggregate taxation, and assuming no election for separate taxation of wife's earnings, the profits were then assessed as the husband's income for 1989-90. It was held in *Elmhirst v IRC*[4] and *Leitch v Emmott*[5] that it followed that the marriage of spouses, or the death of the husband, did not make any difference to the tax year in which a married woman's profits were assessable. In particular, they did not operate as the commencement or cessation of a source of the wife's income.

> Example
>
> Jim and Margaret are husband and wife living together. Margaret carries on business as a hairdresser, and makes up her accounts to a 31st December year end. Her tax adjusted profit for the year ended 31st December 1987 was £12,000, and for the year ended 31st December 1988 £16,000. Jim died on 5th September 1988. For 1988-89 Jim's estate will be assessed on 5/12ths £12,000, the profit earned in the year ended 31st December 1987, notwithstanding that throughout the year in which the profits were actually earned Jim and Margaret were husband and wife living together. For 1988-89 Margaret will be assessed on 7/12ths £12,000, and for 1989-90 she will be assessed on £16,000.

FA 1988 Sch 3 para 25 ensures that the same principle applies during the transition from aggregate to independent taxation. It provides that the principle of aggregate taxation which applied in years prior to 1990-91 is not to affect any question of whether a married woman's income is chargeable to tax for 1990-91 or a later year, or the computation of the amount of her income which is chargeable. Thus, assuming a married woman makes up her accounting profits to 31st December each year, her tax-adjusted profits for the year ended 31st December 1988 will be assessed as her husband's income for 1989-90, and her tax-adjusted profits for the

1   ICTA 1988 s 282B(2).
2   ICTA 1988 s 282B(5).
3   ICTA 1988 s 279(2).
4   (1937) 21 TC 381.
5   (1929) 14 TC 633.

year ended 31st December 1989 will be assessed as her income for 1990-91.

2.3 A wife's business profits and the opening year rules

The profits of a trade or profession taxable under Sch D Case I or II are assessable on a preceding year basis. In the year in which a business commences there are no preceding year's profits, and therefore ICTA 1988 s 61 provides rules designed to convert the assessment of business profits from an actual year basis to a preceding year basis as quickly as possible. In the first year of a new business its profits are assessed on the actual profits arising from the commencement of the business to the following 5th April. The profits shown by the business's first accounts are normally time-apportioned to achieve the assessable amount. For the second year of assessment of a new business the profits of the first twelve months trading are taxed, accounting periods being apportioned if necessary. For the third year of assessment, providing accounts have been prepared annually, a preceding accounts year end basis of assessment can apply. Otherwise the Revenue are free to tax the profits of any twelve months trading providing the period they choose ends in the preceding year of assessment.

The change to independent taxation has no effect on these normal opening year rules if the first three years of assessment of a business started by a wife straddle the change from aggregate to independent taxation. The change merely affects the person on whom the profits are assessable.

Example
On 1st January 1989 Jemima, a married woman living with her husband, commenced business as a hairdresser. She made up her accounts to a December 31 year end, and the tax adjusted profits shown by the first two years' accounts were:

	£
Year ended 31st December 1989	5,000
Year ended 31st December 1990	9,000

The assessments for the opening years will be computed as follows:

1988-89 (1st Jan 1989-5th Apr 1989) 95/365 × £5,000	1,301
1989-90 (first 12 months trading)	5,000
1990-91 (preceding year to 31/12/1989)	5,000
1991-92 (preceding year to 31/12/1990)	9,000

Assuming no election for separate taxation of wife's earnings or separate assessment was in force, the profits for 1988-89 and 1989-90 will be assessed on the husband, but he may claim a wife's earned income allowance against them. Thus the taxable profit for 1988-89 is nil, and the taxable profit for 1989-90 is £2,215 (£5,000 − £2,785). For 1990-91 Jemima will be assessed on £5,000, from which she may deduct her personal allowance of £3,005.

The normal method of taxing profits in the opening years of a business is disadvantageous if profits in the first year are high, but then decline. In the second and third years of assessment the taxpayer is liable to find himself being taxed on higher profits than he actually earned during those years. Accordingly under ICTA 1988 s 62 the taxpayer is given an election. Instead of applying the normal opening year rules, the taxpayer may elect to have both the second and third years of assessment taxed on the basis of the profits actually earned during those years. The profits of relevant accounting periods will be time apportioned to obtain the profits earned between 6th April and 5th April in the second year of assessment and 6th April and 5th April in the third year of assessment. The election must be made not later than seven years after the end of the second year of assessment[1].

Under the system of aggregate taxation of spouses' income, assuming no election for separate taxation of wife's earnings had been made, the only person entitled to make the election was the husband, even if the wife was the proprietor of the business in question. This was because ICTA 1988 s 62(2) gives the right to make the election to the person charged, or liable to be charged, to tax on the profits. Under aggregate taxation that person was the husband. The change to independent taxation has resulted in a transitional provision to transfer the right to make the election to the wife in circumstances in which it would otherwise have remained with the husband. The transitional provision is a new ICTA 1988 s 62(2A)[2] which reads:

> 'Where—
> (a)   the second year of assessment is the year 1989-90,
> (b)   the person charged, or liable to be charged, for that year is a married man, and
> (c)   the person charged, or liable to be charged, for the year 1990-91 is his wife,
>
> subsection (2) above shall have effect as if it conferred the right to give notice on her and not on him.'

The operation of s 62(2A) can best be illustrated by an example:

Example
Hermione, a married woman living with her husband, commenced a business on 1st January 1989 and made up her accounts to 31st December each year. The profits for the first three years trading were:

	£
Year ended 31st December 1989	12,000
Year ended 31st December 1990	4,000
Year ended 31st December 1991	7,000

If no election was made the assessable profits would be:

1988-89 (1st Jan 1989-5th Apr 1989)	
95/365 × £12,000	3,123
1989-90 (first 12 months trading)	12,000
1990-91 (preceding year to 31/12/1989)	12,000
1991-92 (preceding year to 31/12/1990)	4,000
	31,123

If an election is made under ICTA 1988 s62(2) the computation becomes:

	£
1988-89 (1st Jan 1989-5th Apr 1989)	3,123
1989-90 (6th Apr 1989-5th Apr 1990)	
270/365 × £12,000 + 95/365 × £4,000	9,918
1990-91 (6th Apr 1990-5th Apr 1991)	
270/365 × £4,000 + 95/365 × £7,000	4,781
1991-92 (preceding year to 31/12/1990)	4,000
	21,822

1   ICTA 1988 s 62(2).
2   Inserted by FA 1988 Sch 3 para 2.

The election for an actual basis of assessment in the second and third years of assessment is clearly beneficial but, under ICTA 1988 s 62(2A), it must be made by the wife for both years. The consequence of making the election is that the husband's Sch D Case I assessment for 1989-90 will be reduced from £12,000 to £9,918 and the wife's Sch D Case I assessment for 1990-91 will be reduced from £12,000 to £4,781. Although in this example the husband's tax liability is reduced, the same principle applies if the effect of the election is to increase the 1989-90 assessment but reduce the 1990-91 assessment. Obviously it will only be sensible to make an election in these circumstances if there is an overall reduction in the assessable profits.

2.4 The closing years of a business

In a year in which a business ceases, its profits are assessed on an actual year basis, ie the profits actually earned from 6th April in the year of cessation to the date of cessation, time apportioning the tax adjusted profits of the final accounts to obtain the relevant figure. It follows that the profits of the accounting year ended in the year of assessment preceding the year of cessation fall out of charge to tax. To prevent high profits being packed into the year prior to cessation the Revenue are given the right under ICTA 1988 s 63 to reassess both the penultimate and the pre-penultimate years of assessment on an actual year basis rather than a preceding year basis. The actual profits are those earned between 6th April and 5th April in each of the two years of assessment, but the tax adjusted profits of accounting periods covering the two years are normally time apportioned to obtain the relevant figures. It was held by the High Court in *Baylis v Roberts*[1] that, despite the apparently discretionary nature of the wording of ICTA 1988 s 63, its provisions were mandatory, and had to be applied by the Revenue if a reassessment of the profits of the penultimate and pre-penultimate years of a business on an actual year basis would produce higher profits than assessments on a preceding year basis. In *Baylis v Roberts* the taxpayers were a husband and wife carrying on a grocery business in partnership. The business ceased and the Revenue, in accordance with their normal practice, reassessed the penultimate and pre-penultimate years on an actual basis, as this resulted in higher taxable profits than under a preceding year basis of assessment. The taxpayers appealed on the ground that ICTA 1988 s 63 gives the Revenue a discretionary power and, as the inspector had not considered whether to exercise his discretion, the assessments were invalid. This argument succeeded before the General Commissioners but failed in the High Court, where the taxpayers neither appeared nor were represented.

The change to independent taxation has only required minor changes of wording to be made to ICTA 1988 s 63[2]. These changes do not affect the substance of the section, so that if a wife who has been carrying on business on her own account ceases trading in 1990-91, the assessment for

1 [1989] STC 693.
2 See FA 1988 Sch 3 para 3.

1990-91 can only be made on her, but any back assessments under ICTA 1988 s 63 for 1989-90 and 1988-89 must be made on her husband, assuming no election for separate assessment or separate taxation of wife's earnings was in force for those years.

Example

Sarah is a married woman living with her husband. For many years she carried on business on her own account, but the business ceased trading on 31st October 1990. Prior to the cessation, the business had always made up its accounts to 31st December, and the tax adjusted profits of the final four accounting periods were:

	£
Year ended 31st December 1987	5,000
Year ended 31st December 1988	3,000
Year ended 31st December 1989	10,000
Ten months to 31st October 1990	6,000

The Sch D Case I assessment for 1990-91 will be on the actual profits earned between 6th April 1990 and 31st October 1990, and will be made on Sarah, ie

	£
1990-91 209/304 × £6,000	4,125

For 1988-89 and 1989-90 the following Sch D Case I assessments would already have been raised on Sarah's husband:

1988-89 (preceding year to 31/12/1987)	5,000
1989-90 (preceding year to 31/12/1988)	3,000

On an actual year basis the assessments for these two years become:

1988-89 (6th Apr 1988-5th Apr 1989)	
270/366 × £3,000 + 95/365 × £10,000	4,816
1990-91 (6th Apr 1990-5th Apr 1991)	
270/365 × £10,000 + 95/304 × £6,000	9,272

Although the actual assessment for 1988-89 is lower than an assessment based on the previous year's profits, this is more than offset by the increased assessment for 1989-90. Accordingly the Revenue will exercise their rights under ICTA 1988 s 63 and reduce the 1988-89 assessment on the husband by £184 (£5,000 — £4,816), and issue an additional assessment for 1989-90, also on the husband, for £6,270 (£9,270 — £3,000).

2.5 Capital allowances

Capital allowances are normally deducted from the tax adjusted profits of a trade in computing the net amount chargeable to tax. Accordingly under a system of aggregate taxation of spouses' income the husband gained the benefit of any capital allowances deductible from the profits of any trade or profession carried on by his wife, unless an election for separate assessment or separate taxation of wife's earnings had been made. Under independent taxation the benefit of capital allowances will go to the spouse carrying on the trade. Apart from this obvious change, only minor alterations have been needed in the capital allowances legislation as as result of the change to independent taxation. The Capital Allowances Act 1990 s 4(11) (originally FA 1988 Sch 3 para 23) applies if there is a disposal of an industrial building within 25 years of its construction in such a way that a balancing allowance or charge is attracted under CAA 1990 s 4, for example by sale. CAA 1990 s 4(10) limits the amount of any balancing charge to the total amount of industrial buildings allowance given to the taxpayer on the building. CAA 1990 s 4(11) provides that if a husband received industrial buildings allowance before 6th April 1990 on the basis of an interest in the building which belonged to his wife, and there is a disposal of the building by the wife after 5th April 1990 as a result of which she is liable to a balancing charge, the allowance given to the husband is to be deemed to have been given to her for the purposes of computing the maximum balancing charge.

CAA 1990 s 128(8) (originally FA 1988 Sch 3 para 24) contains a similar provision to deal with agricultural buildings allowance. If a husband received agricultural buildings allowance prior to 6th April 1990 on the basis of an interest in a building which belonged to his wife, and the building is disposed of after 5th April 1990 in such a way that a balancing charge falls to be made on his wife, the wife is to be treated as have received the agricultural buildings allowance when computing the maximum balancing charge that can be levied.

If agricultural buildings allowance was given provisionally to a husband prior to 6th April 1990 on the basis of expenditure incurred by his wife and on the assumption that the assets would be used for a qualifying purpose, but the assets are not used for that purpose, the provisional allowance may be recovered from the husband irrespective of the date it becomes apparent that the qualifying purpose requirement has not been satisfied[1].

2.6 Allocation of relief for trading and professional losses

If either spouse is engaged in a trade or profession, whether or not in partnership with another person, and the trade or profession makes a loss, a number of provisions in the income tax legislation enable relief to be claimed for the loss. Under a system of aggregate taxation of spouses' income some of the provisions enabled a trading loss of one spouse to be deducted from the income of the other spouse. The change to independent taxation has resulted in the repeal of these provisions, so that trading losses of one spouse will in future only be deductible from that spouse's income. However, for a transitional period, there may be an overlap between the old and the new rules. The following paragraphs illustrate how loss relief will operate during the transitional period.

2.6:1 Relief under ICTA 1988 s 380 against other income
If a business which makes up its accounts to a regular annual accounting date sustains a tax adjusted loss, the Sch D Case I or II assessment for the following year of assessment will be nil.

---

1 CAA 1990 s 124(2), and see IR 83 para 159.

Example

A trader makes up his business accounts to 31st December each year. For the year ended 31st December 1988 he had a tax adjusted profit of £6,000 and for the year ended 31st December 1989 he had a tax adjusted loss of £11,000. His Sch D Case I assessment for 1989-90 will be £6,000, and his Sch D Case I assessment for 1990-91 will be nil. In the absence of special provisions, the earliest year he could get relief for a loss incurred prior to 31st December 1988 is 1991-92, assuming his business returned to profitability in 1990. This is because, under ICTA 1988 s 385, the normal method of relieving a trading loss is to carry it forward and deduct it from future profits of the same trade.

ICTA 1988 s 380 allows a taxpayer to get immediate relief for trading losses against both his prior year's trading profits and his other income of the year in which the loss was incurred. For the purposes of this relief capital allowances for the period in which the loss was actually incurred may be added to the loss, or used to turn a profit into a loss, provided relief for the capital allowances has not been obtained elsewhere[1]. Under s 380(1) a taxpayer may claim relief for the loss against his other income for the year of assessment in which the loss actually occurs. Although technically the loss must be computed accurately from 6th April to 5th April in the years in which it occurs, in practice the Revenue accept a loss for an annual accounting period ended in a year of assessment as a loss for that year. A claim for relief under s 380 must be made by notice in writing not later than two years after the end of the year of assessment for which the relief is claimed[2]. Under s 380(2) a taxpayer may, but is not obliged to, elect that losses unrelieved against other income of the year the loss was incurred should be carried forward and relieved against other income of the next following year of assessment. Any losses unrelieved after that may only be carried forward and relieved under ICTA 1988 s 385 against future profits of the same trade, unless there are special circumstances, such as the loss being incurred in the opening years of the business. It should be noted that, if relief is claimed under ICTA 1988 s 380, the loss must be set against all available income of the taxpayer until either the loss is fully relieved or the taxpayer's income is exhausted[3]. In particular, it is not possible to restrict the loss relief claim so as to leave into charge to tax sufficient income to cover the taxpayer's personal allowances for the year. As unused personal allowances cannot be carried forward, a claim under s 380 may not always be the most effective way of using trading losses.

Under aggregate taxation of spouses' income, if the taxpayer incurring the loss was married to and living with his spouse, the income from which the loss was to be deducted was governed by ICTA 1988 s 282. The person sustaining the loss could require that the relief be given against his income only, without taking account of the income of his spouse[4]. Thus if a trading or professional loss was incurred by a wife, only she could require that the unrelieved loss should be deducted from her income only without also being deducted from her husband's income. It was often advantageous to

1   ICTA 1988 s 383.
2   ICTA 1988 s 380(1).
3   *Butt v Haxby* (1982) 56 TC 547, and see **2.6:3**.
4   ICTA 1988 s 382(1).

make such a claim, as some personal allowances would normally remain available to deduct from the income of the other spouse. Subject to this right to restrict the relief to the income of the spouse incurring the loss, ICTA 1988 s 382(2) provided that the loss was to be deducted from the income of both spouses, in the following order:

(1) income of the corresponding class of the person incurring the loss;
(2) the other income of the person incurring the loss;
(3) the spouse's income of the corresponding class;
(4) the spouse's other income.

Consequent upon the introduction of independent taxation, FA 1988 Sch 14 Part VIII repeals s 282(1) and (2), and the repeal is stated to have effect 'in relation to relief given for the year 1990-91 or a subsequent year of assessment'. As s 380 relief is given against income of a year of assessment, rather than in respect of a loss, the effect of the repeal appears to be that a loss incurred by one spouse for an accounting year ended in 1989-90 may be relieved against the assessable income of both spouses in 1989-90 but, to the extent that the loss is still unrelieved and further relief is claimed for 1990-91 under ICTA 1988 s 380(2), the unrelieved loss may only be deducted from the income of the spouse incurring the loss. It is clear from IR 83 para 154 that this is also the Revenue's interpretation of the repeal.

Example

Simon and Susan are husband and wife living together. Simon has earned income of £4,000 in both 1989-90 and 1990-91. Susan is in business as a taxidermist, making up her accounts to December 31 each year. For the year ended 31st December 1988 she had a tax adjusted profit of £1,000, and for the year ended 31st December 1989 she had a tax adjusted loss of £15,000. Susan has unearned income of £3,000 in each year. If full relief is claimed under ICTA 1988 s 380(1) and (2) the assessable incomes of both spouses are:

1989-90

				Chargeable
		£		£
Susan	Sch D Case I	1,000		
	Unearned income	3,000		
		4,000		
Less S 380 relief		(4,000)		Nil
Simon	Earned income	4,000		
Less S 380 relief		(4,000)		Nil

leaving £7,000 unrelieved loss available for carry forward to 1990-91.

1990-91

Susan	Sch D Case I	0	
	Unearned income	3,000	
		3,000	
Less S 380(2) relief		(3,000)	Nil
Simon	Earned income	4,000	4,000

Leaving £4,000 unrelieved losses available to carry forward under ICTA 1988 s 385 against future profits of Susan's trade.

In the above example it would not in fact be sensible to elect to deduct Susan's loss from Simon's income in 1989-90, as the married man's allowance of £4,375 is wasted. Indeed, if there is a realistic prospect of Susan's business returning to profit it is probably better not to make any s 380 relief claim, and wait to relieve the loss against future profits of the trade. But the example illustrates how s 380 relief will operate in the years of transition from aggregate to independent taxation.

2.6:2 Relief for opening year losses under ICTA 1988 s 381

Under ICTA 1988 s 381 where an individual incurs a loss in a trade or profession for the year of assessment in which it commenced, or in the following three years of assessment, he may claim to relieve the loss against his income of the three years of assessment prior to that in which the loss was incurred. As with s 380 relief, trading losses may be augmented by capital allowances[1]. Relief is given against the income of an earlier year before the income of a later year[2]. A taxpayer may chose to make a claim either under ICTA 1988 s 380 or under ICTA 1988 s 381, but relief under the section chosen must then be exhausted before any unrelieved losses can be relieved under the other section. Thus in *Butt v Haxby*[3] the taxpayer incurred a trading loss, augmented by capital allowances, of £41,000 for 1978-79, the first year in which he commenced trading. For 1978-79 he had other assessable income of £46,461. He sought to claim relief for the loss under what is now ICTA 1988 s 380 against £35,000 of his income for 1978-79, and carry back £6,000 unrelieved losses under the then equivalent of ICTA 1988 s 381 and set them against against his income for 1975-76. The General Commissioners supported his claim to split his loss relief in this way, but it was rejected by the High Court. If his total income for 1978-79 had only been £35,000 he could, of course, have elected to relieve £35,000 of the loss under ICTA 1988 s 380, and to carry back the unrelieved £6,000 under ICTA 1988 s 381.

Anti-avoidance provisions apply to prevent or restrict relief being claimed under ICTA 1988 s 381 if a business is transferred from one spouse to the other. ICTA 1988 s 381(5) provides that, if a business is transferred between spouses living together, the periods of ownership of both spouses are to be aggregated in determining whether a loss has been incurred in any of the four years of assessment following the commencement of a trade. This provision is not affected by the introduction of independent taxation.

Prior to the introduction of independent taxation, if the proprietor of the business was married and living with his spouse, the order of set-off of losses under ICTA 1988 s 381 was identical to loss relief under ICTA 1988 s 380. Unless the proprietor elected to the contrary, the loss would be relieved against the income of both spouses[4]. The right to relieve a loss against the income of the other spouse is removed by FA 1988 Sch 14 Part VIII, but again only in relation to relief given for 1990-91 or a subsequent year of assessment. As s 381 envisages the carrying back of a loss to relieve it against the income of an earlier year of assessment, it

---

1 ICTA 1988 s 383.
2 ICTA 1988 s 381(2).
3 (1982) 56 TC 547
4 ICTA 1988 s 382(1)(2).

seems that a loss incurred after the introduction of independent taxation can still be carried back and relieved against the income of both spouses of a year prior to the introduction of independent taxation. It is clear from IR 83 para 152 that this is the way the Revenue propose to interpret the legislation.

Example

At all material times Philip and Mary are husband and wife living together. On 1st January 1992 Mary commences a business. The tax adjusted profit for the year to 31st December 1992 is £3,000. The assessable profit for 1991-92 is therefore 95/366 £3,000 = £779. For 1991-92 Mary made a capital allowances claim of £11,000. Deducted from the profit of £779, this gave a loss available for relief of £10,221. Mary may claim under ICTA 1988 s 381 to relieve this loss against the joint income of herself and Philip for 1988-89. To the extent that the loss remains unrelieved, it may be relieved against their joint income for 1989-90. But if there is still an unrelieved loss, it can only be relieved against Mary's income for 1990-91. It should be noted that any tax repayment due as a result of the carry back is technically payable to Philip unless there has been an election for separate assessment or separate taxation of wife's earnings, when any repayment attributable to Mary's income assessable separately would be due to her.

2.6:3 Relief for share losses under ICTA 1988 s 574

Under ICTA 1988 s 574(1) where an individual subscribes for shares in a qualifying trading company and subsequently incurs an allowable loss on the disposal of those shares for capital gains tax purposes, he may claim to deduct that loss from his income for income tax purposes for the year in which the loss was incurred[1]. The relief must be claimed by notice in writing given not more than two years after the year of assessment in respect of which the relief is claimed. If the loss cannot be fully relieved against income of the year in which it was incurred, the unrelieved loss may be carried forward one further year and relieved against income of the next following year, on principles analogous to those in ICTA 1988 s 380. A claim for relief under s 574 is given in priority to a claim for relief under both s 380 and ICTA 1988 s 381[2]. To avoid double relief under the business expansion scheme provisions and s 574, any capital loss must be reduced by any relief claimed for business expansion investment before relief can be claimed under s 574[3].

The rules for relief for married claimants are the same as for relief under ICTA 1988 ss 380 and 381. Accordingly, prior to 1990-91 if the claimant was married to and living with his spouse he could elect that the loss should only be deducted from his own income[4]. If no such election was made, the loss was deducted from the income of both spouses[5]. For 1990-91 and later years relief can only be claimed against the income of the spouse incurring the loss[6].

---

1 ICTA 1988 s 574(1).
2 ICTA 1988 s 574(2)(d).
3 CGTA 1979 s 149(c)(2) and (3).
4 ICTA 1988 s 574(2)(b).
5 ICTA 1988 s 574(2)(c).
6 FA 1988 Sch 14 Part VIII, which repeals (2)(b) and (2)(c) of the original s 574.

A qualifying trading company is a company none of whose shares have ever been quoted on the stock exchange and which is either a trading company on the date the shares are disposed of or was a trading company at some time within the three years preceding the disposal, and has not been an excluded investment company since it ceased trading[1]. Additionally, the company must have been resident in the UK since the date of incorporation, and must either have been a trading company for a continuous period of six years immediately prior to the sale, or, if it has been trading for a shorter period, must not have been an excluded or investment company prior to the commencement of trade[2].

2.6:4 Terminal loss relief under ICTA 1988 s 388

Where a trade or profession is permanently discontinued and there is a loss in the last twelve months of trading a taxpayer may, to the extent that no relief has been given under any other provision, such as ICTA 1988 s 380, claim to carry back that loss and set it against the profits of the same trade in each of the three years of assessment prior to the year in which the trade ceased. Relief is to be given against a later year before an earlier year. If the claimant is married it has only ever been possible to deduct a terminal loss from the claimant's income, as the loss can only be set against earlier years' profits of the same trade. The change to independent taxation therefore has no direct effect on the relief. But if a loss is incurred in, say, 1990-91, the relief will be given against the tax liability on the income of a spouse in a year in which the aggregation principles applied.

2.7 National Savings Bank interest

The first £70 of National Savings Bank deposit interest, other than interest on investment deposits, is exempt from income tax[3]. Husband and wife are, and always have been, entitled to separate £70 limits for the purposes of this exemption, but the exemption available to each spouse can only be set against that spouse's interest. Any unused exemption of one spouse cannot be transferred to the other spouse. As the principle of separate exemptions applies automatically under independent taxation, FA 1988 Sch 14 Part VIII has repealed from 1990-91 onwards that part of ICTA 1988 s 325 which provided for each spouse to have a separate £70 limit.

2.8 Pension receipts

Under independent taxation a wife will be taxed on any state retirement pension to which she is entitled, whether her entitlement derives from her own contributions or from her husband's contributions, and will be able to set her personal allowance against it[4]. Under aggregate taxation a wife's

1 ICTA 1988 s 576(4).
2 ICTA 1988 s 576(4).
3 ICTA 1988 s 325.
4 IR 83 para 70 and [1988] STI 174.

state retirement pension based on her husband's contributions was taxed as the husband's income.

If under the terms of a relevant statutory pension scheme for employees a spouse in receipt of a pension is entitled to transfer all or part of the pension to the other spouse, an irrevocable transfer of pension will result in the transferred pension being taxed as the recipient spouse's income[1]. The transfer will not be caught by the settlements anti-avoidance provision in ICTA 1988 s 683 or ICTA 1988 s 674A[2]. A 'relevant statutory pension scheme' is defined in ICTA 1988 ss 611A and 612 as a scheme established under any enactment, or under statutory regulations, or approved by a Minister or government department, and, if established after 13th March 1989, is listed in a register maintained by the Revenue. The concession is therefore confined to public sector pension schemes, and does not extend to private sector schemes. If an approved private sector scheme permits the transfer of pension during the life of the person who has earned the pension, any pension transferred to a spouse will remain taxable as the transferor spouse's income under ICTA 1988 s 674A[3]. ICTA 1988 s 683(4A), which excludes from both s 683 and s 674A income from property which has been gifted outright from one spouse to another, does not apply if the property transferred is wholly or substantially a right to income[4].

2.9 Ex gratia payments on the termination of an office or employment

Compensation for loss of office, and ex gratia payments on the termination of an office or employment, if they are not otherwise subject to tax under Schedule E, are taxable under provisions contained in ICTA 1988 ss 148, 188 and Sch 11. Any payment to the taxpayer's spouse or relative consequent on the termination of the taxpayer's employment is treated as payment to the taxpayer[5]. The first £30,000 of a compensation payment or ex gratia payment is exempt from tax[6], but any excess over that amount is fully taxable. The marginal relief which used to exist was withdrawn by FA 1988 s 74.

Husband and wife have always been entitled to separate exemptions in respect of termination payments from their respective employments, and the change to independent taxation therefore merely confirms the existing law. However, if a compensation payment was received by a wife, the excess over the exempt limit would, under aggregate taxation, have been added to her husband's income to compute the tax payable on it, unless there had been an election for separate taxation of wife's earnings. Under independent taxation this will no longer happen, and only the wife's income will be taken into account in computing any tax payable by her on compensation payments on the termination of her employment.

1   ICTA 1988 s 685(4C) and s 674A(3).
2   ICTA 1988 s 685(4C) and s 674A(3), and see **4.4** below.
3   Dealt with in detail in **4.4** below.
4   ICTA 1988 s 685(4A)(b).
5   ICTA 1988 s 148(3).
6   ICTA 1988 s 188(4).

2.10 Other Sch E benefits

Even under the system of aggregate taxation of spouses' income, it followed from the principle that the taxable income of a husband and wife was computed as if they were single but taxed as if they were one unit that the amount of a wife's income from employment was always computed separately from that of her husband's, even though it might then be taxed as his. The only change brought about by independent taxation is that the wife's Sch E emoluments can now only be taxed as her income. Thus, for example, under provisions now contained in ICTA 1988 ss 186, 187 and Schs 9 and 10, a company may establish a trust to which it makes grants of money which are used to purchase shares in the company. The trustees then allocate the shares to employees of the company. Provided the shares are retained by the trustees for five years, or until the employee's death, no income tax is payable on the initial value of the shares allocated, and capital gains tax is only payable on the excess of the disposal proceeds of the shares over their value at the time they were allocated, plus indexation relief. The shares cannot normally be disposed of within two years of allocation, and if they are disposed of between two and five years of allocation an income tax charge will usually arise. The maximum value of shares which can be appropriated to an employee in any one tax year is the greater of £2,000 or 10% of the employee's salary for the year or the preceding year, but subject to an overriding maximum of £6,000. If husband and wife are both employees of a company operating such a scheme, these limits are applied to them separately, both under aggregate taxation and under independent taxation.

The Revenue have recently announced two new extra statutory concessions which relate to benefits provided for a member of an employee's family[1]. The first concession deals with the provision of company cars. If husband and wife, or any other member of the family, both have emoluments of at least £8,500 per annum and are employed by the same employer, and each of them is provided with a company car, each of them will be taxed on the scale benefit appropriate to their own car. However, under the legislation, each employee could also be taxed on the benefit arising from the other car provided for use of each member of the employee's family[2]. The concession makes it clear that each employee will only be taxed on a single car benefit in these circumstances. For the concession to apply it must be shown that equivalent cars are made available to employees of similar status who are not related to the taxpayer, and that it is normal commercial practice to provide a company car for a job of the kind undertaken by the employee. Similarly, if a car is shared by two employees, for example a husband and wife, of the same employer, there will only be one scale benefit charge, which will be apportioned between them having regard to all the relevant facts.

The second concession concerns the taxation of an employee on employers' contributions to approved retirement benefits or accident schemes. Most employers' contributions to exempt pension schemes are exempt from taxation as a benefit to the employee under ICTA 1988 s 155(4). However,

1   See [1989] STI 648.
2   ICTA 1988 s 157(1).

although permitted by the Superannuation Funds Office, contributions to provide benefits for members of an employee's wider family, such as his parents, son-in-law and daughter-in-law, are not technically within the tax exemption. The concession confirms what has always been the Revenue practice not to tax the employee on contributions by an employer which may be used to provide benefits for such members of the family.

2.11 Close company loans to participators

Under ICTA 1988 s 419, if a close company makes a loan, otherwise than in the course of a lending business, to a participator or an associate of a participator the company must pay advance corporation tax on the amount of the loan. An associate includes a relative[1], and a relative includes a spouse, whether or not the spouses are living together[2]. The advance corporation tax is recoverable if the loan is repaid[3], but if repayment of the loan is waived then the participator is taxed as if he had received as income the amount written off grossed up at the basic rate of income tax, from which basic rate tax had been withheld at source[4]. The participator cannot recover the basic rate tax if he is a non-taxpayer[5], and will have no further tax liability if he remains a basic rate taxpayer after the addition of the gross amount. However, if the addition of the gross amount puts him into the higher rate tax band, he will have to pay the excess of the higher rate over the basic rate (currently 15%) on the amount liable to higher rate tax.

Under ICTA 1988 s 420(2), as it was in force prior to 6th April 1990, these provisions did not apply to a loan to a participator who was a director or employee of the close company, or an associated company, provided he was a full time working director or employee and he did not have a material interest (roughly 5% of the share capital) in the company and the loan was within certain financial limits. The amount of the loan when added to any other loans made by the close company, or an associated company, to the borrower or his spouse must not exceed £15,000. If the earlier loan was made before 31st March 1971 it had to be for the purpose of enabling the participator to purchase a main residence, and the outstanding amount must not exceed £10,000[6]. If a loan is made on or after 6th April 1990 a prior loan to a spouse of the participator no longer has to be included in determining whether these financial limits have been exceeded[7].

It should be noted that ICTA 1988 s 420(2) only operates to exclude the loan from the close company rules. If the participator director or employee is in receipt of annual emoluments of £8,500 or more he will be taxable under ICTA 1988 s 160 for each year in which the loan is outstanding on the excess of interest at the notional rate on the outstanding loan over

1　ICTA 1988 s 417(3).
2　ICTA 1988 s 417(4).
3　ICTA 1988 s 419(4).
4　ICTA 1988 s 421(1).
5　ICTA 1988 s 421(1)(b).
6　ICTA 1988 s 420(2)(a).
7　FA 1988 Sch 3 para 16.

any interest he pays (see **4.2** below). If the loan is waived, and the amount waived is not taxable under normal Sch E principles, he will have a Sch E taxable benefit under ICTA 1988 s 160(2) of the amount written off. Unlike the close company provisions in ICTA 1988 s 421, the loan is not grossed up, but conversely no basic rate tax is deemed to have been paid, so the employee or director will be liable to both basic rate and higher rate tax on the amount written off.

2.12 The allocation of tax deductible expenditure and charges

With the exception of provisions relating to the deduction of mortgage interest, the legislation is silent on which spouse is entitled to the benefit of tax deductible expenditure and charges on income. In particular, there is no equivalent of ICTA 1988 s 282A to deal with the allocation of payments where the obligation to make the payment is a joint obligation of both husband and wife. As a matter of general principle, a spouse will only be able to get a deduction for expenditure which is otherwise tax deductible if he can establish that (a) he, rather than the other spouse, was under a legal obligation to make the payment, and (b) that he actually made the payment. If the obligation is a joint obligation, but the payee could call upon either spouse to make payment in full, the spouse who actually makes the payment may be able to claim a tax deduction for it. IR 83 paras 115 and 117 indicate that the Revenue are prepared to take a reasonably generous approach in determining who is entitled to tax relief on joint payments.

2.13 Payments under the business expansion scheme provisions

Under statutory provisions contained in ICTA 1988 ss 289-312, as amended, an individual may subscribe for shares in qualifying companies and obtain full tax relief for his subscription. The minimum subscription in any one year which qualifies for tax relief is £500, and the maximum is £40,000[1]. Relief is only given on the making of a claim, and the deduction is made from the taxpayer's income, after making all other deductions including personal allowances, of the tax year in which the shares were issued[2]. However, if the shares are issued before 6th October in a tax year, a taxpayer may elect to carry back part of his subscription and deduct it from his income of the immediately preceding tax year[3]. The amount which can be so carried back is the lower of half the amount subscribed, or £5,000[4]. The limit of £5,000 applies to the aggregate of all amounts which a taxpayer elects to carry back. In certain circumstances BES relief, once granted, may be subsequently withdrawn. In particular, under ICTA 1988 s 299(1), if a subscriber disposes of the shares within five years of their acquisition and the disposal was otherwise than under a bargain at arm's length, the

1 ICTA 1988 s 290.
2 ICTA 1988 s 287(5),(14).
3 ICTA 1988 s 289(6).
4 ICTA 1988 s 289(7).

relief is withdrawn in full. If the disposal was under a bargain at arm's length the relief is withdrawn to the extent of the gross consideration received on the disposal. Any withdrawal of relief is achieved by raising a Sch D Case VI assessment for the tax year in which the relief was given[1]. If, under the carry-back provisions, relief was given for two consecutive years of assessment, relief is withdrawn from the earlier year before the later year[2]. The assessment may be raised at any time within six years of the end of the year of assessment in which the event giving rise to the withdrawal occurred[3], but no assessment can be raised in relation to events occurring after the death of the person to whom the shares were originally issued[4].

Under the system of aggregate taxation of spouses' income, a husband and wife were treated as a single unit for the purposes of the business expansion scheme rules. Thus the limit of £40,000 applied to the joint subscriptions of both of them. Relief was given by deducting the combined qualifying subscriptions of both spouses from the income of the husband, unless an election for separate assessment or separate taxation of wife's earnings had been made. If either of these elections were in force qualifying payments made by the wife had to be deducted from her income. If the combined qualifying subscriptions exceeded £40,000, the tax deductible amount of £40,000 was allocated between the spouses pro rata to their gross payments. These provisions had little practical effect under a separate assessment election, as this election had no overall effect on the spouses' tax bill, but they could be disadvantageous under a separate taxation election. They meant that the payments had to be deducted from the wife's earned income and could not be deducted from her unearned income, which remained aggregated with her husband's income and could be liable to a higher rate of tax than her earned income. Conversely, unless the spouses had separated at the time of the disposal, any withdrawal of relief was made on the spouse who had originally received it, normally the husband. However, if the parties had separated prior to a disposal of the shares within the restricted period of five years, the spouse making the disposal was liable to repay the original tax relief.

Under independent taxation the aggregation rules are repealed[5]. Thus each spouse now has a separate £40,000 maximum limit, and qualifying payments can only be deducted from the income of the spouse making the payment. Consistent with the principle that deductions under the BES scheme are made after all other deductions, including personal allowances, BES contributions are not deductible in computing whether a husband has unused married couple's allowance[6], or unused personal allowance transferable under the transitional provisions[7]. Special provisions are necessary to deal with the situation where either spouse subscribes for shares before 6th October 1990 and elects under ICTA 1988 s 289(6) to carry back part of the relief to 1989-90, the last year of aggregate taxation. If the spouses were living with each other throughout 1989-90 the amount carried back

1   ICTA 1988 s 307(1).
2   ICTA 1988 s 307(1).
3   ICTA 1988 s 307(2).
4   ICTA 1988 s 307(2).
5   FA 1988 Sch 3 para 12(1).
6   ICTA 1988 s 257B(2).
7   ICTA 1988 s 257D(8).

must be deducted from the husband's total income, and single £40,000 and £5,000 overall limits apply to the aggregate subscriptions of both spouses for 1989-90[1]. Despite the wording of FA 1988 Sch 3 para 12, it seems that, if an election for separate assessment or separate taxation was in force for 1989-90, payments made by the wife and carried back to 1989-90 will continue to be deducted from her income, or her earned income[2]. This is because ICTA 1988 s 283, which dealt with separate assessment for 1989-90, provided that tax should be charged as if the spouses were not married, and s 287(7), dealing with separate taxation, said that, notwithstanding anything to the contrary in the Income Tax Acts, payments made under the BES scheme by a wife must be deducted from her earnings.

If any relief under the BES scheme which was given for a tax year before 1989-90 has to be withdrawn in 1990-91, or a later year, as a result of a disposal by the spouse who acquired the shares, the assessment withdrawing the relief is to be made on the spouse making the disposal[3]. This may cause some difficulties where the original acquisition was made by the wife, and no election for separate assessment or separate taxation of wife's earnings was in force, as the original relief will have been given to the husband.

If one spouse who acquired shares under the BES scheme provisions and claimed tax relief on them transfers them to the other spouse that transfer does not result in a withdrawal of relief under ICTA 1988 s 299, provided the spouses are living together at the time of the transfer[4]. However, if tax relief has to be clawed back because of a disposal of the shares by the transferee within five years of their original issue, the assessment clawing back the tax relief must be made on the transferee and not on the spouse who originally subscribed for the shares. This is apparently so even if relief was originally granted in a year in which there was aggregate taxation of spouses' income.

> Example
>
> In October 1988 Dave subscribed £20,000 for shares under the business expansion scheme, and claimed this amount as a deduction against his 1988-89 tax liability. The top slice of his income after the deduction remained taxable at 40%; accordingly the deduction was worth £8,000 in terms of tax relief (£20,000 @ 40%). In June 1990 he gifted the shares to his wife Mary. In May 1991 Mary gifts the shares to their eldest child. The transfer of the shares from Dave to Mary has no BES tax implications but, as the transfer to the child in May 1991 is within five years of their original issue, there will be a clawback of relief under ICTA 1988 s 299(1). Mary will receive a Sch D Case VI assessment for 1988/89 in the sum of £20,000, tax payable £8,000.

2.14 Deeds of covenant to charity

The allocation of tax deductible expenditure may cause problems if a wife has entered into a deed of covenant to charity. Under ICTA 1988 ss 660

---

1   FA 1988 Sch 3 para 12.
2   Confirmed as the Revenue's view by IR 83 para 151.
3   Revised ICTA 1988 s 304(6), inserted by FA 1988 Sch 3 para 12.
4   Revised ICTA 1988 s 304(5), inserted by FA 1988 Sch 3 para 12.

and 683, if a taxpayer makes a deed of covenant in favour of a charity which is capable of lasting for more than four years, payments made under the deed are tax deductible for both basic and higher rate tax purposes. Basic rate tax relief is obtained under ICTA 1988 s 348, which enables the payer to withhold and retain basic rate tax from the gross payment at the rate in force when the payment was due. However, this presupposes that the payer has taxable income in excess of the payments made under deed of covenant. If he does not, some or all of the basic rate tax withheld when the payment was made will have to be recovered by the Revenue either by restricting the payer's personal allowances under ICTA 1988 s 276(1) to leave into charge to tax an amount equal to the gross payment under deed of covenant or, if that is insufficient, by applying ICTA 1988 s 349. Under ICTA 1988 s 349, if a payer's taxable income is less than a payment made under deed of covenant, the payer must withhold basic rate tax at the rate in force at the time the payment is made, and the tax withheld will then be collected by the Revenue by direct assessment on the payer.

With a system of aggregate taxation of spouses' income it was immaterial which spouse made the covenant. Unless an election for separate taxation of wife's earnings had been made, in which case a wife's payments under charitable deed of covenant had to be deducted from her earned income, payments by both spouses under charitable deed of covenant were aggregated and treated as if they had been made by the husband. Provided the combined incomes of husband and wife exceeded the gross amount due under the covenant there was no restriction of personal allowances under ICTA 1988 s 276(1), and no need for a direct assessment under ICTA 1988 s 349. With the change to independent taxation payments made by a spouse under qualifying deed of covenant can only be deducted from that spouse's income. If a spouse's income is less than the payment problems will arise. The problems are aggrevated if the spouse's income includes building society or bank deposit interest which is subject to composite rate tax, as only the net receipt may be used to cover gross payments under deed of covenant[1].

Example

For 1990-91 Julie, a married woman living with her husband, received building society interest of £350. She was obliged under a four year deed of covenant with a charity to pay such sum as, after deducting basic rate tax, should equal £400. Julie paid £400 to the charity. For income tax purposes she is deemed to have made a gross payment to the charity of £533.33 from which she has withheld tax of £133.33 (£533.33 × 25%). Only £350 of this £533.33 is treated as having been paid out of taxable income. Julie has therefore gained excessive tax relief, and the Revenue will raise an assessment under ICTA 1988 s 349 as follows:

		£
	Gross payment	533
Less	Building society interest	(350)
	S 349 assessment	183
	Tax payable @ 25%	45.75

---

1   ICTA 1988 s 476(5)(d); 479(2)(c).

In their booklet IR 80 the Inland Revenue therefore advise married couples to review charitable deeds of covenant if the spouse who has made the covenant has a low taxable income, and to consider whether the higher income earning spouse should enter into the deed of covenant instead. Technically a deed of covenant is a legally enforceable document binding on both parties to it, and it is not open to a spouse to decline to continue payments unilaterally. However, it is improbable that a charity would insist on its strict legal rights, particularly if it was clear that the other spouse would be entering into a new deed of covenant to compensate for the one that was being extinguished.

For the avoidance of any doubt it should be emphasised that it is only a deed of covenant to charity which should be changed in this way. No attempt should be made to vary other deeds of covenant which continue to attract basic rate tax relief only because they were made before 15th March 1988. If these covenants are varied tax relief will be lost completely, and it cannot be transferred from one spouse to the other. Thus, if a spouse is under an obligation to make a payment under a pre 15th March 1988 covenant and has insufficient income to cover the gross covenant, the only realistic solution is for that spouse to generate additional income, perhaps by a transfer of income producing assets from the other spouse, or by taking part-time employment. If additional income is not generated the spouse making the payment under deed of covenant will have the basic rate tax withheld collected by means of an assessment under ICTA 1988 s 349.

If there is a joint deed of covenant to charity the Revenue state in IR 83 para 115 that the amount on which each person is entitled to tax relief is the amount that each person pays. If it is unclear who is making the payments each spouse will be presumed to have paid half the total payments. On this interpretation it seems that if one spouse is a non-taxpayer and there is a joint deed of covenant to charity, full tax relief can be retained by ensuring that only the taxpaying spouse makes the payments. To ensure that the Revenue can be satisfied that payments have been made in this way it is desirable that the payments should be made out of the taxpaying spouse's separate bank account.

2.15 Annual payments between spouses

Annual payments between spouses living together remain ineffective for income tax purposes under independent taxation even if the legal obligation to make the payment was entered into before 15th March 1988[1]. Other provisions in the 1988 Finance Act withdrew tax relief from deeds of covenant entered into on or after 15th March 1988 unless the covenant was in favour of a charity. Existing covenants were not affected, and continue to attract tax relief at the basic rate until they expire. FA 1988 Sch 3 para 32 therefore preserves the tax treatment of annual payments between spouses under aggregate taxation, which was that, since spouses were taxed as a single unit, annual payments between them had no tax consequences.

1   FA 1988 Sch 3 para 32.

2.16 Tax relief for mortgage interest

Tax relief for interest payments is now severely restricted. Relief can only be claimed either where interest is paid on a fixed loan or overdraft which has been applied wholly and exclusively for the purposes of a trade, profession, or vocation, or where interest is paid on a fixed loan (not an overdraft) which has been applied for a limited number of purposes specified in the tax legislation. Of these by far the most common are loans for house purchase, commonly called mortgages, although it is the purpose for which the loan was granted, and not the fact that it is secured on property, that is important for tax relief. For loans taken out after 5th April 1988 tax relief will be granted for interest paid on a loan incurred for the purchase of land, or a large caravan or houseboat, situated in the United Kingdom or the Republic of Ireland if either the land is used as the only or main residence of the borrower or it is rented out on a commercial basis for at least 26 weeks in any 52 week period[1]. Tax relief is also available for loans for the purchase of 'job-related accommodation' under provisions introduced in FA 1977 s 36 and now in ICTA 1988 s 356. If an employee is provided with accommodation as part of his job and if, but only if, that accommodation is exempt from charge on its annual value under one of the three exemptions in ICTA 1988 s 145(4), then the employee may claim tax relief on another house in which he resides (even though it is not his main residence) or which is intended to become his only or main residence. Relief is only allowed on one such property. A loan limit of a maximum of £30,000 applies to loans for the purchase of property for personal occupation or as job-related accommodation, but there is no limit on the interest which can be deducted from the income of property which is rented out. However interest on rented property may only be deducted from the profits of that or any other rented property, and may not be deducted from the taxpayer's other income[2]. Any unrelieved interest may be carried forward and deducted from rental income of future years[3].

Prior to 6th April 1988 tax relief was also available in two other circumstances — loans for home improvements, and loans for the purchase of a house where the occupant was a dependent relative of the borrower or his spouse and the accommodation was provided rent-free, or the occupant was the borrower's former or separated spouse. A dependent relative was defined as a relative of the taxpayer or his spouse who is incapacitated by old age or infirmity from maintaining himself, or his or his spouse's widowed, divorced or separated mother, whether incapacitated by old age or not[4]. Although tax relief was available for a house occupied by a dependent relative or a former or separated spouse, only one £30,000 loan limit was available for the combined loans on the taxpayer's main residence and the house occupied by the dependent relative or the former or separated spouse. FA 1988 s 43 abolished tax relief for home improvement loans made after 5th April 1988. Loans in place before that date continue to qualify for relief until the loan is repaid. New improvement loans may still qualify

1   ICTA 1988 ss 353, 354.
2   ICTA 1988 s 355(4).
3   ICTA 1988 s 355(4).
4   ICTA 1988 s 367(1).

for relief if the loan is for the erection of new buildings on land which previously had no buildings on it, and which are not part of an existing residence. FA 1988 s 44 withdrew tax relief from 6th April 1988 on house purchase loans where the house is occupied by a dependent relative or former or separated spouse. There is continuing relief if the loan was made before 6th April 1988 and the only reason the loan qualified for relief immediately prior to 6th April 1988 was because the house was then being occupied by a dependent relative or a former or separated spouse[1].

2.16:1 The 'only or main residence' of a spouse

For interest relief purposes the 'only or main residence' of an individual is a question of fact. If an individual has more than one residence there is no equivalent for income tax of the capital gains tax provision in CGTA 1979 s 101(5), which enables an individual to elect which of two or more residences is to be his main residence. Until recently there was also no equivalent of CGTA 1979 s 101(6), which restricts husband and wife living together to claiming principal private residence exemption on the same residence. With the introduction of independent taxation, the absence of such a provision would have enabled a husband and wife each to have a £30,000 loan limit on separate houses provided they could establish that the house on which they were claiming relief was in fact their main residence. This might be possible if, for example, a wife is working in Exeter and her husband is working in London. The wife pays the mortgage on a house in Exeter, where she permanently resides. The husband has purchased a flat in London with the aid of a mortgage, and resides there from Monday to Friday, returning to Exeter only at weekends. The Exeter house is clearly the main residence of the wife, but the husband could reasonably claim that the London flat was his main residence. The only reported case on the meaning of 'main residence' in the mortgage interest legislation is *Frost v Feltham*[2]. A taxpayer normally lived in a public house in Essex of which he was the tenant and licensee. Jointly with his wife he purchased a house in Wales, which they visited every month. For 1975-76 and 1976-77, when tax relief for loans to purchase job-related accommodation had not yet been introduced, the taxpayer claimed relief for mortgage interest on the purchase of the Welsh home on the ground that it was his main residence. The General Commissioners held that the home in Wales was the taxpayer's main residence, and the High Court refused to interfere saying that, if a taxpayer has two residences, it was ultimately a question of fact which is the main one.

Legislation was introduced in the Finance Act 1988 to deal with the situation where husband and wife have mortgages on different residences. ICTA 1988 s 356B(5)[3] provides that, if a husband and wife are living together, and the husband pays interest in respect of a residence which he is using as his only or main residence, and the wife is paying interest in respect of a house which she is using as her only or main residence, the house purchased first is to be treated as the only or main residence of both of them, and the house purchased second is to be treated as the only or main

---

1   FA 1988 s 44(2)(3).
2   (1980) 55 TC 10.
3   S 356B(8) for 1988-89 and 1989-90.

residence of neither of them. The new provision applies to payments of interest on or after 1st August 1988, whether or not the relevant loan was taken out before that date[1]. The application of s 356B(5) is disadvantageous if there is a low outstanding mortgage, say £10,000, on the house purchased first, and a high mortgage, say £35,000, on the house being purchased second. Tax relief will only be available on the £10,000, thus leaving £20,000 of the £30,000 loan limit unused. In these circumstances it makes sense, if finance is available, to redeem the first loan. This will enable tax relief to be claimed on the loan to purchase the house acquired second, and unlock an additional £20,000 of loan limit.

2.16:2 Spouses and the £30,000 loan limit

We have seen that the maximum loan on which tax relief can be claimed on a loan for house purchase for personal occupation, or for occupation by a dependent relative or a former or separated spouse, is £30,000. Prior to the Finance Act 1988 husband and wife were treated as a single unit for the purpose of this restriction. A loan made to a wife was deemed to have been made to her husband, and was aggregated with any house purchase loans made to him to determine whether the £30,000 loan limit had been exceeded. If the limit was exceeded tax relief was restricted on the loan which crossed the limit, with each loan being dealt with in date order. However, cohabitees were subject to no such aggregation, and were therefore each entitled to mortgage relief on a loan of £30,000, which gave them a substantial advantage over a married couple. This advantage was removed by the Finance Act 1988 for loans taken out on or after 1st August 1988. Instead of the £30,000 loan limit being a limit per person, with husband and wife counting as one person, it became a limit per residence. The implications of this change for cohabitees are discussed in the chapter on cohabitation; the implications for husband and wife are discussed here.

The new rules were not intended to confer any new advantage on husband and wife. Accordingly for the first two years of their operation, 1988-89 and 1989-90, if no person other than a husband and wife had a qualifying mortgage on the residence, and if no election for separate assessment or separate taxation of wife's earnings was in force, interest paid by a wife living with her husband was deemed to be paid by her husband[2], and a single £30,000 loan limit applied to the aggregate loans to both spouses[3]. As this represented no change from the previous law, the new provisions applied to interest payments made on or after 1st August 1988 even if the loan had been made before that date[4]. If an election for separate assessment or separate taxation of wife's earnings was in force and only one spouse was paying qualifying mortgage interest, that spouse was allocated the full £30,000 loan limit[5]. If each spouse was paying qualifying mortgage interest, each spouse was allocated a sharer's limit of £15,000 and received tax relief on loans up to this amount[6]. Any unused limit of one spouse was automatically transferred to the other spouse[7]. However the spouses

1 ICTA 1988 s 356C(1).
2 ICTA 1988 s 356B(2).
3 ICTA 1988 s 356B(1).
4 ICTA 1988 s 356C(1), the excluding provisions in s 356C(2) not applying.
5 ICTA 1988 s 356A(1).
6 ICTA 1988 s 356A(3).
7 ICTA 1988 s 356A(5)(6).

were permitted jointly to make an 'allocation of interest election', discussed in more detail in the next section, to allocate all or part of both the sharer's limit and interest payments of one spouse to the other spouse[1]. Again, these provisions applied to payments of interest made on or after 1st August 1988, even if the loan was made before that date.

The position was more complicated if spouses were sharing their home with a third party who was also paying qualifying interest on the same residence. There were different rules for loans made before 1st August 1988 and loans made on or after that date. If the loans were made before 1st August 1988, the new provisions did not apply at all to payments made under the pre-August 1988 loans as long as interest payments continued and as long as the third party both retained an interest in the house and paid qualifying mortgage interest[2]. These pre-August 1988 loans are called 'protected loans' by the Revenue. If one loan to a borrower for the acquisition of a residence was a protected loan, all other loans to the same borrower and his spouse, provided the spouses were living together, to acquire the same residence were outside the new system[3]. However all the payers of qualifying interest under protected loans on the same property could jointly elect that the loans should cease to be protected loans and become subject to the new rules[4]. If no such election was made then, under ICTA 1988 s 357(3), a loan made to the spouse of a borrower was deemed to be made to the borrower if the spouses were living together, and a single £30,000 limit had to cover all loans to both spouses. If there was more than one loan the loans were dealt with in the date order in which they were created[5]. Tax relief on a protected loan was restricted to the lower of the loan outstanding on 1st August 1988 or the loan outstanding when the interest was paid[6]. If an election for separate assessment or separate taxation was in force any qualifying interest payments made by a wife had to be deducted from her income, with apparently no option to make an allocation of interest election to treat them as made by her husband.

If the loans were made on or after 1st August 1988 the new rules applied, but the husband was allocated two units in working out his sharer's limit, whether or not his wife was paying qualifying mortgage interest[7].

Example

In September 1988 Oscar and Hannah, a husband and wife living together, decided to purchase a house jointly with a friend Simon, and all were to share it as their main residence. Oscar took out a qualifying mortgage of £32,000 and then Simon took out a qualifying mortgage of £8,000. For 1988-89 and 1989-90 the sharer's limits are:

Oscar	£30,000 × 2/3 = £20,000
Simon	£30,000 × 1/3 = £10,000

1 ICTA 1988 s 356B(4).
2 ICTA 1988 s 356C(2).
3 ICTA 1988 s 356C(4).
4 ICTA 1988 s 356C(5).
5 ICTA 1988 s 357(1).
6 ICTA 1988 s 357(1C).
7 Original ICTA 1988 s 356B(2) and (3).

Oscar is therefore entitled to tax relief on a loan up to £20,000 and Simon is entitled to tax relief on a loan up to £10,000. As the loan to Simon is only £8,000, the unused £2,000 is reallocated to Oscar[1]. Accordingly for 1988-89 and 1989-90 Simon was entitled to tax relief on the whole of each interest payment that he made, whereas Oscar was only entitled to tax relief on 22/32 × each interest payment he made[2].

With the introduction of independent taxation from 6th April 1990 husband and wife are treated as independent taxpayers for the purposes of mortgage interest relief. Accordingly amended rules apply for 1990-91 and later years, and the original ICTA 1988 s 356B has been replaced by a new s 356B[3]. Under the revised provisions husband and wife are treated as separate persons. If only one spouse is liable to pay qualifying interest on a main residence a £30,000 maximum loan limit will be allocated to that spouse[4]. If both spouses are liable to pay mortgage interest on their main residence, and there is no other qualifying borrower, each spouse will be allocated a sharer's limit of £15,000[5]. Interest paid by each spouse on loans up to that amount will qualify for relief to the spouse paying the interest. If the mortgage is a joint mortgage each spouse will be deemed to have borrowed half of the total loan[6]. If either spouse has a loan less than their sharer's limit, the unused limit will automatically be transferred to the other spouse[7]. Additionally, the spouses may jointly make an allocation of interest election to allocate both the sharer's limit and the payments of interest between the spouses in whatever proportions they choose. Where there is no third party involvement, the new provisions apply whether the loan was granted before, on, or after 1st August 1988.

If husband and wife are sharing a house with a person who is also paying qualifying mortgage interest, the position after the introduction of independent taxation depends on the date the qualifying loans were made. If the qualifying loans were made on or after 1st August 1988 the sharer's limit of each of the borrowers is determined by dividing the maximum limit of £30,000 by the number of borrowers, with no distinction being made merely because two of the borrowers are married to each other. Thus if husband and wife are sharing a house with one other person and all three are liable to pay qualifying interest, each will have a sharer's limit of £10,000. If only the husband and third party are liable to pay qualifying interest, it appears at first glance that the husband has a limit of £15,000 and the third party has a limit of £15,000, as the provision in the original ICTA 1988 s 356B(3) allocating the husband two units in these circumstances has been repealed. However this can be avoided if the spouses make an allocation of interest election under ICTA 1988 s 356B(1), discussed below. If the wife has no income and MIRAS does no apply to the loan, to gain maximum tax relief on the mortgage interest paid by the husband it will

1   ICTA 1988 s 356A(4)-(6).
2   ICTA 1988 s 356D(5).
3   FA 1988 Sch 3 para 14.
4   ICTA 1988 s 356A(1).
5   ICTA 1988 s 356A(2) and (3).
6   ICTA 1988 s 356D(8).
7   ICTA 1988 s 356A(5),(6).

be necessary for the spouses jointly to elect under ICTA 1988 s 356B(1)(a) that part of the mortgage loan to the husband should be treated as payable by the wife, thus entitling her to a sharer's limit of $\frac{1}{3} \times £30,000 = £10,000$, and reducing the sharer's limit of the husband and the third party to £10,000 each. The spouses then further elect under ICTA 1988 s 356B(1)(b) that the wife's sharer's limit of £10,000 should be allocated to her husband, thus ensuring that he gets tax relief on a loan up to £20,000.

If the qualifying loans were made to one or both spouses and a third party before 1st August 1988, and payments are still continuing, ICTA 1988 s 356A and s 356B have no application at all[1] unless everyone paying qualifying interest jointly elect that they should apply[2]. The implications of this for husband and wife are not entirely clear. It seems that there can be no allocation of interest election, as the provisions permitting this are in s 356B, which no longer applies. Tax relief can therefore only be given to the spouse who pays the interest. As ICTA 1988 s 357 now applies to the loan to restrict relief to a loan of £30,000[3], and as there has been no amendment to ICTA 1988 s 357(3), a loan made to the spouse of a borrower will be added to any loan made to the borrower, provided the spouses are living together, and a £30,000 limit will be applied to the combined loans. If the loans were made on different dates, an earlier loan will attract tax relief before a later one.

2.16:3 Mortgage payments — allocation of interest election

Under aggregate taxation of spouses' incomes it normally did not matter which spouse was legally liable for payment of tax deductible mortgage interest, because the payments would be treated for income tax purposes as made by the husband and deducted from the combined incomes of husband and wife. But the position was different if the spouses had made an election for separate taxation of wife's earnings under ICTA 1988 s 287. In that event mortgage interest payments made by the wife had to be deducted from her earned income and could not be deducted from her unearned income, which remained aggregated with her husband's income, or from her husband's income. There was evidence that, if the spouses had a joint mortgage, the Revenue treated the interest payments as partly made by the husband and partly made by the wife unless there was clear evidence to the contrary, as where it could be shown that the payments were only made out of one spouse's bank account. This treatment could be particularly unfair if the wife had unearned income and her husband was a higher rate taxpayer, whereas her earned income was liable to basic rate tax only. It effectively meant that an additional penalty for making a separate taxation of wife's earnings election was the loss of higher rate relief on qualifying mortgage interest payments made by the wife. The same principle applied if an election for separate assessment was made under ICTA 1988 s 283, but this was of less significance as (a) the overall bill for the couple was not affected by the election, and (b) the wife's unearned income was allocated to her and not to her husband.

To alleviate the problem the Finance Act 1988 changed the rules for

1   ICTA 1988 s 356C(2).
2   ICTA 1988 s 356C(5).
3   ICTA 1988 s 357(1).

both 1988-89 and 1989-90. ICTA 1988 s 356B(4), inserted by FA 1988 s 42, provided that for both those years, if an election for separate assessment or separate taxation of wife's earnings had been made, the spouses could jointly elect that part or all of one spouse's sharer's limit could be transferred to the other spouse. They could also elect that part or all of the interest payments made by one spouse should be treated for income tax purposes as if they had been made by the other spouse. An election in the prescribed form had to be made not more than twelve months after the end of the tax year to which it related, so that an election for 1989-90 may still be made at any time before 6th April 1991[1]. An election made for 1988-89 also applied for 1989-90, but it could be withdrawn or altered for that year[2]. Under ICTA 1988 s 356C(1) an election for 1988-89 appears only to apply to payments of qualifying interest made on or after 1st August 1988, and it is now clear that this is the way the Revenue propose to interpret the provisions. In Revenue leaflet IR 13 dealing with a wife's earned income election[3] it is stated that, if an election for separate taxation of wife's earnings is made for 1988-89, any mortgage interest paid by the wife before 1st August 1988 can only be set against her earnings. It cannot be set against any other income she may have or any of her husband's income. Conversely mortgage interest paid by a husband cannot be deducted from his wife's earnings. An allocation of interest election is available for mortgage interest payments made on or after 1st August 1988.

The policy of allowing spouses a free choice on the allocation of both a sharer's loan limit and mortgage interest payments for income tax purposes is continued under independent taxation. FA 1988 Sch 3 para 14 inserts a revised ICTA 1988 s 356B, which applies for 1990-91 and later years. An election made for 1988-89 or 1989-90 under the original s 356B does *not* apply for 1990-91; a fresh election is necessary. The revised s 356B closely follows its predecessor. A husband and wife who are not separated may *jointly* elect that qualifying mortgage interest payable or paid by one of them should be treated for income tax purposes as if it had been payable or paid by the other[4]. They may also elect that all or part of the sharer's limit of one of them should be transferred to the other. The election must be made not more than twelve months after the year of assessment to which it relates, or within such longer period as the Revenue may allow; must be in the prescribed form (Form 15(1990)); and has effect for following tax years as well as for the year it was made[5]. In SP 8/89[6] the Revenue state that they will normally exercise their discretion to extend the one year time limit for making the election where it can be demonstrated that the failure to comply with the time limit has been caused by sickness, absence abroad, or by serious personal difficulties, or by the unavailability (within the time limit) through no fault of the taxpayers or their advisers of information essential to the decision to make or revoke an election.

Either spouse may give a notice to withdraw the election for any subsequent tax year, in which event the election will not apply for the

1　ICTA 1988 s 356B(5).
2　ICTA 1988 s 356B(5)-(7).
3　Published in August 1989.
4　ICTA 1988 s 356B(1).
5　ICTA 1988 s 356B(2).
6　A revised version of which was published on 26th January 1990; see [1990] STI 84.

year of withdrawal or any subsequent year[1]. A notice of withdrawal must be in the prescribed form (Form 15-1 (1990)), and must be given not more than twelve months after the year of assessment to which it relates, or within such longer period as the Revenue may allow[2]. A notice of withdrawal does not prejudice the making of a fresh election for any subsequent year[3]. ICTA 1988 s 356B(4)(c) is ambiguously drafted. On one reading, it does not seem possible to make a fresh election in respect of the tax year to which the notice of withdrawal relates. This may prove inconvenient if spouses have elected that a specific amount of mortgage interest should be transferred to one spouse for a particular year, and wish to vary the amounts in the following tax year. This was not the effect of the original s 356B, which allowed an election made for 1988-89 to be withdrawn for 1989-90 and a fresh election to be made for that year. It may therefore be preferable to interpret the words 'subsequent year' in s 356B(4)(c) as meaning a year subsequent to the tax year in respect of which the election was made, rather than a year subsequent to the tax year in respect of which the notice of withdrawal is given, although this intepretation has its own difficulties if an election has been in force for a number of years before it is withdrawn.

However, because of the approach which has been adopted by the Revenue to the variation of an allocation of interest election, the difficulties of interpretation discussed in the preceding paragraph may well be largely academic. The Revenue take the view that, as the terms of the Act do not preclude the making of a fresh election, it is permitted, and that it is not necessary to withdraw the original election before making a fresh election. Accordingly spouses may jointly agree to vary the allocation of sharer's limits and the allocation of mortgage interest payments by filing a new Form 15(1990) specifying the new allocation of sharer's limits and mortgage payments. The new Form 15(1990) must specify the year for which it is to have effect[4]. Provided the new Form 15(1990) is filed not more than twelve months following the end of the tax year, it is clear from IR 83 para 109 that allocation of interest elections may be varied each year to reflect changed circumstances. But it also now seems clear that, provided the twelve month time limit for making the election is complied with, the Revenue will be prepared to accept a variation effective for the same year for which an earlier election had previously been made[5]. Prior to the commencement of independent taxation some inspectors invited taxpayers for whom an allocation of interest election might be beneficial to make the election early in 1990-91. This was resisted by some practitioners because the couple's financial circumstances might not be adequately known at that stage. If a variation election can be made at the end of the year by the joint filing of a fresh Form 15(1990), and the Revenue take the view that it can, this difficulty disappears and there is no objection to complying with the Revenue's request. Nevertheless the position is not entirely a satisfactory one, because the legislation is completely silent on the variation

1   ICTA 1988 s 356B(3).
2   ICTA 1988 s 356B(4).
3   ICTA 1988 s 356B(4)(c).
4   See letter from IR Senior Press Officer (1990) 124 Taxation 377; the penultimate paragraph of the advice given on Form 15(1990); and IR 83 para 109.
5   IR 83 para 109; notes of guidance to Form 5(1990).

of an allocation of interest election; indeed, if anything it implies that a variation is not possible. It was therefore extremely difficult for practitioners to advise their clients effectively until the Revenue's views became known.

An allocation of interest election is a useful tax planning device to enable spouses to deduct mortgage interest paid by either of them from the income of the spouse with the highest marginal rate of tax. If both spouses are basic rate taxpayers no overall tax saving will result from an allocation of interest election. But if one spouse is a higher rate taxpayer, and the other is not, transferring a sharer's limit and allocating mortgage interest from the lower income spouse to the higher income spouse will result in a tax saving of 15p for every pound of mortgage interest transferred. Similarly, if a spouse has little taxable income and has to pay mortgage interest gross because the lender is not a qualifying lender, it may be that the only way in which tax relief can be obtained for the interest payments is to allocate them to the other spouse.

An allocation of interest election may also save tax if one or both spouses are over 65 and so entitled to the higher age allowance. The higher personal allowance is reduced if the total income of the claiming spouse is over £12,300, and the higher married couple's allowance is reduced if the total income of the husband is over £12,300. The gross amount of tax deductible mortgage interest is deductible in computing total income for the purpose of applying the restriction, so if one spouse over 65 has total income, ignoring mortgage interest, in excess of £12,300 and the other does not, additional personal allowances may become available if all qualifying mortgage interest is deducted from the income of the spouse with the higher income, irrespective of who actually pays the mortgage.

2.16:4 Qualifying loans on a house occupied by a dependent relative

The new provisions giving mortgage interest relief on a 'per residence' basis rather than a 'per person' basis do not apply to a loan which qualifies for tax relief only because the property which was being acquired was occupied by a dependent relative or former or separated spouse on 5th April 1988, and has continued to be so occupied[1]. Accordingly in computing the loan limit of the spouse liable to pay interest under the dependent relative loan, prior loans to the borrower's spouse have to be taken into account as if they had been made to the borrower, provided the spouses are living together[2].

However it appears that one consequence of the change to a 'per residence' basis of mortgage interest relief for married couples, even if the loan was taken out before 1st August 1988, is that loans to purchase a main residence no longer enter into cumulation in computing the maximum tax relief available on a loan to purchase a house for a dependent relative *provided* the dependent relative loan was taken out *before* the loan to purchase the main residence. Revenue authority in support of this approach is contained in para 17(b) of a guidance statement issued in July 1988 by the Inland Revenue MIRAS Central Unit. Para 17(b) states:

1   ICTA 1988 s 356C(7).
2   ICTA 1988 s 357(3),(5).

'The residence basis does not apply to loans used to purchase a main residence for a dependent relative etc. If the borrower has a loan on a dependent relative's main residence in respect of which he is obtaining tax relief prior to 1 August 1988, relief will continue after 31 July 1988, even where he is obtaining relief under the residence basis for a loan used to purchase his own main residence, as follows:

(i)   where the loan to purchase a dependent relative's residence was made first, relief on this loan up to £30,000 will be available in addition to relief under the residence basis in respect of the borrower's own residence;

(ii)   where the loan to purchase the borrower's residence was made first, relief in respect of the dependent relative's residence will be restricted by the amount of the earlier loan. For example, if the earlier loan was £20,000 relief will only be available on a loan up to £10,000 (ie £30,000 − £20,000) for the purchase of the dependent relative's residence. The borrower's own residence will be eligible for relief under the residence basis as in (i) above.'[1]

2.16:5 Mortgage interest — anti-avoidance provisions

There are a number of anti-avoidance provisions in the income tax legislation which may operate to deny tax relief on loans for the purchase or development of land.

(1)   No tax relief can be claimed for interest paid on loans for the purchase of land where seller and purchaser are husband and wife who are living together at the time of the sale[2].

(2)   No tax relief can be claimed for interest paid on a loan for the purchase of land where the person is acquiring land, directly or indirectly, from a person connected with him and the price substantially exceeds the value of what is acquired[3]. Husband and wife, irrespective of whether they are living together, are connected persons[4]. Spouses cease to be connected persons following a decree absolute of divorce. For sales between husband and wife the combined effect of ICTA 1988 s 355(5)(a) and (d) is that, as long as husband and wife are living together, no tax relief is available on sales from one to the other. Once they separate, tax relief is available, but only if the sale is not substantially out of line with the market value of the property sold. After a divorce, neither of the above two restrictions apply.

(3)   No tax relief can be claimed if, after 15th April 1969, the purchaser, or the spouse of the purchaser, disposed of the land and it appears that the main purpose of the disposal and reacquisition was to obtain tax relief[5]. A disposal by a spouse is only caught if the spouses were living together, and it seems that the relevant time for ascertaining this is the time the property was reacquired.

(4)   No tax relief can be obtained if the purchasers are the trustees of a settlement and the seller is the settlor, or the wife or husband of the settlor, and it appears that the main purpose of the sale was to

1   For further discussion of the legal reasoning which supports this view see **8.3** below.
2   ICTA 1988 s 355(5)(a).
3   ICTA 1988 s 355(5)(d).
4   ICTA 1988 s 839(2).
5   ICTA 1988 s 355(5)(b).

gain tax relief[1]. Again, spouses are only caught if they are living together at the time of the sale.

(5) If a loan for the development of property is made and it is not caught by the prohibition on tax relief for home improvement loans in ICTA 1988 s 355(2A) and (2B), ICTA 1988 s 355(5) provides that there is to be no tax relief where the person spending the money on the development is connected with the person receiving it, and the money paid substantially exceeds the value of the work done. Again, husband and wife are connected persons, and the restriction applies whether or not the spouses are living together. If does not apply if they are divorced.

2.16:6 MIRAS relief for mortgage interest

Originally loan interest was within the statutory predecessors of ICTA 1988 ss 348 and 349, and was paid net of standard rate tax. This was changed by FA 1969 which, in general, required interest paid by an individual to be paid gross unless paid to a non-resident. Under the revised system tax relief for deductible interest paid has to be given either as a business expense in computing Sch D Case I or II profit, or on a claim from the taxpayer. If the taxpayer is an employee the relief is normally given through his notice of coding, and one of the disadvantages of this system is that, if interest rates change during the year, adjustments are necessary to notices of coding to ensure that the correct relief is given.

In practice a substantial number of interest relief claims involve interest paid on house purchase loans. As from 6th April 1983 (1st April in some cases) new arrangements came into force colloquially known as MIRAS (Mortgage Interest Relief at Source) which enable basic rate relief to be given to the borrower on many house purchase loans by permitting him to deduct and retain basic rate tax on paying the interest[2]. For MIRAS to apply there must be a qualifying borrower, a qualifying lender, and qualifying loan interest. Additionally ICTA 1988 s 374(1) requires that there should either be a notice from the Revenue to the borrower and lender that interest may be paid net of tax, or the loan was originally made under the option mortgage scheme, or is covered by regulations. The relevant regulations are contained in the Income Tax (Interest Relief) Regulations 1982[3]. It is clear from ICTA 1988 s 374(1)(a) as applied by reg 3 that, in respect of loans made after March 1983, only the borrower can unilaterally give a notice to make the scheme apply, and only in respect of very limited types of loans, of which the most important is a loan to purchase his own residence. In all other cases interest, other than interest under the old option mortgage arrangements, even if fully qualifying may only be paid net of tax if the Board of Inland Revenue have given a notice to both lender and borrower that it may be so paid.

A qualifying borrower is any individual[4]. Companies and trusts are therefore never qualifying borrowers. The individual technically does not have to be resident in the United Kingdom, although a non-resident still

---

1 ICTA 1988 s 355(5)(c).
2 ICTA 1988 ss 369-378.
3 SI 1982 No 1236.
4 ICTA 1988 s 376(1).

has to satisfy the 'relevant loan interest' requirements. However where an individual, or his spouse, would be chargeable to tax under Sch E Case I, II or III but for some special exemption, he is not a qualifying borrower[1]. A spouse is only included in the prohibition if she is living with the borrower[2]. This provision is mainly designed to ensure that foreign diplomats resident in the United Kingdom whose salary is exempt from United Kingdom tax do not receive mortgage interest relief as, under the MIRAS scheme, relief is given irrespective of whether the taxpayer has taxable income. Qualifying lenders are listed in ICTA 1988 s 376(4)-(6), and in subsequent statutory instruments, and include building societies, local authorities, and approved banks and insurance companies. Individuals are not qualifying lenders.

Relevant loan interest is interest on loans for:

(1)   the purchase of land situated in the United Kingdom (not the Republic of Ireland) which is used wholly or to a substantial extent as the residence of the borrower, or is job-related accommodation[3]. Interest paid on a loan to acquire property which is let out is not within MIRAS, even though it may qualify for tax relief. In para 13 of Inland Revenue pamphlet IR 11 (1985) on the operation of MIRAS the Revenue have said that they will regard a house as occupied to a substantial extent by a borrower if at least two thirds of it is occupied by him. This should ensure that a family who let out one of their rooms to a lodger do not lose their MIRAS tax relief;

(2)   loans taken out prior to 6th April 1988 for the purchase of property used by a dependent relative, or former or separated spouse, of the taxpayer also qualify (tax relief for these loans was abolished for loans made after 15th April 1988 by FA 1988 s 44). The same applies to home improvement loans made before 5 April 1988[4];

(3)   loans for the purchase of life annuities by people over 65 where the loan is secured on land and would otherwise qualify for relief under ICTA 1988 s 365[5].

For interest within these three classifications to qualify, it must otherwise have been fully deductible under the loan interest provisions of ICTA 1988 s 353, or as business interest, but for this purpose the £30,000 loan limit restriction is ignored[6].

Although there is no prohibition on interest on loans over £30,000 being qualifying interest, certain restrictions apply. The restrictions vary depending both on the date of the loan and on whether the loan exceeding the £30,000 limit is the first loan, or a subsequent loan which exceeds the limit because of the need to cumulate prior loans. If the loan is the first loan it is only within MIRAS if it was made on or after 6th April 1987, or the lender has notified the Board of Inland Revenue that he agrees to

---

1 ICTA 1988 s 376(2). The validity of the prohibition in relation to EEC employees has recently been upheld by the European Court in *Tither v IRC* [1990] STC 416.
2 ICTA 1988 s 376(3).
3 ICTA 1988 s 370(2),(5),(6).
4 ICTA 1988 s 370(2) with FA 1988 s 43.
5 ICTA 1988 s 370(2)(a).
6 ICTA 1988 s 370(2).

the loan being dealt with under MIRAS[1]. If there are prior loans which have to be cumulated, none of the interest on a subsequent loan which exceeds the limit is within the scheme unless[2]:

(a)   the prior loans were made by the same lender; and
(b)   the restricted loan was made on or after 6th April 1987, or the lender agrees.

If these conditions are satisfied, only interest on a loan, or loans, up to £30,000 is eligible for relief under MIRAS[3].

With the introduction of independent taxation, each spouse is normally treated as a separate taxpayer for the purposes of mortgage interest relief, including MIRAS. If only one spouse is paying interest on a qualifying mortgage that spouse is allocated the full £30,000 loan limit. If the loan is below that limit, it will be within the MIRAS system. If the loan exceeds that limit it will be within MIRAS only if the conditions in the preceding paragraph are satisfied, and only interest on the first £30,000 of the loan will qualify for relief. If each of the spouses have a qualifying mortgage loan, and there is no other relevant borrower, each will be entitled to a sharer's limit of £15,000. The same principle will normally apply if there is a joint mortgage[4]. If either spouse has a loan of less than £15,000, that spouse's limit will be allocated to the other spouse. Once the sharer's limit has been allocated, MIRAS then applies in the normal way to each spouse's loan, ie if the loan does not exceed the sharer's limit, MIRAS applies to the whole of the interest payable on the loan. If the loan exceeds the sharer's limit MIRAS will only apply if the conditions set out in the preceding paragraph are satisfied, and then only on interest attributable to the sharer's limit part of the loan. However, the spouses may decide to make an allocation of interest election in respect of their mortgage interest payments. Such an election will have implications for the operation of MIRAS, and these are discussed in the next section.

If MIRAS does apply to payments of mortgage interest the following consequences ensue:

(1)   No deduction can be claimed for the interest under ICTA 1988 s 353[5] or as a business interest expense[6].
(2)   The payer is entitled to deduct and retain basic rate tax on making the payment at the rate in force when the payment became due[7]. This provision is analogous to ICTA 1988 s 348 but, unlike s 348, the payer is entitled to make the deduction whether or not he has any taxable income.
(3)   The lender is treated as having received gross interest under deduction of basic rate tax[8]. The lender can then require the Revenue to refund the tax withheld[9].

1   ICTA 1988 s 373(2).
2   ICTA 1988 s 373(3).
3   ICTA 1988 s 373(5).
4   IR 86 p 1.
5   ICTA 1988 s 353(2).
6   ICTA 1988 s 74(o).
7   ICTA 1988 s 369(1).
8   ICTA 1988 s 369(1).
9   ICTA 1988 s 369(6).

(4)   In computing the borrower's total income a deduction is allowed for the gross mortgage interest but, in addition to his ordinary tax liability, the borrower is assessed to basic rate tax on the gross qualifying interest[1]. This automatically collects the correct tax from both a basic rate taxpayer and a higher rate taxpayer, and gives higher rate relief for the interest, as the worked example in the next section illustrates. If the taxpayer has unused personal allowances he may deduct the unused allowances from any mortgage interest assessable to basic rate tax under ICTA 1988 s 369(3)[2]. In practice this last provision means that most people on low incomes get basic rate tax relief on their mortgage interest whether or not they have sufficient income to cover it.

(5)   Mortgage interest paid under MIRAS is not deductible in computing whether a husband has unused married couple's allowance available for transfer to his wife[3], or, under the transitional provisions, whether he has a transferable personal allowance[4].

2.16:7 MIRAS and an allocation of interest election

If MIRAS applies to the payment of mortgage interest, payments can continue to be made under MIRAS even if the taxable income of the paying spouse is less than the gross mortgage payments[5]. The allocation of interest election applies to MIRAS payments as well as non-MIRAS payments[6], but, as basic rate tax relief will have already been given under MIRAS to the spouse who paid the interest, the practical effect of the election will only be to allow the gross mortgage interest to be deducted from the income of the spouse in receipt of an allocation of interest in computing the higher rate tax liability of the recipient spouse. This will be achieved by deducting the gross qualifying interest in arriving at the recipient spouse's total income, computing the tax due on that total income, and then additionally assessing an amount equal to the gross interest to basic rate tax[7].

Example

Jasper and Sonia are husband and wife living together. For 1990-91 Jasper had earned income of £35,000 and Sonia had earned income of £10,000. Sonia paid £2,250 net mortgage interest under MIRAS on a £25,000 house purchase loan fully qualifying for tax relief. The gross interest was therefore £3,000 on which Sonia has received £750 basic rate relief by withholding under MIRAS. Jasper and Sonia have jointly elected that the mortgage interest paid by Sonia should be treated as paid by Jasper for income tax purposes. Jasper's tax liability for 1990-91 is:

		£
	Earned income	35,000
Less	Mortgage interest	(3,000)
	Total income	32,000

1   ICTA 1988 s 369(3).
2   ICTA 1988 s 369(3) and (4).
3   ICTA 1988 s 257B(1).
4   ICTA 1988 s 257D(8).
5   ICTA 1988 s 369(1).
6   ICTA 1988 s 356B(1)(a).
7   ICTA 1988 s 369(3).

		£	£
Less	Personal allowances		
	personal	3,005	
	married couple's	1,720	(4,725)
	Taxable income		27,275
	Tax payable £		
	20,700 @ 25%		5,175
	6,575 @ 40%		2,630
	27,275		7,805
Add	3,000 @ 25%		750
	Total tax due		8,555

The Revenue have announced a practical relief to deal with the situation where husband and wife take out a new joint mortgage but wish to allocate the mortgage payments unequally. Technically the spouse should file an allocation of interest election on Form 15 with their tax inspector before the lender is able to operate MIRAS, but guidance notes to MIRAS lenders from the Inland Revenue Central MIRAS Central Policy Unit state that, where tax relief on the loan as a whole is not affected, lenders may accept form MIRAS 70 showing an unequal share of relief, and give MIRAS relief, without enquiring whether the spouses have filed Form 15. However both spouses' tax inspectors must be made aware by the lender that there is a need for a Form 15 to be filed, and this is to be done by the filing of form MIRAS 85 in addition to the filing of form MIRAS 70[1].

2.16:8 Mortgage interest relief in the year of marriage

Under independent taxation a man and woman make separate claims for mortgage interest relief, whether or not they are married to each other, but subject to the right of a married couple to make an allocation of interest election in relation to qualifying interest payments made after they marry. Where, prior to marriage, each spouse has been purchasing a main residence with the aid of a loan, each may claim full tax relief on qualifying interest paid prior to the marriage, subject to the usual £30,000 limit per residence or, if the transitional provisions for sharer loans made before 1st August 1988 apply, per taxpayer. There are, however, severe technical problems for mortgage interest payments made after the date of the marriage. If one spouse goes to live in the house of the other he or she will immediately cease to be entitled to mortgage interest relief on the house which has been abandoned, as the abandoned house is no longer the main residence of either spouse. Technically no relief is available under ESC A27, which allows mortgage interest relief to continue for up to four years if there is a temporary absence from mortgaged property, as it is an implicit condition of that concession that the taxpayer should be intending to return to the property. If each spouse retains the house they were acquiring prior to marriage as their respective main residences, they will fall foul of ICTA 1988 s 356B(5), which says that, if each spouse is paying interest on a loan to purchase separate main residences, the house purchased first is to be deemed to the main residence of both of them, and the house purchased later is to be treated as the main residence of neither of them. The consequence

1 Letter from Inland Revenue MIRAS CPU, reproduced in CCH [1990] Taxes 12.

of this is that, in the absence of a concession, the spouse purchasing the later acquired house immediately loses tax relief and, if MIRAS hitherto applied to give basic rate relief, will be under an obligation to notify the lender that the loan interest is no longer qualifying interest[1].

However there are two long-standing concessions which may alleviate the tax problems which arise when a couple purchasing separate houses with the aid of a mortgage subsequently marry and, after marriage, they intend to live in the same main residence. The concessions make use of the bridging loan provisions in ICTA 1988 s 354(5) and (6). Under these provisions a taxpayer who is selling one main residence and purchasing another, and who has to borrow on a bridging loan to finance the purchase of the new house, may claim tax relief for a period of one year after the grant of the new loan (or such longer period as the Revenue may allow) for interest paid on loans for the purchase of both old and new houses. A separate £30,000 limit is applied to the original loan, and the original loan is not aggregated with the subsequent loan in computing whether the £30,000 limit on the subsequent loan has been exceeded. Effectively the taxpayer is able to claim tax relief on two loans of up to £30,000 each. The MIRAS provisions are also applied separately to each loan in working out whether basic rate relief can be obtained by withholding tax from each interest payment[2].

Extra-statutory concession A35 provides that where, on marriage, one spouse goes to live in the house of the other and sells his or her own house, the bridging loan provisions will apply to the house being sold, so that (within the normal £30,000 ceiling) loan interest will continue to qualify for tax relief, provided the house is sold within twelve months after the date it is vacated. The loan on the vacated house will be disregarded in determining what relief is due in respect of interest payable on the property which becomes the matrimonial home. Further, under Statement of Practice 10/80, where both spouses sell their houses and purchase a new property *in joint names* to be used as their joint matrimonial home, the bridging loan provisions will apply to all three houses. It does not matter that a house that is being sold is no longer being used as a main residence. Tax relief may therefore be claimed for up to one year from the grant of the loan to purchase the new matrimonial home (or such longer period as the Revenue may allow) for loans on each house up to a loan limit of £30,000 per house. As the concessions are extending the bridging loan provisions, each of the loans should continue to qualify for payment of interest net of tax under MIRAS to the same extent as if each loan was the only relevant loan, applying ICTA 1988 s 371.

2.17 Loan interest — other qualifying purposes

While loans for house purchase are the most common type of loans which qualify for tax relief, loans for a number of other purposes specified in the legislation also qualify for relief. These purposes are:

(1)   Loans applied by a partner to acquire plant or machinery which is

1   ICTA 1988 s 375(1).
2   ICTA 1988 s 371.

used in the partnership and on which the partnership is entitled to claim capital allowances, and loans used by an employee to acquire plant or machinery which is used in his employment and on which he is entitled to claim capital allowances[1].

(2) Loans applied to acquire share capital in a close company which is not a close investment holding company[2], or a loan to such a company which is used wholly and exclusively for the purposes of the business of the company or an associated company[3], or a loan which is used to repay an earlier loan to the company which qualified for tax relief to the company as a loan used for business purposes, or, if it was an interest free loan, would have so qualified if interest had been paid on it[4]. To qualify for tax relief a number of further conditions have to be satisfied; in particular the lender must have a material interest (roughly 5% of the share capital) in the close company[5].

(3) Loans applied to acquire an interest in a co-operative or shares in an employee controlled company, subject to a number of conditions being satisfied[6], or a loan used for the business purposes of the co-operative, or to pay off prior qualifying loans. If the loan is to acquire shares in an employee controlled company, prior to 6th April 1990 two of the conditions which had to be satisfied were that the individual *or his spouse* had to be a full-time employee of the company, and at least 50% of the share capital and voting control of the company had to be owned by employees *or their spouses*[7]. The references in the legislation to the spouse of an employee have been deleted with effect from 6th April 1990 for payments of interest on or after that date, unless the proceeds of the loan were used before 6th April 1990 to acquire shares in the company, or to pay off an earlier loan which qualified for relief[8]. If the proceeds of the loan were applied in the purchase of qualifying shares before 6th April 1990 the aggregation provisions continue to apply to determine whether interest payments made on or after 6th April 1990 qualify for tax relief.

Under ICTA 1988 s 361 if an employee has a shareholding in excess of 10% in a company, or more than 10% of the voting rights, the excess is treated as belonging to non-employees when working out whether the company is an employee controlled company. Prior to 6th April 1990 the shareholdings of spouses were aggregated for this purpose, whether or not the spouses were living together, unless both spouses were employees of the company[9]. With the change to independent taxation, the aggregation provisions have been repealed, so the shareholdings of spouses will now be considered separately, whether or not they are both employees of the company[10]. However,

---

1 ICTA 1988 s 359.
2 ICTA 1988 s 360(1)(a).
3 ICTA 1988 s 360(1)(b).
4 ICTA 1988 s 360(1)(c).
5 ICTA 1988 s 360(2)(a).
6 ICTA 1988 s 361.
7 ICTA 1988 s 361(4)(d),(5).
8 FA 1988 Sch 3 para 15(1)(2).
9 ICTA 1988 s 361(6), (7).
10 FA 1988 Sch 3 para 15(1)(b).

as with the 50% shareholding rule, the old rules continue to determine whether interest payments after 5th April 1990 qualify for tax relief if the proceeds of the loan were applied for the purchase of shares, or the repayment of an earlier qualifying loan, on or before 5th April 1990. The new rules only apply to payments of interest made on or after 6th April 1990 if the proceeds of the loan were applied for a qualifying purpose on or after that date[1].

If a loan is made on or after 6th April 1990, and is used to pay off an earlier loan which qualified for tax relief, interest on the later loan will only be eligible for relief if either the earlier loan was made on or after 6th April 1990 and qualified for relief, or the earlier loan was made before 6th April 1990, but interest on it would have qualified for relief had it been made on or after that date[2].

(4) Loans to a partner, other than a limited partner, used to acquire an interest in the partnership, or wholly and exclusively for the business purposes of the partnership, or to repay a loan which qualified for tax relief[3].

(5) Loans to personal representatives to pay capital transfer tax or inheritance tax prior to a grant of representation, or to repay a loan used for this purpose[4].

(6) Loans to individuals over 65 which are secured on land in the UK or the Republic of Ireland if at least 90% of the proceeds are used to purchase a life annuity for at least the life of the borrower, whether or not the annuity is a joint life annuity[5].

2.18 Connected persons

There are occasions when the income tax legislation provides that certain tax consequences are to follow if there are transactions between connected persons. One illustration of this was noted when dealing with the anti-avoidance provisions for mortgage interest relief, in that, under ICTA 1988 s 355(5)(d), no tax relief can be claimed for interest paid on a loan for the purchase of land where the person is acquiring land, directly or indirectly, from a person connected with him and the price paid substantially exceeds the value of what is acquired. Another illustration can be found in the capital allowances legislation. If a business is transferred from one connected person to another, the connected persons may jointly elect that, for the purposes of capital allowances on plant and machinery, capital allowances should continue to be granted as if there had been no change in ownership of the business[6]. 'Connected persons' in such provisions are normally defined to include persons connected with each other within the terms of ICTA 1988 s 839, and the statutory provisions just cited conform to this principle.

Under ICTA 1988 s 839(2) the husband or wife of a taxpayer is connected with him for the purposes of provisions which apply ICTA 1988 s 839,

1 FA 1988 Sch 3 para 15(2).
2 FA 1988 Sch 3 para 15(3).
3 ICTA 1988 s 362.
4 ICTA 1988 s 364.
5 ICTA 1988 s 365.
6 CAA 1990 s 77 and ss 157 and 158.

as also is a relative of the taxpayer and the relative's spouse. A relative is a brother, sister, ancestor (parents and grandparents etc), or lineal descendant (children and grandchildren etc). If the connected person rules apply to include a spouse, it is irrelevant whether or not the spouses are living together. Only a decree absolute of divorce can break the link. To this extent the connected person rules are different from many of the rules in the income tax and capital gains tax legislation which deal with husbands and wives. Normally these rules only apply if the husband and wife are living together and do not apply if they are separated, albeit not divorced.

CHAPTER 3

Capital gains tax

3.1 Introduction

Capital gains tax is charged on a gain arising on the disposal of chargeable assets, wherever situated, by persons resident or ordinarily resident in the United Kingdom[1], although persons who are not domiciled in the United Kingdom are not chargeable on foreign source gains which are not remitted here[2]. Gains on the disposal of United Kingdom source assets by a person not resident and not ordinarily resident in the United Kingdom are exempt from tax[3], except where the gain arises through the carrying on of a branch or agency here[4]. The disposal of an asset includes the sale, exchange, grant of a lease, and part disposal of an asset. A gift of an asset is also a chargeable disposal. Thus in *Turner v Follett*[5] the taxpayer had given away 500 shares to one of his children. He argued that there was no liability to capital gains tax because, far from making a gain, he had made a substantial loss. His argument was rejected by the Court of Appeal.

Capital gains tax was introduced in the Finance Act 1965 with effect from 6th April 1965. Until 1982 no allowance was made for the effect of inflation, so that chargeable gains were computed as the excess of disposal proceeds or value over allowable cost, with gains attributable to a period of ownership prior to 6th April 1965 being excluded from charge. The Finance Act 1982 introduced for the first time some relief for the effects of inflation, but the relief was limited. A taxpayer was permitted to increase the allowable cost of a chargeable asset by the increase in the retail prices index (RPI) from one year after acquisition of the asset, or from 31st March 1982 if later, until the date of disposal. Indexation allowance could only be used to reduce a chargeable gain; it could not be used to create or increase an allowable loss, and it had to be applied to the original cost of the asset, even if the asset had been acquired long before April 1982. The 1985 Finance Act further reformed the indexation allowance for disposals of assets on or after 6th April 1985 by individuals (1st April 1985 for companies). The one year waiting period was abolished, so that indexation allowance now applies the increase in the RPI from the date of acquisition of the asset, or 31st March 1982 if later, until the date of disposal. For assets acquired prior to 31st March 1982 a taxpayer was entitled to elect to have the indexation allowance applied to the 31st March 1982 value of the asset rather than

1   CGTA 1979 s 2(1).
2   CGTA 1979 s 14.
3   CGTA 1979 s 2(1).
4   CGTA 1979 s 12.
5   (1973) 48 TC 614.

its cost, and an indexation allowance may now be used to create or increase an allowable loss.

The Finance Act 1988 made two further major changes to the operation of capital gains tax. The first change was the rebasing of CGT. Indexation for inflation only protected gains accruing after 31st March 1982. There was no inflation relief for gains accruing between April 1965 and March 1982. Now, as a result of the 1988 Finance Act, if there is a disposal on or after 6th April 1988 of an asset acquired prior to 1st April 1982, in computing the allowable cost of the asset the taxpayer is deemed to have sold it on 31st March 1982 at its then market value, and immediately reacquired it at that value[1]. Rebasing does not apply if:

(a) Rebasing results in a gain and a lower gain or a loss would accrue if the original acquisition value was taken as the allowable cost[2]. It should be noted that the legislation requires a comparison to be made between the 'gain' arising under the new system and the 'gain' arising under the old system. It does not require a comparison between the 'chargeable gains' under the two systems. This has important implications where part of a gain is an exempt gain, as where the asset disposed of is a principal private residence. The comparison has to be made between the gains arising before applying the exemption (the gain), rather than between the gains arising after the exemption (the chargeable gain).

(b) Rebasing results in a loss but there would be a lower loss or a gain without rebasing[3]. If there is a gain under rebasing but a loss without rebasing, or vice versa, the disposal is to be treated as giving rise to neither a gain nor a loss[4].

(c) Without rebasing the disposal results in neither a gain nor a loss[5].

(d) The disposal is covered by a number of statutory provisions which deem the transfer to take place at neither a gain nor a loss to the transferor[6]. One of the statutory provisions is CGTA 1979 s 44, which deals with a transfer of assets between a husband and wife who are living together[7]. The effect of rebasing and indexation allowances on s 44 transfers is fully discussed in **3.5** below.

These rules mean that a taxpayer has to continue to keep records of acquisition values of assets acquired prior to 1st April 1982 as, without the records, it will be impossible to make the requisite comparison. As a result of pressure during the Committee stage of the Finance Bill 1988, a taxpayer may now elect under FA 1988 s 96(5) that the acquisition value of assets acquired prior to 31st March 1982 shall only be computed by reference to their 31st March 1982 market value. The advantage of such an election is that the cost of assets acquired prior to that date are no longer relevant, and consequently details of the original cost need no longer be kept. The election has the further advantage that a loss under rebasing

1 FA 1988 s 96(2).
2 FA 1988 s 96(3)(a).
3 FA 1988 s 96(3)(b).
4 FA 1988 s 96(4).
5 FA 1988 s 96(3)(c).
6 FA 1988 s 96(3)(d).
7 FA 1988 Sch 8 para 3.

will not be restricted if there would have been a smaller loss, or a gain, without rebasing, but it has the corresponding disadvantage that a gain under rebasing will no longer be limited if there would have been a lower gain or a loss without rebasing. The election may be made by notice in writing to an inspector at any time before 6th April 1990, or within two years after the end of the year of assessment in which the first disposal after 5th April 1988 of an asset acquired before 1st April 1982 occurs[1]. In Statement of Practice No 2 of 1989[2] the Revenue list a number of assets the disposal of which will not be regarded as starting the clock for the purposes of the two year time limit for making the election. The assets listed are mainly ones which do not attract a CGT liability, and so the implications of a disposal on the time limit might be overlooked by a taxpayer. With limited exceptions, which are set out in FA 1988 Sch 8 paras 2 and 12, an election applies to all disposals made on or after 6th April 1988 of assets acquired prior to 1st April 1982, whether the disposal is made before or after the election. One of the exceptions is a disposal between husband and wife living together which is deemed by CGTA 1979 s 44 to result in neither a gain nor a loss to the transferor[3].

For assets acquired prior to 1st April 1982 and disposed of on or after 6th April 1988 indexation allowance is applied to the 31st March 1982 market value of the asset, unless a higher allowance would result from applying it to the original acquisition value and the taxpayer has not elected under FA 1988 s 96(5) to have the acquisition values of all his assets acquired prior to 1st April 1982 deemed to be their 31st March 1982 value[4]. The combination of rebasing to 31st March 1982 plus indexation relief from that date ensures that capital gains tax is now a tax on real gains accruing since 31st March 1982.

The second major change made by the Finance Act 1988 was in the computation of the capital gains tax payable on chargeable gains. For 1987-88, after deduction of an exempt slice (£6,300), the excess of an individual's chargeable gains over the exempt slice was taxed at a flat rate of 30%. This meant that an individual who was only liable to income tax at the basic rate was paying capital gains tax at a higher marginal rate, whereas a higher rate income tax payer was subject to tax on his capital gains at a lower tax rate. For 1988-89 the exempt slice of chargeable gains was reduced to £5,000, where it has since remained[5]. The reason for the reduction was stated to be that a high exemption had previously been given as rough and ready compensation for the lack of adequate protection from the effects of inflation. Now that rebasing and indexation allowance had provided that protection, a lower exempt slice was appropriate. Chargeable gains in excess of the exempt slice are now taxed as if they were additional income, and are subject to income tax at the individual's top rate of income tax[6]. Thus for 1990-91 if an individual's taxable chargeable gains, when added to his taxable income, do not exceed £20,700, the whole of the taxable gains will be taxed at the basic rate of 25%. If the individual is a higher

1 FA 1988 s 96(6).
2 [1989] STI 125.
3 FA 1988 Sch 8 para 2.
4 FA 1985 s 68(4) and (5).
5 CGTA 1979 s 5(1A).
6 FA 1988 s 98.

rate taxpayer for income tax, the whole or his taxable gains will be taxed at the higher income tax rate of 40%. If the individual's taxable income is below £20,700, but the addition of taxable capital gains take him over this threshold, part of his capital gains up to the threshold will be taxed at 25%, and the excess will be taxed at 40%.

Example

For 1990-91 Jim has taxable income, after deduction of personal allowances, of £18,200. He has chargeable gains of £15,000. £5,000 is exempt, to leave £10,000 taxable. The tax payable is:

-£		£
2,500 (£20,700—£18,200) @ 25%		625
7,500 @ 40%		3,000
10,000		3,625

Although income tax rates are now used to calculate the capital gains tax payable on taxable gains, this does not mean that the two taxes have been amalgamated. They remain distinct taxes. Thus it is not possible to deduct unused personal allowances from chargeable gains, and it is not possible to deduct capital losses from income. Capital losses realised in a year of assessment must be deducted from chargeable gains realised in the same year, even if this reduces chargeable gains below the exempt threshold[1], and, if losses exceed gains, the unrelieved losses can only be carried forward and relieved against chargeable gains arising in future years[2]. If unrelieved losses are being carried forward relief for them is given against gains of the first available future year[3], but it is only necessary to use so much of the losses as will reduce the net chargeable gains of a subsequent year to an amount equivalent to the annual exemption[4]. If chargeable gains of a later year do not exceed the annual exemption, no prior year losses are applied against the gains[5]. This ensures that losses only relieve taxable gains, and are not wasted against gains which the £5,000 annual exemption precludes from being taxed. Except where there is an excess of allowable losses over chargeable gains in the year in which a taxpayer dies, unrelieved allowable losses cannot be carried back to an earlier year[6].

3.2 CGT and independent taxation

Following the introduction of independent taxation, as from 1990-91 the chargeable gains and allowable losses of each spouse are computed separately. Allowable losses of one spouse may only be deducted from that spouse's chargeable gains and, if there is an excess of allowable losses, the unrelieved losses may only be carried forward and deducted from future gains of the same spouse[7]. Each spouse is entitled to an annual exemption

1 CGTA 1979 s 4(1).
2 CGTA 1979 s 4(1)(b).
3 CGTA 1979 s 4(1)(b).
4 CGTA 1979 s 5(4).
5 CGTA 1979 s 5(4).
6 CGTA 1979 s 29(5).
7 FA 1988 s 104.

of the first £5,000 of chargeable gains, and the CGT payable is computed separately for each spouse using their own income tax bands.

> Example
>
> For 1990-91 Clive and Anna, who are husband and wife living together, each have chargeable gains of £8,000. After deducting the annual exemption of £5,000, each therefore has taxable gains of £3,000. Clive has taxable income of £25,000 and Anna has taxable income of £10,000. The capital gains tax payable by each of them is:
>
> | Clive | £3,000 @ 40% = £1,200 |
> |-------|-----------------------|
> | Anna | £3,000 @ 25% = £ 750 |

With one important exception, husband and wife living together are now treated for capital gains tax purposes as if they were unmarried. The exception, contained in CGTA 1979 s 44, is that a transfer of assets between them still takes place at a value which ensures that there is neither a gain nor a loss to the transferor spouse. On the eventual disposal of the asset the recipient spouse is then taxed on the total gain over the combined period of ownership. This ability to transfer assets between spouses living together may give spouses significant tax planning advantages over other couples. In the above example there would have been a saving of £450 tax if the assets sold by Clive had first been transferred to Anna and then sold by her. It is, of course, vital to avoid being caught by the new tax avoidance doctrine being enunciated by the courts in cases such as *Ramsay v IRC*[1] and *Furniss v Dawson*[2], and this is discussed in more detail in chapter 4 on tax planning.

If gains are realised on the disposal of assets situated outside the United Kingdom but, because of restrictions imposed by the country in which the gains were realised or because of a lack of foreign currency, the gains cannot be remitted to the United Kingdom, a claim can be made to defer the CGT charge until the gains can be remitted to the United Kingdom[3]. They will then be treated as chargeable gains arising in the year of assessment in which they can be remitted[4]. If a CGT charge on gains realised prior to 6th April 1990 by a married woman was being deferred under CGTA 1979 s 13 consequent on a claim made by her husband, and the gains become remittable on or after 6th April 1990, they can only be assessed on the wife, or her personal representatives, and cannot be assessed on her husband[5].

3.3 Administration of capital gains tax under independent taxation

For years prior to the introduction of independent taxation the Revenue were entitled to require separate returns of their capital gains from both husband and wife[6]. Alternatively, where no election for separate assessment had been made, the Revenue could require the husband to make a return of both his and his wife's gains[7]. CGTA 1979 s 5(5) authorises a simplified

1   (1981) 54 TC 101.
2   (1984) 55 TC 324.
3   CGTA 1979 s 13.
4   CGTA 1979 s 13(2)(b).
5   FA 1988 s 104(3).
6   CGTA 1979 s 45(3) with TMA 1970 ss 8 and 12.
7   CGTA 1979 s 45(3).

reporting requirement if the amount of chargeable gains accruing to an individual do not exceed his annual exemption (£5,000 for both 1989-90 and 1990-91) and total disposal proceeds do not exceed twice the annual exemption. A statement to this effect is sufficient compliance with a request from an inspector to report details of gains, unless the inspector otherwise requires. This obviates the need to compute and report details of gains where, at the end of the day, it is clear that no tax will be payable. For years prior to the introduction of independent taxation the reduced reporting requirements never applied to a man whose wife was living with him if an election for separate assessment of capital gains was in force[1], and it also did not apply to a married woman living with her husband if she was requested to make a return of her gains[2]. However if the husband was a married man whose wife was living with him, and there had been no election for separate assessment, the gains and disposal proceeds of husband and wife could be aggregated and, if the aggregate figures were within the limits, the reduced reporting requirement applied[3].

With the introduction of independent taxation the provisions in CGTA 1979 Sch 1 para 3 limiting the application of restricted reporting for spouses have been repealed with effect from 1990-91[4]. Accordingly each spouse is now responsible for reporting only their own gains, and the limits which attract the restricted reporting requirements are applied separately to each spouse. As the change relates to gains realised in 1990-91 and later years, the first time it will become relevant is when tax returns are sent out after 5th April 1991. The previous rules will apply to tax returns set out in 1990-91, or a later year, which require details of gains realised in 1989-90.

Prior to the introduction of independent taxation, if spouses were living together the husband was liable to pay any tax due on his wife's gains unless an election for separate assessment had been made[5]. If the Revenue were unable to collect tax on a wife's gains from her husband, they had the right to assess the wife and collect the tax from her[6]. If a husband died his executors had the right to disclaim liability for any capital gains tax due on his wife's gains which had not yet been assessed[7]. As from 1990-91 each spouse is separately chargeable on their own gains, and can never be liable to pay unpaid tax on the other spouse's gains[8].

3.4 CGT and husband and wife in 1988-89 and 1989-90

The rebasing provisions and the new method of computing capital gains tax imposed in the Finance Act 1988 took effect from 6th April 1988, two years prior to the introduction of the independent taxation of spouses' gains. For 1988-89 and 1989-90, whether or not an election for separate assessment

1   CGTA 1979 Sch 1 para 3(2)(a).
2   CGTA 1979 Sch 1 para 3(2)(b).
3   CGTA 1979 Sch 1 para 3(1).
4   FA 1988 s 104(1) and (2).
5   CGTA 1979 s 45(1) and (2).
6   CGTA 1979 s 45(4).
7   CGTA 1979 s 45(4).
8   FA 1988 s 104(1).

had been made, a married woman's chargeable gains were computed separately from her husband's but were then taxed as if they were his gains[1]. Losses of one spouse which could not be deducted from that spouse's gains were deducted from the gains of the other spouse[2]. This applied for both current year losses and for unrelieved prior year losses being carried forward, but with the important difference that current year losses had to be deducted from current year gains until the losses or the gains were exhausted, even if this reduced the gains below the £5,000 annual exemption[3], whereas prior year losses being carried forward only had to be used to the extent necessary to reduce current year gains to the exempt threshold of £5,000[4]. However either husband or wife could elect by notice in writing to the inspector before 6th July following the relevant year of assessment that losses of each spouse for that year should be kept separate[5].

A single £5,000 annual exemption was then deducted from the aggregated gains of the husband and wife, and excess gains over the threshold were taxed as if they formed the top slice of the husband's income[6]. For this purpose a husband's income included his wife's unearned income. It also included his wife's earned income unless an election for separate taxation of wife's earnings election had been made, when the wife's earnings did not form part of her husband's income. Thus if in 1988-89 or 1989-90 a married couple had substantial capital gains, a separate taxation election could become advantageous even if it would not have been advantageous if only income tax considerations were taken into account. The following example illustrates the point:

Example

Godfrey and Susan are husband and wife living together. For 1989-90 Godfrey had earned income of £15,000 and Susan had earned income of £13,000. Susan had chargeable gains of £9,000, after deducting the annual exemption of £5,000. Their tax liability with no election for separate taxation of wife's earnings is:

		£	£
Income tax			
Godfrey — income			15,000
Susan — income			13,000
Total income			28,000
Less Personal allowances			
married man's allowance		4,375	
wife's earned income allowance		2,785	(7,160)
Taxable income			20,840
Income tax payable:			
£20,700 @ 25% =	5,175		
140 @ 40% =	56		5,231
£20,840			

1 FA 1988 s 99(1) and (2).
2 CGTA 1979 s 4(2).
3 CGTA 1979 s 4(2).
4 CGTA 1979 s 5(4).
5 CGTA 1979 s 4(2) proviso.
6 FA 1988 s 99(1).

Capital gains tax		£
	£9,000 @ 40%	3,600
Total tax liability		8,831

Their tax liability if an election for separate taxation of wife's earnings is made is:

		£	£
Income tax			
	Susan		
	Income	13,000	
Less	Personal allowance	(2,785)	
	Taxable income	10,215	
	Income tax payable — £10,215 @ 25%		2,553.75
	Godfrey		
	Income	15,000	
Less	Personal allowance	(2,785)	
	Taxable income	12,215	
	Income tax payable — £12,215 @ 25%		3,053.75
			5,607.50

Capital gains tax			
(£9,000 gains added to Godfrey's £12,215 income)			
	£8,485 @ 25%	2,121.25	
	515 @ 40%	206.00	2,327.25
	£9,000 @ 40%		
Total tax liability			7,934.75

Thus, although there has been a net increase of £376.50 in the aggregate income tax liability of Godfrey and Susan as a result of the separate taxation election, this has been more than offset by a saving of £1,272.75 in their capital gains tax liability, giving an overall tax saving of £896.25. The time limit for making a separate taxation of wife's earnings election for 1989-90 is 5th April 1991, or such longer period as the Revenue may allow (see **1.10:2** above), so it is important to give consideration before this deadline to whether a separate taxation election should be made.

For 1988-89 and 1989-90 capital gains tax on the aggregate gains of husband and wife was assessed on, and payable by, the husband. However on or before 5th of July following the relevant year of assessment either spouse could apply by notice in writing to the inspector on Form CG11S to have their capital gains tax liability separately assessed[1]. An election, once made, continued until it was revoked[2]. The effect of an election for separate assessment was that each spouse was responsible both for returning their own chargeable gains and for paying their own capital gains tax liability. However, as with the income tax election for separate assessment, the election had no effect on the aggregate tax payable on the combined taxable gains of husband and wife. Accordingly the CGT liability was computed by apportioning the £5,000 annual exemption between the spouses

1 CGTA 1979 s 45(2).
2 CGTA 1979 s 45(2).

to ascertain their respective chargeable gains[1]. The wife's taxable gains were then added to her husband's, and the combined CGT liability was computed applying the husband's marginal rate or rates of income tax[2]. The combined tax liability was then apportioned between the spouses in proportion to their gains[3]. In a press release on the 1988 Budget proposals[4] the Revenue gave the following example of how the apportionment worked:

> 'In 1988-89 a wife has gains (after indexation) of £10,000 and the husband has gains (after indexation) of £30,000. A separate assessment election is in force. The annual exemption of £5,000 is split between them proportionately to their gains, so that the wife has exemption on £1,250 and the husband on £3,750, leaving chargeable gains of £8,750 and £26,250 respectively. The total capital gains tax chargeable is £12,000. The tax will be split up as follows
>
> Wife's tax: $\dfrac{£\ 8,750}{£35,000} \times £12,000 = £3,000$
>
> Husband's tax: $\dfrac{£26,250}{£35,000} \times £12,000 = £9,000$'

3.5 Transfers between spouses

Special rules apply for transfers between spouses which take place in a year of assessment during which the spouses are married to, and living with, each other. Husband and wife are connected persons for the purposes of capital gains tax (see **3.9** below), and transfers between them would therefore normally be deemed to take place at market value[5]. However where there is a transfer between husband and wife living together CGTA 1979 s 44 deems the transfer to take place at a value which gives neither a gain nor a loss on the disposal, and the transferee takes the transferor's cost base as her acquisition cost for any subsequent disposal. If the asset was originally acquired prior to 6th April 1965 the recipient spouse also takes over the transferor spouse's date of acquisition of the asset for the purposes of computing the gain or loss on the asset when it is disposed of under a transaction which is not within s 44[6]. If the asset was acquired on or after 6th April 1965 but before 31st March 1982, and the inter-spousal transfer takes place after that date, the recipient spouse becomes entitled to the benefit of the 31st March 1982 market value of the asset as the acquisition value if the asset is sold after 5th April 1988[7]. The practical effect of these rules is that, if a gain arises on the disposal, the recipient spouse is taxable on the gain arising over the period of ownership of both spouses, and, if there is a loss, the recipient spouse has the benefit of the loss accruing over their combined period of ownership. The effect of rebasing on transfers within CGTA 1979 s 44 is dealt with in **3.5:2** below, and the application of the indexation allowance to s 44 transfers is dealt with in **3.5:1** below.

1 CGTA 1979 Sch 1 para 2.
2 FA 1988 s 99(3)(a).
3 FA 1988 s 99(3)(b).
4 [1988] STI 208.
5 CGTA 1979 s 29A(1)(a).
6 CGTA 1979 Sch 5 para 17.
7 FA 1988 Sch 8 para 1.

Under CGTA 1979 s 155(2) spouses are 'living together' for capital gains tax purposes if they would be treated as living together for income tax purposes under ICTA 1988 s 282. They are therefore living together unless they are separated under a court order or deed of separation, or are separated in such circumstances that the separation is likely to be permanent. Prior to 1990-91 spouses were also deemed to be separated if one of them was, and one of them was not, resident in the United Kingdom[1], and this provision led to an unusual House of Lords decision in *Gubay v Kington*[2]. On 4th April 1972 the taxpayer's wife permanently left the United Kingdom. On 7th July 1972, in the following year of assessment, the taxpayer transferred assets to her with accrued gains of £1,392,315. On 28th October 1972 the taxpayer himself became non-resident and joined his wife. There would have been no doubt about the CGT treatment of the transactions if the transfer had taken place before 4th April 1972, because the transfer would have taken place at a value which resulted in no gain nor loss to the transferor under the relief for transfers between spouses living together in what is now CGTA 1979 s 44(1). Equally, had the transfer taken place after 5th April 1973, or possibly 28th October 1972 (see ESC D2), there would have been no chargeable gain, because the transferor would not have been resident or ordinarily resident in the UK at the time of the transfer. However the Revenue argued that the wife was not 'living with' her husband at the time of the transfer because at that time Mr Gubay was, but Mrs Gubay was not, resident in the UK. Accordingly both the High Court and the Court of Appeal held that the exemption for inter spousal transfers did not apply and, as Mr and Mrs Gubay were connected persons, Mr Gubay had made a chargeable disposal of the assets at their market value on 7th July 1972.

The House of Lords reversed this decision accepting an argument which had not been raised in the courts below. The proviso to ICTA 1970 s 42(2), which became ICTA 1988 s 282(3) in the 1988 consolidation, read:

'Provided that where this subsection applies and the net aggregate amount of income tax (including surtax) falling to be borne by the husband and the wife for the year is greater than it would have been but for the provisions of this subsection, the Board shall cause such relief to be given (by the reduction of such assessments on the husband or the wife or the repayment of such tax paid (by deduction or otherwise) by the husband or the wife as the Board may direct) as will reduce the said net aggregate amount by the amount of the excess.'

The House of Lords held that the effect of what became CGTA 1979 s 155(2) was to apply for capital gains tax the whole of what became ICTA 1988 s 282, including the proviso. Ignoring the residence provisions in ICTA 1988 s 282(2), no CGT would have been payable on the transfer of assets as the transfer would have been within CGTA 1979 s 44. The proviso therefore required the CGT liability to be reduced to nil.

Following the change to independent taxation, if the facts of *Gubay v Kington* were to occur today the decision would be the same as that reached by the House of Lords, but for different reasons. In the income tax legislation a revised ICTA 1988 s 282, effective from 1990-91, has dropped

1   ICTA 1988 s 282(2).
2   (1984) 57 TC 601.

all reference to the residence status of spouses from the definition of spouses living together. As in *Gubay v Kington* the spouses were not in fact separated, the relief in CGTA 1979 s 44 for assets transferred between spouses who are living together would apply.

The somewhat unusual wording of CGTA 1979 s 44(1) has implications for transfers in the year in which spouses marry, and in the year in which they separate. Section 44(1) applies to disposals between man and wife if 'in any year of assessment' the woman is a married woman living with her husband. In the year of marriage s 44 therefore applies to transfers after the marriage, but probably not to assets transferred prior to the marriage, as at the time of the transfer the man and woman would not then be husband and wife. In the year of separation s 44 applies to transfers throughout the year, including the period after the date of separation, unless the couple divorce before the end of the year. S 44 does not apply to transfers made in a year after separation. From the year following the date of separation until they divorce transfers between spouses are treated as transfers between connected persons, so that the transferor spouse is deemed to have made a chargeable disposal of the asset at its market value at the time of the transfer[1].

The no gain/no loss provisions in CGTA 1979 s 44(1) do not apply if an asset is trading stock of the transferor or is to become trading stock of the transferee[2]. In these circumstances the asset will be deemed to have been transferred at its open market value[3], but the transaction will have income tax as well as capital gains tax consequences. S 44 also does not apply to a gift by way of *donatio mortis causa*,[4] which is a gift in anticipation of imminent death. The reason is that transfers on death are technically not disposals, but the donee nevertheless takes over the asset for capital gains tax purposes at its market value on the date of death[5]. In effect there is an uplift of the base cost of the asset on the death of the owner, but the notional gain is exempt from tax. A transfer by way of *donatio mortis causa* is a disposal for capital gains tax purposes, so that, in the absence of the statutory exclusion, the recipient spouse would acquire the asset at its original cost and, on a subsequent disposal, would be charged to capital gains tax on the total gain arising over the combined period of ownership of both spouses. The effect of the exclusion of a *donatio mortis causa* from s 44(1) is that the transfer takes place at market value under CGTA 1979 s 29A(1)(a), but the transferor's gain is excluded from charge by CGTA 1979 s 49(5).

3.5:1 Indexation allowance and transfers between spouses

As outlined in **3.1** above, an indexation allowance is now available to reduce a gain, or create or increase a loss, to compensate for inflation from the date of acquisition of the asset, or 31st March 1982 if later, to the date of disposal. The allowance is available both for the original acquisition

1   CGTA 1979 s 29A(1)(a); *Aspden v Hildesley* (1981) 55 TC 609; and see also **8.10** below.
2   CGTA 1979 s 44(2)(a).
3   CGTA 1979 s 29A(1)(a).
4   CGTA 1979 s 44(2)(b).
5   CGTA 1979 s 49.

value and for qualifying improvement expenditure incurred subsequently to the acquisition of the asset[1]. The allowance is given as a deduction from the gross gain before applying exemptions such as the principal private residence exemption[2]. An allowance is computed separately for each item of qualifying expenditure according to the formula[3]

$$\frac{RD - RI}{RI}$$

where RD is the retail prices index for the month in which the asset is disposed of, and RI is the retail prices index of the month in which the relevant qualifying expenditure was incurred, or March 1982 if later. The resulting indexation factor is expressed to three places of decimals[4], and is then applied to the relevant qualifying expenditure. If the asset was acquired prior to 31st March 1982, the factor is applied to the 31st March 1982 market value of the asset, unless its application to the original cost would give a higher indexation allowance and the taxpayer has not elected under FA 1988 s 96(5) to have all his pre 31st March 1982 acquisitions deemed to have been acquired on 31st March 1982[5].

Example:

Paul acquired a chargeable asset in July 1975 at a cost of £5,000. The market value of the asset on 31st March 1982 was £12,500. Paul sold the asset on 15th June 1989 for £45,000. His indexation allowance is:

indexation factor	$\dfrac{115.40 - 79.44}{79.44}$	=	0.453
∴ indexation allowance is	£12,500 × 0.453	=	£5,662.50

and his chargeable gain is therefore:

	sales proceeds	£45,000.00
Less	31st March 1982 market value	(12,500.00)
	Gross gain	£32,500.00
Less	indexation allowance	(5,662.50)
	Chargeable gain	£26,837.50

In practice it is not normally necessary to compute the indexation factor, since the Revenue and many professional taxation publications provide the relevant factor for every month from March 1982 to the month of disposal[6].

If an asset originally acquired after 31st March 1982 is transferred between husband and wife living together, so that CGTA 1979 s 44(1) applies to the transfer, the transfer is deemed to take place at a value which, after deducting indexation allowance, results in neither gain nor loss to the transferor[7]. Put another way, the transfer value is acquisition value plus

1   FA 1982 s 86(2)(b).
2   FA 1982 s 86(2)(a) and (4), but see *Smith v Schofield* [1990] STC 602.
3   FA 1982 s 87(2).
4   FA 1982 s 87(4).
5   FA 1985 s 68(4) and (5).
6   See also Revenue pamphlet CGT 16, 1989, capital gains tax: indexation allowance; disposals after 5th April 1988. For the relevant indexation factors for disposals in June 1989, used in these examples, see [1989] STI 622.
7   FA 1982 Sch 13 para 2(3).

indexation allowance. On a disposal of the asset by the transferee spouse indexation allowance is computed from the date of transfer between the spouses to the date of eventual disposal of the asset and, for this purpose only, one ignores the provision in CGTA 1979 Sch 5 para 17 that the transferee spouse should take over the transferor spouse's date of acquisition[1].

Example

In May 1985 Hank acquired 1,000 shares in Pluto plc, a quoted company, for £3,500. In June 1989 he gifted the shares to his wife, Eileen. The transfer value of the shares is:

		£
	allowable cost	3,500
plus	indexation allowance May 1985 — June 1989	
	£3,500 × 0.212 =	742
	Transfer value and allowable cost for Eileen	4,242

Special provisions apply if an asset which was originally acquired prior to 31st March 1982 is subsequently transferred after 5th April 1988 (similar provisions applied to transfers between 5th April 1985 and 6th April 1988) to a spouse living with the transferor. As will be seen in the next section if, after 5th April 1988, an asset which was acquired prior to 31st March 1982 is transferred from one spouse to the other, there is normally no substitution of 31st March 1982 market value for original cost in computing the transfer value. That substitution takes place when the recipient spouse eventually disposes of the asset in a transaction to which CGTA 1979 s 44 does not apply. However the indexation allowance at the time of the transfer between the spouses is computed on the 31st March 1982 value of the asset unless the original acquisition value was higher and the transferor spouse has not elected under FA 1988 s 96(5) to have all his pre 31st March 1982 acquisitions deemed to have been acquired on 31st March 1982[2].

Example:

In 1972, as a result of a bequest in her uncle's will, Sarah acquired shares in a quoted company with a market value of £7,600. The market value of the shares on 31st March 1982 was £16,700. In June 1989 she transferred the shares to her husband, Michael. Sarah has not made any election under FA 1988 s 96(5). The transfer value is:

		£
	allowable cost	7,600
plus	indexation allowance March 1982 — June 1989	
	£16,700 × 0.453 =	7,565
	Transfer value	15,165

Further special provisions in FA 1985 s 68(7), (7A) and (8) deal with the computation of indexation allowance where an asset acquired on or before 31st March 1982 was transferred in a no gain/no loss transfer after that date and is disposed of by the recipient spouse on or after 6th April 1988 in a transfer which is not a no gain/no loss transfer[3]. The immediately

---

1   FA 1982 Sch 13 para 2(4).
2   FA 1985 s 68(4)(5) with FA 1982 Sch 13 para 2.
3   Equivalent provisions existed in the original FA 1985 s 68 to deal with a disposal to a third party between 6th April 1985 and 5th April 1988.

preceding example illustrates why special provisions are necessary, as the recipient spouse's acquisition value is currently an amalgam of the original 1972 cost of the shares plus indexation allowance based on the 31st March 1982 value of the shares. On the chargeable disposal on or after 6th April 1988 the transferee's indexation allowance is computed as if the transferee owned the asset on 31st March 1982, ie indexation relief is given from 31st March 1982 to the date of disposal. However any indexation allowance taken into account in computing the transferee's acquisition cost of the asset at the time of the no gain/no loss transfer is deducted from the transferee's acquisition cost of the asset in computing the chargeable gain. Put another way, any indexation allowance given at the time of the no gain/no loss transfer is ignored when computing the gain on the ultimate disposal of the asset, but indexation allowance is computed from 31st March 1982 and not from the date of the inter spousal transfer. For practical purposes the reduction of acquisition cost will only matter if, after reduction, it is still higher than the 31st March 1982 market value of the asset, as this value will now normally be substituted for cost. While indexation allowance will normally be computed on the 31st March 1982 value of the asset, it can be computed on the original cost if this gives a larger allowance provided there has been no election under FA 1988 s 96(5) to rebase all pre-31st March 1982 acquisitions to 31st March 1982[1].

Example
John acquired shares in a quoted company in 1980 for £9,000. The market value of the shares on 31st March 1982 was £12,000. In February 1986 he gifted the shares to his wife, Jane. The transfer value was £9,000 plus indexation allowance of £2,592 = £11,592, which became Jane's acquisition cost. In June 1989 Jane sold the shares for £25,000. In computing Jane's chargeable gain her acquisition cost is reduced by £2,592 to £9,000. As this is lower than the 31st March 1982 market value of the asset, the chargeable gain will be computed using the 31st March 1982 market value, and computing indexation allowance from that date. The computation is:

		£
	Sales proceeds	25,000
Less	31st March 1982 market value	(12,000)
	Gross gain	13,000
Less	indexation allowance £12,000 × 0.453	(5,436)
	Chargeable gain	7,564

3.5:2 Rebasing to 31st March 1982 and transfers between spouses

If an asset originally acquired before 31st March 1982 is transferred on or after 6th April 1988 between spouses who are living together, there is no rebasing of acquisition value at the time of this transfer[2] unless the transferor spouse has elected under FA 1988 s 96(5) to have all his assets owned on 31st March 1982 rebased to their 31st March 1982 value, in which case the transfer value will be the market value of the asset on 31st March 1982[3] plus indexation allowance from that date. If no election under FA

1   FA 1985 s 68(5).
2   FA 1988 s 96(3)(d).
3   FA 1988 s 96(5) and (2).

1988 s 96(5) has been made, indexation allowance on the inter spousal transfer will still be computed on the 31st March 1982 value of the asset unless its application to the original acquisition value would give a higher allowance[1]. The transfer value will therefore normally be the original cost of the asset plus indexation allowance from 31st March 1982 applied to the 31st March 1982 market value of the asset.

If after 5th April 1988 one spouse disposes of an asset which had been acquired from the other spouse at any time after 31st March 1982 under a no gain/no loss transfer within CGTA 1979 s 44, and that other spouse owned the asset on 31st March 1982, then on the ultimate disposal of the asset the recipient spouse is treated as owning the asset on 31st March 1982 for the purpose of rebasing the acquisition value[2]. For this provision to apply, all disposals of the asset between 31st March 1982 and the relevant disposal must have been no gain/no loss disposals by virtue of one of a number of enactments listed in FA 1988 Sch 8 para 1(3), which list includes CGTA 1979 s 44[3]. The last example in **3.5:1** above of John and Jane also illustrates the operation of this provision. The practical effect of these provisions is that there is normally no uplift of acquisition value to 31st March 1982 market value if an asset acquired prior to 31st March 1982 is transferred to a spouse, but the acquisition value will be uplifted to the 31st March 1982 market value when the recipient spouse disposes of the asset.

Special rules deal with the application to transfers between husband and wife living together of an election under FA 1988 s 96(5) for all assets owned on 31st March 1982 to be rebased to that date. If, on or after 6th April 1988, an asset which was acquired prior to 31st March 1982 is transferred between husband and wife living together, only an election by the transferor spouse to have FA 1988 s 96(5) applied to his assets will affect the acquisition value of the asset. If the transferor does make a s 96(5) election, it will apply to the asset transferred to his spouse, whether or not the recipient spouse has made a s 96(5) election[4], and whether the transferor spouse makes a s 96(5) election before or after the inter spousal transfer[5]. Consequently, on the eventual disposal of the asset by the recipient spouse, acquisition value will be the 31st March 1982 market value of the asset. Conversely, if the transferee spouse has elected under s 96(5) to have all her assets acquired prior to 31st March 1982 deemed to have been acquired on that date, any assets which she received on or after 6th April 1988 under a no gain/no loss transfer from her spouse are excluded from the election[6]. If there are successive no gain/no loss transfers on or after 6th April 1988 between spouses living together, only the spouse who owned the asset on 5th April 1988 can make a s 96(5) election covering that asset until the asset is acquired other than in a no gain/no loss transfer[7].

If an asset owned by one spouse on 31st March 1982 was transferred to the other spouse in a no gain/no loss disposal prior to 6th April 1988,

1   See **3.5:1** above.
2   FA 1988 Sch 8 para 1.
3   FA 1988 Sch 8 para 1(b).
4   FA 1988 Sch 8 para 2(2)(a).
5   FA 1988 Sch 8 para 2(1).
6   FA 1988 Sch 8 para 2(2)(a).
7   FA 1988 Sch 8 para 2(3).

only an election under FA 1988 s 96(5) by the recipient spouse will apply
to the asset.

3.5:3 Part disposals and transfers between spouses
Under the capital gains tax legislation the disposal of part of an asset
is, in general, a chargeable event. The acquisition value of the asset is
apportioned between the part disposed of and the part retained applying
the following formula[1]:

$$\text{original cost} \quad \times \quad \frac{\text{sales proceeds or market value of part disposed}}{\begin{array}{ccc} \text{sales proceeds or} & & \text{market value} \\ \text{market value of} & + & \text{of part} \\ \text{part disposed} & & \text{retained} \end{array}}$$

Where part of an asset is transferred by one spouse to another in
circumstances in which CGTA 1979 s 44(1) applies, the cost of the part
disposed of is first determined according to the above rule[2]. The
apportionment is made before computing indexation allowance[3], and then
the normal inter-spousal rules apply so that the recipient spouse takes over
the part at that base cost, plus indexation allowance.

If the asset was originally acquired prior to 31st March 1982 and a part
disposal occurs on or after 6th April 1988 in a transfer between husband
and wife living together, FA 1988 s 96 will apply to substitute 31st March
1982 market value for original cost in the above formula only if the transferor
spouse has made an irrevocable election under FA 1988 s 96(5) to have all
his assets acquired prior to 31st March 1982 valued at their 31st March
1982 market value[4]. Otherwise the rebasing provisions in FA 1988 are ignored
until the eventual disposal of the part transferred[5].

If between 31st March 1982 and 6th April 1988 there was a part disposal
of an asset owned on 31st March 1982, in computing under CGTA 1979
s 35 the acquisition value of the part retained if it is sold on or after 6th
April 1988, the original apportionment of acquisition value made at the
time of the part disposal has to be recomputed on the assumption that
the rebasing provisions in FA 1988 s 96(2) were in force[6]. This principle
will also be relevant in computing the acquisition value of the part
transferred if the part disposal between 31st March 1982 and 6th April 1988
was a no gain/no loss transfer between spouses within CGTA 1979 s 44.

If there is a small part disposal of land, CGTA 1979 s 107 may permit
a taxpayer to elect to exclude the part disposal rules and instead deduct
the consideration received for the part disposal from the acquisition value
of the land, both retained and sold[7]. The reduced acquisition value then
becomes the allowable base cost when the retained land is ultimately disposed
of[8]. S 107 applies if the consideration for the part disposal does not exceed

1   CGTA 1979 s 35(1)(2).
2   CGTA 1979 s 35(5)(a).
3   FA 1982 Sch 13 para 1.
4   FA 1988 s 96(3) and (5).
5   FA 1988 s 96(3)(d).
6   FA 1988 Sch 8 para 8.
7   CGTA 1979 s 107(2).
8   CGTA 1979 s 107(2).

£20,000[1] or 20% of the total market value of the land immediately prior to the part disposal[2], whichever is the less. Additionally, total proceeds of all land disposals in the relevant year must not exceed £20,000[3]. The election in s 107 *is not available* if the part disposal is between husband and wife living together so that CGTA 1979 s 44 applies to it[4]. Accordingly the cost of the part disposed must be determined using the formula, and that cost, together with indexation allowance, then becomes the acquisition value of the recipient spouse.

3.5:4 Shareholdings and transfers between spouses

The introduction of indexation allowance in 1982, its amendment in 1985, and the rebasing of capital gains tax to 31st March 1982, have resulted in considerable complication in the identification and valuation of shares of the same class in the same company which have been acquired at different times. The current rules are principally contained in FA 1985 Sch 19 as supplemented by an extra statutory concession and Statement of Practice 5/89. The legislation has to deal with (1) shares acquired before 6th April 1965, (2) shares acquired between 6th April 1965 and 6th April 1982 (3) shares acquired on or after 6th April 1982. The legislation is relevant to a book on family taxation as it will apply whenever shares are transferred between husband and wife living together, particularly when only part of a holding is transferred. Briefly, the rules are as follows[5]:

(1)   Shares acquired prior to 6th April 1965 remain separate, although the shareholder has the right to elect to bring quoted shares into the pool of shares acquired between 6th April 1965 and 5th April 1982[6]. The acquisition value of these shares is uprated to their market value on 31st March 1982, and indexation allowance is effectively computed on the increase in the RPI from March 1982 to the month in which the disposal occurs.

(2)   Shares acquired between 6th April 1965 and 5th April 1982 form part of a single pool which is frozen at 5th April 1982[7]. As a result of rebasing the value of the pool is increased to the market value of the shares on 31st March 1982 plus any additions between then and 5th April 1982. A shareholder may therefore be maintaining separate pools of shares in the same company because some of them were acquired before 6th April 1965. In certain circumstances this could affect the valuation of the shares as at 31st March 1982. For example, assume a shareholder in an unquoted company has a 60% shareholding, 30% of which was acquired prior to 6th April 1965 and 30% was acquired between 6th April 1985 and 31st March 1982. As the law stands each holding would have to be valued, both for rebasing and indexation allowance, as a 30% minority holding, the aggregate value of which

1   CGTA 1979 s 107(3)(a).
2   CGTA 1979 s 107(1)(a).
3   CGTA 1979 s 107(1)(a).
4   CGTA 1979 s 107(1)(b).
5   The rules on the allocation of shares are particularly complex. The reader needing a more detailed exposition is referred to one of the major works on CGT.
6   FA 1985 Sch 19 para 6(3).
7   FA 1985 Sch 19 para 6(1),7(1).

would be less than a 60% shareholding valued as a controlling interest. However in an extra-statutory concession[1] the Revenue have said that all shares held in a company at 31st March 1982 will be aggregated and valued as a single holding for rebasing and indexation allowance. If there is a part disposal on or after 6th April 1988 of such a holding the acquisition value and indexation allowance of the part disposed of will be based on the proportion that the part disposed of bears to the total shareholding.

Similar relief is given under SP 5/89 if a shareholder owned shares on 31st March 1982 and, after that date, received additional shares of the same class in the same company under a no gain/no loss transfer from a shareholder who owned the shares on 31st March 1982. All the shares will be valued as a single holding when the transferee disposes of them. If there is a disposal of some of the shares then the allowable cost and indexation allowance will be based on the proportion that the shares disposed of bears to the total holding.

Example

On 31st March 1982 Shaun owned 30% of the ordinary share capital in a company, and his wife Lucy owned 25%. In May 1987 Shaun transferred his shareholding to Lucy. In valuing Lucy's shareholding, both for rebasing and for indexation allowance, the value per share will be computed on the assumption that she had a 60% shareholding.

(3)   The final category is shares of the same class in the same company acquired on or after 6th April 1982, called 'new holdings' in the legislation. Rebasing is irrelevant to such shares, but for indexation allowance they are deemed to form part of a single pool[2], with separate pools for each category of shares. The qualifying expenditure of a pool is the acquisition value of the shares[3]. On the disposal of all the shares in a category 3 pool the indexation allowance is computed by deducting the qualifying expenditure of the pool from the indexed pool[4]. The concept of the indexed pool is that every time some of the shares in the pool are disposed of, or additional shares are acquired, indexation allowance is applied to the whole pool to increase its value to reflect the increase in the RPI from the last disposal or acquisition to the current chargeable event. For shares acquired between 6th April 1982 and 6th April 1985 the initial value of the indexed pool is the acquisition value of the shares plus indexation allowance to 6th April 1985 computed under FA 1982 s 87 on the assumption that the shares had been disposed of at that time and immediately reacquired[5]. For shares acquired on or after 6th April 1985 the initial value of the indexed pool is the acquisition value of the shares[6]. If there have been acquisitions or disposals of pool shares after 6th April 1985, on a current disposal it will only be necessary to compute indexation allowance from the month of the most recent relevant transaction

1   [1989] STI 432.
2   FA 1985 Sch 19 para 9(1)(2).
3   FA 1985 Sch 19 para 12.
4   FA 1985 Sch 19 para 11(3).
5   FA 1985 Sch 19 para 13(2).
6   FA 1985 Sch 19 para 13(3).

to the month of disposal[1].

If there is a part disposal of shares in a pool then the allowable cost of the shares is apportioned between the part transferred and the part retained applying the normal part disposal rules discussed in **3.5:3** above[2], ie the total acquisition value of the pool is allocated to the part transferred in the ratio that the current market value of the part transferred bears to the current market value of the whole of the pool. The indexed pool must also be apportioned on the same basis between the part retained and the part transferred[3]. The indexation allowance on the part disposal is the difference between the apportioned part of the indexed pool and the apportioned part of the acquisition value of the part disposed[4].

Example

In March 1986 Peter purchased 500 shares in Blanco plc for £350. The RPI was then 96.73. In September 1987 he purchased a further 300 shares for £250. The RPI was then 104.40. In June 1989 he gave 200 shares to his wife Mary. The market value of the shares was then £1 per share, and the RPI was 115.40. In September 1987 the allowable cost of the pool became:

No	Value £
500	350
300	250
800	600

and the indexed pool became[5]:

	No		Value £
	500		350
	$+ £350 \times \dfrac{104.40 - 96.73}{96.73}$		28
	300		250
	800		628

On the part disposal to Mary, Peter's holding is revalued as follows:

	No		Value £
Allowable cost			
	800		600
Less disposal	(200)	$£600 \times \dfrac{200}{200 + 600}$	(150)
	600		450
Indexed pool			
	800		628
	$+ £628 \times \dfrac{115.40 - 104.40}{104.40}$		66
			694
Less disposal	(200)	$£694 \times \dfrac{200}{200 + 600}$	(173)
	600		521

1 FA 1985 Sch 19 para 14(1).
2 FA 1988 Sch 19 para 10.
3 FA 1988 Sch 19 para 11(2).
4 FA 1988 Sch 19 para 11(2)(b).
5 FA 1985 Sch 19 para 13(5) and 14.

Under FA 1985 Sch 19 para 11(2)(b) the indexation allowance on the part disposal to Mary is therefore £173 — £150 = £23. Under CGTA 1979 s 44 Mary is deemed to acquire the shares at Peter's base cost plus indexation allowance, ie £173. If Mary already has shares of the same class in the same company acquired on or after 6th April 1982, she must revalue her own indexed pool of shares to June 1989, and then add to both the acquisition value pool and the indexed pool an additional 200 shares with an acquisition value of £173.

If, because shares were acquired on different dates, a shareholder has different pools of shares of the same class in the same company, and he subsequently disposes of some of the shares, the rules for matching a disposal with an acquisition are set out in FA 1985 Sch 19 para 19. They override any allocation made by the transferor[1], and basically operate under a last in, first out principle. Disposals are therefore matched with acquisitions in the following order:

(1) Category 3 acquisitions, ie shares acquired on or after 6th April 1982;
(2) Category 2 acquisitions, ie shares acquired between 6th April 1965 and 6th April 1982;
(3) Category 1 acquisitions, ie shares acquired before 6th April 1965 which the shareholder has not elected to bring within category 2.

3.5:5 Business expansion scheme shares and transfers between spouses

There is neither a chargeable gain nor an allowable loss for capital gains tax purposes on the first disposal of shares issued after 18th March 1986 which qualified for relief under the business expansion scheme provisions when they were first issued[2]. For the exemption to apply the BES relief must not have been withdrawn. If there is a transfer of such shares between husband and wife living together so that the transfer is a no gain/no loss transfer under CGTA 1979 s 44, this transfer does not count as the first disposal for the purposes of this provision. The exemption is instead given on a disposal of the asset by the recipient spouse[3].

If business expansion scheme relief was given for shares issued before 19th March 1986 there is no exemption from capital gains tax on the first disposal of the shares. The acquisition value for the purpose of computing any gain on a disposal is the cost of the shares ignoring any relief under the business expansion scheme provisions. However if the allowable cost of the shares exceeds the disposal proceeds, so that there would otherwise be a loss, the allowable cost is reduced by the lower of the excess or the relief given under the business expansion scheme[4]. These provisions do not apply to a transfer between husband and wife living together within CGTA 1979 s 44[5]. On such a transfer the recipient spouse will acquire the shares at their cost to the transferor spouse, ignoring any relief under the business expansion scheme provisions[6], plus indexation allowance from the date of acquisition, or 31st March 1982, if later. The identification rules for disposals of shares discussed in the previous section do not apply

1 FA 1985 Sch 19 para 16(2).
2 CGTA 1979 s 149C(2).
3 CGTA 1979 s 149C(6).
4 CGTA 1979 s 149C(3).
5 CGTA 1979 s 149C(3).
6 CGTA 1979 s 33(3).

to disposals of shares on which business expansion scheme relief has been given and not withdrawn[1].

3.5:6 Gifts relief and transfers between spouses

Under FA 1980 s 79 if an asset was transferred between individuals otherwise than under a bargain at arm's length, the individuals could elect that the disposal proceeds of the transferor and the acquisition value of the recipient should be reduced by the amount of the gain. Effectively the capital gain was rolled over and the charge deferred until the recipient disposed of the asset. As persons who are not resident and not ordinarily resident in the United Kingdom are exempt from capital gains tax, it would have been easy to avoid a CGT charge altogether by transferring assets, electing for hold-over relief, and having the transferee become non-resident. FA 1981 s 79 therefore provided that, if the transferee was an individual and became not resident and not ordinarily resident in the United Kingdom within six years of the end of the year of assessment in which the transfer was made without having disposed of the asset, the held-over gain should immediately become chargeable to tax. A disposal by the transferee to his spouse did not count as a disposal to a third party for the purpose of the six year rule, but any subsequent disposal by the spouse to a third party was treated as if it was a disposal by the transferee[2]. Although the general relief for gifts was abolished by FA 1989, FA 1989 s 124(3) provides that the repeal of the gifts relief provisions is not to affect the operation of any enactment when that enactment operates in consequence of gifts relief having been given. Consequently, the anti-avoidance provisions in FA 1981 will continue to apply to claw back gifts relief until at least 1994-95.

3.6 The CGT charge on family trusts

The normal rate of CGT on gains on a disposal by trustees of trust assets is 25% where a beneficiary is entitled to the income of the trust[3], and the rate of tax payable on gains realised by a discretionary or accumulation trust is 35%[4]. For a taxpayer liable to income tax at 40% capital gains tax savings could be made by putting assets into trust and realising future gains in the trust, but anti-avoidance provisions in FA 1988 Sch 10 counteract this possibility. If a settlor retains an interest in trust property any gains realised by the trustees are taxed as gains of the settlor taxable at his top marginal rate of capital gains tax, and he is liable to pay the CGT[5]. However the settlor is entitled to recover from the trustees any CGT he has to pay under these provisions[6]. The anti-avoidance provisions only apply if the settlor and trustees are resident or ordinarily resident in the United Kingdom[7].

1   FA 1988 Sch 19 para 16(3)
2   FA 1981 s 79(3).
3   FA 1988 s 98(1).
4   FA 1988 s 100(1).
5   FA 1988 Sch 10 para 2.
6   FA 1988 Sch 10 para 5.
7   FA 1988 Sch 10 para 4.

For 1988-89 and 1989-90 there are provisions to calculate the tax paid on imputed trust gains where the settlor and his spouse are living together, so that their gains are aggregated to compute the tax payable[1]. If, after aggregation, any higher rate tax has to be paid on the gains, settlement gains are treated as the top slice of the chargeable gains[2]. If both spouses have taxable settlement gains then (1) the settlement gains are aggregated and treated as the top slice of their joint gains for the purposes of computing the tax paid on them, and (2) the total tax payable is then apportioned between the respective spouses' trusts pro rata to the trust gains[3].

Example:

For 1989-90 Mark had chargeable gains, after deducting the annual exemption, of £7,000. Mark had imputed settlement gains of £6,000, and his wife Mary had imputed settlement gains of £4,000. Mark had taxable income, after deducting personal allowances, of £11,000. Their combined CGT liability is:

			£
Personal gains			7,000
Imputed trust gains			10,000
			17,000
CGT payable:			
basic rate	£20,700 − £11,000 = £ 9,700 @ 25%		2,425
higher rate	7,300 @ 40%		2,920
	£17,000		5,345
Recoverable from the trustees:			
	£ 7,300 @ 40%		2,920
	2,700 @ 25%		675
	£10,000		3,595

of which 6/10, or £2,157, is recoverable from the trustees of Mark's settlement and 4/10, or £1,438, is recoverable from the trustees of Mary's settlement.

The circumstances in which a settlor will be deemed to have retained an interest in a trust are set out in FA 1988 Sch 10 para 2, and are wide ranging. A settlor will be deemed to have retained an interest if:

'(a) any property which may at any time be comprised in the settlement or any income which may arise under the settlement is, or will or may become, applicable for the benefit of or payable to the settlor or the spouse of the settlor in any circumstances whatsoever, or

(b) the settlor, or the spouse of the settlor, enjoys a benefit deriving directly or indirectly from any property which is comprised in the settlement or any income arising under the settlement.'

A settlor does not retain an interest if he can only derive a benefit on the bankruptcy of a third person, or there is an assignment or charge of the settled property, or, if the trust is a marriage settlement, the parties to the marriage and their children die[4]. Finally, a settlor is not deemed

---

1 FA 1988 Sch 10 para 5(3).
2 FA 1988 Sch 10 para 5(4)
3 FA 1988 Sch 10 para 5(5).
4 FA 1988 Sch 10 para 2(2).

to retain a benefit if the only circumstance in which he can derive a benefit is on the death of a trust beneficiary under the age of 25[1]. There is no charge in the year in which the settlor dies[2], but benefits received by a settlor's spouse continue to be relevant until there is a decree absolute of divorce[3].

3.7 The family home

The capital gains tax legislation contains provisions to exempt the whole or any part of a gain arising on the disposal of property which has at any time throughout the transferor's period of ownership been his only or main residence[4]. The relief is also extended to land up to one acre, or such larger area as the Revenue may allow where they are satisfied that the larger area is required for the reasonable enjoyment of the house[5]. Where an individual has two or more residences he may determine which is to be treated as his main residence for any period by serving notice in writing on the inspector within two years from the beginning of the period, and may vary the notice in respect of any period beginning not more than two years before the notice of variation[6]. If a taxpayer with more than one residence fails to give notice of his main one to an inspector within the requisite time limit, the inspector is entitled to determine the issue for him[7]. The determination may cover the whole, or only specified parts, of the taxpayer's period of ownership. Notice of any determination by an inspector must be given to the taxpayer, who has a right of appeal to the General or Special Commissioners within thirty days of its service[8]. Although it is not spelt out in the legislation, it would seem that the Appeal Commissioners' jurisdiction is confined to deciding which residence is, on the facts, the taxpayer's main residence.

A husband and wife living together may only have one principal private residence between them for exemption purposes[9], and the introduction of independent taxation has not altered this principle. Where there are two or more residences both spouses must sign a notice of election designating one residence as the main one, unless all the residences are wholly owned by one of the spouses. As it is now increasingly common for a spouse to acquire an equitable interest in property, even if she does not have legal ownership, it would seem preferable for both spouses to make the election as a matter of course. Similarly, any notice given by an inspector in respect of 'a residence owned by the husband and a residence owned by the wife' must be given to each spouse, and each spouse has a right of appeal[10].

1   FA 1988 Sch 10 para 2(2)(c).
2   FA 1988 Sch 10 para 3(1).
3   FA 1988 Sch 10 para 3(2).
4   CGTA 1979 s 101(1).
5   CGTA 1979 s 101(1)(b), (2) and (3).
6   CGTA 1979 s 101(5)(a).
7   CGTA 1979 s 101(5)(b).
8   CGTA 1979 s 101(5)(b).
9   CGTA 1979 s 101(6)(a).
10 CGTA 1979 s 101(6)(b).

CGTA 1979 s 101(6)(b) is unhappily phrased, as it implies that one residence must be wholly owned by the wife, and the other residence wholly owned by the husband. The same principle should apply where there is joint ownership, legal or equitable, of two or more houses.

Where the principal private residence has been occupied as such throughout the transferor's period of ownership, or throughout that period except all or part of the last twenty-four months, the whole of any gain after deducting indexation allowance[1] is exempt from tax[2]. The taxpayer is permitted to be absent from the property for certain periods without losing any of his exemption. These periods are cumulative, and are[3]:

(1)   three years for any purpose, plus
(2)   unlimited absence due to an employment or office the duties of which are performed wholly abroad, plus
(3)   four years, where residence elsewhere is in consequence of the taxpayer's place of work, or in consequence of a condition imposed by his employer requiring him to reside elsewhere, provided the condition is reasonably imposed to secure the effective performance of his duties of employment.

Under ESC D3 if either of the last two conditions is satisfied by one spouse it will also be treated as satisfied by the other spouse provided the spouses are living together. Thus if a principal private residence is owned by a wife who accompanies her husband when he takes up a three year contract of foreign employment, none of the exemption will be lost.

To take advantage of the provisions in CGTA 1979 s 102(3) which enable periods of absence to be ignored, a taxpayer must have occupied the house both before and after the period of absence which it is sought to ignore[4]. Additionally, principal private residence relief must not be claimed on any other house during the period of absence[5]. Thus there is no relief for a period of absence between the acquisition of a house and its first occupation, and there is also normally no relief for a period of absence if the house is not reoccupied, even if the absence would otherwise be within one of the exemptions. However, under ESC D4, the condition of reoccupation is treated as satisfied for the purposes of periods (2) and (3) if the taxpayer is unable to resume residence because the terms of his employment require him to reside elsewhere.

Occupation of a house as a main residence is also deemed to be continuous where a taxpayer resides in 'job-related accommodation' and intends eventually to occupy the house as his only or main residence[6]. Job-related accommodation is defined in accordance with the income tax provisions in ICTA 1988 s 356, which give mortgage interest relief for interest paid

1   FA 1982 s 86(4).
2   CGTA 1979 s 102(1).
3   CGTA 1979 s 102(3)
4   CGTA 1979 s 102(3).
5   CGTA 1979 s 102(3)
6   CGTA 1979 s 101(8).

on a loan used to acquire job-related accommodation. If the taxpayer, or the taxpayer's spouse, is an employee, it is accommodation which is necessary for the proper performance of the duties of the employment, or is for the better performance of the duties of employment and the employment is one in which it is customary for accommodation to be provided[1], or is accommodation provided as part of security arrangements in force because there is a special threat to the employee's security[2]. There are additional requirements set out in ICTA 1988 s 356(4) if the taxpayer is a director. If the taxpayer, or his spouse, is self-employed, job-related accommodation is accommodation which the self-employed individual is required to occupy under a contract entered into at arm's length which obliges the individual to carry on the trade on particular premises and to live either in those premises or in other premises made available by the employer[3]. The accommodation must not be provided by a company in which the self-employed individual or his spouse has a material interest, or by any partner of the self-employed individual or his spouse[4]. The capital gains tax exemption for job related occupation of the self-employed is restricted to periods of occupation after 5th April 1983[5], but the rebasing of capital gains tax to 31st March 1982 has limited the effect of this restriction. If property qualifies as a residence because of the relief for job-related accommodation in CGTA 1979 s 101(8), it appears that it is irrelevant whether the property is left unoccupied or let out, as CGTA 1979 s 101(8) says without qualification that, while the owner continues to reside in job-related accommodation, CGTA 1979 ss 101-105 shall apply as if the dwelling house or part of a dwelling house were at that time occupied by him as a residence.

Complications can arise if a house, Blackacre, is acquired by a husband and wife in their joint names but is lived in by neither of them because the husband is required to live elsewhere as part of the duties of employment, and the house provided by the employer is occupied by both spouses, even though the wife has no job related need to live in the alternative accommodation. Assuming the husband does intend eventually to reside in Blackacre, it will be treated as occupied by him as a residence under CGTA 1979 s 101(8). But what is the position of the wife? It seems clear from CGTA 1979 s 101(6) that spouses can only have one main residence between them, and from the definition of job related accommodation in ICTA 1988 s 356(3) that Blackacre is a residence of both spouses for this purpose. Accordingly Blackacre is a qualifying residence as far as the wife is concerned, whether or not she in fact occupies it. If she is in fact occupying another residence, it may be desirable for her and her husband to serve a notice on the inspector under CGTA 1979 s101(5)(a) specifying that Blackacre is to be treated as the main residence of both of them for the purposes of the capital gains tax exemption. If the spouses have to sell Blackacre without ever having occupied it,

---

1 See *Vertigan v Brady* [1988] STC 91.
2 ICTA 1988 s 356(3)(a).
3 ICTA 1988 s 356(3)(b).
4 ICTA 1988 s 356(4).
5 CGTA 1979 s 101(8A).

for example following a marital breakdown, the whole of any gain should be exempt provided the sale takes place not more than two years after the cessation of the intention eventually to live in the house or, in the case of the wife only, after the date of separation, if earlier[1].

The rebasing of capital gains tax to 31st March 1982 has had important implications for the computation of the principal private residence exemption where the house was used as a main residence for a period prior to 31st March 1982, but was not so used for a period after 31st March 1982. On a disposal on or after 6th April 1988 of a main residence originally acquired before 31st March 1982 the gain will be computed by deducting the 31st March 1982 market value of the house from the sales proceeds, and a further deduction will then be made for indexation allowance computed on the 31st March 1982 market value of the house. For the purpose of computing the principal private residence exemption, ownership of the house is deemed to have begun on 31st March 1982[2]. Accordingly, if the taxpayer has continuously occupied the house as his main residence since that date, the whole of the gain will be exempt from tax, even if the house was not so occupied for periods prior to 31st March 1982. Conversely, if the house was not so occupied, including permitted absences, continuously from 31st March 1982, only part of the gain may be exempt. The exemption is computed by dividing the period of actual occupation since 31st March 1982, but *inclusive in any event of the last twenty-four months of ownership*[3], by the total period of ownership since 31st March 1982. It should be noted that the taxpayer is entitled to deemed occupation of the last twenty-four months of ownership even if the only time he occupied the premises as his main residence was prior to 31st March 1982. This is because CGTA 1979 s 102, which gives the exemption, applies to any gain to which s 101 applies; and s 101 applies to the disposal of a house which has during his period of ownership been the taxpayer's main residence. 'Period of ownership' in s 101 is not restricted to periods of ownership after 31st March 1982[4], and CGTA 1979 s 102 therefore applies to a principal private residence which was so occupied at any time, even if the period of occupation was wholly prior to 31st March 1982[5].

The effect of the rebasing rules is that any principal private residence exemption accrued through residence prior to 31st March 1982 has been lost, so that, if there was substantial occupation prior to 31st March 1982, but little after it, the taxpayer may end up with a higher chargeable gain than if the FA 1988 changes had never been made, which seems somewhat unfair.

1 The relief under s 101(8) would cease at this point but, under s 102(2)(a), an owner of a house which has at any time been his main residence is deemed to have occupied it for his last twenty-four months of ownership.
2 CGTA 1979 s 102(4).
3 CGTA 1979 s 102(2).
4 The restriction to 31st March 1982 in s 102(4) only applies for the purposes of s 102, and then only to compute the period of ownership for time apportionment.
5 For an excellent explanation of this see 'The basic problem', David Smailes FCA, *Taxation* 21st October 1988 p 50.

Example

In June 1972 Simon acquired a main residence at a cost of £10,000. In June 1981 he ceased to occupy it. The 31st March 1982 market value of the house was £30,000. In June 1989 Simon sold the house for £95,000. Under the new rules his chargeable gain will be:

		£
	Sales proceeds	95,000
Less	31st March 1982 market value	(30,000)
	Gross gain	65,000
Less	indexation allowance — £30,000[1] × 0.453	(13,590)
	Gain	51,410
Less	PPR exemption — $\dfrac{0 + 24}{87} \times £51,410$	(14,182)
	Chargeable gain	37,228

If the rebasing provisions in the Finance Act 1988 had not been enacted the chargeable gain would have been:

		£
	Sales proceeds	95,000
Less	allowable cost	(10,000)
	Gross gain	85,000
Less	indexation allowance — £30,000 × 0.453	(13,590)
	Gain	71,410
Less	PPR exemption — $\dfrac{108 + 24}{204} \times £71,410$	(46,206)
	Chargeable gain	25,204

The FA 1988 changes have therefore resulted in Simon realising an additional £12,024 chargeable gains which, if he is a higher rate income tax payer, will give rise to an additional CGT liability of £4,809.60. Yet there seems to be no way out of the impasse, for two reasons. First, CGTA s 102(4) requires 31st March 1982 to be treated as the date of initial ownership in computing the principal private residence exemption for all disposals made on or after 6th April 1988, whether the old or the new rules for computing gain are used. Secondly, although FA 1988 s 96(3) allows a taxpayer, assuming no irrevocable election to the contrary has been made under FA 1988 s 96(5), to compute a gain using original cost if that is higher than 31st March 1982 market value, it is *the gain* under both systems that must be compared for this purpose, and not the *chargeable gain*. 'Gain' and 'chargeable gain' are different concepts in the capital gains tax legislation, as a gain is the amount taxable before the application of an exemption, and a chargeable gain is the amount chargeable after application of any relevant exemption. That FA 1988 s 96(3) means to use 'gain' in its strict sense is borne out by FA 1988 Sch 8 para 8, which, in the application of s 96(3) to an asset acquired prior to 6th April 1965, deems the gain for the purposes of s 96(3)(b) to be the chargeable gain, which indicates that, apart from this specific exemption, the draftsman meant the word 'gain'

1   Since 1985 a taxpayer has had the right to compute indexation allowance on the 31st March 1982 market value of the asset.

in FA 1988 s 96(3) to be interpreted strictly. Thus in the above example the gain under rebasing was £51,410 and the gain under the old rules was £71,410. As the gain under rebasing is lower, the option in FA 1988 s 96(3) to use original cost is not available[1].

Relief from capital gains tax may be available if the whole, or any part, of a main residence is let as residential accommodation. If a room in a house is let to a lodger who shares the remaining living accommodation with the family and takes his meals with them, the whole of the house remains the owner's principal private residence and none of the exemption is lost[2]. If a tenant does not qualify as a lodger then the gain attributable to the part let, for the period let, is not exempt under the principal private residence exemption, except to the extent that it includes the last two years' ownership of the property. However, under FA 1980 s 80, any gain attributable to the part let will be chargeable only to the extent that it exceeds the lower of the gain that is exempt from tax under the principal private residence exemption or £20,000.

Example
In October 1983 Paul acquired a house for £20,000. He occupied it as his main residence until October 1986. In October 1986 he let the house. In June 1989, on the tenant vacating it, he sold the house for £85,000. In the absence of relief under FA 1980 s 80 Paul's chargeable gain would be:

		£
	Sales proceeds	85,000
Less	allowable cost	(20,000)
	Unindexed gain	65,000
Less	indexation allowance £20,000 × 0.336	(6,720)
	Gain	58,280
Less	PPR exemption £58,280 × $\frac{36 + 24}{68}$	(51,424)
	Chargeable gain	6,856

As the £6,856 chargeable gain is below both the exempt gain of £51,424 and £20,000, it will be wholly exempted from tax by virtue of FA 1980 s 80.

In SP 15/80 the Revenue make clear that the relief only applies if the property let is the whole or part of the taxpayer's main residence. No relief is available if what has been let is in fact a separate residence from the taxpayer's main residence. If part of a house is let as rooms or a flat with minimal structural alteration the relief will apply, even if the tenants have separate washing and cooking facilities. But the relief does not extend to property which, although it may be part of the same building, forms a dwelling house separate from that which is, or has been, the owner's (for example, a fully self contained flat with its own access from the road). However if the property let forms an integral part of a building which is also the taxpayer's main residence it seems that the relief is available on a generous basis. Thus in *Owen v Elliott*[3] the Court of Appeal, reversing a decision of the High Court, held that the relief in FA 1980 s 80 extended

1 For good articles on the problem see 'The basic problem', David Smailes FCA, *Taxation* 21st October 1988 p 50 and 'A nasty shock', Roy Parker and Malcolm Gunn FTII, *Taxation* 8th December 1988 p 222.
2 SP 14/80 Capital gains tax: relief for owner occupiers.
3 [1990] STC 469.

to a private hotel which was also occupied by the proprietors as their main residence as the phrase 'let by him as residential accommodation' should be interpreted broadly.

Special rules apply where husband and wife are living together and one disposes of his interest in the principal private residence to the other. The disposal takes place on the normal no gain/no loss basis, plus indexation allowance, but when the transferee subsequently disposes of the interest the exempt portion of the gain is computed on the basis that her ownership began with the transferor's ownership[1], and the transferor's occupation is deemed also to be her occupation[2]. Effectively ownership and occupation of both are combined and treated as being by a single taxpayer.

One aspect of these rules deserves comment. CGTA 1979 s 101(7)(a) enacts that the special provisions apply:

> '... if one disposes of, or of his interest in, the dwelling-house or part of a dwelling-house which is their only or main residence to the other, *and in particular if it passes on death to the other as legatee...*'

It is difficult to see the reason for the words underlined. Death is not a disposal for capital gains tax purposes, and it is therefore odd to have a particular event which is not within the preceding general category. On death the personal representatives acquire the deceased's assets at their current market value[3]. The effect is to exempt from charge gains accruing on death. It is difficult to see why, if a husband transfers his principal private residence to his wife on death, any part of the wife's subsequent exemption should be reduced by reference to her husband's prior ownership. A simple example will illustrate the point.

Example

In March 1983 H purchased a house for £20,000. From March 1983 to March 1986 the house was unoccupied. In March 1986 H married W and went to live with W in the house as their main residence. In March 1989 he died and bequeathed the house (then market value £90,000) to W. W lived in the house until March 1991, when she sold it for £120,000. Ignoring indexation allowance, and attempting to apply CGTA 1979 s 101(7), W's chargeable gain is

		£
	Sales proceeds	120,000
Less	acquisition value (CGTA 1979 s 49)	(90,000)
	Gain	30,000
Less	PPR exemption $\frac{60}{96} \times £30,000$	(18,750)
	Chargeable gain	11,250

It is unclear why W's gross gain, which relates solely to her period of occupation of the house as her main residence after H's death should be apportioned. If W was a cohabitee of H, or a child of H, then on H's death there is no disposal[4], and hence no chargeable gain, but the personal

1   CGTA 1979 s 101(7)(a).
2   CGTA 1979 s 101(7)(b).
3   CGTA 1979 s 49.
4   CGTA 1979 s 49(1)(b).

representatives, and subsequently the beneficiaries, acquire the house at its then market value[1]. As the beneficiaries occupy the house as their main residence throughout their period of ownership, the whole of any subsequent gain is exempt. There seems no logic in this distinction between spouses and others. It can, admittedly, work to the advantage of a recipient spouse as well as to her disadvantage. For example if a residence owned by one spouse and occupied by him as his main residence is bequeathed to the other spouse who does not thereafter use it as her main residence, on its eventual disposal she can, apparently, claim partial principal private residence exemption based on her husband's occupation prior to his death[2]. But, again, there seems no logic in this, since the wife's acquisition value of the property will be its market value on her husband's death, so that the whole of any gain prior to his death has been exempted from charge to tax. The words highlighted were in the original capital gains tax legislation as part of FA 1965 s 29(8)(b), when disposals on death were chargeable events. It may be that, when disposals on death ceased to be chargeable events by virtue of provisions in FA 1971, the draftsman inadvertently omitted to make a consequential amendment to the principal private residence exemption. CGTA 1979 s 101(7) would certainly read much better if the words highlighted were omitted.

3.8 Residences for dependent relatives

The relief in CGTA 1979 s 105 for gains arising on the disposal of a house occupied by a dependent relative was abolished by FA 1988 s 111(1) for disposals on or after 6th April 1988, and it might therefore appear no longer to be of any relevance. However the repeal does not apply if there was a period of occupation by a dependent relative prior to 6th April 1988[3]. Occupation by a dependent relative prior to 6th April 1988 will qualify for exemption when the house is eventually sold, as also will occupation on or after that date by the same dependent relative if he was in occupation of the premises on 5th April 1988[4]. Once the occupation of the dependant relative ceases, any further occupation by that, or another, dependent relative will not qualify for exemption[5].

A dependent relative means any relative of the taxpayer's or of his spouse, whether or not the spouses are living together, who is incapacitated by old age or infirmity from maintaining himself, or his or his spouse's mother, whether incapacitated or not, but provided she is widowed, living apart from her husband, or single following the divorce or annulment of her marriage[6]. 'Relative' is not further defined, but it should be noted that, unlike the equivalent provisions which used to exist for mortgage interest relief, no relief can be claimed merely because a house is being occupied by a former or separated spouse. A separated spouse is no doubt a relative of the taxpayer (a divorced spouse would not be), but she would have to

1 CGTA 1979 s 49(1)(a).
2 See Whiteman and Wheatcroft, *Capital Gains Tax* (4th edn) pp 16-29.
3 FA 1988 s 111(2).
4 FA 1988 s 111(3).
5 FA 1988 s 111(3).
6 CGTA 1979 s 105(5)(6).

be incapacitated by old age or infirmity from maintaining herself before the relief could be relevant.

It is a further condition for qualification for relief that the house must have been provided rent free and without any other consideration[1]. In ESC D20 the Revenue have stated that this condition will be regarded as satisfied even if the dependent relative pays all or part of the occupier's rates and the cost of repairs to the dwelling house attributable to normal wear and tear. The condition will also be treated as satisfied even if the dependent relative makes payments to the taxpayer or to a third party, provided no net income is received by the taxpayer, taking one year with another. In practice, payment by the dependent relative of a mortgage on the premises would normally bar the relief.

If the exemption applies the additional residence is treated as if it were the taxpayer's main residence during the period of residence by the dependent relative, and occupation by the dependent relative is treated as occupation by the taxpayer[2]. The relief is additional to any relief for the actual main residence of the taxpayer[3]. It should follow from the way CGTA 1979 s 105(2) is worded that the gain attributable to the last twenty-four months of ownership of a house at some time occupied by a dependent relative is also exempt, even if the house is sold after 5th April 1988 and the occupation by the dependent relative was all prior to that date. Only one additional residence may be claimed by each taxpayer at any one time[4]. For this purpose husband and wife living together are treated as one person and, for any one period, may only have one additional residence between them[5]. This restriction is unaffected by the introduction of independent taxation. An inspector may require a spouse making a claim for relief to show that the claim will not preclude a claim by the other spouse or, if it will, that the other spouse's claim has been relinquished[6]. There are no provisions for resolving conflicts between spouses where both are providing houses for dependent relatives, but in practice such disputes are likely to be rare.

3.9 The 'connected person' rules

There are important provisions in the capital gains tax legislation dealing with the consequences of transfers between people who are 'connected' with each other. As many of these connected persons are other members of the family, the provisions are worth considering in some detail. The following people are connected with each other:

(1)   A husband and wife[7]. It is important to note that there is no limitation to husband and wife living together. Thus husband and wife remain connected persons after separation[8], although they cease to be connected

1   CGTA 1979 s 105(1) and FA 1988 s 111(2).
2   CGTA 1979 s 105(2).
3   CGTA 1979 s 105(2).
4   CGTA 1979 s 105(3).
5   CGTA 1979 s 105(3).
6   CGTA 1979 s 105(4).
7   CGTA 1979 s 63(2).
8   *Aspden v Hildesley* (1981) 55 TC 609; *Gubay v Kington* (1984) 57 TC 601.

persons after a decree absolute of divorce has taken effect. Transfers between husband and wife living together take place on a no gain/ no loss basis by virtue of CGTA 1979 s 44, but transfers in the year after separation until divorce will be subject to the connected person rules.

(2)   An individual and his, or his spouse's, relative, or the husband or wife of a relative[1]. A relative means brother, sister, ancestor, or lineal descendant[2]. Thus a taxpayer's children always remain connected with him, irrespective of their age. On the wording of the legislation, a taxpayer is connected with his wife's sister-in-law, but not with his, or his wife's, nephews.

(3)   Trustees of a settlement and the settlor, or any person connected with the settlor, or a company which is connected with the settlement for income tax purposes[3].

(4)   An individual and his partners, their spouses and relatives, except in relation to the acquisition and disposal of partnership assets pursuant to bona fide commercial arrangements[4]. This provision can be of particular importance if a husband and wife are in a business partnership and the marriage breaks down. Although they will cease to be connected persons by virtue of their relationship after decree absolute, they will remain connected persons for the purposes of dealings in the partnership assets, and, if there is a transfer of partnership assets as part of a financial settlement following the marriage breakdown, it is likely to be difficult to establish that it was made pursuant to a bona fide commercial arrangement.

(5)   Companies with other companies and individuals where there is mutual control[5].

Some of the more significant consequences for capital gains tax purposes of transactions between persons who are connected with each other are as follows:

(1)   Transactions between connected persons are deemed to be otherwise than by way of bargain at arm's length[6]. It follows from this that the disposal proceeds are deemed to be the market value at the time of disposal of the asset transferred irrespective of the actual consideration[7], although special rules apply to the transfer of assets between husband and wife living together (see **3.5** above). 'Market value' is defined to mean the price which the assets might reasonably be expected to fetch on a sale in the open market, with no reduction being made for any fall in price due to all the assets being placed on the market at the same time[8]. Where an asset is transferred between connected persons subject to a right or restriction enforceable by the transferor, the market value is to be computed ignoring the restriction,

1   CGTA 1979 s 63(2).
2   CGTA 1979 s 63(8).
3   CGTA 1979 s 63(3).
4   CGTA 1979 s 63(4).
5   CGTA 1979 s 63(5) and (6).
6   CGTA 1979 s 62(2).
7   CGTA 1979 s 29A(1)(a).
8   CGTA 1979 s 150(1) and (2).

but is then to be reduced by the lower of[1]:

(a)   the market value of the right or restriction, or

(b)   the amount by which the extinction of the right or restriction would increase the value of the asset.

If the right or restriction is of such a nature that its enforcement would destroy or substantially impair the value of the asset without a countervailing benefit to the transferor, or a person connected with him, it is to be totally ignored[2]. The value of any option to repurchase or, in the case of an incorporeal property such as a right of way, the right to extinguish the asset, is also to be ignored[3]. These provisions do not apply in relation to rights exercisable on breach of covenant in a lease of land or other property, or in mortgages[4], and the value of any such rights therefore continues to be taken into account in computing the market value of the asset.

(2)   Transfers between connected persons may result in a restriction of loss relief. If the person disposing of an asset to a connected person incurs an allowable loss, the loss can only be relieved against chargeable gains on future disposals to the same connected person at a time when they are still connected persons[5]. This rule does not apply to certain trusts for educational purposes[6]. Where a transferor grants an option to a transferee who is a connected person, and the transferee subsequently disposes of that option at a loss, the loss will only be an allowable loss if the disposal is under an arm's length transaction to a person who is not connected with the transferee[7].

(3)   Under CGTA 1979 s 7A, CGT payable following the gift of land, or a controlling shareholding, or a shareholding in an unquoted company can be paid by instalments over ten years (see **3.11** below). These deferral provisions apply if the transfer is to a person connected with the transferor, but any unpaid instalments and interest become immediately payable if the asset is subsequently disposed of for valuable consideration, whether or not by the original transferee. Thus if a father gifts some land to his son, the father will be deemed to have disposed of the land at its market value, and a chargeable gain is likely to accrue. The father may elect to defer payment of tax on this chargeable gain over ten years. If the son gifts the land to his wife, that transfer will have no effect on the father's deferred CGT liability. But if the wife then sells the land, the father will immediately become liable to pay any outstanding instalments of CGT attributable to the original transfer to the son, plus arrears of interest.

(4)   The connected person rules also have important implications in those limited circumstances, discussed in the next section, when gifts roll-over relief remains available.

1   CGTA 1979 s 62(5).
2   CGTA 1979 s 62(5).
3   CGTA 1979 s 62(5).
4   CGTA 1979 s 62(6).
5   CGTA 1979 s 62(3).
6   CGTA 1979 s 62(3), proviso.
7   CGTA 1979 s 62(4).

3.10 Roll-over relief for gifts of assets

FA 1980 s 79 introduced a relief under which, if an individual made a disposal otherwise than under a bargain at arm's length to an individual resident or ordinarily resident in the United Kingdom, the transferor and the transferee could jointly elect to deduct the gain which would otherwise have been chargeable from the acquisition value of the transferee. The effect was to roll over the gain until the eventual disposal of the asset by the transferee. The 1981 and 1982 Finance Acts extended the roll over provisions to transfers into trust, and to transfers between trusts, and to transfers out of trusts to a resident beneficiary. Gifts roll-over relief therefore became an invaluable tool in tax planning for the family. Indeed it could often be used to eliminate a gain from charge to tax altogether, as where land which had not been the main residence of one member of the family, say the father, was gifted to another member of the family, say the son, and became the son's main residence. However, following the abolition of an immediate inheritance tax charge on most inter vivos gifts in the Finance Act 1986, the Chancellor of the Exchequer eventually decided that there was no longer any justification for such a generous CGT relief for gifts. Accordingly for disposals after 13th March 1989, FA 1979 s 124(1) repealed the general relief for gifts in FA 1980 s 79 and subsequent Finance Acts, and replaced it with a much more limited relief. The new provisions cover gifts of business assets plus gifts of other assets in limited circumstances.

The provisions dealing with gifts of business assets are in an amended CGTA 1979 s 126 and Sch 4. The section applies if an individual disposes of a business asset otherwise than under a bargain at arm's length. A business asset is defined as an asset used for the purposes of a trade, profession, or vocation carried on by the individual, or by his family company, or by a member of a trading group of which the holding company is his family company[1]. Agricultural property and commercial woodlands are covered[2]. The definition also includes shares or securities in a trading company, or the holding company of a trading company provided the shares are not quoted on the Stock Exchange or the Unlisted Securities Market or, if they are so quoted, the trading company or holding company is the transferor's family company[3]. 'Family company' means a company in which either at least 25% of the voting rights are exercisable by the individual, or at least 50% of the voting rights are exercisable by the individual's family, with at least 5% exercisable by the individual himself[4]. An individual's family is comprised of his spouse and both his and his spouse's parents and remoter ancestors, children and remoter descendants, and brothers and sisters[5]. Roll-over relief therefore remains a useful planning tool if a family business is being transferred to the next generation. However no relief is available to the extent that a gain is exempt from CGT under the retirement relief provisions in FA 1985[6], or on the disposal of certain qualifying corporate bonds[7], or if the disposal is one which attracts an immediate

1   CGTA 1979 s 126(1A)(a).
2   CGTA 1979 s 126(4) and Sch 4 Part 1.
3   CGTA 1979 s 126(1A)(b).
4   CGTA 1979 s 126(7)(a) and FA 1985 Sch 20 para 1(1).
5   FA 1985 Sch 20 para 1(1).
6   CGTA 1979 s 126(2)(a) and (b).
7   CGTA 1979 s 126(2)(c).

inheritance tax charge, for example a transfer into a discretionary trust, so that a roll-over claim can be made under CGTA 1979 s 147A[1]. There are anti-avoidance provisions to prevent or restrict relief if there is a transfer to a non-resident[2], or to a foreign controlled company[3], or to trustees who subsequently become non-resident[4]. Unlike the original provisions, there appears to be no clawback of relief if there is a gift of business assets to an individual who is initially resident but subsequently becomes non-resident.

If s 126 applies, the transferor and transferee, or the transferor alone if the transfer is into trust, may elect to reduce the transferee's acquisition value by the chargeable gain, computed after indexation allowance, which would otherwise accrue to the transferor[5]. There are provisions in CGTA 1979 Sch 4 to deal with the computation where an asset was not a business asset throughout the transferor's period of ownership, or was a non-business asset of a company in which the transferor had at least a 25% shareholding or, if the transferor is an individual, was his family company, and where retirement relief exempts part of the gain.

Transfers into trust are fully covered by CGTA 1979 s 126 provided the transferor satisfies the conditions, and only the transferor is entitled to make the election. Relief for transfers between trusts and transfers out of trust is governed by CGTA 1979 Sch 4 para 2. Relief is available if the asset transferred is an asset used for the purposes of a trade or profession carried on by the trustees or by a beneficiary who had an interest in possession in the trust immediately before the transfer[6]. Relief is also available for the transfer of shares or securities of a trading company where either the shares are not quoted on the Stock Exchange or the USM or at the time of disposal at least 25% of the voting rights in the company are exercisable by the trustees[7]. If a qualifying transfer is made from one trust to another, only the transferor trustees can make the election, but if the transfer is to a beneficiary both the trustees and the beneficiary must join in the election.

If there is actual consideration for a transfer which would otherwise qualify for roll-over relief and the actual consideration exceeds the allowable cost of the asset, the excess of actual consideration over the allowable cost is a non-deferrable chargeable gain, but the excess gain may be deferred[8].

Example

In 1983 a father acquired shares in an unquoted trading company for £5,000. In 1990, when the shares have a market value of £30,000, the father sells the shares to his son for £15,000. Father and son are connected persons. It follows that the disposal proceeds on the transfer to the son are deemed to be the market value of the shares, £30,000, and the actual sales proceeds of £15,000 are ignored. Assuming an indexation allowance of £2,300 the chargeable gain is therefore:

1   CGTA 1979 s 126(2)(d).
2   CGTA 1979 s 126A.
3   CGTA 1979 s 126B.
4   CGTA 1979 s 126C.
5   CGTA 1979 s 126(3).
6   CGTA 1979 Sch 4 para 2(2)(a).
7   CGTA 1979 Sch 4 para 2(2)(b).
8   CGTA 1979 s 126(6).

	£
Market value	30,000
Less allowable cost	(5,000)
Gross gain	25,000
Less indexation allowance	(2,300)
Chargeable gain	22,700

Of this, the amount which can be held over is the amount by which the chargeable gain exceeds he difference between actual sales proceeds and allowable cost, ie £22,700 — (£15,000 — £5,000) = £12,700 held over and £10,000 immediately chargeable. It will be noted that, on the wording of CGTA 1979 s 126(6), it seems that the indexation allowance must first be used to reduce the held over gain, and only when that is completely eliminated can it be used to reduce the chargeable gain.

The other occasions when gifts roll-over relief remains available are set out in CGTA 1979 s 147A, and mainly concern occasions when property is transferred into trust or out of trust and there is, at least potentially, an immediate inheritance tax charge. The relief applies to disposals otherwise than by way of a bargain at arm's length by individuals and trustees if any of the following conditions are satisfied:

(1)   The transfer is a chargeable transfer for inheritance tax purposes and, ignoring the £3,000 annual exemption, is neither an exempt transfer nor a potentially exempt transfer[1]. A potentially exempt transfer is defined in the Inheritance Tax Act 1984 s 3A(1) as a transfer made by an individual to another individual or to an accumulation and maintenance trust or a disabled trust. As ITA 1984 s 49(1) deems a person beneficially entitled to an interest in possession in settled property to be beneficially entitled to the property, the definition in ITA 1984 s 3A(1) effectively covers transfers into fixed interest trusts. However transfers into discretionary trusts and ordinary accumulation trusts are excluded from the definition, and hence qualify for CGT roll-over relief under s 147A. At a meeting between the English and Scottish Law Societies and the Revenue held on 14th June 1989 the Revenue confirmed that gifts relief was preserved for transfers both into and out of a discretionary trust. There had been some doubt on whether transfers out of discretionary trust qualified, but Parliamentary Counsel's view was that the legislation was clear and did not need changing[2].

(2)   The transfer is exempt from inheritance tax because it is a transfer to a political party, or for the public benefit, or to a maintenance fund for historic buildings, or which is certified as a designated transfer by the Treasury because the property comprised in it is of national importance. Also included are interests in possession which are transferred to a maintenance fund for historic buildings, transfers of works of art which are exempt under ITA 1984 s 78(1), and disposals of interests in settlements where there is a reduced charge to inheritance tax because assets are transferred to maintenance funds for historic buildings[3].

1   CGTA 1979 s 147A(2).
2   'Notes of Meeting' published by the Law Society, para 19.
3   CGTA 1979 s 147A(2)(b), (c), (e), and (f).

(3)   A beneficiary becomes entitled to, or to an interest in possession in, an accumulation and maintenance settlement as defined in ITA 1984 on or before attaining the specified age, or dies before attaining the specified age[1]. The inter-relationship between inheritance tax and capital gains tax as they apply to accumulation and maintenance trusts is a matter of some difficulty, and is considered in greater depth in the chapter on children.

If CGTA 1979 s 147A applies, the chargeable gain, computed after deducting indexation allowance, may be held over by reducing both the chargeable gain of the transferor and the acquisition value of the recipient[2]. If actual consideration is given for the transfer, the amount that can be held over is reduced by the excess of the actual consideration over the allowable cost[3]. If retirement relief is claimed under FA 1985 Sch 20, the held-over gain must be reduced by the amount of the relief[4].

Whether or not hold-over relief is claimed, if there is a disposal within CGTA 1979 s 147A(2)(a), ie CGT is chargeable on it and it is neither exempt nor potentially exempt, a deduction may be made in computing the chargeable gain of the lower of the inheritance tax payable in respect of the asset or the chargeable gain[5].

3.11 Deferral of a capital gains tax liability

If roll-over relief cannot be claimed for a transfer under either CGTA 1979 s 126(3) or s 147A(3) it may be possible to spread payment of any CGT liability over a period of ten years. FA 1979 Sch 14 para 5 inserted a new s 7A into CGTA 1979 to achieve this, but the new provisions closely mirror provisions which were originally in CGTA 1979 s 8 but were repealed by FA 1984 s 63(1). The deferral provisions only apply to a gift of specified assets, which is a narrower concept than a transfer otherwise than under a bargain at arm's length, the concept used in both CGTA 1979 s 126 and s 147A. The relief also applies if a trust beneficiary becomes absolutely entitled as against trustees, or if there is a termination of a life interest on death within CGTA 1979 s 55(1) in the unlikely event of there being a CGT charge[6].

Deferral of a CGT liability may be claimed if there is a gift of[7]:

(1)   land, or an estate or interest in land, or
(2)   shares or securities which, immediately before the disposal, gave control of the company to the transferor, or
(3)   any other shares in a company which is not quoted on the Stock Exchange or on the USM,

and a claim could not be made to roll over the gain under either CGTA

---

1   CGTA 1979 s 147A(2)(d).
2   CGTA 1979 s 147A(3)(4).
3   CGTA 1979 s 147A(5).
4   CGTA 1979 s 147A(5).
5   CGTA 1979 s 147A(7).
6   CGTA 1979 s 7A(1)(a).
7   CGTA 1979 s 7A(3).

1979 s 126(3) or s 147A(3)[1] or, if it could, the held-over gain is less than the total chargeable gain which would have accrued without hold-over relief[2].

If CGTA 1979 s 7A applies, the transferor may elect by notice in writing to the inspector to pay any CGT liability attributable to the asset transferred by ten equal yearly instalments[3], the first instalment to be due on the normal due date[4], ie 1st December following the year of assessment in which the gain accrued, or 30 days after the issue of the assessment, if later[5]. Interest is chargeable on the deferred instalments, and is added annually to the instalment due in that year[6]. The transferor may pay the outstanding instalments, with any accrued interest, at any time[7]. If the transferee, or any subsequent transferee, disposes of the assets for valuable consideration within the ten year deferral period, the original transferor immediately becomes liable to pay any outstanding instalments plus accrued interest[8].

1 CGTA 1979 s 7A(1)(b)(i).
2 CGTA 1979 s 7A(1)(b)(ii).
3 CGTA 1979 s 7A(2).
4 CGTA 1979 s 7A(4).
5 CGTA 1979 s 7.
6 CGTA 1979 s 7A(5).
7 CGTA 1979 s 7A(6).
8 CGTA 1979 s 7A(7).

CHAPTER 4

Tax planning for independent taxation

4.1 Income tax planning under independent taxation

For income tax purposes the objectives of tax planning under the new system of independent taxation should be to ensure that both spouses take full advantage of their personal allowances and the married couple's allowance, and that taxable income is allocated between the spouses in such a way that any higher rate tax liability is minimised. This may be achieved either by reallocating income or by reallocating expenditure, and the tax planning possibilities of an allocation of mortgage interest election should not be overlooked. Under the new system, the combined incomes of the spouses will have to be in excess of £49,130 before there is any need to pay higher rate tax, but to achieve this the spouses' taxable incomes will have to be roughly equalised. If one spouse currently has a high income and the other does not, tax planning techniques will be needed to divert income and expenditure between the spouses. If one of the spouses is elderly, tax may be saved if that spouse's income can be reduced so as to take maximum advantage of the higher age allowance. In short, tax planning will be needed to move income and expenditure between the spouses, a tax planning requirement which has long been familiar to those dealing with taxation of the family. As might be expected, there are a significant number of anti-avoidance provisions designed to stop the movement of income from one spouse to another, and the introduction of independent taxation has increased the number of these provisions. The sections of this chapter on tax planning for income tax therefore deal first with the employment of a spouse and the taking of a spouse into partnership, where the anti-avoidance provisions have little impact, before dealing with other transfers of income where the anti-avoidance provisions are more pervasive. For ease of exposition, it will be assumed that the husband is the higher income spouse, but the same principles apply if the wife is the higher income spouse.

Before discussing particular planning devices in depth, it should be emphasised that the practical realities of a transaction that is proposed for tax planning purposes must be taken into account as well as any tax advantages that are expected to accrue from it. A transaction that is a sham, or is subject to an enforceable obligation that any financial benefits are to return to the transferor spouse, is unlikely to be effective for tax purposes. Therefore effective tax planning for spouses will normally involve the transfer of assets and income from one spouse to the other on a long-term basis. Such a transfer may pose few problems for a happily married couple, but unfortunately not all marriages enjoy this state, and the spouse with the higher income and greater assets may not be particularly appreciative of his professional advisers if a significant percentage of his assets have been transferred to the other spouse to reduce tax liabilities, and the marriage then breaks down. It is therefore important to maintain a sense of perspective, and preferably also a good personal knowledge of the clients to whom advice is being given.

4.2 Employing a spouse in a business

For many years it has been routine tax planning for a self-employed taxpayer, whether working on his own account or in a partnership, to employ his wife in the business if she has no other job. Under aggregate taxation the main advantage to be gained was that the wife's earned income allowance could be claimed if a wife had earned income. If she received earnings as an employee of her husband's business the earnings would normally be tax deductible in computing the husband's business profits, thus resulting in the removal of up to £2,785 (using 1989-90 allowances) from the husband's top marginal rate of tax. If the wife's duties were insubstantial there was generally little point in paying her a salary higher than the single person's allowance, as the the loss of the married man's allowance would make an election for separate taxation of wife's earnings disadvantageous, even if the husband was a higher rate taxpayer, and there was the further disadvantage that employer's and employee's national insurance contributions had to be paid on the wife's earnings. Indeed, to avoid the national insurance trap, it was often sensible planning to pay a wife a salary below the national insurance threshold (£43 per week or £2,236 pa for 1989-90), which was usually slightly below the wife's earned income allowance.

The tax system under independent taxation is much more favourable to income splitting between spouses by the employment of one spouse by the other because the wife's earnings will now be treated as her separate income for all tax purposes without any loss of married couple's allowance, the effective penalty for making a separate taxation election under the system of aggregate taxation of spouses' incomes. If the husband is a higher rate taxpayer there will therefore be a tax saving of 15p in the pound if income which would otherwise have been taxed at 40% in the hands of the husband can be transferred to the wife and taxed at 25%. There will also be a tax saving of £1,202 (£3,005 @ 40%). on the first slice of earnings up to the single person's allowance. However in making any computation of tax savings it remains necessary to take account of national insurance contributions. For 1990-91 the rate of contributions for a non-contracted out employee are[1]:

earnings below £46 per week	Nil
earnings between £46 and £350 per week	
percentage on the first £46	2%
percentage on earnings above £46	9%

1   See [1989] STI 855.

An employer's contributions for a non-contracted out employee are:

earnings below £46 per week	Nil
earnings between £46 and £79.99 per week	5% on all earnings
earnings between £80 and £124.99 per week	7% on all earnings
earnings between £125 and £174.99 per week	9% on all earnings
earnings above £175 per week	10.45% on all earnings

For wages or salary paid to an employee to be tax deductible in computing the profits of a business the payment has to satisfy the requirement in ICTA 1988 s 74(a) that it is wholly and exclusively expended for the purposes of the business. Cases have held that a salary will not be treated as paid wholly and exclusively for the purposes of the business unless salary paid is reasonably justifiable in relation to the work done. Thus in the leading case of *Copeman v William Flood & Sons Ltd*[1] there was a family business in which the son and daughter were employed. The daughter, aged 17, was paid £2,600 (about £501,800 in today's money) for four months duties which consisted mainly of answering telephone enquiries. The son, aged 24, was paid £2,600 for a year's work which consisted mainly of calling on farmers to purchase pigs. The High Court held that such a high salary could in no way be justified by the work that the children had done, and sent the case back to the Appeal Commissioners to determine how much of the salary was paid for services rendered[2].

Similar principles have been applied in interpreting what is now ICTA 1988 s 75, which allows a deduction for the expenses of management of an investment company. In *LG Berry Investments Ltd v Attwooll*[3] an investment company had three directors and shareholders. One of the directors was the principal shareholder's sister and another was his octogenarian mother. For 1960-61 the income less expenditure before directors' fees was £1,800, and directors fees of £600 to each of the three directors were voted to extinguish this balance. This reflected the policy of the Board of Directors to extinguish taxable profits by salaries paid to directors, and no attention was paid to the services performed by a director for the company. Apart from informal discussions of outstanding and new mortgages, four properties were inspected, and there were seven formal board meetings, of which the mother attended only two. The Special Commissioners held that only £600 could be justified as an expense of managing the company and the High Court refused to interfere.

Normally if the Revenue can demonstrate that an item of claimed expenditure has not been wholly or exclusively incurred for the purposes of the business the whole of that expenditure is disallowed in computing the profits of the business unless part of the expenditure can be specifically allocated to business purposes[4]. Thus if a taxpayer uses his home telephone to make business calls the actual cost of the business telephone call will be deductible because the whole of the expenditure was for a business purpose and the whole of the expenditure can be identified. However none of the telephone rental is deductible as it cannot be specifically allocated to business

1   (1940) 24 TC 53.
2   See also *Stott and Ingham v Trehearne* (1924) 9 TC 69.
3   (1964) 41 TC 547.
4   See eg *Murgatroyd v Evans-Jackson* (1966) 43 TC 581.

use and non-business use[1]. If the expenditure in dispute is salary paid to an employee the courts have been prepared to direct apportionment of the total expenditure if they consider it excessive, although without articulating why it is considered that part of the expenditure is specifically allocable to business purposes and part is not so allocable[2].

It is unclear what the tax position of an employee is who is initially paid a salary, from which tax will have been deducted under PAYE and on which national insurance contributions will have been paid, but where it is later held that not all of that salary is tax deductible to the employer because it cannot be justified by the work that the employee has undertaken. If the whole of the salary remains taxable in the hands of the employee, what started out as a tax avoidance arrangement will have exactly the opposite consequence, as the employee will now be in receipt of taxable income which has to be paid out of taxed income. It would have been preferable not to pay the additional salary at all. It is arguable that a sum paid to a member of the family which is later disallowed as a business expense in computing the profits of the employer is in truth a gift to the employee and not an emolument arising from the employment. Accordingly it is not assessable to tax under Sch E. In practice it is likely to be difficult to disentangle the PAYE and national insurance contributions already paid and, if the total amount paid to the employee exceeds £8,500 and the employer is a company, it may be impossible. This is because under the special statutory provisions which apply to employees earning £8,500 per annum or more and directors, all sums paid to an employee by his employer in respect of expenses, and all benefits provided to an employee by his employer, *are deemed to be provided by reason of the employment* unless the employer is an individual and it can be shown that the benefit was provided in the normal course of his domestic, family or personal relationships[3]. The person providing a benefit is the person at whose cost the provision is made[4]. Thus if payments made by a company to an employee take the employee over the £8,500 threshold, the employee seems to have no defence to a Sch E assessment, and it should be remembered that, for the purpose only of computing whether the employee is higher paid, one has to add together the employee's pay, all expense reimbursements without any deduction for Sch E expenses, and all fringe benefits valued on the assumption that he is higher paid[5]. The only possible defence is provided by the case of *Hamblett v Godfrey*[6]. The Government decided that GCHQ employees, for reasons of national security, should no longer be able to be members of a trade union, or have recourse to the employment protection legislation. The employees were given the option of transferring to another part of the Civil Service, or of renouncing their right to belong to a trade union. If they renounced trade union membership they became entitled to an *ex gratia* payment of £1,000. The taxpayer, who was a higher paid employee and so subject to the special statutory rules, received a payment of £1,000 but claimed that it was not taxable. It might seem that she had

1   *Lucas v Cattell* (1972) 48 TC 353.
2   *Copeman v Flood* (1940) 24 TC 53.
3   ICTA 1988 s 168(3).
4   ICTA 1988 s 154(3).
5   ICTA 1988 s 167(2).
6   (1986) 59 TC 694.

no defence because the payment was automatically caught by the deeming provision, but the Court of Appeal held that the payment was taxable as an emolument under the general Sch E principles, and deliberately did not decide the case by applying the special statutory provisions relating to higher paid employees. As Purchas LJ put it[1]:

> 'Having reached that conclusion [that the payment was a Sch E emolument], I find it unnecessary to consider the somewhat more complicated issues which would or might have arisen under s 61 of the 1976 Act [now ICTA 1988 s 154], for instance, whether a payment in cash can be a benefit in kind. I am grateful not to have to resolve those difficult problems.'

The argument against treating cash payments as benefits in kind within ICTA 1988 s 154 is based mainly on the grounds that the benefits listed in s 154(2) are benefits in kind, and the valuation provisions in s 156 seek to determine 'the cash equivalent' of any benefit chargeable under the special rules. It is argued that it is not meaningful to talk about a benefit in cash having a cash equivalent, and so the statutory provisions must be confined to benefits in kind. Nevertheless, it is anticipated that if the courts are asked to determine whether the special statutory provisions for employees with emoluments of £8,500 pa or more apply to cash benefits, they will hold that they do.

Additional problems may arise if a family business is conducted through the medium of a closely owned family company of which one spouse is the principal shareholder and the other spouse is employed by the company with emoluments of £8,500 pa or more, or is a director[2]. The employee will be subject to the special statutory rules for higher paid employees and directors, one of which is ICTA 1988 s 160 which applies to interest-free or reduced rate loans made to an employee by reason of the employment, and treats as an emolument the difference between interest at the notional rate on the loan and any interest paid by the employee. There is no taxable benefit if the notional interest does not exceed £200 or, if there are two or more loans, the total notional interest on all the loans does not exceed £200. Loans which are covered by ICTA 1988 s 160 are detailed in ICTA 1988 Sch 7 Part I. They include loans from the employer unless the employer is an individual and the loan is made in the ordinary course of his domestic, family or personal relationships. If the employer is a closely-owned family company the requirement that the employer must be an individual is obviously not satisfied and any loans made by the company will be caught[3]. ICTA 1988 Sch 7 Part I para 1(4) additionally includes a loan *made in any case* where the employer was, or had control over, or was controlled by, a close company and the loan was made by a person who had a material interest in the close company or its holding company. Thus if a husband has a shareholding in excess of 5% in a close company and his wife is employed by the company at emoluments of £8,500 pa or more, or is a director, any interest-free loan made to her by her husband will be caught, even if the loan is made in the course of the husband's domestic

---

1 (1986) 59 TC 694 at 724.
2 ICTA 1988 s 167(5), which excludes directors from charge in certain circumstances, is not applicable as the taxpayer, with her associates, controls more than 5% of the share capital of the company.
3 See also **2.11** above.

responsibilities. The lender is an individual and the loan is made in fulfilment of his domestic responsibilites, but the exemption for domestic responsibilities loans only applies if the loan is made by the employer. For the purposes of the rules a loan includes the assumption of the rights and liabilities of the person who originally made the loan, and the arranging, guaranteeing, or in any way facilitating the continuation of a loan already in existence[1]. Spouses caught by these provisions must therefore keep a careful eye on their domestic financial arrangements.

The employment of a spouse in a family business mainly for the purpose of taking advantage of the more liberal tax system can have tax advantages, but, unless considerable care is taken, the disadvantages may well outweigh the advantages. There are unlikely to be problems if one spouse is employed at a salary of £2,391 (£45.99 × 52), which takes maximum advantage of the spouse's personal allowance while remaining below the threshold at which national insurance contributions become payable. One cannot expect much in the way of duties for an annual salary of £2,391, so there should be no difficulty in satisfying the Revenue that the remuneration paid to the spouse is comensurate with the work she has performed. But if it is intended to pay a salary in excess of this amount it is essential to be able to establish to the Revenue's satisfaction that the work done by the spouse justifies the salary paid. If this cannot be done, the excess salary will be disallowed as a Sch D expense, but there may be considerable difficulty in ensuring that the spouse escapes a Sch E charge on the payment. If a spouse is being employed with emoluments of £8,500 pa or more, or is the director of a family company, attention must also be paid to the impact of the fringe benefits rules for such employees.

4.3 Husband and wife partnerships

Many of the difficulties noted when considering the tax implications of the employment of a spouse with the main objective of transferring income to her from the other spouse can be overcome if the spouses are able to go into business in partnership. Indeed a husband and wife partnership is likely to become a very attractive tax planning tool under the new system of independent taxation, and is therefore also likely to come under closer Revenue scrutiny than it has hitherto. In many cases a partnership will be impractical, as where a family business is carried on through a company, or where special qualifications are required before a person can be admitted into partnership. There are also risks involved in entering into a partnership, in that a partner normally accepts unlimited liability for the debts of the partnership.

Nevertheless if a partnership can be established, two principal advantages arise. First, the profits for tax purposes of a partnership are initially computed on the basis that the partnership is an entity distinct from the partners[2]. Ignoring transitional provisions in the opening years, the partnership is then assessed on the profits actually earned in the preceding year of assessment[3]. If the partnership makes up its accounts annually to

1   ICTA 1988 Sch 7 para 2(a).
2   ICTA 1988 s 111.
3   ICTA 1988 s 60(1).

a regular accounting date, the relevant profits are the tax adjusted profits for the accounting year ended in the preceding year of assessment[1].

Example

A partnership makes up its accounts each year to 30th April. Its tax adjusted profits for the year ended 30th April 1989 were £25,000. Those profits will be assessed as its Sch D case I or II profits for the year of assessment 1990-91.

However in computing the tax payable by the partnership the partnership profits are apportioned between the partners in their profit sharing ratios for the year the profits are assessable, not their profit sharing ratios for the year the profits were actually earned[2]. Thus, especially if the partnership's accounting year ends early in the tax year, there is plenty of time for tax planning by adjusting the profit sharing ratios of the partners for the year the profits are assessable to allocate the partnership profits between the partners in the way which is most beneficial for tax purposes. The second major attraction of a partnership over employment is that, provided a genuine partnership can be established, there is as yet no rule that the share of profits allocated to a partner has to be commensurate with the services that the partner has rendered or capital he has provided. If an allocation is significantly higher than can be justified by services rendered or capital provided, the Revenue may be able to argue successfully that a portion of the allocated profits are unearned, rather than earned, income. But with the abolition of any distinction in the tax treatment of earned and unearned income, this is likely to have few practical consequences. Indeed the only consequence of note is that, in computing profits to which to apply the $17\frac{1}{2}\%$ maximum limit for deductible retirement annuity or personal pension premiums[3], only earned income qualifies, so that a partner's share of profits which cannot be justified by the services he has rendered would probably not count.

If a partner's share of profits is greatly in excess of what can be justified by capital she has provided or services she has rendered it might be possible for the Revenue to argue that the partnership was a settlement within one of the anti-avoidance provisions considered in detail in 4.4:1 below. Hitherto no such argument has been taken, and the point was not raised in cases such as *Alexander Bulloch & Co v IRC*[4] where the issue was whether a minor child was a partner, but the increased attractiveness of husband and wife partnerships following the introduction of independent taxation may tempt the Revenue to move in that direction. Nevertheless it is suggested that the risk of such a challenge is a risk worth taking because, even if the argument was successful, its effect will only be to nullify the tax planning, but without increasing the tax liability above what it would have been in the absence of any tax planning, whereas the tax advantages flowing from a successfully established partnership are substantial.

The advantages of a husband and wife partnership are additional to the normal advantages of self-employment over employment — the ability to

1   ICTA 1988 s 60(3).
2   ICTA 1988 s 272(2); *Lewis v IRC* (1933) 18 TC 174.
3   ICTA 1988 ss 619(2) and 640. The $17\frac{1}{2}\%$ maximum limit is raised for partners over 50; see ICTA 1988 ss 626 and 640.
4   (1976) 51 TC 563.

receive income gross and to withdraw profits from the partnership without the application of any withholding tax; more liberal expense rules; assessment on a preceding year basis rather than an actual year basis with, because of the effects of inflation, a consequent real reduction in tax liabilities; and the ability to manipulate the opening and closing rules for the assessment of partnership profits to ensure that the profits which are assessed are lower than the profits which have been earned. Under independent taxation the creation of a husband and wife partnership, if it is practical, offers considerable advantages for tax planning purposes with few disadvantages. It is therefore important to consider in some detail what facts need to be proved to establish a partnership.

A partnership is defined in the Partnership Act 1890 s 1 as:

> 'The relationship which subsists between persons carrying on a business in common with a view to profit.'

In *IRC v Williamson*[1] Lord President Clyde expanded on this, saying:

> 'My Lords, you do not constitute or create or prove a partnership by saying that there is one. The only proof that a partnership exists is proof of the relations of agency and of community in losses and profits and of the sharing in one form or another of the capital of the concern; the only proof of a partnership consists in proof of these things.'

If a partnership can be proved applying these tests it will not be rendered ineffective for tax purposes merely because the principal reason for establishing it was to reduce tax liabilities. Lord President Clyde commented in a famous dictum in another case, *Ayrshire Pullman Motor Services and D M Ritchie v IRC*[2]:

> '[The partnership was formed] I think one may reasonably add, to create a state of legal relations between the family and this business which would render the position of the family, as entitled to its profits, favourable in relation to the Inland Revenue both with regard to Income Tax to some extent, certainly with regard to Super-tax, and still more clearly with regard to Death Duties.
>
> So far as my point of view is concerned, the agreement is neither better nor worse for that reason. No man in this country is under the smallest obligation, moral or other, so to arrange his legal relations to his business or to his property as to enable the Inland Revenue to put the largest possible shovel into his stores.'

This statement of principle as it applies to a partnership should be unaffected by the recent developments in the courts' approach to tax avoidance evidenced by cases such as *Ramsay (WT) Ltd v IRC*[3] and *Furniss v Dawson*[4].

The courts have held that the issue of whether or not a partnership exists is primarily an issue of fact rather than an issue of law[5]. In tax appeals the final arbiters on issues of fact are the Appeal Commissioners, as an appeal from them to the courts is only permitted on an issue of law. The

---

1 (1928) 14 TC 335 at 340.
2 (1929) 14 TC 754 at 763.
3 (1981) 54 TC 101.
4 (1984) 55 TC 324.
5 *Taylor v Chalklin* (1945) 26 TC 463; *Saywell v Pope* (1979) 53 TC 40; *IRC v Williamson* (1928) 14 TC 335 at 339; and *Alexander Bulloch & Co v IRC* (1976) 51 TC 563 at 567.

principles laid down by the House of Lords in the leading case of *Edwards v Bairstow*[1], as developed by later decisions[2], therefore severely limit the ability of the unsuccessful party to an appeal before the Appeal Commissioners on the issue of whether a partnership exists to appeal further to the courts. The High Court can only interfere if either there is a misstatement of law in the reasons given by the Appeal Commissioners for their decision, or the decision is perverse in the sense that no reasonable Appeal Commissioners, properly directed on the law, could have reached the decision in the light of the primary facts. The High Court is not free to substitute its own view of the facts if there is evidence which can justify the conclusion drawn by the Appeal Commissioners. On the issue of whether or not a partnership exists the taxpayer has the choice of appealing either to the General Commissioners or to the Special Commissioners, but there seems to be no particular advantage in appealing to the Special Commissioners, and it is suggested that it is normally preferable for the appeal to be heard by the General Commissioners.

A number of factors have been considered as relevant by the courts when deciding whether or not a partnership exists. No one fact is, of itself, decisive; what is important is their cumulative effect.

(1)   The existence of a partnership agreement. A partnership may be formed as a result of an oral agreement, but it is easier to persuade the relevant authorities that there is a partnership if the agreement is in writing. Thus in *Taylor v Chalklin*[3] the appellant and his son were farmers on 225 acres of rented land. There was no written partnership agreement but evidence was given of an oral agreement. Nevertheless the courts held that, taking into account the other facts, there was insufficient evidence of a partnership. If a written partnership agreement is drawn up it is suggested that this is best done by a solicitor[4].

(2)   Compliance with a partnership agreement. If a partnership agreement exists but its terms are in practice largely ignored, the courts may view sceptically a claim that there is a partnership in law. As an illustration, in *Dickenson v Gross*[5] a farmer entered into a formal deed of partnership with his three sons with the main purpose of reducing his tax liability. The agreement provided, *inter alia,* that two farms owned by the farmer should be let to the partnership, that accounts should be prepared annually, that profits should be divided equally between the partners, and that each partner should have the right to sign and endorse cheques on behalf of the firm. In practice no rent was ever paid by the partnership, no partnership accounts

1   (1955) 36 TC 207.
2   *Furniss v Dawson* (1984) 55 TC 324; *Lim Foo Yong Sdn Bhd v Comptroller-General of Inland Revenue* [1986] STC 255; *Richfield International Land and Investment Co Ltd v IRC* [1989] STC 820.
3   (1945) 26 TC 463.
4   It was the consideration of a partnership agreement drawn up by an accountant that moved Harman LJ to remark in *Harrison-Broadley v Smith* [1964] 1 All ER 867 at 870, that 'accountants are the witch-doctors of the modern world and they appear indeed willing to turn their hands to any kind of magic'. See also *Miles v Clarke* [1953] 1 WLR 537 at 539 and *Re TR Technology Investment Trust plc* (1988) 4 BCC 244 at 255 for similar observations on the magical powers of accountants.
5   (1927) 11 TC 614.

were kept, profits were not distributed, cheques were signed only by the farmer, and many trading receipts were paid into the farmer's private bank account. The court held that, despite the partnership agreement, there was no partnership in law.

(3) Services performed by an alleged partner. If a partner has not supplied capital for a partnership it is likely to be difficult to establish that a partnership exists in law if an alleged partner spends insignificant amounts of time on the partnership business. This has proved a problem in attempts to establish that a child is a partner, but the same principles should apply to husband and wife partnerships. Thus in *Alexander Bulloch & Co v IRC*[1] a deed of partnership purported to bring two children aged 17 and 18 into an off-licence business. After the execution of the partnership deed both children did routine work at one of the shops, but continued at school, drew no salary and received only pocket money. The Appeal Commissioners held that they were not partners for the relevant tax year, and the High Court refused to interfere.

(4) The supply of capital. It is not essential for an alleged partner to have introduced capital into the partnership, but if this is not done it has been suggested in point three that it does then become essential for the partner to devote significant time to partnership business. The converse is that, if a partner has introduced significant capital, the existence of a partnership is unlikely to be prejudiced if he only spends a small amount of time on partnership business.

(5) The partnership notepaper. All partners should be listed, or referred to, on the partnership notepaper. If a person is not so listed, that is a factor pointing against his being a partner.

(6) The partnership banking arrangements. If a partnership is alleged one would normally expect there to be a partnership bank account with specified cheque signatories, and that all partnership transactions should be conducted through the partnership bank account rather than through the partners' private bank accounts.

(7) Accounts should be prepared on a partnership basis.

In practice if it is desired to establish a husband and wife partnership a formal partnership agreement is likely to be essential, and any attempt to allege that the partnership commenced before the date of the partnership agreement is likely to be fraught with difficulty. In *Saywell v Pope*[2], one of the only reported cases in which a husband and wife partnership was in issue, a firm had been started in 1960 by three people, one of whom later left. The wives of the two remaining partners were employed by the firm under an oral agreement and received small salaries. In January 1973 the firm's business expanded significantly, and the wives became more actively involved. On the advice of the firm's accountants the wives entered into a written partnership agreement dated in June 1975 stating that a partnership between them and their husbands had commenced on 6th April 1973. Accounts were eventually prepared for the two years to April 1974 and April 1975 and they credited the wives with a share of the profits for

1 (1976) 51 TC 563.
2 (1979) 53 TC 40.

those years. During the two years in question neither wife introduced any capital into the business or made any drawings from it. Neither wife could sign cheques or draw on the firm's bank account. No notice of the change in the partnership in 1973 had been given either to the partnership's bank or to its creditors or to its customers. The firm's notepaper did not state that the wives were partners. On these facts the Appeal Commissioners held that the wives were not partners for the two years to April 1975, and the High Court refused to interfere. *Saywell v Pope* is a particularly useful case illustrating the facts that need to be established if a judicial tribunal is to be persuaded that a genuine partnership exists. If a partnership is found not to exist, any profits that have been provisionally allocated to the disqualified 'partner' will be reallocated to the genuine partners in their profit sharing ratios.

As an alternative to a full partnership it is possible to have a 'salaried partnership'. A salaried partnership is distinct from a limited partnership formed under the Limited Partnerships Act 1907, under which a partner who is introducing capital to the partnership but takes no active part in the running of the partnership business may limit his liability to the amount of capital which he subscribes[1]. If an individual is a genuine 'salaried partner' he will be taxed as an employee and PAYE tax will be withheld from his salary, which will be taxed under Sch E on an actual year basis. However, a partner who is only entitled to a fixed salary may have accepted sufficient responsibility for the running of the partnership business to be a full partner in law, with the consequence that he is entitled to be taxed under Sch D. The leading recent case on salaried partners is *Stekel v Ellice*[2] where Megarry J explained as follows the law on the distinction between a salaried partner who was a mere employee and a salaried partner who was a genuine partner:

> 'It seems to me impossible to say that as a matter of law a salaried partner is or is not necessarily a partner in the true sense. He may or may not be a partner, depending on the facts. What must be done, I think, is to look at the substance of the relationship between the parties; and there is ample authority for saying that the question whether or not there is a partnership depends on what the true relationship is and not on any mere label attached to that relationship. A relationship that is plainly not a partnership is no more made into a partnership by calling it one than a relationship which is plainly a partnership is prevented from being one by a clause negativing partnership ...
>
> If, then, there is a plain contract of master and servant, and the only qualification of that relationship is that the servant is being held out as being a partner, the name "salaried partner" seems perfectly apt for him; and yet he will be no partner in relation to the members of the firm. At the other extreme, there may a full partnership deed under which all the partners save one take a share of the profits, with that one being paid a fixed salary not dependent on profits. Again, "salaried partner" seems to me an apt description of that one: yet I do not see why he should not be a true partner, at all events if he is entitled to a share of the profits in a winding up.... It may be that most salaried partners are persons whose only title to partnership is that they are held out as being partners; but even if "salaried partners"

---

1 See ICTA 1988 s 117 for the taxation of a limited partnership.
2 [1973] 1 All ER 465 at 473, and see also the unreported Court of Appeal decision in *Darker v Pim* (1988) Lexis Transcript, 23rd November.

who are true partners, though at a salary, are in a minority, that does not mean that they are non-existent.'

The formation of a partnership can be an attractive tax-avoidance vehicle under the new system of independent taxation. But if the partnership is to be effective it must be constructed with care, and as many as possible of the factors mentioned in the previous paragraphs should be incorporated to provide the best chance of the partnership escaping intact if it comes under the scrutiny of the Inland Revenue.

4.4 Transfers of income

In many cases it may not be practical to transfer income from a high income spouse to a low income spouse by employing the spouse or taking her into partnership. It may therefore be desired to save tax by transferring income from one spouse to the other. Any attempt to achieve this successfully for tax purposes is complicated by a myriad of settlements anti-avoidance provisions enacted at different times over many years and now contained in ICTA 1988 Part XV. These anti-avoidance provisions were further amended by FA 1989 ss 108 and 109 partly to take account of the change to independent taxation. It will be necessary to consider a number of the provisions in some detail, but it may be preferable to state at the outset the Revenue's view of the tax effectiveness of transfers of income and assets from one spouse to the other. The intention is that, if there is a transfer of complete beneficial ownership of an asset from one spouse to the other, any income derived from that asset after the date of transfer will be taxed as income of the recipient spouse. However if the transferor spouse retains any benefit from the asset transferred the income from it remains taxable as the transferor's income. A transfer of the right to receive income, for example an annuity, from one spouse to the other is wholly ineffective for tax purposes, even if the transfer is an outright transfer. An exception arises where there is an irrevocable allocation of pension rights by one spouse to the other under the terms of a public sector pension scheme[1].

It is now clear from IR 83 para 118 that the Revenue are prepared to accept a transfer of assets from one spouse into the joint ownership of both spouses as a transfer of a share of the assets and related income to the recipient spouse. There will be no problem if the transfer is into the joint ownership of the spouses as tenants in common, but there are indications in IR 83 para 120 that a transfer to the spouses as joint tenants will also be acceptable despite the possibility of the transferee's half share reverting to the transferor on the transferee's death under the doctrine of survivorship. Nevertheless, if it is practical to do so, it may be preferable for a transfer of assets from one spouse into joint ownership to be made to the spouses as tenants in common. An advantage for the transferor spouse of transfers into joint ownership is that he retains some control over the asset while ensuring that some of the income from it is taxed as income of the recipient spouse.

Whether an asset is transferred absolutely from one spouse to the other,

1   See **2.8** above.

or is transferred by one spouse into the joint names of both spouses, there will normally be no inheritance tax, capital gains tax, or stamp duty implications. For inheritance tax transfers between spouses are exempt transfers until a decree absolute of divorce[1]. For capital gains tax gifts of property from one spouse to the other, or into joint names, will be exempt from tax provided the spouses are living together at the time of the transfer[2].

For stamp duty voluntary transfers[3] are exempt from duty provided the transfer contains a certificate in writing signed by the transferor or his solicitor or other duly authorised agent specifying that the transfer is exempt from duty because it is a transfer of property operating as a voluntary conveyance within category L of the Stamp Duty (Exempt Instruments) Regulations 1987[4]. If the certificate is signed by an authorised agent other than a solicitor it must contain a statement of the capacity in which the agent is signing, that he is authorised so to sign, and that he gives the certificate of his own knowledge of the facts stated in it[5]. Documents transferring property by way of gift which do not contain the appropriate certificate remain liable to a 50p duty, and are not properly stamped unless they are adjudicated[6].

In a recent Statement of Practice, SP 6/90[7] the Revenue have pointed out that complications can arise where an asset subject to an outstanding financial liability to a third party is transferred from one spouse to the other and the recipient spouse assumes liability for payment of the outstanding obligation. A typical example is a house subject to a mortgage, with the recipient spouse assuming liability to pay the remaining mortgage instalments. If this happens the transfer is regarded for stamp duty purposes as a sale rather than a gift, and it is therefore not entitled to the benefit of the exemption for gifts in Category L of the Stamp Duty (Exempt Instruments) Regulations 1987. The consideration given for the transfer is the outstanding financial liability payment of which has been assumed by the transferee spouse. If the transferee has only assumed liability for part of the debt the consideration will be restricted to that amount. If the asset is land, stamp duty may still be avoided if a certificate of value can be attached certifying the total consideration at less than £30,000. Special exemptions in FA 1985 s 83(1) and Category H of the Stamp Duty (Exempt Instruments) Regulations 1987 ensure that no duty is payable on transfers in connection with divorce or separation even if the transferee assumes liability for an outstanding financial obligation.

4.4:1 The anti-avoidance provisions
The statutory authority for the Revenue's approach to transfers of income and assets between spouses is contained in ICTA 1988 s 674A inserted by FA 1989 s 109. S 674A applies to all income arising on or after 14th March

1 ITA 1984 s 18(1).
2 CGTA 1979 s 44. The exemption applies throughout the year of separation even if the transfer is made after the date of separation.
3 Schedule to Stamp Duty (Exempt Instruments) Regulations 1987, SI 1987 No 516, category L.
4 Ibid para 3.
5 Ibid para 3(c)(ii).
6 FA 1985 s 82(5).
7 [1990] STI 414.

1989 under a settlement made on or after that day[1]. If a settlement confers entitlement to income on a spouse of the settlor s 674A also applies to income arising on or after 6th April 1990 whenever the settlement was made[2]. However it does not apply to payments made under legally enforceable maintenance arrangements entered into before 15th March 1988 which comply with the transitional arrangements for then existing maintenance payments set out in FA 1988 s 36(3) and (4)[3]. S 674A provides that where, during the life of the settlor income is under the settlement, and in the events that occur, payable to or applicable for the benefit of any person other than the settlor then, unless under the settlement and in those events one of a number of specified exemptions apply, the income is to be treated for all the purposes of the income tax Acts as the income of the settlor and not as the income of any other person[4]. For present purposes the most important exemption is contained in s 674A(d), which excludes income which:

> '. . . is income from property of which the settlor has divested himself absolutely by the settlement.'

In interpreting this phrase s 674A(3) incorporates into s 674A the interpretation provisions in ICTA 1988 s 685(1)(2)(3) and (4A)-(4C)[5]. As applicable to s 674A these provisions are:

'(1) For the purposes of [section 674A], the settlor shall not be deemed to have divested himself absolutely of any property if that property or any derived property is, or will or may become, in any circumstances whatsoever, payable to or applicable for the benefit of the settlor or *the wife or husband of the settlor.*

(2) For those purposes, the settlor shall not be deemed not to have divested himself absolutely of any property by reason only that the property or any derived property may become payable to or applicable for the benefit of the settlor, or *the wife or husband of the settlor,* in the event of —

    (a) the bankruptcy of some person who is or may become beneficially entitled to the property or any of the derived property; or

    (b) an assignment of or charge on the property or any of the derived property being made or given by some such person; or

    (c) in the case of a marriage settlement, the death of both parties to the marriage and of all or any of the children of the marriage; or

    (d) the death under the age of 25 or some lower age of some person who would be beneficially entitled to the property or the derived property on attaining that age.

(3) In subsections (1) and (2) above [and subsection 4B below] "derived

---

1 ICTA 1988 s 674A(5)(a).
2 ICTA 1988 s 674A(5)(b).
3 ICTA 1988 s 674A(5).
4 ICTA 1988 s 674A(1).
5 ICTA 1988 s 685(4A)-(4C) were added by FA 1989 s 108 and only apply for 1990-91 and later years.

property", in relation to any property, means income from that property or any other property directly or indirectly representing proceeds of, or of income from, that property or any income therefrom.

(4A) References in [section 674A] to a settlement do not include references to an outright gift by one spouse to the other of property from which income arises unless —
  (a) the gift does not carry a right to the whole of that income, or
  (b) the property given is wholly or substantially a right to income.

(4B) For the purposes of subsection (4A) above a gift is not an outright gift if it is subject to conditions, or if the property given or any derived property is or will or may become, in any circumstances whatsoever, payable to or applicable for the benefit of the donor.

(4C) References in [section 674A] to a settlement do not include references to the irrevocable allocation of pension rights by one spouse to the other in accordance with the terms of a relevant statutory scheme (within the meaning of Chapter I of Part XIV).'

In a joint meeting between the Revenue and the English and Scottish Law Societies the Revenue, commenting on the application of ICTA 1988 s 685(4A) and (4B), said that the purpose of ICTA 1988 s 685(4A)(a) was to define an outright gift between husband and wife to ensure that such gifts were taken outside the scope of the settlements legislation. A gift of income-bearing property would be regarded as an outright gift if it carried the right to the whole income from the property, it was not just a right to income (without any underlying capital), it was not subject to conditions and it was property of which the donor had divested himself absolutely[1]. The Revenue confirmed that ICTA 1988 s 685(4A)(b) meant that gifts of life interests and annuities would not be treated as outright gifts. The object of s 685(4A)(b), which was drafted in general terms, was to ensure that the mere assignment of income without its underlying capital should not take an asset outside the scope of the settlements legislation[2].

It will be noted that, even if there is an outright gift of an income producing asset, the gift is ineffective if the property given, or any derived property, which is defined in s 685(3) to include income from the property given, may in any circumstances whatsoever be applicable for the benefit of the donor. Interpreted literally this would debar all gifts, since it is quite possible that a wife will use income from an asset transferred to her by her husband to provide a benefit for the husband, for example by buying food which he consumes for his dinner, or buying him a Christmas present. However such a strict interpretation would make a nonsense of the relieving provision for outright gifts, and it seems clear from case law that ICTA 1988 s 685(4B) has to be rewritten to read:

'. . . if, *under the terms of the gift*, the property given or any derived property is or will or may become, in any circumstances whatsoever, payable to or applicable for the benefit of the donor.'[3]

---

1 Para 12 of 'Notes of Meeting' held on 14th June 1989 at Somerset House with the Law Societies of England & Wales and Scotland, obtainable from the office of the Legal Practice Directorate, the Law Society, 50 Chancery Lane, London WC2A 1SX.
2 'Notes of Meeting' between the Revenue and the Law Societies, above, para 13.
3 ICTA 1988 s 674A, which s 685(4B) is interpreting, only applies if *under the settlement* income is payable to the settlor.

Mere voluntary applications of the property, or income from it, by the recipient for the benefit of the donor are not caught. In *Glyn v IRC*[1] an equivalent provision in what is now ICTA 1988 s 673 was considered. S 673 taxes as the income of the settlor income of a settlement in which the settlor retains an interest to the extent that the income remains undistributed. A settlor is deemed to retain an interest in a settlement if any income or property which may at any time arise under or be comprised in that settlement is, or will or may become, payable to or applicable for the benefit of the settlor or the wife or husband of the settlor in any circumstances whatsoever. The Special Commissioners accepted the argument that these words could not be read as including the possibility of a mere voluntary application of income by a beneficiary of the settlor, outside the provision of the settlement altogether, and Singleton J appeared to agree with this view, although any discussion of it was strictly obiter.

In *Jenkins v IRC*[2] the Court of Appeal considered a provision now in ICTA 1988 s 665 which defines 'irrevocable' for provisions which enact that an irrevocable accumulation settlement by a parent on a minor child is effective for income tax purposes. S 665(1) provides that a settlement 'shall not be deemed to be irrevocable if its terms provide for payment to the settlor or, during the life of the settlor, to the wife or husband of the settlor for his or her benefit ... of any income or assets in any circumstances whatsoever during the life of the settlor's child'. Both Macnaghten J in the High Court and Lord Greene MR in the Court of Appeal held that a payment did not come within the phrase 'in any circumstances whatsoever' if it arose from circumstances extrinsic to the terms of the settlement[3]. This view was followed by Pennycuick J in *Muir v IRC*[4]. Dealing with the phrase 'in any circumstances whatsoever' in what is now ICTA 1988 s 673, he said[5]:

> 'Section [673] is in very wide terms, but it must, I think, be confined to cases where income or property "will or may become payable to or applicable for the benefit of the settlor" either under the trusts of the settlement itself or under some collateral arrangement having legal force ...'

In IR 83 para 120 the Revenue have now confirmed that, assuming there are no special conditions attached to it, they will regard an outright gift of an asset from one spouse to the other as effective for tax purposes even though the donee might voluntarily decide to use the capital or income in a way which benefited the donor, or the property might return to the donor following the death of the donee (either by will or intestacy, or as a result of the normal rules of survivorship on the death of a joint life tenant).

1   (1948) 30 TC 321.
2   (1944) 26 TC 265.
3   Per Lord Greene MR, (1944) 26 TC 265 at 281.
4   (1966) 43 TC 367.
5   (1966) 43 TC 367 at 381.

In addition to the exemption for transfers of property of which the donor has divested himself absolutely, ICTA 1988 s 674A(1) specifies a number of other circumstances in which a transfer of assets will not be regarded as a settlement for the purposes of deeming subsequent income to remain income of the donor for income tax purposes. These circumstances are:

(1)   A settlement the income from which consists of annual payments made under a partnership agreement to or for the benefit of a former member, or the widow or widower or dependants of a deceased former member, of the partnership, provided the payments are made under a liability incurred for valuable consideration, as most partnership annuities are[1].

(2)   Payments made in connection with the acquisition of the whole or part of a business, or top-up payments within certain limits under a partnership annuity scheme even if the payments cannot strictly be said to have been made for valuable consideration[2].

(3)   Maintenance payments for a spouse following separation or divorce provided the maintenance is payable to or applicable for the benefit of the other party[3].

(4)   Covenanted donations to charity which are capable of lasting for more than three years[4].

(5)   Payments which are taxed as income of the settlor under any other provision in the income tax Acts[5].

Although ICTA 1988 s 674A is likely to be the statutory provision most commonly deployed by the Revenue to render ineffective for income tax purposes arrangements seeking to transfer income between spouses, there are a number of other anti-avoidance provisions which may be relevant for settlements created by spouses and which need to be mentioned briefly. The first important point to note is that all the provisions, including ICTA 1988 s 674A, apply only if there is a 'settlement'. Settlement is widely defined in ICTA 1988 s 681(4) to include 'any disposition, trust, covenant, agreement or arrangement'. It is implicit in the way ICTA 1988 s 685(4A) has been drafted that Parliament considered that this definition is wide enough to include an outright gift of an asset. However this assumption may be challengeable in an appropriate case. The definition of settlement in ICTA 1988 s 681(4) is materially different from the definition of settlement in ICTA 1988 s 670(1), where settlement is defined for the purpose of anti-avoidance provisions dealing with settlements on minor children as including 'any disposition, trust, covenant, agreement, arrangement *or transfer of assets*'. In *Thomas v Marshall*[6] the House of Lords held that a transfer of an asset by a parent to a minor child did constitute a settlement so that income from the asset remained taxable as income of the transferor parent and not as income of the child[7]. But it was a fundamental part of the ratio of the House of Lords decision that a gift was deemed to be a settlement because of the inclusion of the words 'transfer of assets' in

1   ICTA 1988 s 674A(1)(a).
2   ICTA 1988 s 674A(1)(b).
3   ICTA 1988 s 674A(1)(c).
4   ICTA 1988 s 674A(1)(e).
5   ICTA 1988 s 674A(1)(f).
6   (1953) 34 TC 178.
7   See also *Hood-Barrs v IRC* (1946) 27 TC 385.

the definition section. Without those words the decision might well have been different. As Lord Morton, who gave the leading judgment, put it[1]:

> 'It is true that an absolute gift of money or of an investment would not ordinarily be regarded as a "settlement", but it is expressly enacted that in Section 21 the expression "settlement" includes, inter alia,
> "Any ... transfer of assets."
> For my part, I see no escape from the conclusion that the Appellant made a transfer of assets, in the ordinary sense of that phrase, when he used his own money to make a payment into Michael's bank account and to purchase Defence Bonds in Michael's name.'

As the words 'transfer of assets' do not appear in ICTA 1988 s 681(4), the relevant definition section for the purpose of husband and wife settlements, it may be possible to argue that the outright transfer of an asset from one spouse to another is not a settlement. This will be particularly important where the asset transferred is a right to income, for example where a husband gifts an annuity to his wife, or irrevocably transfers to her a life interest under a settlement. However an argument that such a transfer does not constitute a settlement within the statutory provisions should be regarded as a defence of last resort and no tax planning should be based on it, as it is clearly the Revenue's view that a gift of assets is prima facie a settlement, whether or not the words 'transfer of assets' are used in the definition section, and only ceases to be a settlement if it comes within the exception in ICTA 1988 s 685(4A) and (4B) for outright gifts of assets other than an outright gift of a right to income.

Under ICTA 1988 s 672 if and so long as under the terms of a settlement any person has, or may have, power to revoke a settlement, whether or not with the consent of some other person, and on revocation the settlor, or the wife or husband of the settlor, may become entitled to all or part of the settlement property or to the income from it, the settlement is ineffective for income tax purposes and the income of the settlement remains taxable as income of the settlor. A power to revoke a settlement includes a power to diminish the payments to be made under it[2]. If the power to revoke is unexercisable for a period of at least six years after property first becomes comprised in the settlement, the anti-avoidance section does not apply until the power becomes exercisable[3]. It will be noted that the section applies if, on revocation, property or income may become payable to a husband or wife of the settlor. A widower or widow is not a husband or wife[4], so payments to a spouse that can only become payable after the death of the settlor are not caught. However a potential future spouse may be covered, even though the settlor is not married at the time of the settlement. Thus in *IRC v Tennant*[5] a female settlor, at a time when she was not married, transferred property into trust, but retained the power to revoke the trust with the consent of the trustees and create new trusts in favour of any person except herself. The High Court held that the settlement was caught by the section, as the settlor could use the power to transfer property

1 (1953) 34 TC 178 at 201.
2 ICTA 1988 s 672(3).
3 ICTA 1988 s 672(2).
4 *Vesteys's Executors v IRC* (1949) 31 TC 1.
5 (1942) 24 TC 215.

to a husband whom she might subsequently marry. In Statement of Practice A30[1] the Revenue state that they take the view that the decision in *IRC v Tennant* applies:

> '(a)   where, although a settlor is not at the material time a party to a subsisting marriage, the terms of the settlement are such that a benefit may be conferred on substantially any person who may become the wife or husband of the settlor in future, or
>
> (b)   where, whether or not the settlor is married, the terms of the settlement are such as to indicate a specific intention that a future wife or husband of the settlor may be enabled to benefit.'

It follows that a properly-drawn settlement must exclude the ability of both husband and wife, and any future husband and wife, to benefit from the settlement.

Under ICTA 1988 s 673 if and so long as a settlor retains an interest in any settled property, any undistributed income of the settlement is taxed as the settlor's income. Subject to some minor exceptions[2], a settlor is deemed to have retained an interest if any property comprised, or becoming comprised, in the settlement, or any income from it, may become payable to or applicable for the benefit of the settlor, or a husband or wife of the settlor, in any circumstances whatsoever[3]. In Statement of Practice 1/82 the Revenue state that a settlor will not be treated as entitled to a benefit merely because the trustees of the settlement have power to, or do in fact, pay inheritance tax on assets put into the settlement.

Under ICTA 1988 s 674 if any person has under the terms of a settlement the power, whether exercisable immediately or in the future, to pay or apply or secure any of the settlement property or income from it for the benefit of the settlor or the husband or wife of the settlor, then the income from the settlement remains taxable as the income of the settlor. Thus it is essential when creating a discretionary trust to exclude the settlor, or any current or future husband or wife of the settlor, from any possibility of benefit under the terms of the settlement.

General provisions dealing with the consequences of income being taxed as income of the settlor under any of these anti-avoidance provisions, including ICTA 1988 s 674A, are contained in ICTA 1988 s 675. The settlor is to be assessed to tax under Sch D Case VI, and is entitled to claim the same allowances to which he would have been entitled had the income in fact been received by him. The settlor is entitled to recover from the trustees, or from whoever is actually entitled to the income, any income tax paid by the settlor. In computing this tax the settlement income is deemed to be the highest part of the settlor's income[4], and the settlor is entitled to a certificate from his inspector of taxes specifying both the amount of settlement income on which he has been taxed and the amount of tax paid[5]. The certificate is conclusive evidence of the facts stated in it[6]. If, unusually, a settlor becomes entitled to a tax refund as a result of settlement

---

1   Issued as a press release on 18th June 1979.
2   Set out in ICTA 1988 s 673(3).
3   ICTA 1988 s 673(2).
4   ICTA 1988 s 675(5).
5   ICTA 1988 s 675(3)(b).
6   ICTA 1988 s 675(3).

income being imputed to him, he must pay the tax refunded to the trustees or other person actually entitled to the income[1]. In order to obtain any relevant information for the purposes of these anti-avoidance provisions, an inspector is empowered to require any person who is a party to the settlement to furnish him, within a period of not less than twenty-eight days, with such information as he may require[2].

If any of the above anti-avoidance provisions apply, their effect is to deem the income from the assets transferred (or the income caught by the provision) to be the income of the settlor's for all income tax purposes. There are two additional provisions which if they apply, and no other more onerous provision applies, deem income from a settlement[3] to be the income of the settlor for the purposes of higher rate tax only, with the income remaining taxable as income of the recipient for the purposes of basic rate tax. The two sections, ICTA 1988 s 683 and s 684, are inter-related, as one deals with settlements made after 6th April 1965 and, with relatively minor differences, the other deals with settlements made before 7th April 1965 but after 9th April 1946. The introduction of ICTA 1988 s 674A is likely to render these sections superfluous for settlements by one spouse in favour of the other, as from 1990-91 s 674A is retrospective in its application to inter-spousal settlements and it is more onerous than either ICTA s 683 or 684. But if the recipient of income is a person other than a spouse, ICTA 1988 s 674A does not apply to settlements made before 14th March 1988, so that ICTA 1988 s 683 and s 684 may continue to be relevant.

ICTA 1988 s 683 applies to income from a settlement made on or after 6th April 1965 which, during the life of the settlor, is payable to a person other than the settlor. Unless one of a number of exemptions apply, the income is deemed to be income of the settlor for the purposes of higher rate tax. The exemptions are set out in s 683(1), and closely follow the exemptions set out in ICTA 1988 s 674A(1), which have been discussed in detail earlier in this section. In particular, there is no charge if the settlor has divested himself absolutely of the settlement property, and the meaning of 'divested himself absolutely' is set out in ICTA 1988 s 685 which provides a common definition both for these provisions and for the more onerous ICTA s 674A.

The settlement anti-avoidance provisions are complex, and the wording of each provision must be carefully considered if any tax planning is undertaken following the introduction of independent taxation which goes beyond a simple transfer of assets, other than a right to income, from one spouse to another, or to another member of the family. Although a different stance can be taken in any negotiations with the Revenue, it may often be sensible during the planning stage to assume that an anti-avoidance provision does apply and consider whether, in that event, the proposed tax planning transaction would be disadvantageous in comparison with doing nothing at all. If it would not be disadvantageous, but would clearly be advantageous if the anti-avoidance provision did not apply, then tax

---

1   ICTA 1988 s 675(4).
2   ICTA 1988 s 680.
3   Given the same definition as in the other provisions, and thus not including a transfer of assets.

planning may be beneficial provided the taxpayer is aware of any risks. If the application of an anti-avoidance provision would make the proposed planning positively disadvantageous, it may be better to think again.

4.5 Planning for a spouse with a low income

One of the objectives of tax planning for independent taxation is to ensure that the personal allowance of each spouse and the married couple's allowance are fully utilised. It is therefore important to ensure that each spouse has taxable income of at least this amount and that any tax withheld at source on the income can be reclaimed from the Revenue. It is possible that a spouse with a low income will derive some of that income from a building society deposit account or a bank deposit account, and a well-known disadvantage with these accounts is that the composite rate tax withheld at source cannot be recovered if the taxpayer's income, including the interest, is less than his personal allowance. Building society and bank deposit accounts are therefore potentially unattractive investments to a low-income spouse, but it needs to be emphasised that a problem only arises if all or part of bank deposit or building society interest, *when treated as the highest part of the spouse's income,* is still below the personal allowance threshold. Thus if a wife has earned income of £3,500 the fact that she may also have building society interest has no adverse affects on her tax liability as the whole of her personal allowance of £3,005[1] can be deducted from her earnings and none needs to be set against the building society interest. The fact that tax withheld on the building society interest cannot be recovered then becomes immaterial.

Following changes announced in the March 1990 Budget the problem of the inability to reclaim composite rate tax on building society and bank deposit interest will cease to exist as from 6th April 1991, as composite rate tax will be abolished from that date. It is envisaged that most taxpayers will thereafter have basic rate tax withheld at source from bank and building society interest, but will be able to reclaim the tax withheld if the interest turns out not to be liable to income tax. If it is clear at the outset that interest will be covered by a depositor's personal allowance (and the depositor has no other income which, when added to the interest, would result in his personal allowance being exceeded), the depositor will be able to sign a certificate which will authorise a bank or building society to pay interest gross, without deduction of tax. The precise details of these new arrangements have yet to be finalised in discussions between the Inland Revenue and the banks and building societies, and statutory provisions setting out the ground rules for these discussions are contained in FA 1990 s 30 and Sch 5. As the changes will only take effect in 1991-92 composite rate tax remains a problem for 1990-91.

If a spouse does need to find an alternative investment to a building society account there are various options. The first is to transfer the investment into another UK investment which withholds tax at source, but the tax withheld can be reclaimed from the Inland Revenue. Examples are dividends on shares and unit trusts. Disadvantages of such a change

---

1 It is assumed there is no transferred married couple's allowance.

of investment are that (*a*) it may not be possible to obtain as high an income yield from shares or unit trusts and (*b*) the income is initially received under deduction of tax, so that a repayment claim has to be made to the Revenue with the inevitable delay and increased administration that that entails. An alternative is to transfer funds to an investment which pays interest gross. Within the UK the main choices are National Savings and Government Stock which is listed on the National Stock Register, but the yields from such an investment may be unattractive. Alternatively it may be possible to deposit funds with building societies or banks registered outside the UK, and institutions registered in the Channel Islands or the Isle of Man qualify for this purpose. It is not yet clear whether building societies in these countries will be over-enthusiastic about receiving funds deposited with them primarily to circumvent the rule that UK building societies and banks must pay interest under deduction of a non-refundable tax. Evidence to date suggests that customers will have to seek out off-shore building society accounts, and that they will not be actively marketed.

If funds in a building society account are transferred to an account which pays interest gross it must be remembered that the basis of assessment of the new interest will be quite different from the basis of assessment of UK building society interest, and tax planning will need to take particular account of the special basis of assessment in the opening years of the new account. As UK building society interest has tax withheld at source, a recipient is assessable to tax on the interest for the year of assessment in which it is credited to his account[1]. Interest from a source in the UK which pays interest gross, such as National Savings, is taxable under Sch D Case III. Interest from a source situated outside the United Kingdom is taxable under Sch D Case V as income from a foreign possession. In both cases the interest is assessable under rules set out in ICTA 1988 ss 64-68. Assuming the recipient is resident, ordinarily resident, and domiciled in the United Kingdom the normal basis of assessment is a preceding year basis of assessment, ie the recipient is taxed for a year of assessment on the income credited to his account in the preceding year of assessment[2]. There is no time apportionment of interest[3], so that interest credited to an account on 30th April 1989 will be assessable for 1990-91 as income of the spouse entitled to it, and it is immaterial that most of the interest related to 1988-89 and that the whole of the interest was earned during a period when aggregate taxation of spouses' unearned incomes was in force.

Special rules apply in both the opening and the closing years of a Sch D Case III or Sch D Case V source. In the year in which he first receives interest paid gross, regardless of the year the source of the interest commenced, a taxpayer will be taxed on the actual interest credited[4]. In the second year of assessment he will be taxed on the actual interest credited in the second year unless interest was first credited on 6th April in year one, in which case a preceding year basis of assessment applies[5]. In the third year of assessment the taxpayer will be taxed on a preceding year

1   ICTA 1988 s 476(5)(c).
2   ICTA 1988 ss 64 and 65.
3   *Whitworth Park Coal Co Ltd v IRC* (1961) 38 TC 531.
4   ICTA 1988 s 66(1)(a).
5   ICTA 1988 s 66(1)(b).

basis. The taxpayer may however elect within six years from the end of the third year of assessment to have the third year of assessment assessed on an actual year basis[1]. If there is a new source of Sch D Case III or V income, or an addition to an existing source, the opening year rules apply to the new or additional source[2]. If there is an additional deposit in a bank or building society account there is authority that the deposit of money is the source of the interest, so that additional deposits attract the opening year rules to interest attributable to that addition[3]. In practice the Revenue are unlikely to apply this rule strictly to a fluctuating deposit account, and will treat it as a single source. But if there is a large additional deposit they may seek to invoke the strict law[4].

In the closing year of a source of Sch D Case III or V income a taxpayer is assessed on the actual income credited in the year in which the source ceased[5]. The Revenue have the right to reassess the penultimate year on an actual basis if it is beneficial to do so[6]. There are special rules to deal with the situation where income from a source ceases but the source itself does not cease, as otherwise a taxpayer would inevitably be taxed on more income than he actually received because, since one year's actual income was taxed twice at the commencement of the source, it is essential to have a drop-out year at the end. Accordingly, if there is no income for the last two years immediately preceding the cessation of the source, a taxpayer may elect to have the year the income ceased treated as the year the source ceased[7]. Any such election must be made within two years of the cessation of the source, but cannot be made more than eight years after the end of the year of assessment in which income last arose[8]. If the source does not in fact cease, a taxpayer can elect to deem the source to have ceased when he has had no income from it for six consecutive years[9]. The election must be made not later than two years after the end of the six years[10]. After electing for a deemed cessation, a taxpayer can make the further election to relate back the deemed cessation to the year in which income was last received.

4.6 Mortgage interest planning

Under independent taxation if one spouse is liable to tax at the the higher rate of income tax and the other is not, it is efficient tax planning to make an allocation of interest election to ensure that, irrespective of which spouse actually pays the interest, the mortgage interest is deducted from the income of the spouse liable to higher rate tax. Full details of the requirements surrounding an allocation of interest election are set out in **2.16:3** above.

1 ICTA 1988 s 66(1)(c). The election applies to the second year if that was the first year
   to be assessed on a preceding year basis.
2 ICTA 1988 s 66(3).
3 *Hart v Sangster* (1957) 37 TC 231.
4 In *Hart v Sangster* the additional deposit was £2,000,000.
5 ICTA 1988 s 67(1)(b).
6 ICTA 1988 s 67(1)(b).
7 ICTA 1988 s 67(1)(c).
8 ICTA 1988 s 67(4).
9 ICTA 1988 s 67(5).
10 ICTA 1988 s 67(5).

Planning may also bring tax savings where spouses occupy separate main residences and there are outstanding mortgages on both residences. Under the law the house which was purchased first is deemed to be the main residence of both of them and the house which was purchased second is deemed to be the main residence of neither of them. If the mortgage on the first house is below £30,000 and the mortgage on the second house is above the £30,000 threshold the result could be a significant loss of tax relief. It may therefore be beneficial to pay off the mortgage on the first house in order to claim tax relief up to the £30,000 loan limit on the second house (see further **2.16:1** above).

4.7 Income tax planning for retired couples

In practice the new system of independent taxation may well prove to be of greatest benefit to retired couples, as neither spouse is likely to have any earned income, apart from a pension, and any pension payable to a wife as a result of her husband's contributions did not count as the wife's earned income for the purposes of a claim to wife's earned income allowance[1]. Consequently under the system of aggregate taxation a wife's unearned income was added to her husband's and taxed at his marginal rate of income tax, and there was often no possibility of making use of the wife's earned income relief. Only one higher married age allowance was available, and this was subject to reduction if the combined incomes of the spouses exceeded £11,400[2]. Under independent taxation the position is very much better. First, each spouse is taxed separately on their incomes, earned and unearned, so that, even without the benefit of any personal allowances, their combined taxable incomes would have to exceed £41,400 before payment of higher rate tax became unavoidable. Second, each spouse now qualifies for a personal allowance based on their respective ages, and the incomes of the spouses are treated separately when working out whether age allowance has to be reduced because the total income of a spouse exceeds £12,300. A wife aged 65 with an unearned income of £6,000 qualifies for the higher age allowance of £3,670 irrespective of the income of her husband, thus eliminating this amount of income from charge to tax with a consequent reduction in the tax liability of at least £917.50[3] in comparison with the tax liability on the income in 1989-90. Third, the higher married couple's allowance is based on the age of the older spouse, and in determining whether it has to be reduced because total income exceeds the income limit of £12,300 only the husband's income is taken into account. A husband aged 77 with income below this threshold therefore qualifies for a personal allowance of £3,820 plus a married couple's allowance of £2,185. His wife will additionally qualify for a personal allowance based on her own age.

Tax planning for elderly married couples should be geared to the following objectives. First, ensure that no higher rate tax is paid by either spouse. Second, ensure that each spouse has sufficient taxable income to

1   ICTA 1988 s 257(7)(b).
2   The income limit for 1989-90.
3   £3,670 @ 25%. The reduction will be £1,468 if the aggregate income of the spouses was liable to higher rate tax in 1989-90.

cover their personal allowance and, in the case of a husband, the married couple's allowance. It will be recalled that for 1990-91 bank deposit and building society interest subject to composite rate tax are not effective for this purpose as the tax withheld cannot be reclaimed. Third, ensure that the total income of neither spouse exceeds £12,300 as above that level the higher age allowances start to be reduced by £1 for every £2 of excess income[1]. If it is unavoidable for one spouse to exceed the limit, it will normally be advantageous for it to be the wife, as this will have no effect on the higher married couple's allowance. For elderly couples whose incomes are not already divided in a way that is tax efficient, it will normally only be possible to achieve these objectives by an outright transfer of income producing assets from one spouse to the other.

4.8 Capital gains tax planning under independent taxation

For capital gains tax independent taxation presents significant opportunities for tax planning, as spouses are much better placed under the new system than they were under aggregate taxation, and they are also much better placed than a couple who are living together as husband and wife but who are not married to each other. Each spouse has an annual exemption of £5,000, thus doubling the aggregate annual exemption that was available to spouses in 1989-90, and a wife's chargeable gains are now taxed separately at her own marginal rate of income tax instead of being added to her husband's income. The only significant disadvantage under independent taxation is that one spouse's allowable losses can no longer be deducted from the other spouse's chargeable gains, but, as will be seen shortly, there are ways around this. Over and above these new advantages, which only put spouses in the same position as cohabitees have always been, spouses living together retain the ability to transfer assets from one spouse to the other at no gain/no loss to the transferor spouse[2], something that is denied to cohabitees. CGTA 1979 s 44 is therefore likely to be the key to much tax planning for capital gains realised by spouses.

The objectives of capital gains tax planning should be to ensure that both spouses take full advantage of their £5,000 annual exemption, and that any CGT payable is only charged at 25% rather than 40%. If one spouse is a higher rate taxpayer and the other is only taxable at the basic rate it should usually be possible to achieve this by ensuring that gains in excess of the annual exemption are realised by the spouse with the lower income. If the assets in question in fact belong to the spouse with the higher income they should be gifted to the other spouse under CGTA 1979 s 44, and that spouse should then realise the gain. In the same way, although there may be a theoretical bar to the losses of one spouse being deducted from the gains of the other spouse, there is no practical bar, as the spouse with assets which have unrealised gains merely transfers those assets to the spouse who is about to realise losses, and that spouse sells all relevant assets in the same tax year. Unlike the income tax legislation, there are few if any relevant anti-avoidance provisions for capital gains tax, so the only cloud

1   See further **1.5** above.
2   CGTA 1979 s 44.

on the horizon is the anti-avoidance doctrine recently developed by the courts in cases such as *WT Ramsay Ltd v IRC*[1] and *Furniss v Dawson*[2].

Prior to the decision of the House of Lords in *WT Ramsay Ltd v IRC* it had been assumed by tax planners that, if there were a series of transactions none of which was a sham, the tax treatment of each transaction had to be determined in isolation from the other transactions. This view was rudely shattered by the House of Lords in *Ramsay*. They held that, when faced with a pre-planned scheme which had no business purpose other than the avoidance of tax, courts could consider the scheme as a whole and could apply tax consequences to the net effect of the scheme. This new approach was affirmed by the House of Lords in *IRC v Burmah Oil Co Ltd*[3]. However the schemes considered in *Ramsay* and *Burmah Oil* were circular self-cancelling schemes. It remained unclear whether similar principles would apply if there was a transaction which was not circular and which had enduring legal and financial consequences, but which had a step or steps inserted in it which had no commercial purpose other than the avoidance of tax. This issue arose in *Furniss v Dawson*. The taxpayers were shareholders in a family company. They wished to sell their shares to a third party. If nothing was done the sale would result in a substantial chargeable gain of the difference between the sales proceeds and the original cost of the shares. The sale was therefore effected by:

(1)   The formation of a new company, G Ltd, incorporated and resident in the Isle of Man, and the transfer to it by the taxpayers of their shares in the family company in exchange for shares in G Ltd. Under the CGT legislation this was not a chargeable disposal, but the taxpayers were deemed to have acquired G Ltd shares at the cost base of the family company shares.

(2)   G Ltd sold the family company shares to the third party. As G Ltd was not resident or ordinarily resident in the UK there was no chargeable gain.

If each step was taxed in isolation the effect of the scheme was to defer a capital gains tax charge until the taxpayers disposed of their shares in G Ltd, but the interposition of G Ltd as a step in the sale had no commercial purpose other than to avoid tax. The Court of Appeal held that the *Ramsay* principle only applied where there was a circular self-cancelling scheme. It did not apply where, as here, there was a non-circular scheme with enduring effects. Accordingly the scheme succeeded. The House of Lords held that this was a misunderstanding of what *Ramsay* decided. *Ramsay* applies to all cases where, as Lord Diplock put it in *Burmah Oil*[4], there is 'a pre-ordained series of transactions (whether or not they include achievement of a legitimate commercial end) into which there are inserted steps which have no commercial purpose apart from the avoidance of a liability to tax which in the absence of those particular steps would have been payable.' Commenting on this statement in *Furniss v Dawson*, Lord Brightman explained the effect of the decisions as follows[5]:

1   (1981) 54 TC 101.
2   (1984) 55 TC 324.
3   (1981) 54 TC 200.
4   (1981) 54 TC 200 at 214.
5   (1984) 55 TC 324 at 401.

'The formulation by Lord Diplock in *Burmah* expresses the limitation of the *Ramsay* principle. First, there must be a pre-ordained series of transactions; or, if one likes, one single composite transaction. This composite transaction may or may not include the achievement of a legitimate commercial (ie business) end. The composite transaction does, in the instant case; it achieved a sale of the shares in the operating companies by the Dawsons to Wood Bastow [the third party]. It did not in *Ramsay*. Secondly, there must be steps inserted which have no commercial (business) *purpose* apart from the avoidance of a liability to tax — not "no business *effect*." If those two ingredients exist, the inserted steps are to be disregarded for fiscal purposes. The court must then look at the end result. Precisely how the end result will be taxed will depend on the terms of the taxing statute sought to be applied.'

The most recent House of Lords judgments on the new approach to tax avoidance evidenced by *Ramsay* are in *Craven v White*[1]. In fact three separate cases were involved, *Craven v White, IRC v Bowater Property Developments Ltd* and *Bayliss v Gregory*, but they all involved the same general issue, and were grouped together for the purposes of appeal. The Law Lords reached unanimous conclusions on *IRC v Bowater Property Group* and *Bayliss v Gregory*, but divided 3-2 on *Craven v White*. In *Craven v White*, the most controversial of the three cases, the taxpayers owned all the shares in a company (Queensferry) which owned and operated supermarkets. From 1973 onwards they had attempted to sell or merge the business. In 1976 they commenced negotiations with C Ltd and in March 1976 explored the possibilities of establishing a company in the Isle of Man to act as a holding company for the proposed merger. In June 1976 a company (Millor Ltd) was incorporated in the Isle of Man and on 19th July 1976 Millor Ltd acquired the issued share capital of Queensferry in exchange for its own shares. Meanwhile the taxpayers began negotiations with another company, J Ltd, and temporarily abandoned negotiations with C Ltd until it appeared that the negotiations with J Ltd would not succeed. Later on 9th August 1976 the taxpayers and J Ltd reached an agreement and Millor Ltd sold the shares in Queensferry to J Ltd for over £2 million. The scheme was essentially the same as that which had been unsuccessful in *Furniss v Dawson*, and had the effect of deferring a capital gains tax liability on the disposal of the Queensferry shares until the shares in Millor Ltd were disposed of. Meanwhile Millor Ltd, whose sole assets were the proceeds of sale of the Queensferry shares, loaned this amount to the taxpayers on interest free loans. The Inland Revenue assessed the taxpayers to capital gains tax on the basis of a direct disposal by them of the Queensferry shares to J Ltd for £2,000,000.

In all three cases the Revenue argued (1) that the crucial requirement for the application of the *Ramsay* principle to a scheme for the avoidance of tax was that the inserted step in the series of transactions, which was for fiscal purposes to be ignored, should be embarked on for no commercial purpose; (2) that a series of transactions might properly be regarded as one composite transaction if they were intended to take place in a planned sequence and as machinery by which tax could be avoided, albeit in achieving a commercial end.

The majority of the House of Lords held that, for the *Ramsay* principle

1   [1988] STC 476.

as developed in *Dawson* to be applied to a series of transactions containing an intermediate transaction designed to avoid tax, it was essential (*a*) that the series was, at the *time the intermediate transaction was entered into*, pre-ordained in order to produce a given result; (*b*) that the intermediate transaction had no other purpose than the avoidance of taxation; (*c*) that there was, at the time, no practical likelihood that the pre-planned events would not take place in the order pre-ordained, so that the intermediate transaction was not even contemplated practically as having an independent life; and (*d*) that the pre-ordained events did in fact take place (per Lord Oliver at 507, with whom Lord Jauncey expressed his agreement). Lord Keith, the third majority judge reached the same conclusion, saying[1]:

> 'But I do not think that the transaction embodied in the final disposal can be said to be pre-ordained, a matter to be ascertained as at the time of the share exchange [the inserted step], when at that time it is wholly uncertain whether that disposal will take place, or a fortiori when neither the identity of the purchaser nor the price to be paid nor any of the other terms of the contract are known. In my opinion both the transactions in the series can properly be regarded as pre-ordained if, but only if, at the time when the first of them is entered into the taxpayer is in a position for all practical purposes to secure that the second also is entered into.'

All the Law Lords agreed that it was essential for the *Ramsay* doctrine to apply that the step which had been inserted for tax avoidance purposes should be part of a composite scheme. Thus if the ultimate disposal of the asset was completely independent of the tax avoidance step the *Ramsay* doctrine would not apply. This was the case in both *IRC v Bowater Property Development Ltd* and *Bayliss v Gregory*, and the Revenue's appeals in these cases were unanimously dismissed. The Law Lords unanimously rejected the Revenue's argument that any transaction which was only undertaken for tax avoidance purposes could be ignored. They therefore gave unanimous support for strategic tax planning — ie arranging assets in a way which will enable maximum advantage to be taken of the available tax breaks when those assets are eventually sold.

Applying these principles as they have so far been developed by the courts[2] to a transfer of an asset from one spouse to the other primarily to attract a lower capital gains tax rate on the disposal of the asset to a third party, the position would appear to be as follows. If a sale of the asset has been agreed in principle by one spouse and a transfer of the asset is made to the other spouse to gain a tax benefit, and the recipient spouse agrees to hand over the proceeds of sale to the donor, then the transfer to the recipient spouse will be ineffective for tax purposes, either because the transfer was a sham or because the principles in *Furniss v Dawson* apply. But if the recipient spouse is entitled to keep the proceeds of sale, then it is suggested that *Furniss v Dawson* would not apply provided no legally binding contract to sell the asset had been entered into by the donor prior to the transfer of the asset to the recipient spouse. Although the facts are superficially similar to those in *Furniss v Dawson*, the recipient spouse is not in the same position as the inserted company in *Furniss v Dawson* as she is not

---

1 [1988] STC 476 at 481.
2 The development is far from complete — see *Shepherd v Lyntress Ltd* [1989] STC 617, which may well be destined for the House of Lords.

under the control of her husband in the way that a company is under the control of its majority shareholder. Accordingly the correct analysis for capital gains tax would seem to be that one spouse has made a gift of an asset to the other spouse and that other spouse has then sold the asset. The same principle should apply if, before any prospective purchaser has been found, one spouse transfers an asset to the other spouse with a purpose of reducing capital gains tax on the eventual sale of the asset even if there is an expectation, which must not be legally enforceable, that when the recipient spouse does sell the asset she will transfer part or all of the sale proceeds to the donor.

Capital gains tax planning for married couples has therefore been greatly assisted by the introduction of independent taxation. Provided professional advice is taken at an early enough stage, it should be possible to achieve significant reductions in capital gains tax which would otherwise have been payable on the disposal of an asset by a spouse. Most of the planning is likely to revolve around a tax free transfer of an asset between the spouses prior to a sale to a third party, taking advantage of CGTA 1979 s 44. A further advantage of s 44 transfers, for reasons explained in 4.4 above, is that there will normally be no stamp duty or inheritance tax implications.

CHAPTER 5

Cohabitation

5.1 Cohabitation versus marriage

Not all couples who are living together choose to marry. Cohabitation is becoming increasingly common either out of choice, or as a preliminary to eventual marriage, or because marriage is impossible, for example when one of the cohabitees is lawfully married to someone else. Prior to the introduction of independent taxation, and other relevant changes made by the Finance Act 1988, cohabitees enjoyed significant tax advantages over their married counterparts, as they were always taxed as single persons whereas a married couple were normally taxed as a single unit. With the introduction of independent taxation, when added to other recent changes in the tax treatment of cohabitees, the differences in the tax treatment of marriage and cohabitation have been considerably reduced. Nevertheless there still are significant differences and, before considering some aspects of the taxation of cohabitation in more depth, the tax advantages and disadvantages of cohabitation over marriage are considered briefly here.

The advantages of cohabitation
(1)   Cohabitees are not associated or connected persons for the purposes of the income tax and capital gains tax legislation. Spouses normally are.
(2)   Many of the provisions in the settlements anti-avoidance provisions apply if the settlor *or his spouse* can derive any benefit. A cohabitee is not a spouse for this purpose, and thus it may be possible to confer benefits on her without falling foul of the legislation.
(3)   If cohabitees have two separate residences, with separate mortgages on each residence, each cohabitee may be able to claim mortgage interest relief on a loan up to £30,000 on the separate residence, provided it can be shown that each house is the main residence of one of the cohabitees. The circumstances in which this is likely to apply are where the cohabitees work in different places, and one of them purchases a home near his place of work where he resides during the working week. At weekends he resides at the other house, where his partner resides throughout. If the couple were married only the house purchased first could qualify as the main residence of both of them[1]. No mortgage interest relief could be claimed on the second house.
(4)   For capital gains tax cohabitees may be able to claim principal private residence exemption on two houses on facts similar to those outlined

1   ICTA 1988 s 356B(5).

in the previous paragraph. Spouses can only claim exemption for one principal private residence between them[1].

(5)   If cohabitees took out mortgage loans to purchase the same residence before 1st August 1988 they continue to be entitled to a loan limit of £30,000 per person for interest relief purposes so long as the loan is outstanding. A married couple are only entitled to one £30,000 loan limit between them.

The disadvantages of cohabitation

(1)   If cohabitees have no children they will each only be entitled to a single person's allowance. A married couple can additionally claim the married couple's allowance, an extra £1,720 allowances for 1990-91. This disadvantage is removed if cohabitees have children, as they may then claim the additional personal allowance[2] which is the same amount as the married couple's allowance. A married couple gain no additional tax allowances if they have children.

(2)   Cohabitees are unable to make an 'allocation of interest election' to allocate mortgage interest between them in the way that is most efficient for tax purposes. The ability to make this election is confined to spouses.

(3)   Assets transferred between spouses living together are transferred on a no gain/no loss basis for capital gains tax by virtue of CGTA 1979 s 44(1). Cohabitees cannot take advantage of this provision, and therefore transfers of assets from one to the other may result in a chargeable gain. This will be disadvantageous if the transferor has fully utilised his annual CGT exemption of £5,000 against other disposals, as capital gains tax will then be payable on the transfer to the cohabitee, whereas it would not have been payable had the couple been married. It will be advantageous if the chargeable gain on the transfer to the cohabitee remains within the £5,000 annual exemption, as no CGT will be payable on the transfer but the recipient will acquire the asset at its market value at the date of transfer. A married couple cannot use the annual exemption in this way to increase the base cost of assets transferred from one to the other.

(4)   On the death of a cohabitee there is no exemption equivalent to the exemption for bequests from one spouse to the other. Inheritance tax will therefore be chargeable if the deceased cohabitee's estate exceeds £128,000 whether or not all or part of it is left to the surviving partner. Estate planning may therefore be more important for cohabitees than spouses, but any planning for inter vivos transfers will have to take account of the possibility of capital gains tax at 25% or 40% on the chargeable gain arising on any chargeable assets transferred. Transfers inter-vivos between cohabitees will only be potentially exempt transfers for inheritance tax so that some inheritance tax may become payable if the transferor dies within seven years. Inter vivos transfers between spouses are exempt transfers.

1   CGTA 1979 s 101(6)(b).
2   See **5.2** below.

5.2 Tax allowance for the children of cohabitees

If cohabitees have children they may qualify for additional personal allowance, which is an allowance designed to give single parent families the same total personal allowances as a married man. The amount of the allowance is therefore the same as the married couple's allowance[1], £1,720 for 1990-91.

The conditions for claiming additional personal allowance are set out in ICTA 1988 ss 259 and 260. If the claimant is a woman she must show that she is not throughout the year of assessment a married woman living with her husband[2]. If the claimant is a man he must show either that he is not married to and living with his wife at any time during the year and is not entitled to claim married couple's allowance under ICTA 1988 s 257F because his wife is wholly maintained by voluntary maintenance payments[3] or that, although married to and living with his wife, she is totally incapacitated by physical or mental infirmity throughout the year[4]. Cohabitees will normally satisfy these requirements. A claimant must also prove that he has a qualifying child residing with him for the whole or part of the year[5]. A qualifying child is a child under 16 at the start of the year of assessment or, if over that age, is receiving full-time educational instruction at any university, college, school or other educational establishment[6]. A child who is undergoing training for a period of not less than two years for a trade profession or vocation is deemed to be undergoing full-time instruction at an educational establishment[7]. Additionally the child must *either* be the claimant's *or* be under the age of 18 at the start of the year of assessment and be maintained by the claimant for the whole or part of the tax year[8].

Under ICTA 1988 s 259(8) the claimant's child includes a stepchild, an illegitimate child where the two parents marry after the child's birth, and an adopted child provided the child was under 18 when adopted. It seems clear from this definition that a child who is born out of wedlock and is not within the three exceptions is not the 'child' of his parents for the purposes of a claim for additional personal allowance. A parent can therefore only claim additional personal allowance on the basis that he is maintaining the child. If further follows that no claim can be made in respect of the child after he reaches the age of 18, even if he is still continuing in education.

This continued discrimination against non-marital children may seem strange in an era when family law legislation has sought to remove any such discrimination[9], but the history of the additional personal allowance legislation seems to compel this result. ICTA 1988 s 831(4) provides that the interpretation of 'child' in the Taxes Acts is to be determined without regard to provisions in the Family Law Reform Act 1987, which sought

1   ICTA 1988 s 259(2).
2   ICTA 1988 s 259(1)(a).
3   ICTA 1988 s 259(1)(b).
4   ICTA 1988 s 259(1)(c).
5   ICTA 1988 s 259(2).
6   ICTA 1988 s 259(5)(a).
7   ICTA 1988 s 259(6).
8   ICTA 1988 s 259(5)(b).
9   See the Family Law Reform Act 1987.

to equate the legal position of children born outside marriage with those born in it. In particular FLRA 1987 s 1 enacted that, in any reference to a child in legislation passed after the coming into force of s 1, it shall be irrelevant, unless there is a contrary intention, whether or not the child's parents are, or have been, married to each other. The distinction between legitimate and illegitimate children therefore remains relevant for tax purposes.

Before child tax allowances were abolished it was a pre-condition to a claim for additional personal allowance that the claimant was entitled to a child tax allowance in respect of the child for whom he was claiming. Children included both children of the claimant and children of whom he had custody and was maintaining[1]. The consolidation of the income tax legislation in 1918 defined child as follows[2]:

> 'The expressions "child" and "children" in this provision include a stepchild or stepchildren, but do not include an illegitimate child or children: Provided that where the parents of any illegitimate child or illegitimate children shall, after the birth of such child or children, have married each other, such illegitimate child or children shall be included in the expressions "child" and "children".'

In the 1952 consolidation this was shortened to[3]:

> 'In this provision "child" includes a stepchild and an illegitimate child whose parents have married each other after his birth'

without, it is thought, any change of meaning. This definition was repeated in ICTA 1970 s 10. With the abolition of child tax allowances, F(No 2)A 1979 amended the requirements for a claim for the additional personal allowance to their present form, but these amendments were stated to be consequential on the withdrawal of child tax allowances[4], and the definition of children in Sch 1, now ICTA 1988 s 259(8), was transposed from the definition for child tax allowances. The definition of 'child' in these provisions should be compared with the definition of 'child' in the settlements anti-avoidance legislation where it is stated that[5]:

> '"Child" includes a stepchild and an illegitimate child.'

Where more than one claimant is entitled to an allowance in respect of the same child the additional personal allowance is apportioned between the claimants in such proportions as they agree or, in default of agreement, in proportion to the length of time that the child resides with each claimant during the tax year[6]. If these proportions cannot be agreed they are to be determined by General Commissioners nominated by the Revenue, but the Commissioners must cover the area in which at least one of the applicants resides[7]. If none of the claimants is resident in the United Kingdom, the apportionment is made by the Special Commissioners[8]. Where a claimant

1 · See ICTA 1970 s 10(1).
2   ITA 1918 s 12(1).
3   ITA 1952 s 212(1).
4   F(No 2)A 1979 s 11.
5   ICTA 1988 s 670.
6   ICTA 1988 s 260(1) and (3).
7   ICTA 1988 s 260(3).
8   ICTA 1988 s 260(3).

is exclusively entitled to an allowance in respect of one child, he or she is debarred from claiming an allowance for any child in respect of whom another person is also entitled to an allowance[1].

Each qualifying child can support a claim for additional personal allowance for that child, but no claimant is entitled in total to more than one allowance for each tax year[2].

Prior to changes made in the Finance Act 1988 these provisions were of considerable advantage to cohabitees who had at least two children. The children might be their own, or from a former marriage of one of the cohabitees but whom the other cohabitee was now also at least partly maintaining. One cohabitee made a claim for additional personal allowance in respect of one child and the other cohabitee made a claim in respect of the other child. The effect was that each cohabitee became entitled to the equivalent of the married man's allowance giving them larger personal allowances than if they were married, when the maximum allowances would have been the married man's allowance and the wife's earned income allowance. To counteract this provisions were enacted in FA 1988 s 30, effective from 1989-90, which provide that, where a man and a woman are cohabiting, a claim for additional personal allowance may only be made for the youngest child in respect of whom either of them is entitled to claim. The provisions are now contained in ICTA 1988 s 259(4A), which reads:

'Where —
(a) a man and woman who are not married to each other live together as husband and wife for the whole or any part of a year of assessment, and
(b) apart from this subsection each of them would on making a claim be entitled to a deduction under subsection (2) above,
neither of them shall be entitled to such a deduction except in respect of the youngest of the children concerned (that is to say, the children in respect of whom either would otherwise be entitled to a deduction).'

In IR 92 'A guide for one parent families'[3] the Revenue state that if both partners can claim for the youngest child one of them can give up their claim or the allowance can be split between them. If only one partner is entitled to claim for the youngest child the other partner gets no allowance, even if there are other qualifying children in respect of whom he would otherwise be entitled to claim.

The restriction to a single allowance applies for the year in which the partners commence cohabitation, and it also applies for the year cohabitation ceases, so that for both these years the cohabitees are limited to a single additional personal allowance between them. The restrictions are confined to heterosexual relationships, and will not prevent both parties to a homosexual relationship claiming additional personal allowance if there are two qualifying children living with them. Finally, the new provisions have no effect on a claim to additional personal allowance by both husband and wife after divorce or separation where neither has remarried and their children reside with both of them for at least part of the year[4].

1 ICTA 1988 s 260(6).
2 ICTA 1988 s 260(2)
3 December 1989.
4 See **7.3** below.

5.3 Mortgage interest relief for loans made after 31st July 1988

Prior to changes made by the Finance Act 1988 one of the main advantages that cohabitees had over a married couple was that loans made to them for the purpose of house purchase were not aggregated in computing whether the £30,000 loan limit had been exceeded. It followed that a cohabiting couple could get tax relief on loans up to £60,000, whereas the maximum limit for loans to a married couple was £30,000. In his 1988 Budget the Chancellor Nigel Lawson said that he was determined to end this discrimination against marriage. Legislation was enacted in the Finance Act 1988 to change the £30,000 loan limit to a limit per residence rather than a limit per person. However the changes were not retrospective, and did not affect loans which were in place on 1st August 1988, which was one of the contributory factors to the explosion in house prices in 1988 from which the housing market has not yet recovered. Different provisions therefore apply to loans taken out on or after 1st August 1988 and loans made before that date, commonly called protected loans. The law relating to new loans is dealt with here; the law relating to protected loans is dealt with in the next section.

ICTA 1988 s 356A(2) provides that where 'qualifying interest' is 'payable by' two or more people for 'any period' in relation to 'a residence' the maximum loan on which each borrower is entitled to tax relief is to be determined according to their sharer's limit. 'Qualifying interest' is interest which qualifies for tax relief because the loan was used to purchase either the borrower's main residence or accommodation which is job related accommodation[1]. 'Payable by' is concerned with the question of who is under a legal obligation to pay the interest, and not with who in fact pays it. Thus if there is a joint mortgage loan to cohabitees there are two sharers even if, in practice, only one of the cohabitees actually pays the mortgage interest. 'Any period' is defined in ICTA 1988 s 356D(3) to make it clear that a new period starts at the beginning of each tax year and every time there is a change in the persons paying qualifying loan interest. 'A residence' is defined as[2]:

> '. . . a building, or part of a building, occupied or intended to be occupied as a separate residence, or a caravan or house boat; but a building, or part of a building, which is designed for permanent use as a single residence shall be treated as a single residence notwithstanding that it is temporarily divided into two or more parts which are occupied or intended to be occupied as separate residences.'

It will take litigation to determine how temporary an alteration to a building has to be for it to be caught by this provision. It seems clear that if a large house is subdivided into flats by a developer and those flats are then sold to different purchasers, each flat is a separate residence, as the division of the original house is not temporary. Conversely, if cohabitees

---

1   ICTA 1988 s 356D(1).
2   ICTA 1988 s 356D(2).

were to subdivide a house and claim to live in separate parts primarily to qualify for separate £30,000 limits, it is probable that their claim would fail.

If there is only one person liable to pay qualifying interest in relation to a residence, that borrower is allocated the whole of the £30,000 limit[1]. If there are two or more borrowers the sharer's limit of each of them has to be computed[2]. This is done by dividing the qualifying maximum for the year, currently £30,000, by the number of individuals who are liable to pay qualifying interest[3].

> Example
>
> In December 1989 Peter and Mary, who are cohabiting, agree to purchase a house jointly with Mary's friend Jill. Jill is to have exclusive use of a bedroom, a sitting room, and one of the two bathrooms. An additional room is to be converted for her exclusive use as a kitchen. All three borrow money to finance the purchase. The division is likely to be regarded as temporary, so there will be three sharers. Peter, Mary and Jill will therefore each have a loan limit of £10,000.

Each borrower is then entitled to tax relief for interest paid on a loan up to their sharer's limit, provided that the borrower actually pays the interest in respect of which he is claiming relief[4]. If cohabitees both have mortgage loans they therefore need to be particularly careful to ensure that each of them actually pays the interest due on their loan, or their share of the loan if it is a joint loan. If, in the above example, Peter were to pay the mortgage interest due on his and Mary's loans, he would get tax relief on a loan up to £10,000 but Mary would be entitled no relief, and Peter would be unable to claim it on her behalf. Only Mary is entitled to tax relief in respect of interest payments due on her loan, and she can only get tax relief if she can prove that she paid the relevant interest. Qualifying lenders under the MIRAS system have been instructed that, if they have reason to suspect that a qualifying borrower is not paying his share of the interest, a report should be made to the Revenue on form MIRAS 85[5]. In this respect cohabitees are in a worse position than a married couple, as a married couple can make an allocation of interest election transferring both interest payments and sharer's limit from one spouse to the other. However there is some evidence that the Revenue may be more interested in the mechanics of how interest is paid rather than in the substance of who is bearing the cost of paying it. Example 4 of a series of examples in guidance notes from the MIRAS Central Unit issued on 7th December 1989[6] reads:

---

1   ICTA 1988 s 356A(1).
2   ICTA 1988 s 356A(2).
3   ICTA 1988 s 356A(3).
4   ICTA 1988 s 356A(2).
5   Guidance notes on MIRAS relief issued by the MIRAS Central Policy Unit on 25th July 1988; see 1989-90 CCH *Tax Legislation* vol I p 3141.
6   See CCH [1990] Taxes 12.

'D and Mrs F Smith who previously lived at 120 High Street, Somewhere, jointly (on 1 December 1989) buy a house at 72 Good Road, Moneytown for £120,000 with a single borrower George Jones who previously lived at 125 High Street Somewhere. A loan of £117,000 is taken out with lender X on 1 December 1989.

Mrs F Smith is a housewife who does not work. She pays her share of the mortgage out of the housekeeping given to her by her husband.

Relief due:
D Smith — on £10,000 of loan (£117,000)
Mrs F Smith — on £10,000 of loan (£117,000)
G Jones — on £10,000 of loan (£117,000)'

The fact that Mrs Smith is a married woman does not appear material to the example, as under independent taxation husband and wife are treated separately for the purposes of mortgage interest relief, but with the right to make an allocation of interest election. No allocation of interest election has been made, or is relevant, in the example. Accordingly if cohabitees have a joint mortgage but one of them does not have sufficient income to pay her share of the mortgage payments it is important that the other gifts to her sufficient cash to enable her to pay her share of the mortgage, and that both cohabitees then pay their own liabilities. In this way maximum tax relief will be preserved, whereas part of it may be lost if one of the cohabitees simply pays the liability of both of them.

If the sharer's limit of each borrower is less than the outstanding loan of each borrower, then no adjustment can be made to the sharer's limits. Each borrower gets tax relief on interest computed applying the formula[1]:

$$\text{Total interest paid} \times \frac{\text{Sharer's limit}}{\text{Outstanding loan}}$$

However if the outstanding loan of one sharer is less than his sharer's limit, the limit is reduced to the amount of that sharer's loan[2], and the unused limit is reallocated to the other sharers[3]. If only one one other sharer has a loan in excess of the limit the unused balance is allocated to that sharer[4]. If two or more other sharers have loans in excess of their limits, the unused sharer's limit is allocated to them in proportion to their respective excesses[5].

Example

Continuing the example of Peter, Mary and Jill, assume that Peter takes out a loan of £50,000, Mary takes out a loan of £6,000 and Jill takes out a loan of £20,000. The initial sharer's limit of each is £10,000 but, as Mary only has a loan of £6,000, her limit will be reduced to £6,000, and the whole of the interest that she pays will qualify for tax relief. Peter has an excess loan over his £10,000 limit of £40,000, and Jill has an excess of £10,000. Accordingly Jill's £4,000 unused limit will be reallocated as follows:

1   ICTA 1988 s 356D(5).
2   ICTA 1988 s 356A(5)(a).
3   ICTA 1988 s 356A(5)(a).
4   ICTA 1988 s 356A(6).
5   ICTA 1988 s 356A(7) & (8).

	£	£		£
Peter	4,000 ×	$\dfrac{40,000}{50,000}$	=	3,200
Jill	4,000 ×	$\dfrac{10,000}{50,000}$	=	800

The qualifying interest of each will be computed:

		£
Peter	Total interest paid ×	$\dfrac{13,200}{50,000}$
Jill	Total interest paid ×	$\dfrac{10,800}{20,000}$

If there is a joint mortgage the total amount borrowed is allocated equally between the borrowers for mortgage interest relief purposes, subject to the right given to a married couple to elect for an unequal allocation[1]. For cohabitees this marks a significant change in the law in comparison with the pre-August 1988 system. Under the old system, where there was a joint loan for the purchase of a house as a main residence, or as job related accommodation, to persons other than husband and wife living together, the loan was apportioned to the borrowers in the ratio that interest paid by a borrower bore to the total interest paid on the loan[2]. This meant that cohabitees could effectively choose how to allocate tax relief for mortgage interest on a joint mortgage by varying the interest payments each of them actually made. Tax relief could then be directed to the cohabitee with the highest marginal rate of income tax. Under the new system each cohabitee will be deemed to have a loan of half the joint loan, and tax relief will be given to each on half the loan or their sharer's limit, whichever is the less. To gain this relief each cohabitee will have to show that he has made the interest payments for which he is claiming relief.

Under ICTA 1988 s 356D(10) it is provided that in determining whether the amount of a loan exceeds a sharer's limit no account is to be taken of so much (if any) of that limit as consists of interest which has been added to capital and which does not exceed £1,000. If there is a joint loan this £1,000 limit is a limit per borrower, and not an overall limit, so that if there are three joint borrowers the arrears can amount to £3,000 before s 356D(10) is excluded. A good illustration of this is provided in example 1 on arrears of interest added to a loan in guidance notes issued by the Revenue's MIRAS Central Policy Unit on 25th July 1988[3].

'Example

Joint loan of £29,700 taken out on 1/9/89 and shared equally between unmarried borrowers A, B and C. Each is entitled to a sharer's limit of £9,900. Unpaid arrears at 31/12/89 total £2,700. The sharer's limit in this case is extended to 3 × £10,800, ie the total relief due would be on a total loan of £32,400.'

1 ICTA 1988 s 356D(8).
2 ICTA 1988 s 357(3).
3 1989-90 CCH *Tax Legislation* vol I p 3142.

If the total arrears exceeded £3,000 the arrears which have been added to capital cannot be ignored, so that the sharer's limit of each of the three borrowers would be £10,000.

5.4 Mortgage interest relief for protected loans made before 1st August 1988

The restriction of mortgage interest relief to a residence basis does not apply to loans to sharers, other than husband and wife living together, if the loan was made before 1st August 1988[1] and on that date at least two sharers (other than husband and wife living together) were entitled to claim mortgage interest relief on a loan to purchase the same residence[2]. Each sharer will continue to qualify for mortgage interest relief on a per person basis so long as he continues to pay interest on the same loan *and* there continues to be at least one other person entitled to mortgage interest relief on the same residence. If at any time the house is occupied by a single sharer the new 'per residence' basis applies immediately, even if the loan was taken out before 1st August 1988. So long as there remains only one claimant, this has little practical effect as he will be entitled to a £30,000 loan limit. But if he should subsequently sell an interest in the house to another person who finances the purchase by mortgage and resides in the house as his main residence, each of borrowers will be subject to a £15,000 loan limit. However there is no withdrawal of relief for the original borrower provided that at all times the house has been occupied by two or more people paying interest under qualifying loans, even if the loan of the only other sharer was taken out on or after 1st August 1988. The new sharer's loan will, of course, be subject to his sharer's limit.

> Example
>
> Simon and Samantha cohabited in Bluebell Cottages, which they purchased in February 1988 with the aid of separate mortgages of £40,000 each. Both loans are protected loans, and a £30,000 loan limit is available to each. The relationship breaks down, and in May 1990 Samantha leaves selling her half share to James for £60,000, financed by a mortgage. Provided James moves into the house before, or at the same time as, Samantha moves out Simon will remain entitled to his protected loan limit of £30,000. James will, however, be under the new rules and so restricted to a sharer's limit of £15,000. If there is a gap in occupation Simon will lose tax relief on £15,000 of his loan, so timing is obviously crucial![3]

If a loan is a protected loan the provisions governing tax relief in respect of interest paid on it are contained in ICTA 1988 s 357. The maximum loan limit is £30,000 or the amount of the loan outstanding immediately before 1st August 1988, whichever is the less[4]. If a loan, although made on or after 1st August 1988, qualifies for relief because it resulted from

1   The date a loan was made is defined in ICTA 1988 s 356C(3).
2   ICTA 1988 s 356C(2).
3   For Revenue authority for this see Examples 1 and 2 on protected loans in guidance notes issued by the Revenue's MIRAS Central Policy Unit on 25th July 1988, 1989-90 CCH *Tax Legislation* vol I p 3139.
4   ICTA 1988 s 357(1B).

a written offer made before 1st August 1988 to defray money committed in pursuance of a binding contract made before that date[1], the amount of the loan on the date on which interest first becomes payable is deemed to be the amount of the loan immediately prior to 1st August 1988[2]. It is not intended that the £30,000 loan limit for protected loans should be increased in line with any general increase in the mortgage loan limit, and the protection will only continue so long as interest remains payable on the same loan.

As discussed in the previous section, joint loans to cohabitees for the purchase of a main residence are treated quite differently if they are protected loans in comparison with their treatment under the residence basis. For protected loans remaining under the old system a joint loan is apportioned between cohabitees in the proportions in which they actually pay interest on it[3]. This in turn appears to determine the amount of the loan of each of the cohabitees immediately before 1st August 1988.

Example

Fred and Sue, who are not married, purchased a house in 1987 with the aid of a joint endowment mortgage of £60,000. Interest is payable monthly on the 15th of the month. The interest payment for 15th July 1988 was £700 of which Fred paid £500 and Sue paid £200. The loans to each cohabitee immediately prior to 1st August 1988 are therefore deemed to be:

	£		£		£
Fred	60,000	×	$\dfrac{500}{700}$	=	42,857
Sue	60,000	×	$\dfrac{200}{700}$	=	17,143

The maximum loan limit for Fred and Sue is therefore permanently fixed at £30,000 and £17,143 respectively, and Sue has permanently lost £12,857 of her maximum £30,000 loan limit. Provided Fred continues to pay at least one half of the interest on the loan there will be no further loss of tax relief even if the ratio in which the cohabitees subsequently pay interest varies.

Once the loan limits at August 1st 1988 have been established, in determining whether that loan limit has been exceeded no account need be taken of unpaid interest which has been added to capital provided the amount added does not exceed £1,000[4]. For joint mortgages any arrears of interest will have to be allocated to the loan apportioned to each borrower, and the test applied separately to each borrower. Thus if arrears of interest allocated to a borrower do not exceed £1,000 and, ignoring those arrears, the borrower's outstanding loan does not exceed his limit, full tax relief will be given for interest paid on the loan, including interest paid on the arrears of interest.

As with loans on the residence basis, tax relief can only be claimed for interest which is actually paid, and interest is not paid if it is merely added to capital[5]. However the Revenue have recently announced that they are

1 See ICTA 1988 s 356C(3).
2 ICTA 1988 s 357(1C).
3 ICTA 1988 s 357(2).
4 ICTA 1988 s 357(6).
5 *Paton v IRC* (1938) 21 TC 626.

now prepared to accept that payment by way of a loan from the *same* lender which advanced the 'qualifying loan' will be regarded as payment by the borrower out of his own resources *even where* that payment is made direct from the second loan account to the qualifying loan account without it first going through the borrower's normal payment account. The second account from which the interest payment is being made must be kept independent from the qualifying account, and interest on the second account will never qualify for tax relief[1].

5.5 Cohabitees and tax relief under MIRAS

Cohabitees are entitled to tax relief under MIRAS in the same way, and to the same extent, as a married couple. The only complication that appears to arise is where there is a joint loan to cohabitees. ICTA 1988 s 373(6) provides:

> 'Where a loan on which interest is payable by the borrower was made jointly to the borrower and another person who is not the borrower's husband or wife, the interest on the loan is not relevant loan interest unless —
> (a)   each of the persons to whom the loan was made is a qualifying borrower; and
> (b)   in relation to each of them considered separately, the whole of that interest is relevant loan interest, in accordance with sections 370 to 372 and this section.'

The exclusion of a husband and wife is confined to a husband and wife who are living together[2], but is not affected by the change to independent taxation.

The exact application of this provision is not completely clear, and this lack of clarity can cause problems. Is the provision to be applied to the part of the loan which is apportioned to each cohabitee, or is it to be applied to the whole loan? For example, assume that cohabitees take out a joint loan of £20,000 for the purchase of a house for use as their main residence, and that the new residence basis applies. Each cohabitee will have a sharer's limit of £15,000. The whole of the interest on their own share qualifies for relief because their share of the loan does not exceed their sharer's limit. If this narrow interpretation of ICTA 1988 s 373(6) is correct MIRAS can be applied to give tax relief at source to payments of interest on the loan. But neither cohabitee could claim tax relief on the whole of the loan interest on a loan of £20,000 because this exceeds their respective sharer's limit and, although loans made after 5th April 1987 are now brought within the MIRAS system even if they exceed the limit[3], it is specifically provided that only so much of the interest that qualifies for tax relief is relevant loan interest[4]. The whole of the loan interest on the joint loan is therefore not relevant loan interest and the condition in s 373(6)(b) is not satisfied. Consequently MIRAS does not apply

1   Guidance notes from the Revenue MIRAS CPU, 7th December 1989, [1990] CCH Taxes 14.
2   ICTA 1988 s 373(7).
3   ICTA 1988 s 373(2).
4   ICTA 1988 s 373(5).

to the loan at all, interest must be paid gross, and tax relief claimed in a PAYE notice of coding or in an assessment. The same point applies to protected loans where the total loan exceeds £30,000. However it seems clear from the notes of guidance to MIRAS lenders issued by the Revenue's MIRAS Central Policy Unit that in practice these technical difficulties are ignored, and if MIRAS can be operated to give basic rate tax relief to cohabitees on a joint loan, then it will be operated, even if the loan apportioned to a cohabitee exceeds that cohabitee's sharer's limit, or the £30,000 limit if it is a protected loan[1]. MIRAS relief will, of course, be restricted to interest paid on so much of the loan as is within the limit.

5.6 Tax planning for cohabitees

With few exceptions the general principles set out in chapter 4 relating to tax planning for married couples are equally relevant for cohabitees. If one cohabitee is a higher rate taxpayer and the other is not, tax savings will result if income can be diverted from the higher income cohabitee to the lower income cohabitee. The same applies if one of the cohabitees is not working. There will be tax savings if sufficient income, which for 1990-91 must not include building society or bank interest, is transferred from one cohabitee to the other to cover the other cohabitee's personal allowance of £3,005. If there is a joint mortgage it is vital that each cohabitee pays their own share of the interest, as otherwise the cohabitee who does not pay will lose tax relief, and it will not be possible to transfer this relief to the other. This problem can be overcome by a cash gift to the non-working cohabitee, which she can then use to pay her share of the mortgage, with no loss of MIRAS relief.

Prior to changes made in the 1988 Finance Act, a simple tax planning technique for cohabitees was for one cohabitee to make a seven year deed of covenant in favour of the other. The covenant was effective to transfer income from one to the other for basic rate tax purposes only[2], but it was not effective for higher rate tax purposes as income paid under the covenant was deemed to be the donor's, and not the recipient's, for the purposes of any rate other than the basic rate[3]. It was therefore useful where one cohabitee had income less than her personal allowance, but it was of no assistance where one cohabitee was a higher rate taxpayer and the other was a basic rate taxpayer. The use of a deed of covenant was not available to transfer income from one spouse to the other. FA 1988 s 36 inserted a new ICTA 1988 s 347A which blocked the use of deeds of covenant for tax avoidance. Payments under a deed of covenant made on or after 15th March 1988 from one individual to another individual are neither tax deductible to the payer nor income of the recipient[4]. The new provisions do not apply to deeds of covenant made before 15th March 1988 provided particulars of the covenant were received by an inspector of taxes before

1 See eg example 6 of the guidance notes issued on 7th December 1989, [1990] CCH Taxes 12.
2 ICTA 1988 s 660(1).
3 ICTA 1988 s 683.
4 ICTA 1988 s 347A(1).

30th June 1988[1]. Payments under these covenants will continue to be tax deductible to the payer and income of the recipient for basic rate tax purposes only until the covenant expires[2]. To preserve this favourable tax treatment it is essential that the covenant is not varied in any way.

Apart from employment and partnership, where the principles for married couples and cohabitees are identical and have been discussed in chapter 4, effective tax planning for cohabitees is likely to involve the transfer of income producing assets from one cohabitee to the other. As for married couples, the major hurdle to be overcome is ICTA 1988 s 674A (inserted by FA 1989 ss 108 and 109) which treats income arising under a settlement as the settlor's for all income tax purposes unless, inter alia, it is income from property of which the settlor has divested himself absolutely under the settlement[3]. In one respect cohabitees have an advantage over married couples in the application of this section, because the provisions apply to income arising after 5th April 1990 under a settlement by one spouse in favour of the other irrespective of when the settlement was made. A settlement by one cohabitee on another is only caught by ICTA 1988 s 674A if the settlement is made on or after 14th March 1989[4]. Thus if prior to 14th March 1989 a cohabitee had the foresight to transfer assets into settlement under which the income from the assets was to be payable to his companion until they ceased to live together, the settlement remains effective for income tax purposes and the income will be taxed as income of the companion for basic rate purposes, although it is likely to remain taxable as income of the settlor for higher rate tax purposes by virtue of ICTA 1988 s 683[5].

For transfers on or after 15th March 1988 complete ownership of assets will have to be transferred if income from them is thereafter to be taxed as the income of the recipient cohabitee. In making such a transfer cohabitees are at a disadvantage in comparison with married couples, in that they will have to take into account the capital gains tax implications of the transfer, whereas a transfer of assets from one spouse to the other is exempt from CGT under CGTA 1979 s 44. A transfer of assets from one cohabitee to the other constitutes a disposal of the assets for capital gains tax purposes, and a chargeable gain will arise of the market value of the assets at the time of transfer, less their allowable cost plus indexation allowance. If, when added to chargeable gains on other disposals made by the transferor in the same tax year, the chargeable gain exceeds £5,000 capital gains tax will be payable at 25% or 40% of the excess, depending on the marginal income tax rate of the transferor. Careful planning is therefore needed to ensure that transfers from one cohabitee to the other do not result in the capital gains tax annual exempt amount being exceeded.

Cohabitees are in the same position as a married couple in relation to the stamp duty implications of any transfer of assets made to save income tax, as voluntary transfers are exempt from duty whoever makes the transfer provided the transfer contains a certificate in writing signed by the transferor

1   FA 1988 s 36(3) and (4).
2   Although the covenant is a settlement it escapes ICTA 1988 s 674A because it was made before 14th March 1989 and does not confer a benefit on the donor's spouse; s 674A(5).
3   ICTA 1988 s 674A(1)(d).
4   ICTA 1988 s 674A(5)(a).
5   See 4.4:1 above.

or his solicitor or other duly authorised agent specifying that the transfer
is is exempt from duty because it is a transfer of property operating as
a voluntary conveyance within category L of the Stamp Duty (Exempt
Instruments) Regulations 1987[1]. A transfer from one cohabitee to another
will be a potentially exempt transfer for inheritance tax purposes[2], so that
the death of the donor within seven years of the transfer will result in
all or part of the amount transferred being included as part of the donor's
estate. However for many cohabitees this possibility will be a risk worth
taking, and an insurance policy can be taken out if a potential liability
is large.

1 Stamp Duty (Exempt Instruments) Regulations 1987, SI 1987 No 516 para 3.
2 ITA 1984 s 3A.

CHAPTER 6

Children

6.1 Tax planning for children

Any tax planning for children must take account of a number of anti-avoidance provisions. These provisions are mainly contained in ICTA 1988 ss 660 to 685. Provisions of special relevance to arrangements for children are discussed in this chapter and the remaining provisions have been discussed briefly in 4.4:1 above. However it should be emphasised that the Revenue are likely to view with suspicion any arrangement designed to reduce an adult taxpayer's income by causing income to be transferred to a minor child, and any such arrangement needs to be carefully checked against all the settlement anti-avoidance provisions before being implemented.

The most important anti-avoidance provision is ICTA 1988 s 663 which provides that income from a settlement made by a parent on a child is deemed for income tax purposes to be the income of the parent, and not of the child, if, at the time of payment, the child is under 18 and unmarried[1]. Income imputed to a parent under ICTA 1988 s 663 is to be treated as the highest part of the parent's income[2], but if the income is trust income the parent is entitled to recover the tax he has to pay from the trustees[3]. The section does not apply if the total income received by the child does not exceed £5[4], or if the parent is not chargeable to United Kingdom income tax because he is a non-resident[5]. As from 1991-92 FA 1990 s 82 increases the £5 income limit to £100. This change will enable parents to deposit significant amounts of money in building society accounts in the name of their children without the interest credited being treated as income of the parent. Assuming the child's total income does not exceed his personal allowance it should be possible to have the interest credited gross. A child includes a stepchild, an adopted child, and an illegitimate child[6]. Thus the provisions apply equally to the children of cohabitees and the children of a married couple. Where a person with children divorces and remarries the children become stepchildren of the new spouse, irrespective of whether the other natural parent is still alive[7]. In this event a settlement by either of the natural parents or by the step-parent is covered by the provisions.

---

1 ICTA 1988 s 663(1).
2 ICTA 1988 s 667(3).
3 ICTA 1988 s 667(1).
4 ICTA 1988 s 663(4).
5 ICTA 1988 s 663(5).
6 ICTA 1988 ss 670 and 832(5).
7 *IRC v Russell* (1955) 36 TC 83.

Although the section is confined to income from 'settlements', 'settlement' is widely defined to include any disposition, trust, covenant, agreement, arrangement, or transfer of assets[1]. Thus it includes income derived from assets transferred into trust by a parent[2], and income derived from any arrangement made by a parent from which a child receives gratuitous benefit. However it is a defence that a payment was made to a child in pursuance of a bona fide commercial arrangement which does not contain an element of bounty[3].

In the most recent case, *Butler v Wildin*[4], Vinelott J held, on unusual facts, that once the Revenue had conceded that a child not born at the time of a settlement of shares in a family company, and not within the contemplation of the settlement, had paid full market value to acquire shares from her father, the transfer of the shares was not a settlement. If full market value was not paid a settlement arose under s 663. However he also warned against treating as if they were words in a statute the principle that there could be no settlement if there was no element of bounty. The facts of *Butler v Wildin* ultimately involved six children, of whom four were alive at the time the arrangements were made. Two brothers, one of whom was a chartered accountant and the other a surveyor, each had two children all of whom were under 18 at the relevant time. The brothers purchased an 'off-the-peg' company with a share capital of £100 divided into £1 shares. At the time of acquisition of the company the brothers had formed the view that land could be acquired from British Rail and profitably developed, and had started negotiations to this end. On acquisition of the company 19 shares were allocated to each child, and each child paid £19 for these shares using their own resources, money in a building society account provided by their grandparents. The parents acted as unpaid directors to the company, ran the business, and guaranteed loans made to it, and one of them made a £30,000 loan to it. The children's only risk was the possible loss of their £19 investment. Using borrowed funds, the company acquired the land and developed it. In somewhat artificial circumstances (it only had the cash to make the payment because the children lent it money) it paid an interim dividend of £84 per share. Tax repayment claims were made for the tax credits attaching to the dividends received by the children, but the Revenue resisted the claims on the grounds that the whole arrangement constituted a settlement within what is now ICTA 1988 s 663. One defence was that there was no settlement because the children had paid out of their own resources the full market value of the shares at the time they were alloted to them. The Special Commissioner held that this defence succeeded and further held that funds had not been provided by the brothers, so that the dividends received by the four children were not caught by s 663. In the High Court Vinelott J disagreed, and reversed the decision. Viewing the arrangement as a whole the parents had clearly provided bounty because they had borne all the risk and undertaken all the relevant work. The arrangement therefore

---

1 ICTA 1988 s 670.
2 *Hood-Barrs v IRC* (1967) 27 TC 385, CA; *Thomas v Marshall* (1953) 34 TC 178, HL.
3 *Copeman v Coleman* (1939) 22 TC 594; *Bulmer v IRC* (1966) 44 TC 1; *IRC v Plummer* (1979) 54 TC 1, HL: *Chinn v Collins* (1980) 54 TC 311, HL; *IRC v Levy* (1982) 56 TC 68; *Harvey v Sivyer* (1985) 58 TC 569; *Butler v Wildin* [1989] STC 22.
4 [1989] STC 22.

constituted a settlement as regards the four children who were alive when the arrangements were made, and the parents were parties to it.

A person is a settlor for the purposes of these provisions if he has actually made the settlement or if, directly or indirectly, he has provided funds for the settlement[1]. The application of this latter provision is well illustrated by the cases of *Copeman v Coleman*, above, and *Crossland v Hawkins*[2]. In *Copeman v Coleman* the taxpayer and his wife were controlling shareholders and directors of a family company. The company issued additional share capital in the form of twenty-five 10% preference shares of £200 each, of which only £10 was called. One share was issued to each of the taxpayer's two infant children, who paid the £10 for it out of their own funds. Subsequently the children received dividend income. The court held that the arrangement was a settlement and that the father had directly or indirectly provided funds for it. The dividend income was therefore taxable as his income. Similarly in *Crossland v Hawkins* the taxpayer entered into a contract with a service company to provide acting services for much less than their market value. The company resold his services at their market value. The taxpayer's father-in-law then settled £100 on trust for the taxpayer's infant children, and this fund was used to purchase shares in the service company. The court held that dividends paid by the service company to the trustees, which were then applied for the benefit of the taxpayer's children, must be taxed as income of the taxpayer. The creation of the service company, the service contract with the taxpayer, and the creation of the trust amounted to an 'arrangement' and the taxpayer had indirectly provided funds for the arrangement because profits from his work as an actor had been used to pay the dividends[3].

If more than one settlor is involved in the creation of a settlement, as was the case in *Butler v Wildin*, ICTA 1988 s 668 provides that the settlement shall have effect in relation to each settlor as if he were the only settlor[4]. Only income paid to a child of the settlor which is income from property originating from the settlor or income provided directly or indirectly by the settlor can be taxed as the settlor's income under ICTA 1988 s 663[5]. In *Butler v Wildin* the Special Commissioner appeared to consider that this section precluded the dividends paid by the company to the children from being taxed as income of the parent because they were not in any sense derived from income or property provided by the parent. However in the High Court Vinelott J considered this approach to be a fundamental misconception of ICTA s 668. He emphasised that s 668 is not a charging section; the charging section is ICTA s 663. If that section applies and there are two or more settlors, s 668 operates to attribute to each of them income which has been distributed.

It is not possible for a taxpayer to avoid ICTA 1988 s 663 by entering into a mutual arrangement with a friend under which the friend settles

---

1 ICTA 1988 s 670.
2 (1961) 39 TC 493.
3 See also *Mills v IRC* (1974) 49 TC 367, HL, where a similar arrangement was entered into by a child, and income distributed by the service company to the trustees to be held for her benefit was held taxable as the child's income under ITA 1952 s 405, subsequently ICTA 1970 s 447, and now ICTA 1988 s 673. See also *Butler v Wildin* above.
4 ICTA 1988 s 668(1).
5 ICTA 1988 s 668(2)(a) and (5).

property on a child of the taxpayer in return for the taxpayer making a similar settlement on a child of the friend. Under general law the reciprocal arrangements can be looked at as a whole and treated as one settlement[1], and under ICTA 1988 s 668(6)(a) income provided by the friend is to be treated as indirectly provided by the taxpayer.

6.2 Accumulation trusts

It is possible for a parent to create a tax effective trust for a minor child if he creates an accumulation trust. The mere fact that the trust requires an accumulation of income is not, of itself, sufficient, as under ICTA 1988 s 664(1) income which is being accumulated but to which a child will or may become entitled in the future is to be treated as current income of the child, and income of a discretionary trust which is not specifically allocated to a child is to be treated as divided equally between each of the children to or for the benefit of whom the income or assets representing it will or may become payable or applicable[2].

For an accumulation trust to be taken outside the anti-avoidance provisions the trust must both be an accumulation trust and additionally be an irrevocable trust[3]. It is a further requirement that funds provided by the settlor to create the trust must not be deductible to him for income tax purposes[4], although, with the withdrawal of tax relief for payments under deed of covenant, this requirement is unlikely to pose many problems now. The trust must satisfy the general law of irrevocability[5], and the statutorily-extended meaning of irrevocable in ICTA 1988 s 665. Of the general law approach to irrevocable Lord Greene MR in *Jenkins v IRC* said[6]:

> '... the distinction between a revocable and an irrevocable settlement is the veriest ABC in legal language; and nobody familiar with the language of lawyers, and in particular with those concerned with settlements, could have the slightest doubt, I should have thought, when finding the word "irrevocable" used in relation to a settlement, what that word was intended to mean. It seems to me quite illegitimate to take a word which has a technical and precise meaning in conveyancing and then argue that it has some extended meaning.'

In conveyancing terms a trust would not be irrevocable if a right is given to someone to bring the trust to an end, and one would normally expect that right to be contained in the terms of the trust.

The specially extended statutory definition of irrevocable is contained in ICTA 1988 s 665(1). A trust will not be deemed to be irrevocable if, under its terms:

(1)   the settlor or, during the settlor's life, his spouse, may derive any benefit from the settlement during the life of the settlor's child[7].

1   *IRC v Clarkson-Webb* (1933) 17 TC 451.
2   ICTA 1988 s 664(1)(b).
3   ICTA 1988 s 664(2).
4   ICTA 1988 s 664(2)(a).
5   *IRC v Warden* (1938) 22 TC 416; *Jenkins v IRC* (1944) 26 TC 265.
6   (1944) 26 TC 265 at 281.
7   ICTA 1988 s 665(1)(a).

Effectively, therefore, a clause should be inserted in the trust excluding the settlor and his spouse from any possible benefit under the trust;

(2) the trust may be determined by the act or fault of any person[1]. A trust which consists of shares in an existing family company of which the settlor retains control should not be caught by this provision merely because the settlor could use his control over the company to wind it up[2], although the position might be different if the creation of the company was intertwined with the creation of the trust[3]. However the trust may provide for determination if, on any determination, no benefit can be conferred during the life of the child on the settlor or his spouse[4];

(3) the settlor has to pay a penalty if he fails to comply with the provisions of the trust[5].

On the other hand a trust will not be deemed to be revocable merely because:

(1) the settlor or his spouse may benefit if the child becomes bankrupt, or assigns or charges his interest[6];

(2) the trust permits the property to be held on protective trusts under the Trustee Act 1925 s 33, unless the trust period is less than the life of the child or there is some special provision in the trust which would deprive the child of income were it payable to him absolutely during the trust period[7].

If a settlor does establish an irrevocable accumulation trust for his minor child, the income which is accumulated will not be taxed as income of the parent. Any income which is distributed to the minor child, for example to assist with his education, will be taxed as the parent's income, except to the extent that the distribution is greater than the total undistributed accumulated income[8]. It should be noted that there is no inherent objection to giving the trustees a power of maintenance. ICTA 1988 s 664 only protects income which is accumulated; it does not require all income to be accumulated.

To determine how the accumulated income is to be taxed a distinction must be drawn between a trust in which a child only has a contingent interest in accumulated income and a trust in which he has a vested interest. This distinction is taken from trust law, and upon it turns what is to happen to accumulated income if the child dies under the age at which he would be entitled to receive it.

6.2:1 Contingent accumulation trusts

If a child merely has a contingent interest in income and dies under age the accumulations will not form part of his estate, but will pass either

1   ICTA 1988 s 665(1)(b).
2   *Jenkins v IRC* (1944) 26 TC 265.
3   *Crossland v Hawkins* (1961) 39 TC 493.
4   ICTA 1988 s 665(2)(a) and (b).
5   ICTA 1988 s 665(1).
6   ICTA 1988 s 665(2)(a).
7   ICTA 1988 s 665(2)(c).
8   ICTA 1988 s 664(2)(b).

under the terms of the trust or, if undisposed of by the trust, will revert to the settlor or his estate. A simple illustration of a contingent accumulation trust is a settlement of property on a minor child A, currently aged 8, if he attains the age of 18, income in the meantime to be accumulated but with power to apply it for A's maintenance. If A dies under 18, then the property is to be held on trust for B absolutely. The income tax effect of such a trust is that the income accumulated during the child's minority is not his for tax purposes unless it is distributed to him under the power of maintenance, in which case it will be taxed as income of the parent if the parent is the settlor[1] and otherwise as income of the child. However any income which is accumulated will be taxable income of the trust, taxable at both the basic rate and the additional rate[2], a combined rate of 35% for 1990-91. Any chargeable capital gains realised by the trustees will also be taxed at 35%[3]. If the accumulated income is retained in the trust until the child reaches 18 there is no way of recovering this tax, as the right of the child on becoming 18 to relate the trust income back to the years it was accruing, set his personal allowances against it, and make repayment claims was abolished by FA 1969 s 11(5) in respect of tax paid in years of assessment after 1968/69.

In summary, where the settlor of a *contingent* accumulation trust for a minor child is the child's parent, such a trust will only be beneficial for income tax purposes if the parent's marginal rate of tax is greater than 35%, the rate of tax the income will bear in the trust, and the tax saving will be the difference between the two rates. As the top rate of income tax is now 40%, any tax savings are likely to be small. If the settlor is a person other than the child's parent the tax savings are likely to be greater if the income is actually distributed to a child under the power of maintenance. Any such distributions would be net of tax at 35%, but the grossed up income would be taxed as income of the child and not as income of the parent[4]. Assuming the child has no other taxable income, he can then set his personal allowance against the gross trust income and reclaim basic rate tax on income up to the single person's allowance of £3,005. Admittedly a sufficiently large distribution may result in a liability to higher rate tax, but with the 40% tax threshold currently only applying to taxable incomes of £20,700 or more, the occasions on which this happens are likely to be rare. Any tax liability is the liability of the child, but if he fails to pay, the parent becomes liable[5].

6.2:2 Vested accumulation trusts

If, instead of being given a contingent interest in the trust property, a minor child is given a vested interest, the income tax position appears to be quite different. If a child has a vested interest the trust law effect is that, if he dies under the age of 18, the trust assets and accumulated income form part of his estate for devolution purposes and do not pass under the trust. There is no trust law objection to establishing a trust of

1 ICTA 1988 s 664(2)(b).
2 ICTA 1988 s 686.
3 FA 1988 s 100.
4 ICTA 1988 s 687(2).
5 TMA 1970 s 73.

assets for a minor child absolutely, the trust income to be accumulated until the child reaches 18, capital and accumulated income then to be paid to him, and to be treated as his if he dies under that age. There is a rule of trust law, known as the rule in *Saunders v Vautier*[1], that if a trust beneficiary is *sui juris* and absolutely entitled to the trust capital he can call for the trust assets to be transferred to him, even if the settlement directs continued accumulation of the trust income, assuming such direction complies with the maximum accumulation periods set out in Law of Property Act 1925 s 164, as amended by the Perpetuities and Accumulations Act 1964 s 13. This rule, however, is only applicable if the trust beneficiary is of full age[2], and so could not be used by a minor child with a vested interest to demand payment of the trust capital to him. On attaining the age of 18 he would be entitled to insist that the trust assets should be transferred to him, even if the settlement required continued accumulation of income until, for example, the child attains 21. The practical likelihood of such a demand being made may not be great, as it presupposes that an 18 year old child has a sophisticated knowledge of trust law, or feels the need to employ his own professional advisers.

The income tax advantages of giving a child a vested interest in trust income appear considerable where the annual gross trust income is not so great as to be liable to higher rate tax if taxed as part of the child's income. It is suggested that, where a child has a vested interest in trust income, that income is the child's for income tax purposes, even though the income is being accumulated.

Authority for this view can be found in three cases, *Edwardes Jones v Down*[3], *Stanley v IRC*[4] and *IRC v Berrill*[5]. In *Edwardes Jones v Down* a grandparent settled shares on trust for an infant grandchild to accumulate the dividends during infancy, and to transfer both the shares and accumulated dividends to the child when she married or became 21. The High Court held that the child had a vested entitlement to the dividends from the commencement of the trust, so that the trustees could have made tax repayment claims on her behalf every year. As they had failed to make any claims until she attained her majority, they were restricted to claiming repayments of tax for the preceding six years.

In *Stanley v IRC* a father devised a vested life estate in certain property to his minor child. The will was silent as to what was to happen to the income from the property until the child came of age, but this omission was rectified by the Trustee Act 1925 s 31 which requires the income to be accumulated[6], except to the extent that it is used for the child's maintenance, education, or benefit[7]. If the infant currently has a vested interest in the trust capital and, on attaining the age of 18, becomes absolutely entitled to it, the accumulated income is to be held in trust for him absolutely[8], but where, as in *Stanley v IRC*, he only has a limited interest

1   (1841) Cr & Ph 240.
2   *Saunders v Vautier*, above; *Re Somech* [1957] Ch 165.
3   (1936) 20 TC 279.
4   (1944) 26 TC 12.
5   (1981) 58 TC 429. See also *Dale v Mitcalfe* (1927) 13 TC 41 at 55, per Sargant LJ.
6   Trustee Act 1925 s 31(2).
7   Trustee Act 1925 s 31(1).
8   Trustee Act 1925 s 31(2)(i)(b), (3).

in trust capital on attaining his majority, the Trustee Act 1925 s 31(2)(ii) provides that:

'... the trustees shall, notwithstanding that such person had a vested interest in such income, hold the accumulations as an accretion to the capital from which such accumulations arose, and as one fund with such capital for all purposes...'

The Crown claimed that the income being accumulated by the trustees during the child's minority constituted taxable income of the child, but the Court of Appeal held that the words quoted had changed the law to make the child's interest in accumulated income contingent rather than vested, and thus not his income for income tax purposes. However it was not doubted that, had the child had a vested interest in income, it would have been taxed as his income notwithstanding the accumulation. As Lord Greene MR said[1]:

'... By Sub-section (2) "total income" in relation to any person means "the total income of that person from all sources" estimated as there provided. Apart from any special provision in the instrument under which an infant derives his interest and apart from statutory provisions, an infant who has a vested interest in possession is the person entitled to the income. It is his income although he cannot give a good receipt for it. On his death under 21 [the then age of majority], income which has accumulated during his minority goes to his legal personal representatives. In such a case there can be no doubt that the income accruing during minority is the income of the infant. He is accordingly chargeable with Sur-tax in respect of it ... If, on the other hand, the infant is only entitled contingently on his attaining twenty-one he has no title to any income until that event takes place.'

The same point was made by Vinelott J in *IRC v Berrill*[2]. Under FA 1973 s 16(2)(b), now ICTA 1988 s 686(2)(b), additional rate tax is only imposed on trust income which is being accumulated if it 'is neither (before being distributed) the income of any person other than the trustees nor treated for any of the purposes of the Income Tax Acts as the income of a settlor.' Vinelott J said[3]:

'I accept [counsel for the Crown's] explanation of the reason for including these words. There are cases (although since 1925 they are comparatively rare) where, for instance, an infant has a vested interest in possession in settled property and the income so far as not paid to or applied for the maintenance or benefit of the infant falls to be accumulated but on his death before attaining full age the accumulations are payable to his or her personal representatives. In such cases, as Lord Greene MR pointed out in *Stanley v IRC* ..., the income formerly fell to be included in the infant's total income for surtax purposes and would now attract additional and higher rate tax as part of his or her total income. The words in para (b) "(before being distributed)" were necessary to exclude such income from the ambit of the charge in [s 686(1)] since such income would fall within para (a) (the trustees having a discretion as to payment of the income to or for the maintenance or benefit of the infant) and unless excluded from para (b) there would have been a

1 (1944) 26 TC 12 at 17.
2 (1981) 58 TC 429.
3 (1981) 58 TC 429 at 440.

double charge to additional rate tax under [s 686(1)] and as part of the infant's total income under [ICTA 1988 s 1].'

The creation of a trust under which a child has a vested interest in accumulated income is, at least potentially, particularly advantageous where the settlor is the child's parent. ICTA 1988 s 664(2) only requires an *irrevocable accumulation* trust to be created to ensure that the trust income is not to be treated as the income of the parent for income tax purposes. The section is silent on whether the child's interest in the trust must be vested or contingent. Although it is true that if the Trustee Act 1925 s 31 applies to the trust the objective of creating a vested interest in income may be defeated[1], the settlor is free to exclude the Trustee Act 1925 s 31[2], and an express direction in the trust instrument to accumulate income is evidence of an intention to exclude[3]. Similarly, in *Re Delamere's Settlement Trusts*[4] the Court of Appeal held that a direction to hold income in trust for the settlor's six infant grandchildren 'absolutely' evidenced a sufficient intention to exclude s 31[5]. As the effect of the exclusion of the Trustee Act 1925 s 31 is to delete the statutory power of maintenance, it will be necessary to insert an express power of maintenance in the deed of trust. The direction to accumulate should not preclude the statutory power of advancement in the Trustee Act s 32[6].

Applying these principles it ought to be possible to construct a trust under which a parent settles assets of a value of, say, £50,000 on trust for his minor child absolutely, the income to be accumulated until the child reaches 18, but where the child is to have a vested interest in the accumulations. The trustees must be given an express power to apply any of the accumulated income for the maintenance, education, or benefit of the child, and there will have to be a clause excluding the settlor, and any spouse of the settlor, from any possible benefit under the trust. The transfer into trust must completely dispose of the settlor's interest in the property, as otherwise income from the assets transferred would be taxed as income of the settlor under ICTA 1988 s 674A. As the whole of the trust assets and accumulated income are to be paid to the child at 18, it would be unwise to put more into the trust than the parent considers the child can be entrusted to handle at that age. There is no objection to postponing distribution to a later age, say 21, but, because of the rule in *Saunders v Vautier*[7], any such postponement cannot prevent the child from claiming the trust assets at age 18.

The income tax effect of such a trust should be that, even though the income is accumulated by the trustees, it is the child's for income tax purposes[8]. It cannot be deemed to be the income of the parent because it is being accumulated under an irrevocable trust within ICTA 1988 s 664(2),

1   *Stanley v IRC* (1944) 26 TC 12.
2   Trustee Act 1925 s 69(2) and *Re Turner's Will Trusts* [1937] Ch 15.
3   *Re Stapleton* [1946] 1 All ER 323; *Re Ransome's Will Trusts* [1957] Ch 348.
4   [1984] 1 All ER 584.
5   Cf *Swales v IRC* [1984] STC 413 where s 31 was held to apply, to the considerable advantage of the taxpayer.
6   *IRC v Bernstein* (1960) 39 TC 391 at 404 per Harman LJ, although on the special facts of this case the statutory power of advancement was also held to be excluded.
7   (1841) Cr & Ph 240.
8   *Stanley v IRC*; *IRC v Berrill*.

and it is not being paid out to the child so as to be caught by ICTA 1988 s 664(2)(b). Any income which is in fact paid to the child, or for his benefit, under the express power of maintenance will be taxed as income of the parent[1]. The trustees will pay income tax at the basic rate only[2] on the gross trust income, but will then issue a certificate to the child beneficiary, or his parent on his behalf, to include the gross trust income in his total income. If he has no other income, and provided the trust income is not so high as to render him liable to higher rate tax, he can reclaim income tax at the basic rate on so much of the gross trust income as is covered by his personal allowance.

There is some doubt as to how such a trust would be treated for inheritance tax purposes. The inheritance tax legislation draws a sharp distinction between the tax treatment of trusts where there is an interest in possession and trusts where there is no such interest, and the leading case on the meaning of 'interest in possession' is the House of Lords decision in *Pearson v IRC*[3]. In *Pearson v IRC*, under a trust created in 1964, the settlor settled a trust fund on such one or more of his children and their issue as the trustees should appoint during a stated period defined to comply with the rule against perpetuities. Pending such appointment, and in the events that happened, the trustees were to accumulate so much (if any) of the income of the trust fund as they saw fit during a permitted accumulation period of 21 years from the creation of the trust. To the extent that the income was not accumulated it was to be divided equally between the settlor's three daughters, who were all over the age of majority. In fact all the income was accumulated. The issue was whether the daughters had an interest in possession in the trust property, and the House of Lords held, by a 3-2 majority, that they had not. The majority held that a person only has an interest in possession for inheritance tax purposes (the tax was then called capital transfer tax) if he is currently entitled to the trust income, and that a right to enjoy income subject to a power given to the trustees to accumulate it is not such a right. Whether or not there is an interest in possession depends on whether the beneficiary has a present right to the income.

It is not completely clear that the same principle would apply if the only thing preventing the current enjoyment of income is the inability of a minor child to give a valid receipt. The reasoning in *Pearson*, particularly the judgment of Lord Keith, suggests that the child does not have an interest in possession in these circumstances. However it is not unarguable that the position should be different where a minor child has a vested entitlement to income, and the doubt is highlighted in the original Revenue statement on their interpretation of the meaning of 'interest in possession', subsequently confirmed as basically correct by *Pearson v IRC*, which read in part[4]:

> 'An interest in possession in settled property exists where the person having the interest has the immediate entitlement (subject to any prior claim by the trustees for expenses or other outgoings properly payable out of income) to any income produced by that property as the income arises; but that a discretion

1 ICTA 1988 s 664(2)(b).
2 *IRC v Berrill*.
3 [1981] AC 753.
4 [1976] British Tax Review 418.

or power, in whatever form, which can be exercised after income arises so as to withhold it from that person negatives the existence of an interest in possession. For this purpose a power to accumulate income is regarded as a power to withhold it, *unless any accumulations must be held solely for the person having the interest or his personal representatives.*'[1]

If the correct view is that a child beneficiary of a vested accumulation trust does not have an interest in possession for inheritance tax purposes then (a) the trust assets will not be part of the child's estate for inheritance tax purposes if he dies under age, and (b) it will be possible to take advantage of the accumulation and maintenance trust provisions in ITA 1984 s 71[2], so that there will be no ten year charge, and no charge when the child becomes 18.

If the correct view is that the child does have an interest in possession, then the provisions relating to accumulation and maintenance trusts cannot apply. If the child dies under age the trust assets will form part of his estate[3] but, provided the total net estate does not exceed £128,000[4], no inheritance tax will be chargeable. If the child survives to 18 no inheritance tax charge can arise, as the child is treated throughout as the owner of the underlying assets[5]. Whichever approach is correct, an accumulation trust should cause few inheritance tax problems where the trust assets are valued at less than £128,000 and the settlor has made no prior transfers which have to enter into cumulation.

Potentially, therefore, a small accumulation trust for a minor child in which the child has a vested interest, rather than a contingent interest, appears to have considerable attractions from a tax viewpoint. It ensures that the income is taxed as the child's, rather than the parent's or the trust's, thus enabling maximum advantage to be taken of the child's personal allowance and basic rate band.

6.2:3 Accumulation and maintenance trusts and inheritance tax
Although, as indicated above, there may still be some doubt as to whether a trust in which a child has a vested interest in income can qualify as a trust in which there is no interest in possession for the purposes of the special inheritance tax provisions relating to accumulation and maintenance trusts, there is no doubt that a trust in which a child has a contingent interest, or is a discretionary beneficiary, does qualify. As the relief given to accumulation and maintenance trusts can be a useful source of inheritance tax planning for children, the provisions relating to such trusts are considered here.

The qualifying conditions for an accumulation and maintenance trust are now set out in ITA 1984 s 71. The primary requirements are that one or more beneficiaries *must*, on or before attaining an age not exceeding 25, become beneficially entitled to the trust property, *or to an interest in possession in it*[6], and no interest in possession currently subsists in the

1   Author's italics.
2   See **6.2:3** below.
3   ITA 1984 s 49(1) and s 4.
4   ITA 1984 Sch 1.
5   ITA 1984 s 53(2).
6   ITA 1984 s 71(1)(a).

trust, and the trust income is to be accumulated so far as not applied for the maintenance, education or benefit of a beneficiary[1]. A power given to trustees to revoke an accumulation and maintenance trust will preclude the trust from qualifying, although the mere inclusion of a power of advancement will not do so[2]. To prevent accumulation and maintenance trusts lasting too long, it is further provided in ITA 1984 s 71(2) that not more than twenty-five years must have elapsed since the start of the trust or, if later, the time the trust would otherwise have qualified as an accumulation and maintenance trust[3]. If the trust satisfied the requirements for an accumulation and maintenance trust on 15th April 1976 the twenty-five year period runs from that date[4], so that the trust will continue to qualify until 15th April 2,001. As an alternative to the twenty-five year rule, everyone who is or has been a trust beneficiary must have been either[5]:

(1)   the grandchildren of a common grandparent; or
(2)   children, widows or widowers of such grandchildren who died below the age when they would have taken a qualifying interest in the property.

'Children' include illegitimate children, adopted children, and stepchildren[6]. If the trust was created before 15th April 1976 it is sufficient if the conditions were satisfied on that date[7].

It will be noted that it is only necessary for a child to take an *interest in possession* in the trust property before he attains the age of 25 for the trust to qualify as an accumulation and maintenance trust. It is therefore possible to postpone the vesting of capital to a much later age. For example, provided all children become entitled to the trust income on attaining the age of 18, the trust qualifies, even if the trust provides that a child shall only be entitled to his share of the trust capital if he attains the age of 30[8]. However, if the child dies between 18 and 30, his share of the trust assets will be treated as part of his estate for inheritance tax purposes despite that fact that his death under 30 deprives his estate of any entitlement to trust capital.

An application of this principle is illustrated by the Trustee Act 1925 s 31, which has already been referred to in **6.2:2** above. This section applies where property is being held in trust for a minor, whether the minor has a vested or contingent interest in trust capital, where the trust contains no express provision directing trust income to be accumulated, and does not otherwise exclude the Trustee Act 1925 s 31. For dispositions *made* on or after 1st January 1970 the relevant age for the purposes of the section is 18; for dispositions made before that date the relevant age remains 21[9]. The Trustee Act 1925 s 31(1) gives the trustees power to pay maintenance for a child beneficiary during his minority, and sub-s(2) directs that income

---

1 ITA 1984 s 71(1)(b).
2 *Lord Inglewood v IRC* [1983] STC 133.
3 ITA 1984 s 71(2)(a).
4 ITA 1984 s 71(6).
5 ITA 1984 s 71(2)(b).
6 ITA 1984 s 71(8).
7 ITA 1984 s 71(8).
8 There are now CGT problems with this type of trust, see **6.2:4** below.
9 Family Law Reform Act 1969 s 1(2)(b).

not required for maintenance shall be accumulated. Section 31(1)(ii) provides:

> 'if such person on attaining the age of eighteen [21 for pre 1970 dispositions] has not a vested interest in such income, the trustees shall thenceforth pay the income of that property and of any accretion thereto under sub-section (2) of this section to him, until he either attains a vested interest or dies, or until failure of his interest.'

The effect of this provision is that if, for example, property is devised to A, a minor, contingently on his reaching the age of 30, the income, in so far as it is not applied for his maintenance, must be accumulated until he is 18, but thereafter all income must be paid to him. For inheritance tax purposes the effect is that there is no interest in possession in the trust property until the child becomes 18[1], but thereafter A has an interest in possession even though he may never become entitled to trust capital. This is the view of s 31 taken by the Revenue[2] and is supported by *Re Jones' Will Trusts*[3]. In this case a testatrix had left her residuary estate in trust for her nephew contingently on his attaining 25. The nephew was killed in action when he was over 21 but under 25. Estate duty would have been avoided if it had been established that he did not have an interest in possession in the property. The judge held, however, that the effect of the Trustee Act 1925 s 31 was that he was entitled to the whole of the trust income at the time of his death and he therefore had an interest in possession. Similarly in *Swales v IRC*[4] Nicholls J held that, if the Trustee Act 1925 s 31(1)(ii) applied, its effect was to give the beneficiary entitled to the trust property an interest in possession in the trust property, so that there was no capital transfer tax charge when she later acquired a vested entitlement to the trust capital.

Although the settlor can exclude Trustee Act 1925 s 31[5], it should be remembered that there are limitations on the maximum period for which accumulation of income may be directed or permitted. The limits are listed as a number of alternatives by the Law of Property Act 1925 s 164 as amended by the Perpetuities and Accumulations Act 1964 s 13. Where a gift is by will the effect of these limitations is that an accumulation period cannot last for more than twenty-one years. Where the gift is inter-vivos the life of the settlor is a permitted period, and this may obviously last longer than twenty-one years. The restrictions apply whether there is a power to accumulate, as in *Pearson v IRC*, or where a will or gift inter-vivos effectively directs accumulation, eg *Re Rochford's Settlement Trusts*[6]. Where a direction to accumulate is given which cannot exceed the perpetuity period (life or lives in being plus twenty-one years) but does exceed the accumulation period, it is valid until the end of the period and then becomes void. In those circumstances the court chooses a permitted accumulation period which appears to approximate most closely to what the testator intended and directs accumulation for that period[7]. At the end of the period the

---

1 *Pearson v IRC* [1981] AC 753.
2 Press release 24th September 1975, [1975] British Tax Review 436.
3 [1947] Ch 48.
4 [1984] STC 413.
5 Trustee Act 1925 s 69(2); *Re Turner's Will Trusts* [1937] Ch 15.
6 [1965] Ch 111.
7 *Re Ransome's Will Trusts* [1957] Ch 348.

income from the property must be distributed even though no-one is yet entitled to the capital. If the trust beneficiary has a vested interest in the capital he will be entitled to the income. Otherwise it will go to the person entitled to residue or, if residue is directed to be accumulated or is undisposed of, to the next-of-kin as on intestacy[1]. The application of these principles may cause a trust for a minor child to comply with the statutory requirements of an accumulation and maintenance trust for inheritance tax purposes.

It should be noted that it is not a pre-condition of the inheritance tax provisions relating to accumulation and maintenance trusts that the shares of the trust beneficiaries should be predetermined at the outset. Thus if a settlor is establishing an accumulation trust for a number of minor children, it is permissible to leave the trustees a discretion as to the shares in trust capital the children are to take until each of them in turn becomes entitled to an interest in possession, which must not be at an age over 25. This possibility of the use of a discretionary trust may be of assistance where it is unclear when the trust is created which children are likely to use substantial transfers of capital wisely. There is no objection to a child being given an interest on protective trust[2].

If an accumulation and maintenance trust is created which complies with ITA 1984 s 71 the transfer of assets into the trust is a potentially exempt transfer, so that there will be no inheritance tax charge provided the settlor survives for seven years after the transfer[3]. There is no ten year charge on the assets while they remain in the trust. There is also no exit charge on a distribution of trust assets, or the termination of the trust, in favour of a beneficiary who has become entitled to, or to an interest in possession in, the trust property on attaining the specified age, or dying under that age[4]. In general there will be an inheritance tax charge if trust property in an accumulation and maintenance trust ceases to be subject to the trust, or there is a distribution which reduces the value of the trust other than a distribution which is exempt under ITA 1984 s 71(4)[5]. There is no charge if the distribution is to cover administration expenses[6], or if the distribution constitutes taxable income of someone[7], or in certain other limited circumstances set out in ITA 1984 s 70(4)[8]. If there is a charge the value transferred is the reduction in value of the trust property[9] grossed up by the inheritance tax payable if this is borne by the trust[10]. This value is then taxed at special rates, which are[11]:

(a)   0.25% for each of the first forty complete successive quarters in the relevant period;

1 See eg R H Maudsley *The Modern Law of Perpetuities* (1979) and *Brotherton v IRC* (1977) 52 TC 137.
2 ITA 1984 s 88. For problems with an earlier version of this subsection see *Egerton v IRC* [1983] STC 531.
3 ITA 1984 s 3A(1)(c), (3) and (4).
4 ITA 1984 s 71(4).
5 ITA 1984 s 71(3).
6 ITA 1984 ss 70(3)(a) and 71(5).
7 ITA 1984 ss 70(3)(b) adn 71(5).
8 As applied by ITA 1984 s 71(5).
9 ITA 1984 s 70(5)(a).
10 ITA 1984 s 70(5)(b).
11 ITA 1984 s 70(6).

(*b*)   0.20% for each of the next forty;
(*c*)   0.15% for each of the next forty;
(*d*)   0.10% for each of the next forty;
(*e*)   0.05% for each of the next forty.

The relevant period commences on the day the accumulation and maintenance trust was established, or the relevant property was added to it, or 13th March 1975, whichever is the later[1].

Accumulation and maintenance trusts provide a useful method of protecting assets from inheritance tax while leaving the final entitlement to those assets in suspense for a substantial period of time. Effectively the assets are exempt from inheritance tax from the time they leave the settlor, assuming he survives for seven years, until after they have vested absolutely in the child beneficiary. However the inheritance tax advantages must be weighed against the possible income tax disadvantages of such a trust discussed in the preceding section and the capital gains tax difficulties discussed in the following section when deciding whether, overall, an accumulation and maintenance trust is beneficial.

6.2:4 Accumulation trusts and capital gains tax

Prior to changes made in the Finance Act 1989 accumulation and maintenance trusts were also very tax-efficient for capital gains tax, because advantage could be taken of the roll-over relief for gifts in FA 1980 s 79 to defer any charge to capital gains tax when the assets were transferred into the trust[2], and roll-over relief was also available when the beneficiary became absolutely entitled as against the trustees to the trust assets[3]. The withdrawal of gifts roll-over relief for assets other than business assets, including shares in unqoted companies (see **3.10** above), has severe implications for accumulation and maintenance trusts. A new CGTA 1979 s 147A continues to provide gifts roll-over relief where the transfer results in an immediate charge to inheritance tax. This is sufficient to cover transfers both into and out of discretionary trusts[4], but it does not cover transfers into an accumulation and maintenance trust, because such transfers are potentially exempt transfers by virtue of ITA 1984 s 3A(3). The creation of an accumulation and maintenance trust therefore now results in a disposal of the assets by the settlor at their market value at the time of the transfer into trust[5]. The assets are then deemed to be acquired by the trustees at this value[6].

As originally drafted CGTA 1979 s 147A would also have denied gifts roll-over relief when the assets were transferred out of the trust to a beneficiary, as this transfer will normally be exempt from an inheritance tax charge by virtue of ITA 1984 s 71. This was thought to be particularly unfair for accumulation and maintenance settlements which had been established on the basis of the law as it existed before the Finance Bill 1989, but which were now impossible to unravel. An amendment was

---

1   ITA 1984 ss 70(8) and 71(5).
2   FA 1980 s 79(1) with FA 1982 s 82(1).
3   FA 1982 s 82(1).
4   See **3.10** above.
5   The settlor and the trustees are connected persons for CGT; CGTA 1979 s 63(3).
6   CGTA 1979 ss 62(2) and 29A.

therefore made during the passage of the Finance Bill through Parliament. CGTA 1979 s 147A(2)(d) provides that roll-over relief will be available on a transfer out of trust if the transfer is exempt from inheritance tax under ITA 1984 s 71(4). In the absence of s 71(4) an inheritance tax charge would arise on a beneficiary becoming entitled to the trust assets on attaining the specified age or becoming entitled to an interest in possession in the trust assets. Only the former event is also a chargeable disposal for capital gains tax. Thus if, as not uncommonly happens, an accumulation and maintenance trust is established for a child, with the child entitled to the assets when he reaches twenty-five, but entitled to the income from the assets when he reaches 18, ITA 1984 s 71(4) operates to preclude the charge that would otherwise arise under ITA 1984 s 71(3) when the child attains an interest in possession in the trust assets on reaching 18. This event gives rise to no capital gains tax consequences. On the child reaching 25 there is a deemed disposal of the trust assets for capital gains tax because a trust beneficiary has now become absolutely entitled as against the trustees to the trust assets[1]. The transfer of assets from the trustees to the beneficiary when he attains twenty five is exempt from inheritance tax, but it is exempt by virtue of ITA s 53(2), not s 71(4). Accordingly, as the transfer is not a chargeable transfer for inheritance tax and is not exempt by virtue of ITA 1984 s 71(4), the CGT relief in CGTA 1979 s 147A does not apply, and the trustees will be chargeable to capital gains tax on the basis that they made a disposal of the trust assets on the day the beneficiary became twenty five, and so entitled to the trust assets as against the trustees. As the trust is by this stage neither an accumulation trust nor a discretionary trust within FA 1988 s 100, the rate of CGT will be 25%[2]. At a meeting between the English and Scottish Law Societies on 14th June 1989 the Revenue confirmed that the denial of roll-over relief in these circumstances was intentional, although the matter would be looked at again as part of a general review of the taxation of trusts which was currently taking place[3].

In summary, assets transferred into an accumulation and maintenance trust will often be subject to a CGT charge both when they are put into the settlement and when they emerge from it. With capital gains tax at either 25% or 40%, depending on the settlor's income, when the trust is created, and 25% when the child becomes entitled to the trust property, this may be a significant disincentive to the creation of such trusts. These disadvantages do not apply if the assets transferred into trust are business assets, which include shares in a family trading company. Roll-over relief, both into and out of a trust, continues to be available under CGTA 1979 s 126 and Sch 4 (see **3.10** above), and an accumulation and maintenance trust remains an attractive option for these assets.

---

1   CGTA 1979 s 54.
2   FA 1988 s 98(1).
3   Paras 15 and 16 of the 'Notes of Meeting' published by the Law Society obtainable from the office of the Legal Practice Directorate, 50 Chancery Lane, London WC2A 1SX.

6.3 Transfer of resources to children over 18

The settlement anti-avoidance provisions in ICTA 1988 s 663 only apply where payments out of a trust are made to a child of the settlor when the child is under 18. They do not apply to payments made once the child has reached 18, and they do not apply if the settlor was someone other than the child's parent, eg a grandparent, whatever the age of the child when the payments are made. Unfortunately other anti-avoidance provisions have recently been enacted to prevent excessive advantage being taken of these loopholes.

Prior to FA 1988 a common tax planning device was for a parent to enter into a seven year deed of covenant to make annual payments to his child, who had to be over 18 to avoid ICTA 1988 s 663, of an amount not exceeding the child's personal allowance for the year. This was a popular method of funding the parental contribution of students in higher education, as the covenant was only required to be capable of lasting for more than six years, so that a covenant which was to last for seven years or as long as the child continued in higher education, whichever should be the shorter, satisfied the requirement. The principle applied equally to deeds of covenant by grandparents to minor children. Payments made under the deed of covenant were tax deductible to the payer for basic rate tax purposes only[1], and were income of the child. So long as the gross amount covenanted, when added to any other income, did not exceed the child's personal allowance for the year, income tax withheld from the covenanted payments could be reclaimed by the child. The practical effect was to convert income which would otherwise have been taxed at the basic rate into tax free income.

FA 1988 s 36 inserted a new ICTA 1988 s 347A which, with limited exceptions not presently relevant, enacts that an annual payment made by an individual which would otherwise be taxable under Sch D case III shall neither be deductible to the payer nor be taxable income of the recipient. The new provisions apply to payments made on or after 15th March 1988 unless they are due under a deed executed before that date details of which were provided to the inspector before 1st July 1988[2]. Payments under deeds of covenant which satisfy this requirement continue to attract tax relief at the basic rate until the legal liability to make the payments ceases. In this connection it should be noted that the Revenue take the view that, if two alternative durations are specified for the duration of a covenant without the addition of the words 'whichever is the later', the legal obligation to make the payments terminates on the happening of the earlier event[3]. Thus if, before 15th March 1988, a parent had entered into a covenant to make annual payments to his child for seven years or until the child ceased higher education, the legal obligation to make the payments, and hence the tax relief, terminates once the child ceases to be in higher education if that is before the end of the seven year period. It is irrelevant whether or not the parent in fact continues to make the payments. Parents of children in higher education are protected to some extent from the impact of these

1 ICTA 1988 s 683.
2 FA 1988 s 36(3) and (4).
3 See the Family Division *Practice Direction* on school fees, June 1987, [1987] 2 All ER 1084.

changes provided their child is entitled to at least some means-tested grant above the minimum grant, as the parental contribution has been reduced, and the grant increased, by the tax relief to which the parent would have been entitled if he had paid his parental contribution under deed of covenant[1].

With the abolition of tax relief for deeds of covenant, the next tax planning technique developed was the transfer of income-producing assets into trust for the benefit of a child over 18 for a specified period which had to be capable of lasting for more than six years[2], for example for seven years or until the child finished higher education. Thereafter the assets reverted to the parent. This was not caught by ICTA s 347A since the parent was making no payments and, although the parent had retained an interest in the trust property so that ICTA 1988 s 673 applied, this had no adverse consequences, as s 673 only taxes as income of the settlor trust income which has not been distributed. Here all the trust income was distributed to the child. The trust income was therefore taxed as the income of the child for basic rate income tax purposes and not as the income of the parent. For higher rate income tax purposes it remained the income of the parent by virtue of ICTA 1988 s 683. To counteract this FA 1989 s 109 inserted ICTA 1988 s 674A, which has been considered in detail in **4.4:1** above. This section provides that income from a settlement remains taxable as the settlor's income unless, inter alia, he has divested himself absolutely of the settlement property. The trust outlined above would not satisfy this requirement. Again, apart from settlements by one spouse on the other, ICTA 1988 s 674A is not retrospective, so that trusts established before 14th March 1989 continue to attract favourable tax treatment until they expire.

To divert income from a parent to a child over 18 it is therefore now necessary for the parent to divest himself absolutely of the ownership of the income and the underlying assets. This may either be done by way of outright gift to the child or it may be done by the creation of a trust in which the child has a limited interest with the remainder going to someone other than the settlor or his spouse. In this respect cohabitees may be in a better position than a married couple, as a settlement by a cohabitee of property on trust for his 18 year old child for 7 years or so long as the child is in higher education, whichever is the shorter, remainder to the other cohabitee, should be effective for tax purposes. As an additional benefit, since the settlor has divested himself absolutely of the trust property, the income from the trust assets will not be taxed as his income for higher rate tax purposes[3].

6.4 Commercial arrangements for children

Where a parent is self-employed it may be possible to employ a child in the business and pay him or her a wage. The wage should then be tax deductible in computing the profits of the business and be taxable income of the child. The effect is to turn income which would have been taxed

1 The Education (Mandatory Awards) Regulations 1989 (SI 1989 No 1458) Sch 3 para 4(2).
2 To avoid ICTA 1988 s 660.
3 ICTA 1988 s 683(1)(d).

at the parent's top marginal rate of income tax into tax free income up to the child's personal allowance, and to reduce the rate of tax to the basic rate if the child's personal allowance is exceeded, assuming that the child does not become liable to higher rate tax. However a number of pitfalls need to be avoided. First, it is illegal to employ children under the age of 13[1], although local authority bye-laws may permit the relaxation of this rule in certain cases. Although illegality will not of itself preclude a tax deduction of wages paid to an under-age child, it was a factor taken into consideration by the General Commissioners in *Dollar v Lyon*[2] when they held that sums paid to, or applied for the benefit of, the children of a farmer were paid as pocket money and not as wages, and the High Court refused to interfere. Second, a business can only claim a deduction for expenditure if it is established that the expenditure is incurred wholly and exclusively for the purposes of the business[3]. If expenditure on wages is excessive, that portion of the wages which is excessive will be disallowed[4]. It is considered that, where a child is under 18, wages paid ought not to be disallowed solely by virtue of ICTA 1988 s 663, as there is authority that the settlement anti-avoidance provisions do not apply to payments made in pursuance of a bona fide commercial arrangement which does not contain an element of bounty[5].

An alternative to employing a child is to take him or her into partnership, but where the child is still a minor it may be difficult to satisfy the courts that the child is a genuine partner. The mere fact that a child is named as a partner in the partnership agreement does not necessarily mean that he is a partner[6]. Thus, for example, in *Alexander Bulloch & Co v IRC*[7] a deed of partnership purported to bring two children aged 17 and 18 into partnership in an off-licence business. After the execution of the partnership deed both children did routine work at one of the shops, but continued at school, drew no salary and received only pocket money. The Appeal Commissioners held that they were not partners for the relevant tax year, and the High Court refused to interfere[8]. In practice it may be extremely difficult to persuade a court that young children are genuine partners in a business, even if so called in a partnership deed. Where the children are under 18 and the other partners are their parents it may also be possible for the Revenue to achieve the same result by applying ICTA 1988 s 663. If the children are held not to be genuine partners then for income tax purposes the total partnership profits will be divided between the remaining partners in the remaining partners' profit sharing ratio. If the children are held to be genuine partners, then they will be taxed in their own right

1　Children and Young Persons Act 1933 s 18 as amended by the Children and Young Persons Act 1963 s 34.
2　(1981) 54 TC 459.
3　ICTA 1988 s 74(a).
4　*Copeman v William Flood & Sons Ltd* (1941) 24 TC 53, discussed in detail in **4.2** above. See also *Stott and Ingham v Trehearne* (1924) 9 TC 69.
5　*Copeman v Coleman* (1939) 22 TC 594; *Bulmer v IRC* (1966) 44 TC 1; *IRC v Plummer* (1979) 54 TC 1; *Chinn v Collins* (1980) 54 TC 311; *IRC v Levy* (1982) 56 TC 68; *Harvey v Sivyer* (1985) 58 TC 569; *Butler v Wildin* [1989] STC 22.
6　*IRC v Williamson* (1928) 14 TC 335 at 340, per Lord President Clyde.
7　(1976) 51 TC 563.
8　See also *IRC v Williamson*; *Dickenson v Gross* (1927) 11 TC 614; *Waddington v O'Callaghan* (1931) 16 TC 187.

on their share of the partnership profits, which can have very beneficial tax consequences in spreading income round the family.

6.5 Child care expenses

Expenditure incurred in employing a home help to look after children is disallowable for income tax purposes where the taxpayer is an employee, even if the expenditure is essential to enable the employee to go to work[1]. The expenditure is not incurred 'in' the performance of the taxpayer's duties, as required by ICTA 1988 s 198. Although the self-employed only have to satisfy the less rigorous requirement that the expenditure should be incurred wholly and exclusively 'for the purposes of' the trade, profession or vocation[2], the Special Commissioners are reported to have held that child care expenditure is not incurred for the purpose of a profession and, even if it is, the expenditure is still disallowable under ICTA 1988 s 74(b) because it is private expenditure[3]. These rules are unaffected by provisions in the Finance Act 1990 dealing with the provision of creche facilities.

6.6 Creche facilities

It is becoming increasingly common for employers to provide creche facilities to encourage women with children to remain in, or return to, employment. The creche facilities may be provided by the employer directly, or by a third party under contract to the employer. The creche facilities may be free to the employee or, more commonly, the employee may be required to make some payment for them. In considering the tax liability of the employee on these facilities a distinction has to be drawn between employees with emoluments of less than £8,500 pa and employees with emoluments at or above this rate and most directors. To compute whether the £8,500 threshold has been exceeded one has to add together salary *plus* all fringe benefits valued on the assumption that the employee is paid in excess of £8,500 *plus* all expense reimbursements without any deduction for expenditure necessarily incurred in performing the duties of employment[4]. The only exception to this is that expense reimbursements which are covered by a dispensation negotiated between the employer and the Revenue do not have to be included[5]. Thus an employee with a salary apparently below the £8,500 threshold may be taken above it when the fringe benefits and expense reimbursements are added in.

If, after this calculation, the employee still remains lower paid, no taxable benefit will arise if the creche facilities are provided direct by the employer or by a third party under contract to the employer[6]. However any sums paid by the employee for the use of the facilities will not be tax deductible, and the employee will remain taxable on her gross salary even if a compulsory

1 *Halstead v Condon* (1970) 46 TC 289.
2 ICTA 1988 s 74(a).
3 *Itzin v IRC* (8 June 1978, unreported).
4 ICTA 1988 s 167(2).
5 ICTA 1988 s 166(1).
6 *Tennant v Smith* (1892) 3 TC 158.

deduction is made by her employer from her salary for the provision of creche facilities[1]. If the employee initially pays for the creche facilities and is then reimbursed part of the cost by her employer, the amount reimbursed will be a taxable emolument of the employee, and she will not be entitled to any tax relief for the payments she makes[2]. From the recent Privy Council decision in *Glynn v CIR*[3] it seems that this will also apply if the employee effectively chooses the creche even if a direct contract for the provision of creche facilities is then made between the employer and the creche. In *Glynn v CIR*, a case which came to the Privy Council on appeal from Hong Kong where there are no special statutory provisions for higher paid employees, the taxpayer was entitled under his contract of employment to have the education of his children paid for by his employer. The taxpayer chose the school his child was to attend, but a contract for the child's education was then concluded between the employer and the school, and the employer assumed contractual liability to pay the school fees. The Privy Council held that Hong Kong law on the nature of an emolument was the same as English law, and further held that the amount paid was an emolument of the taxpayer's employment, because it was an identifiable benefit to which a particular employee was entitled under the terms of his contract. The Privy Council accepted that the position would have been different if the employer had provided benefits which could not be specifically allocated to any one employee, such as the provision of nursery school facilities for the children of all employees.

Prior to changes made in the 1990 Finance Act, if an employee had emoluments of £8,500 or more she was taxable on the cost to the employer of providing creche facilities[4], and was entitled to deduct any amount paid to her employer for the provision of the facilities. However limited relief has now been provided from 1990-91 by a new ICTA 1988 s 155A, inserted by FA 1990 s 21. An employee is to be exempt from tax under the special rules for employees with emoluments of £8,500 pa or more, and most directors, on the provision of care facilities for children if the following conditions are satisfied:

(a) The care facilities are provided for a child under 18[5] for whom the employee has parental responsibility, or is resident with the employee, or is a child of the employee, including a stepchild, and maintained at his expense[6]. 'Parental responsibility' is defined in terms of the Children Act 1989[7], and will include both natural parents of a child born in wedlock, but only the mother of a non-marital child unless the father has obtained a parental responsibility order or agreement[8].

(b) The care facilities must not be provided in premises which are wholly or mainly used as a private dwelling[9].

1 *Heaton v Bell* (1969) 46 TC 211; *Machon v McCoughlin* (1926) 11 TC 83.
2 *Nicholl v Austin* (1935) 19 TC 531; *Richardson v Worrall* [1985] STC 693.
3 [1990] STC 227.
4 ICTA 1988 s 154 with s 156(1), and see IR press release of 24th April 1985, [1985] STI 246.
5 ICTA 1988 s 155A(8).
6 ICTA 1988 s 155A(3) and (7).
7 ICTA 1988 s 155A(8).
8 CA 1989 ss 2 and 4.
9 ICTA 1988 s 155A(2)(b) and (8).

(c) If the premises in which the care facilities are provided or the person providing the facilities are required by law to be registered with a local authority, they must be so registered[1].

(d) The care facilities must *either* be provided in premises made available by the employer alone[2] *or* the care must be provided under arrangements made between persons who include the employer on premises provided by one of those persons and, under the arrangements, the employer must be wholly or partly responsible for financing *and* managing the provision of the care[3].

(e) Care includes any form of supervised activity, whether or not provided on a regular basis, but excludes supervised activity provided primarily for educational purposes[4]. The provisions are therefore wider than the normal concept of creche facilities, as they include care facilities provided for an older child during the school holidays. They do not, of course, include the provision of regular education for a child.

In practice the most restrictive of these requirements are likely to be (b) and (d), especially the latter. No relief is available under ICTA 1988 s 155A if the employer makes a block booking with a creche over which he otherwise has no control, and no relief is available if the employer provides his employees with vouchers which can be exchanged for the provision of creche facilities by a third party. It remains to be seen how strictly the Revenue propose to interpret the requirement that an employer must be partly responsible for managing the creche facilities if they are not provided on his own premises but, at first sight, ICTA 1988 s 155A does not give much encouragement to those who wish to set up in business as providers of care for the children of women who are in employment.

6.7 Scholarship schemes and school fees

Until recent anti-avoidance legislation an attractive benefit was for a company to establish a scholarship fund for its employees' children. The schemes had many variations, but a common one, and one illustrated by litigation, was as follows: a company establishes an independent trust which is not charitable, and transfers funds to it. The trustees award scholarships to children of the company's employees of the difference between a full LEA grant for study in higher education and the amount actually paid under a means-tested grant.

A child in receipt of a scholarship is exempt from tax on the scholarship under ICTA 1988 s 331, and there is no tax charge on the employee parent if the parent's emoluments do not exceed £8,500 as the scholarship cannot be converted into money or money's worth. But in *Wicks v Firth*[5] the House of Lords held that the exemption for scholarship income in ICTA 1988 s 331 exempted the scholarship for all income tax purposes, so that an employee parent with emoluments of £8,500 or more could not be taxed

1　ICTA 1988 s 155A(2)(d) and (6).
2　ICTA 1988 s 155A(2)(c) and (4).
3　ICTA 1988 s 155A(2)(c) and (5).
4　ICTA 1988 s 155A(8).
5　(1982) 56 TC 318.

under the special statutory provisions in ICTA 1988 s 154. The House of Lords agreed unanimously that, were it not for the scholarship exemption in ICTA s 331, the cost of providing the scholarship would have been a benefit taxable as income of the parent taxable under s 154 whether the employer provided the scholarship directly or used a trust, as under either route the employer was providing the funds for the scholarship, and thus the deeming provisions in ICTA 1988 ss 168(3) and 154(3) deemed the benefit to be provided by reason of the parent's employment.

The effect of this decision was to exempt from income tax parents participating in all variety of scholarship schemes, including the direct award of scholarships by employer companies. The Government therefore enacted legislation to counteract this in FA 1983, with amendments in FA 1984, and the provisions are now in ICTA 1988 s 165. The changes do not affect the exemption for the child, but the exemption for scholarship income in ICTA 1988 s 331 is now only to apply to the scholarship holder[1]. It should be noted that if the scholarship holder is an employee with emoluments of £8,500 pa or more or a director the scholarship is exempt from tax. Thus if a company gives one of its executives one year's leave of absence to pursue an MBA degree and awards him a scholarship to cover tuition and living costs, the scholarship income should remain exempt from tax by virtue of ICTA 1988 s 331.

The award of a scholarship to a member of the family or household of an employee with emoluments of at least £8,500 pa is now deemed to be provided by reason of the employee's employment if it is provided as a result of arrangements entered into by the employer, whether or not the employer is required to contribute funds[2]. A person's family or household comprises his spouse, his sons and daughters and their spouses, his parents, and his servants dependants and guests[3]. However this rule does not apply to scholarships awarded by a trust fund or scheme if, in the year the scholarship payment is made, not more than 25% of the total scholarships awarded are taxable as emoluments and the scholarship is not, in fact, ignoring the deeming provisions, paid by reason of the employee's employment[4]. This exemption should apply, for example, if an employer sets up a scholarship scheme for children whom it hopes eventually to persuade to become employees, and awards a scholarship to a child who, fortuitously, happens to be the child of an existing employee.

ICTA 1988 s 165 applies to all payments made under scholarships awarded on or after 15th March 1983, but transitional relief applied to scholarships awarded before that date and taken up before 6th April 1984. The transitional relief expired on 5th April 1989 unless the child has continuously since 15th March 1983, or the date the scholarship commenced if later, been attending the same educational establishment, in which case the transitional relief will continue so long as he remains at the same educational establishment[5].

If an employer provides subsidised education for the children of his higher

1   ICTA 1988 s 165(1).
2   ICTA 1988 s 165(2).
3   ICTA 1988 s 168(4).
4   ICTA 1988 s 165(3).
5   ICTA 1988 s 165(4).

paid employees and is in the business of providing education to the general public for fees, for example a public school, it had until the recent case of *Pepper v Hart*[1] been assumed that the employee was only taxable on the marginal cost of providing the education for his children. This assumption was held to be wrong by Vinelott J in *Pepper v Hart*. He held that the taxable benefit was the average cost to the employer of providing education for a child of an employee, to be found by dividing the total costs of providing the education by the number of pupils, whether or not children of employees, who benefited from it. In *Pepper v Hart* the taxpayers were the bursar and nine assistant masters at Malvern College. Under a concessionary scheme they were entitled to have their children educated at the school for 20% of the full fees. The children had to meet the normal educational admission standards of the the school and, even then, the reduced fees scheme was entirely discretionary. Most of the children attended as day pupils, but there were a few boarders. During the period under consideration the school was not operating at maximum capacity, and no full fee paying children were refused admission. No additional staff were required to teach the taxpayers' children, and there would have been no reduction in the teaching staff if none of the taxpayers' children had been admitted. On these facts the Special Commissioner held that the taxable benefit was the additional direct cost of educating each child. For a boarder this would include the cost of food and drink consumed, laundry services, stationery, chemicals and other materials used, hot water, and affiliation fees where these were based on a per capita basis. From this taxable amount the employee could, of course, deduct the 20% fees which he paid to the employer.

In the High Court Vinelott J held that this approach gave insufficient weight to ICTA 1988 s 156(2) which provides:

> '... the cost of a benefit is the amount of any expense incurred in or in connection with its provision, and (here and in those subsections) *includes a proper proportion of any expense relating partly to the benefit and partly to other matters.*'[2]

He held that this provision, and in particular the part emphasised, required that the total cost incurred by the employer in providing education for all pupils, whether paying full or subsidised fees, must be ascertained, and the employee of a subsidised child was taxable on an appropriate proportion of that total cost. The employee may deduct from the taxable benefit as so computed the fees which he actually pays for the child's education.

Pepper v Hart is one of the most significant Sch E cases for many years. It has ramifications far beyond the taxation of school teachers whose children receive subsidised education. In particular it will result in higher paid employees of passenger transport undertakings who are entitled to free or subsidised transport being taxed on the average cost to the employer of providing the transport. The exemption in ICTA 1988 s 141(6) for employees in the passenger transport industry from taxation under the statutory provisions relating to the vouchers exchangeable for goods and services

1   [1990] STC 6.
2   Emphasis added.

only applies for the purposes of a charge under s 141. It does not confer exemption from a tax charge under ICTA 1988 s 154, the section which taxes fringe benefits of employees earning £8,500 pa or more. If *Pepper v Hart* goes to appeal it is to be hoped that the Court of Appeal will find a way to sustain the decision of the Special Commissioner.

CHAPTER 7

Marriage breakdown and income tax

7.1 Marriage breakdown and independent taxation

As a husband and wife are now taxed separately the breakdown of a marriage will have fewer income tax implications than it had under the system of aggregate taxation of spouses' incomes. However it would be a misconception to suggest that a marriage breakdown has no income tax implications. The right to claim married couple's allowance and to make an allocation of mortgage interest election will be lost, whereas the right to claim additional personal allowance may become available for the first time. The right to specify the shares in which jointly owned property is beneficially owned also ceases. Once the spouses divorce they will cease to be connected or associated persons for income tax purposes unless they are connected to each other for some reason other than their marriage, for example because they remain in partnership.

Of much greater significance than the introduction of independent taxation were changes made in the 1988 Budget and subsequent Finance Act to the tax treatment of maintenance. Prior to these changes maintenance due under legal obligation from one spouse to the other was tax deductible to the payer spouse and taxable income of the recipient spouse so that, if the payer spouse was a higher rate taxpayer and the recipient spouse was not, maintenance payments would result in an overall tax saving. If maintenance was directed to be paid under a court order by a parent to a child the maintenance was tax deductible to the parent and taxable income of the child even if the child was under 18. The practical effect was that income up to the child's personal allowance could be transferred from being taxed at the parent's top marginal rate of income tax into tax free income. It was even possible for a parent to apply to have a court order made against himself solely to achieve this beneficial tax result[1]. The 1988 Budget and Finance Act swept all this away for maintenance arrangements first made on or after 15th March 1988[2]. Under the new system, with very limited exceptions, maintenance payments are neither tax deductible to the payer nor taxable income of the recipient. The 1988 Budget changes were not retrospective and, with some important exceptions, do not affect continued tax relief for maintenance arrangements which were in place before 15th March 1988 and which were notified to the Revenue before 1st July 1988. The transitional provisions also apply to subsequent variations to those arrangements whenever the variation is made. In practice the continuing effect of these transitional arrangements causes more problems for

---

1 See *Sherdley v Sherdley* [1987] STC 217.
2 Budget day 1988.

professional advisers than maintenance payments which are subject to the new system.

7.2 Personal allowances following separation

Under independent taxation each spouse is entitled to a personal allowance, £3,005 for 1990-91. The separation of the spouses has no effect on this allowance so that, in the year in which they separate, each spouse remains entitled to a personal allowance. For many married couples this tax treatment under independent taxation will be less generous than under aggregate taxation. Under aggregate taxation in the year in which spouses separated the husband was taxable on his wife's income up to the date of separation, and remained entitled to claim wife's earned income allowance against her earnings prior to the date of separation. The wife was treated as a separate taxpayer as from the date of separation, and entitled to a personal allowance to set against her income, earned and unearned, accruing after that date. Provided the date of separation occurred some months after the start of the tax year, the practical effect was that two personal allowances were available to set against the wife's income in the year of separation. Under independent taxation only one personal allowance is available.

Marriage breakdown will, however, result in the loss of the married couple's allowance, which can only be claimed if a husband has his wife living with him for the whole or part of a tax year[1]. Spouses are living together for income tax purposes until they are separated under a court order or written agreement or are in fact separated in such circumstances that the separation is likely to be permanent[2]. In the year in which spouses separate the husband remains entitled to the full married couple's allowance. If he has insufficient income to absorb the allowance the unused allowance may be transferred to his wife to the same extent as if the spouses had remained together throughout the year of separation[3]. This also applies to any personal allowance which a low income husband is able to transfer to his wife under the transitional arrangements discussed in **1.7** above. In the year in which spouses separate the wife, but not the husband, may claim additional personal allowance if she has a child living with her for all or part of the period that she is separated from her husband[4].

In years following the year of separation each spouse is entitled to a personal allowance. The husband is not entitled to claim married couple's allowance. This is a change from the law under aggregate taxation, as a husband remained entitled to claim married couple's allowance until decree absolute of divorce if the wife was wholly maintained by maintenance payments from the husband which did not qualify for tax relief[5]. Maintenance payments do not qualify for tax relief if they are made voluntarily, ie not under legal obligation[6]. To ensure that a husband separated before 6th April 1990 is not prejudiced by the withdrawal of

---

1   ICTA 1988 s 257A(1).
2   ICTA 1988 s 282, and see **1.4** above.
3   ICTA 1988 s 257B(1).
4   See IR 83 para 36 and **7.3** below.
5   ICTA 1988 s 257(1)(a)(ii).
6   *Craddock v Greenwood* (1934) 18 TC 551.

married couple's allowance for years following the year of separation, transitional relief is provided by ICTA 1988 s 257F. A married man may claim married couple's allowance if:

(a) he separated from his wife before 6th April 1990, but they remain married; and
(b) his wife has been wholly maintained by him since the separation; and
(c) the maintenance payments are not tax deductible; and
(d) he was entitled to the married man's allowance in 1989-90 (whether the separation occurred in 1989-90 or an earlier year) and, if the claim is for a year later than 1990-91, he has been entitled to claim married couple's allowance for every intervening year.

If these conditions are satisfied the husband is entitled to married couple's allowance under ICTA s 257A as if his wife were living with him. This means that if either spouse is over 65 or 75 the higher allowance can be claimed, but subject to reduction if the husband's total income exceeds £12,300[1]. If the husband is entitled to transitional relief under ICTA 1988 s 257E to give higher personal allowances because in 1989-90 his wife was, but he was not, over the age of 65 or 75[2], that transitional relief continues to be available if the above conditions are satisfied. But a husband claiming transitional relief under ICTA 1988 s 257F is not entitled to transfer any unused married couple's allowance to his separated wife and, if he is on a low income and has unused personal allowance, he is not entitled to transfer the unused personal allowance under the transitional provisions in ICTA 1988 s 257D[3]. Any transitional relief being given under ICTA 1988 s 257F will automatically terminate when the spouses divorce.

In practice the conditions laid down for the application of the transitional relief in ICTA 1988 s 257F are likely to prove extremely difficult to satisfy. Under the original provisions in ICTA 1988 s 257(1)(a)(ii) the Revenue were known to take the view that it was not sufficient that the whole of any maintenance for the wife should be paid voluntarily; it was an additional requirement that, apart from a de minimus exemption, the wife's only source of income had to be the voluntary maintenance payments. If, for example, a wife had earned income, the allowance was not available even if the maintenance was paid voluntarily. The wording of s 257(1)(a)(ii) is reproduced in s 257F with the additional requirement that this state of affairs must have existed continuously since the date of separation. In many cases this requirement will be impossible to satisfy.

7.3 The additional personal allowance after separation

The requirements for claiming additional personal allowance are contained in ICTA 1988 ss 259 and 260, and they have already been considered in detail in **5.2** above. The allowance is equivalent to the married couple's allowance of £1,720. It is therefore worth £430 to a basic rate taxpayer

1 See **1.5** above.
2 See **1.5:1** above.
3 ICTA 1988 s 257F, and see **1.7** above.

in cash terms, and £688 to a higher rate taxpayer. Briefly, if the claimant is a man he must show that he is not entitled to a married couple's allowance or that his wife is totally incapacitated[1] and that he has a qualifying child living with him for all *or part* of the tax year[2]. If the claimant is a woman she must not be married to and living with her husband throughout the year of claim[3] and must have a qualifying child resident with her for all or part of the tax year. A qualifying child must be under 16 at the start of the tax year or, if over that age, be undergoing full time education, which includes training for a trade or profession provided the period of training is at least two years[4]. Additionally the child must either be the child of the claimant or, if not the claimant's child, must be under the age of 18 at the start of the year of assessment and be maintained by the claimant for the whole or part of the tax year[5].

Where more than one claimant is entitled to an allowance in respect of the same child the allowance will be apportioned between them in such proportions as they agree[6] or, in default of agreement, pro rata to the period of residence that the child spends with each claimant during the tax year[7]. If a claimant is exclusively entitled to an allowance in respect of one child he is debarred from claiming an allowance in respect of any other child[8].

An allowance is claimable for each qualifying child[9], but no claimant is entitled in total to more than one allowance in any tax year[10].

The provisions in ICTA 1988 s 259 give scope for tax planning. If in tax years after the year of separation there are at least two children it should be possible to ensure that each parent obtains an additional personal allowance.

> Example
>
> In 1988-89 Bert and Sandra, a married couple, separated and Bert left the matrimonial home. Bert has since purchased a new home for his own use. Sandra has custody care and control of their two children, Kate and Allie (both under 16), but Bert has liberal access including staying access. In practice the children spend three weeks with him in the summer, plus a week during the Christmas and Easter school holidays.

In this example Sandra is clearly entitled to claim additional personal allowance in respect of both children as they are her children and they reside with her for most of the year. However under ICTA 1988 s 259(3) Sandra's maximum claim is restricted to a single allowance of £1,720. Kate and Allie are as much Bert's children as they are Sandra's and, under the arrangements for access, they reside with Bert for part of the tax year. Bert has therefore satisfied the requirements of ICTA 1988 s 259(2) in respect of both children, as the subsection only requires that the children reside with the claimant for the whole *or part* of the tax year. Consequently Bert

---

1   ICTA 1988 s 259(1)(b) and (c).
2   ICTA 1988 s 259(2).
3   ICTA 1988 s 259(1)(a).
4   ICTA 1988 s 259(5)(a) and (b).
5   ICTA 1988 s 259(5)(b).
6   ICTA 1988 s 260(1) and (3).
7   ICTA 1988 s 260(3).
8   ICTA 1988 s 260(6).
9   ICTA 1988 s 259(2).
10 ICTA 1988 ss 259(3) and 260(2).

and Sandra should agree between them that Sandra will claim additional personal allowance for Kate and that Bert will claim the allowance for Allie. The same principle applies if there is only one child but the mother has remarried, and so cannot claim additional personal allowance herself. These principles are not affected by the changes to the additional personal allowance introduced by FA 1988 s 30 and now ICTA 1988 s 259(4A)[1] which restrict a couple living together as husband and wife to one additional personal allowance between them. This restriction has no application to a couple, whether married or not, who are living apart.

On occasions the Revenue have been known to question whether a child who resides at the house of one parent for infrequent periods during the year is in fact residing there or just visiting. They will often be satisfied that the child is residing there if the parent maintains a bedroom which is always available for the use of the child, and the child keeps some clothes in the room. However it is ultimately a question of fact for decision by the Appeal Commissioners whether a child is residing with a parent for part of the year. The controversy over the circumstances in which a parent of a child who does not normally reside with that parent can claim additional personal allowance has existed since the new rules for additional personal allowance were introduced in F(No 2)A 1979, and it is surprising that no test case has yet reached the courts to provide an authoritative ruling on the issue.

In the year in which spouses separate the husband cannot claim additional personal allowance as he remains entitled to married couple's allowance for that year. However a wife can claim the allowance if, during the part of the tax year in which she was separated from her husband, a qualifying child is resident with her[2]. Thus if a married couple with children separate in 1990-91 and the husband leaves the matrimonial home with the wife and children remaining, the wife will be entitled to a personal allowance and an additional personal allowance for 1990-91. But if the wife leaves the matrimonial home and thereafter the children do not reside with her in another house, the wife will not be entitled to claim additional personal allowance[3].

7.4 Life assurance relief

Life assurance relief was abolished for contracts entered into or varied after 13th March 1984, but premiums paid under contracts entered into before that date continue to attract tax relief until the contract expires[4]. The current rate of relief is $12\frac{1}{2}\%$[5], and is normally given by deduction from the premium payments[6]. A taxpayer is entitled to tax relief for premiums paid under a contract of insurance on the life of himself or his spouse[7]. Following a decree absolute of divorce premiums paid on a policy on the life of a

---

1   Discussed in **5.2** above.
2   ICTA 1988 s 259(4), and see IR 83 para 36.
3   ICTA 1988 s 259(4).
4   ICTA 1988 s 266(3)(c).
5   ICTA 1988 s 266(5)(a).
6   ICTA 1988 s 266(5)(a).
7   ICTA 1988 s 266(2)(b).

spouse would, in the absence of a relieving provision, cease to qualify for tax relief. Accordingly ICTA 1988 Sch 14 para 1 provides that references to an individual's spouse include any person who was that individual's spouse at the time the contract was made, unless the marriage was dissolved before 6th April 1979. This ensures that life assurance relief on a spouse's life can continue after divorce. By extra-statutory concession A-31 this treatment is extended to premiums paid by a divorced person on a policy which was taken out prior to the marriage.

7.5 Maintenance arrangements — the new rules

The Finance Act 1988 made major changes to the tax treatment of maintenance payments which first became due under a legally binding obligation entered into on or after 15th March 1988. In this section such maintenance payments are referred to as 'new' maintenance payments. Under the rules for new maintenenance payments, which are contained in ICTA 1988 s 347A and s 347B:

(*a*)   the recipient of maintenance is exempt from income tax on the maintenance[1]. This applies whether the recipient is a spouse or a child;

(*b*)   with a single limited exception, a payer of maintenance gets no tax relief for maintenance payments[2]. All maintenance is paid gross without deduction of income tax whether or not it qualifies for a tax deduction[3].

The rules governing the single limited exception when a payer of 'new' maintenance remains entitled to a tax deduction are set out in ICTA 1988 s 347B. The provisions are neutral as between spouses, but for ease of exposition it will be assumed that a husband/father is the payer of maintenance and that a wife/mother is the recipient. A payer of maintenance is entitled to a tax deduction for new maintenance payments provided:

(*a*)   The maintenance is payable under a binding written legal obligation for which the proper law is the law of the United Kingdom[4]. A court order is not necessary, although payments ordered by a UK court clearly qualify. Payments due under voluntary arrangements, oral agreements, and foreign court orders or agreements do not qualify for relief. At the time the maintenance is paid the payer and recipient must not be a married couple who are living together[5].

(*b*)   The legal obligation must require payment of maintenance by a spouse to or for the benefit and for the maintenance of a former or separated spouse, or to a former or separated spouse for the maintenance of a child of the family[6]. Payments of maintenance direct to a child under a court order no longer qualify for relief, and the standard tax planning

1   ICTA 1988 s 347A(1)(b).
2   ICTA 1988 s 347A(1)(a).
3   ICTA 1988 s 347A(1)(a).
4   ICTA 1988 s 347B(1)(c)(i).
5   ICTA 1988 s 347B(1)(c)(i).
6   ICTA 1988 s 347B(1)(b).

prior to the FA 1988 changes of arranging for maintenance to a child to be paid to the child under a court order is therefore no longer relevant. If maintenance for the mother is not likely to exceed the maximum deduction it is now good tax planning to require by written agreement maintenance for a child to be paid to the mother for the maintenance of the child. Maintenance for any 'child of the family' qualifies[1], and a child of the family is defined as a person under 21 who is either a child of both spouses or has been treated by both spouses as a child of the family and has not been boarded out with them by a public or local authority[2]. This definition brings the tax legislation into line with the family law legislation in the Matrimonial Causes Act 1973. However it should be noted that no deduction is available for maintenance paid in respect of a child who is over 21.

In one small respect these rules are less restrictive than those they replaced. Under the old rules maintenance for a spouse would not have qualified for tax relief unless it was payable to her. Maintenance paid for her benefit did not count. Under the new rules it does. Thus if a husband continues to pay the mortgage on the former matrimonial home in which his wife is still residing, or pays any other outgoing, the payments qualify for deduction even if the husband is merely discharging his own contractual obligations. However the low limit on the maximum tax deduction for new maintenance payments will ensure that this change has minimal impact.

(c) The recipient spouse must not have remarried[3]. Under family law legislation the remarriage of a spouse automatically terminates any legal obligation to pay further maintenance for the spouse[4]. It does not terminate an obligation to pay maintenance to the spouse for the maintenance of a child of the family. Nevertheless the remarriage of the recipient spouse will result in the payer's tax deduction for both types of maintenance being withdrawn. The remarriage of the payer has no effect on his tax deduction for maintenance payments in respect of a former marriage. Consequently if he remarries the payer may claim both the married couple's allowance and the maintenance deduction.

(d) The maintenance must not qualify for tax relief under any other provision in the taxes legislation[5].

If all these conditions are satisfied the payer of maintenance is entitled to a deduction in computing his total income of *the lower* of an amount equivalent to the married couple's allowance for the year, £1,720 for 1990-91, or the maintenance he actually pays[6]. If the payer is entitled to tax relief under the old rules for maintenance due under a legal obligation undertaken before 15th March 1988, which includes maintenance payable to a child under court order, these payments must be deducted from the married couple's allowance to compute the maximum deduction for new

1   ICTA 1988 s 347B(1)(b)(ii).
2   ICTA 1988 s 347B(7).
3   ICTA 1988 s 347B(1)(c)(ii).
4   MCA 1973 s 28(1).
5   ICTA 1988 s 347B(1)(d).
6   ICTA 1988 s 347B(3) as amended by FA 1988 Sch 3 para 13.

maintenance payments[1]. The maintenance deduction can be claimed for the year of separation in respect of maintenance payments made after the date of separation[2]. For that year a husband is therefore entitled both to a married couple's allowance and to a maintenance deduction.

The new rules are much more restrictive than those they replaced. The maximum tax relief for all new maintenance payments is now limited to the married couple's allowance; under the old system tax relief for maintenance was unlimited. The new rules at least have the practical advantage of simplicity in that, with the minor exception of the husband's maintenance deduction, tax is no longer a relevant factor in determining how much maintenance should be paid by a spouse following a marriage breakdown. The change should also hasten the final demise of the 'one third rule' as a principle for computing maintenance. Under this rule a wife was entitled to receive by way of maintenance such a sum as would bring her actual income up to one third of the spouses' joint gross incomes. The computation was based on the gross income of the spouses, the justification being that maintenance was tax deductible to the payer spouse and taxable income of the recipient spouse, and was accordingly paid and received out of gross income. Now that this is no longer the case the trend towards concentrating on the effect of maintenance payments on the net resources of the spouses after tax is likely to be accentuated[3].

The changes are likely to be most beneficial where there are no children and the spouse in receipt of maintenance already has taxable income, apart from the maintenance, in excess of her personal allowances for the year. With basic rate tax at 25%, under the old rules it was necessary to order a husband to pay £1,000 maintenance to ensure that his wife received £750 cash after tax. Because the husband got tax relief for the payments, the cash cost to him of making them was £750, or £600 if he was liable to higher rate tax at 40%. Under the new rules it is only necessary to order that a wife be paid £750 to ensure that she receives £750 cash. Consequently, all other things being equal, one would expect to see a drop of 20% — 25% in maintenance awards in 1990-91 over their 1988-89 level if both spouses already have other taxable income in excess of their personal allowances. This reduction is solely to adjust for the effect of the tax changes in the Finance Act 1988, without any significant increase or decrease in the net resources of either spouse.

The new rules are, however, clearly disadvantageous where the recipient spouse has no income and there are dependent children. Under the old system a husband could gain tax relief on payments to his wife of £4,725 (£3,005 personal allowance + £1,720 additional personal allowance) without the recipient being taxed on the payments. Under the new rules his maximum deduction is £1,720, a net reduction of £3,005, which represents a net cash loss of £1,202 to a higher rate taxpayer. For each child under the old system up to £3,005[4] could be paid as tax deductible maintenance without the child having to pay tax on it. Under the new system, assuming at least £1,720 maintenance is being paid to the spouse, no relief at all is available

---

1   ICTA 1988 s 347B(4) and (5).
2   ICTA 1988 s 347B(1)(c)(i).
3   See the comment written by Johnson J in (1990) 20 Fam Law 3.
4   The child's personal allowance, using 1990-91 figures.

for child maintenance, an annual cash loss per child of £1,202 to a higher rate taxpayer. For a higher rate taxpayer maintenance payments, whether to a spouse or a child, above the personal allowance threshold of the recipient now cost an additional 15p for each pound of maintenance. Under the old system the payments would have attracted tax relief at the payer's marginal rate of 40%, but the recipient would only have been taxed on them at the basic rate of 25%, a net saving of 15%. While the FA 1988 changes may not have much practical effect where both spouses have incomes and there are no children, they have made the cost of marriage breakdown significantly greater for a family with children where the husband is the sole income earner.

7.6 Maintenance — transitional arrangements

The changes to the tax treatment of maintenance in the Finance Act 1988 were not retrospective, and do not apply to maintenance arrangements in place on 15th March 1988[1], or to subsequent variations of those arrangements irrespective of when the variation is made. However the amount on which a payer can claim relief is 'capped' at the total maintenance on which the payer obtained tax relief in 1988-89, and the amount on which the recipient is taxable is similarly limited to the amount on which she was taxable in 1988-89. Excess maintenance over the payer's limit is not tax deductible; conversely any excess over the recipient's limit is not taxable.

The requirements with which maintenance payments must comply to remain within the old rules are set out in FA 1988 s 36(4) and cover:

(a) Court orders made by a court, whether in the UK or elsewhere, before 15th March 1988[2].
(b) An application for a court order made on or before 15th March 1988 provided the order was granted before 1st July 1988[3].
(c) A legally binding agreement made before 15th March 1988 provided the agreement (or written details of it if it is oral) was received by an inspector of taxes before 1st July 1988[4].
(d) A court order (whether in the UK or elsewhere) or written agreement made on or after 15th March 1988 which replaces, varies or supplements an order or agreement which qualified for transitional relief under one of the preceding three headings[5]. The variation order or agreement must be an obligation to pay maintenance[6]:
   (i) by one spouse to or for the benefit of a former or separated spouse and for the maintenance of that separated spouse, or
   (ii) to any person under 21 for his own benefit, maintenance or education, or
   (iii) to any person for the benefit, maintenance or education of a person under 21.

1 FA 1988 s 36(3).
2 FA 1988 s 36(4)(a).
3 FA 1988 s 36(4)(a).
4 FA 1988 s 36(4)(b) and (c).
5 FA 1988 s 36(4)(d).
6 FA 1988 s 36(5)(a).

Additionally, the variation order or agreement must be for the benefit maintenance or education of the same person as in the order or agreement which is being varied[1].

Category (d) is the only category which applies to current changes to maintenance arrangements, but the capping of maintenance at 1988-89 levels stops the freedom to vary being used to obtain significant additional tax relief. A variation of an existing 'direct to child' court order will preclude any tax relief from being available after the child reaches 21 so that, if there is any likelihood of maintenance under an existing order being paid to a child over that age, any proposal to vary the order should be considered with care. This problem is considered in greater detail in **7.12** below on maintenance arrangements for children under the transitional provisions.

7.7 Tax treatment in 1990-91 of 'old' maintenance for a spouse

This section is concerned solely with the tax treatment of maintenance payments for a former or separated spouse which continue to qualify for tax relief under the old rules because they are due under a qualifying order or agreement made before 15th March 1988, or under a variation of such an agreement or order. As from 1989-90 all maintenance, whether subject to the new or the old rules, is paid and received gross[2]. The small maintenance payments rules have no further relevance and have been repealed, and tax on 'old' maintenance not within the small maintenance payments rules is no longer withheld under ICTA 1988 s 348 or s 349. This change to payment of maintenance gross rather than net[3] only affects the way in which tax relief is given and maintenance is taxed; it does not affect the substance of whether or not maintenance is tax deductible or taxable. Nevertheless the change from a net to a gross method of payment can have considerable practical implications for spouses who had hitherto been used to paying and receiving maintenance under deduction of basic rate tax.

To compute the maximum maintenance deduction for a payer of old maintenance in 1990-91 one adds together the gross amount of all maintenance for which he was given tax relief in 1988-89 in respect of[4]:

(i)   maintenance for a former or separated spouse;
(ii)   maintenance due to a child under 21 under a court order;
(iii)   maintenance paid to another person, normally the other spouse, for the benefit maintenance or education of a child under 21.

The aggregate of these three amounts is the *maximum* maintenance deduction for 1990-91. It must be emphasised that it is the aggregate amount that is relevant and not the separate amounts of the three components. Thus if in 1990-91 variation orders decrease maintenance for a spouse and increase by the same amount maintenance due to a child under a court order, the payer will suffer no loss of tax relief even though the maintenance

1   FA 1988 s 36(5)(b).
2   FA 1988 s 38(7); ICTA 1988 s 347A(1)(a).
3   Apart from small maintenance payments, which were paid gross under the pre-1988 legislation.
4   FA 1988 s 38(3).

he is paying to his child is now higher than it was in 1988-89. There has been no aggregate increase in maintenance payments.

Having computed the maximum maintenance deduction by reference to maintenance payments in 1988-89 one then adds together the aggregate maintenance payments due in 1990-91 which qualify for tax relief under the transitional arrangements. The maintenance deduction to which the payer is entitled in 1990-91 is *the lower of* his maximum deduction and maintenance due in 1990-91 under the old rules and which is paid[1]. Tax relief will be given by a deduction in the payer's notice of coding if he is an employee, or otherwise in an assessment.

Example

Clark was divorced from his wife Mabel in 1985. In 1988-89 in compliance with court orders he paid £3,000 gross maintenance to Mabel and £1,400 to each of his two children. As Mabel has since remarried her maintenance entitlement has ceased, but the court orders in favour of the children have been varied to increase the maintenance payable to each of them to £2,500. Both children are under 21 throughout 1990-91, and Clark pays all the maintenance he is obliged to. Clark's maintenance deduction is:

		£
(a)	1988-89 maintenance cap	
	maintenance to spouse	3,000
	maintenance to children	2,800
	Maximum maintenance deduction	5,800
(b)	1990-91 maintenance payments	
	maintenance to spouse	0
	maintenance to children	5,000
	Maintenance paid	5,000

The maintenance deduction to which Clark is entitled in 1990-91 is therefore £5,000, and it is irrelevant that the child maintenance in 1990-91 exceeds the amount paid in 1988-89 by a significant amount. It should also be noted that it makes no difference to this example whether the maintenance for the children is payable direct to the children or to the mother for the maintenance of the children. Under the transitional rules the remarriage of one spouse does not prevent the other spouse from claiming a tax deduction for maintenance payments he is legally obliged to continue to make to her, as where maintenance is payable to the other spouse for the maintenance of minor children.

A recipient of maintenance which remains under the old rules is taxable in 1990-91 on *the lower of* the maintenance to which she is entitled in 1990-91, provided it is paid, or the maintenance on which she was assessable for 1988-89[2]. Any increase in maintenance since 1988-89 is tax free. It is important to note that these rules are applied separately to each recipient of maintenance even if the maintenance for all of them is paid by the same person[3]. Thus in the last example the maintenance on which each child can be taxed in 1990-91 is limited to £1,400, the amount on which each child was taxable in 1988-89. It has already been seen that this does

---

1 Payments made late are related back for income tax purposes to the year they were due.
2 FA 1988 s 38(4).
3 FA 1988 s 38(4).

not prejudice the payer's ability to claim a tax deduction for the £5,000 maintenance since the increase in the children's maintenance has been more than offset by the reduction in maintenance payable to the other spouse. This difference in tax treatment between payer and recipient can provide a useful tax planning tool when variation orders are under consideration.

If a taxpayer is receiving maintenance from two or more persons the maintenance payments from each person have to be kept separate, and a taxable amount for each person is computed by taking the lower of the payments due and paid by that person in 1988-89 and the payments made by him in 1990-91[1].

If a recipient of maintenance is a former or separated spouse who has not remarried an additional deduction may be claimed from any maintenance that is taxable for 1990-91[2]. The deduction is an amount equivalent to the married couple's allowance, £1,720 for 1990-91. The extra deduction is claimable against maintenance to which the former or separated spouse is entitled for her own maintenance, or maintenance payable to her for the maintenance of a child of the family under 21[3]. Any such maintenance is technically taxable income of the wife[4]. The deduction is also available against any maintenance from a foreign source assessable under Sch D Case V[5]. No deduction is available for maintenance which is taxable as the income of a child because it is payable to him under court order, and no deduction can be claimed if the recipient spouse remarries even if she continues to receive maintenance for the child of a former marriage[6].

Example

Samantha was divorced in 1986, and has not remarried. For 1988-89 the maintenance to which she was entitled under a court order was £5,000 p.a. In July 1989 the court order was varied by consent to increase her maintenance to £8,000 p.a. All payments due under the order have been made by her former husband. For 1990-91 the amount on which Samantha is taxable is:

		£
	maintenance assessable for 1988-89	5,000
	(lower than 1990-91 entitlement)	
less	maintenance deduction	(1,720)
	Assessable maintenance	3,280

Maintenance received under a foreign court order made before 15th March 1988 is taxable, but is included in the capping provisions[7]. Thus the recipient's taxable amount is limited to the lower of the maintenance assessable for 1990-91[8] or the maintenance from the same payer assessable for 1988-89. Even though it is received gross, maintenance due under a UK court order or agreement is assessable under Sch D Case III on the amount

---

1   FA 1988 s 38(4).
2   FA 1988 s 38(5) and (6).
3   FA 1988 s 38(6).
4   *Stevens v Tirard* (1940) 23 TC 321; *Spencer v Robson* (1946) 27 TC 198; *Morley-Clarke v Jones* (1984) 59 TC 567, High Court rather than Court of Appeal.
5   FA 1988 s 38(1)(c), (2)(b) and (5).
6   FA 1988 s 38(6)(b)(ii).
7   FA 1988 s 38(1)(a) and (c).
8   For foreign maintenance this will normally be the maintenance to which the recipient was entitled in 1989-90, see further **9.8** below.

to which the recipient was entitled for the year, provided that it is actually paid[1]. The significance of this wording is that maintenance which is paid late is taxable income of the year it was due to be paid and not the year in which it was actually paid, if this is a later tax year. The preceding year basis which normally applies to Sch D Case III income received gross does not apply to maintenance payments. If the maintenance is foreign source maintenance it will be assessed under Sch D Case V, and the normal preceding year basis of assessment for Sch D Case V income applies.

A payer of maintenance under the transitional provisions is entitled to elect to transfer from the old system to the new system[2]. If he so elects all maintenance payments for the year of assessment for which the election is made cease to be taxable income of the recipient[3]. The payer becomes entitled to a deduction of an amount equivalent to the married couple's allowance or the maintenance paid, whichever is the less, provided the maintenance is payable to or for the benefit of a former or separated spouse who has not remarried, whether for her own maintenance or for the maintenance of a child of the family who is under 21. In the early years of the new system it will not normally be advantageous to make the election, because maintenance payments in 1988-89, the year which sets the maximum limit for deduction for later years, will often be greater than the married couple's allowance, the maximum amount deductible under the new system. However as the married couple's allowance increases in line with inflation it may overtake the maintenance paid in 1988-89 and, if maintenance payments have similarly increased, more relief may be available under the new rules.

An election to change from the old to the new rules can only be made by the payer[4]. It must be made on the prescribed form 142 not later than twelve months after the end of the first year of assessment for which it is to have effect[5]. Thus the latest date for making an election to be effective for 1990-91 is 5th April 1992. The election must cover *all* maintenance payments due under pre-15th March 1988 obligations[6]. The payer cannot elect to bring maintenance payments to a former spouse under the new system but leave maintenance payments direct to a child under the old system. The person making the election must give notice of the election to each recipient of maintenance who is affected by it not later than 30 days after the election has been made[7]. Once made, an election is irrevocable and has effect for the year for which it is made and all subsequent years[8].

7.8 'Net of tax' maintenance arrangements

All new maintenance orders or agreements first made on or after 15th March 1988, whether for a cash amount or payment of an amount equivalent

1 FA 1988 s 38(8).
2 FA 1988 s 39.
3 FA 1988 s 39(1).
4 FA 1988 s 39(1).
5 FA 1988 s 39(2)(a) and (b).
6 FA 1988 s 39(1).
7 FA 1988 s 39(3).
8 FA 1988 s 39(2)(c) and (d).

to expenditure such as mortgage instalments, should be expressed as a gross amount with no reference to income tax. All payments under new maintenance orders or agreements are tax free to the recipient, and therefore any reference to tax is both superfluous and potentially confusing.

Many pre-15th March 1988 maintenance arrangements require the payer to pay a net of tax amount as maintenance to the recipient, ie such sum as, after deducting income tax at the basic rate, equals the amount ordered. This is especially likely to be the case where household expenses such as mortgage payments, rates, and electricity have been ordered to be paid as additional maintenance. This type of payment was not within the small maintenance payments rules because it was not a fixed monthly or weekly amount, and it therefore had to be paid under deduction of tax. If the recipient was to receive sufficient cash to enable her to pay the bills, it was necessary to order payment of the actual bill grossed up at the basic rate of income tax.

Pre-15th March 1988 'net of tax' maintenance arrangements cause considerable problems for both payers and recipients now that all maintenance is paid and received gross. Under the new system the first step is to construe the agreement or order to establish whether the payer has been ordered to pay a gross or a net amount. If the order or agreement requires payment of 'such sum as, after the deduction of income tax at the basic rate, equals' a particular sum or expenditure, the natural construction of the order is that the payer is required to pay the net sum grossed up at the basic rate of income tax. As tax is no longer withheld at source, this gross amount must be paid over to the recipient. However in relation to school fees orders, where the same problem arises[1], the Revenue have said that, until there is an authoritative ruling from a court on the correct interpretation of this type of net order under the new system, they will accept whatever interpretation of the order the parties agree best implements the intended effect of the order. Although the Revenue's statement was confined to school fees orders, it may be that they will be willing to apply the same approach to net of tax maintenance orders received by a spouse. Whether the parties agree that a gross or a net sum is required by the order or agreement, the total amount ordered must be paid by the payer spouse to the recipient spouse without deduction of income tax. The payer spouse will get tax relief on the gross payment in a notice of coding or an assessment, but within the overall maintenance cap of the maintenance for which he was entitled to tax relief in 1988-89. Conversely the recipient will be taxable on the gross payment, subject to a maximum taxable amount for her total maintenance of the maintenance on which she was taxable for 1988-89. Any excess maintenance over the 1988-89 limit is tax free. The recipient will have paid no tax by withholding at source on any of the maintenance she receives, and will have a tax liability to the Revenue to the extent that her maintenance, when added to any other taxable income, exceeds her personal allowances. This needs to be borne in mind if spouses seek to persuade the Revenue that only the net amount is payable under an order or agreement which appears to order payment of the net amount grossed up at the basic rate of income tax. Even if the Revenue accept the spouses' contention, the recipient spouse remains liable to income tax

1 See **7.13** below. Everything written in that section is equally relevant here.

on the net amount, and thought needs to be given as to how she is going to pay this liability. The one thing that is clearly not possible is to continue to pay and receive maintenance net of tax.

7.9 'Free of tax' maintenance

While it is preferable to avoid any reference to income tax in new maintenance agreements or orders first made on or after 15th March 1988, the addition of the words 'free of tax' should have no effect on the amount ordered, as all maintenance under new orders is now free of tax.

'Free of tax orders' are more problematic under the transitional arrangements for pre 15th March 1988 maintenance arrangements. Under the old rules if a payment 'free of tax' was directed to be made by a court order, it was construed as an order to pay a 'net of tax' amount, ie such sum as, after deducting income tax at the basic rate, equalled the sum stated in the order[1]. The recipient was under no duty to account to the payer for any tax repayment she received if the payment was covered by her personal allowances[2]; conversely the payer had no further liability if the recipient was liable to higher rate tax on the maintenance. The position was less clear if 'free of tax' maintenance was required under a written agreement rather than a court order. The payment was initially treated as a payment net of basic rate tax, as in a court order[3], but it remains an open question whether the wife is entitled to retain, or must pay over to the husband, any tax repayment to which she may be entitled, and whether the husband is liable to pay any higher rate tax.

Under the transitional provisions these problems are complicated by the capping of the amount of maintenance on which a recipient can now be taxed at the amount on which she was taxable for 1988-89. If a 'free of tax' maintenance order exceeds this amount, part of the maintenance will be free of tax, and there would seem to be no justification for grossing up this portion. However this is a problem which can probably only be sorted out by a court. In *Jefferson v Jefferson*[4] and *J-PC v J-AF*[5] the Court of Appeal indicated that 'free of tax' orders were undesirable in maintenance arrangements, and the transitional arrangements for old maintenance only add emphasis to that view.

7.10 Household expenses

Maintenance arrangements which incorporate an obligation to pay household expenses such as mortgage payments or heating costs are straightforward to draft under the new rules for maintenance arrangements first made on or after 15th March 1988. The payer is simply ordered to pay maintenance equivalent to the relevant expenditure, with no reference

1   *Jefferson v Jefferson* [1956] P 136.
2   *Jefferson v Jefferson*, above.
3   *Ferguson v IRC* (1969) 46 TC 1, HL.
4   [1956] P 136.
5   [1955] P 215.

being made to income tax. Any household expense payments are tax free to the recipient. However, provided they are for the benefit and maintenance of a former or separated spouse who has not remarried, they count as maintenance payments in computing the payer's maintenance deduction for the year of the lower of maintenance paid or the married couple's allowance[1]. There is no requirement under the new rules that payments for household expenses should be made to the recipient spouse for them to qualify for tax relief.

The transitional arrangements for household expenses required by maintenance arrangements first made before 15th March 1988 are more complicated. Quite apart from the problem considered in the previous section of how to deal with payments of household expenses ordered as 'net of tax' amounts, there is now some doubt as to which payments qualify for transitional relief and which do not. Under the old rules the only reason maintenance payments were tax deductible, whether for household expenses or otherwise, was because they were an annual payment *from* one taxpayer *to* another taxpayer. If a husband agreed to pay an expense for which he remained contractually liable to a third party the payment did not constitute an annual payment for tax purposes even if it conferred a benefit on a divorced or separated wife. It had not been made *to* her[2]. On the other hand, provided payment of additional maintenance to cover household expenses was actually made to a divorced or separated spouse, there was no objection to the maintenance being a variable amount in the sense that it increased in line with the household bills[3].

It seems clear that these rules apply in computing the maintenance payments for which a payer was entitled to tax relief in 1988-89, and which constitute the maximum tax relief he can claim in a later year. For 1988-89 FA 1988 s 36(4) simply excluded existing obligations from the new rules without saying anything about the tests to be applied to determine whether, under the old rules, the payments were tax deductible. Consequently payments of household expenses for which a husband remained contractually liable were neither deductible to him nor taxable income of his former or separated spouse, even if they conferred a benefit on her. For 1989-90 and later years, subject to the overriding maximum of the amount deductible in 1988-89, tax relief for maintenance payments is governed by FA 1988 s 38. This section applies to *any annual payment* which, inter alia, is made by one of the parties of a marriage to *or for the benefit of* the other party to the marriage and for the maintenance of the other party. Suppose that, under a variation of a maintenance order in force prior to 15th March 1988, a husband is obliged to pay the electricity bills for the former matrimonial home which is occupied by his divorced wife. The house remains in the husband's name, and the contract to supply electricity is between him and the electricity board. Under the general law of income tax the payments do not constitute annual payments because the husband is discharging his own contractual obligations and the payments are not

1   ICTA 1988 s 347B(1)(b).
2   *IRC v Compton* (1946) 27 TC 350.
3   *R v Income Tax Special Comrs ex p Shaftesbury Homes and Arethusa Training Ship* (1923) 8 TC 367; *Earl of Normanton v IRC* (1939) 23 TC 403; *IRC v Black* (1940) 23 TC 715; *IRC v Payton* (1940) 23 TC 722.

pure income profit of the electricity board. They could have been converted into annual payments if the wife had taken over contractual liability to the electricity board and the husband had been ordered to pay to her an amount equal to the electricity bills. The payments do, however, comply fully with the requirements of FA s 38(1)(b)(i), in that they are for the benefit of the wife, even though not made to her, and for her maintenance. It is therefore unclear whether they count as tax deductible expenditure, and taxable income, of the later year, although it may be safer to assume that the requirements for an 'annual payment' have to be satisfied as well as the requirements of FA 1988 s 38(1)(b)(i).

7.11 Maintenance payments for children — new arrangements

It is maintenance arrangements for children that have felt the greatest impact of the tax changes announced in the March 1988 Budget. Prior to the Budget, provided certain formalities were complied with, maintenance payments to children were fully tax deductible to the payer and were income of the child. If the child's marginal income tax rate was lower than the marginal income tax rate of the parent paying the maintenance there was an overall tax saving. For maintenance payments up to the child's personal allowance this saving was often substantial. Under the new rules for maintenance arrangements first made on or after 15th March 1988 no tax deduction is available for maintenance required to be paid directly to a child, even if ordered by a court order. Conversely the maintenance is not taxable income of the child. The only way tax relief can now be obtained for maintenance for children is to require, either in a written agreement or a court order, maintenance to be paid to the other parent for the maintenance by that parent of a child of the family[1]. A child of the family is defined in ICTA 1988 s 347B(7) as a person under 21 who is either the child of both spouses or has been treated by both of them as a child of their family and has not been boarded out with them by a public authority or voluntary organisation. The maintenance remains tax free to the recipient but, provided the recipient spouse has not remarried, the maintenance can be included with any maintenance paid for the recipient spouse in computing the payer's maximum maintenance deduction for the year of the lower of maintenance due and paid or the equivalent of the married couple's allowance, £1,720 for 1990-91. If a separated or divorced wife is receiving maintenance for herself, the addition of maintenance for children is unlikely to be of much assistance, as the maintenance for the spouse will often exhaust the £1,720 limit. But if a divorced or separated spouse is not receiving maintenance there is a tax advantage in directing in a written agreement maintenance for children of the family under 21 to be paid to the mother for the maintenance of children. A court order, while acceptable, is not necessary, but there must at least be a legally enforceable agreement in writing. Payments for children over 21 do not qualify for relief, and neither do payments made after the recipient spouse remarries.

1 ICTA 1988 s 347B(1)(b)(ii).

7.12 Maintenance payments for children — transitional arrangements

For maintenance arrangements for children made before 15th March 1988 to be effective at all for income tax purposes they had to avoid the anti-avoidance section ICTA 1988 s 663[1] which taxes income from a settlement by a parent on a minor child as income of the parent. In practice the four main ways in which maintenance for children could be arranged, and their income tax consequences, were as follows:

(1)   Voluntary payments by the father. These had no income tax consequences, in that they were neither tax deductible to the father nor taxable income of the child.

(2)   Payments under court order or legally binding agreement to the wife or former wife for the maintenance of a child. Such payments were fully tax deductible to the father, but were taxable income of the mother and not of the child[2]. Often this was not the best way of using the child's personal allowance.

(3)   Payments under an agreement or court order in trust for the child. Such payments have been held to be due under a settlement within ICTA 1988 s 663[3]. They therefore remained taxable income of the parent making them, and were not income of the child.

(4)   Payments under court order direct to a minor child. A court order was essential, as payments due to a minor child under a written agreement were held to be caught by ICTA 1988 s 663[4]. However it was the practice of the Revenue not to regard payments due to a child under a court order as due under a settlement and, although the validity of the practice has never been tested in court, the House of Lords in *Sherdley v Sherdley*[5] were prepared to take note of it when they agreed an application by a father for a court order against himself for payment to his children, of whom he had custody, of their school fees. Maintenance payments satisfying these requirements were tax deductible to the father but were taxable income of the child, and not of the mother. This meant that the child's personal allowance could be used to eliminate the first slice of maintenance from charge to tax completely.

Maintenance payments under methods (2) or (4) which are due under obligations entered into before 15th March 1988 continue to attract tax relief under the old rules, and remain taxable income of the recipient under the old rules[6]. However the maximum amount on which the payer can claim tax relief in a later year is restricted to the total maintenance payments for which he was entitled to tax relief in 1988-89[7]. Conversely, the maximum

1   See **6.1** above.
2   *Stevens v Tirard* (1940) 23 TC 321; *Spencer v Robson* (1946) 27 TC 198; *Morley-Clarke v Jones* (1984) 59 TC 567, High Court (the case went to the Court of Appeal on other issues).
3   *Yates v Starkey* (1951) 32 TC 38.
4   *Harvey v Sivyer* (1985) 58 TC 569.
5   [1987] STC 217.
6   FA 1988 s 38(1).
7   FA 1988 s 38(3).

maintenance on which the recipient can be taxed in a later year is the amount on which he was taxable in 1988-89[1]. If maintenance is payable to a divorced or separated parent who has not remarried for the maintenance of the child, so that it is taxable income of the parent, it qualifies for the maintenance deduction of £1,720 which the parent is entitled to claim as a deduction from her taxable maintenance payments[2]. If the parent remarries but continues to receive 'old' maintenance for a child, it remains taxable as her income, but no deduction is available. If 'old' maintenance is payable direct to a child under a court order it remains taxable income of the child subject to a maximum of the amount on which the child was taxable in 1988-89, but no £1,720 deduction can be claimed. Nevertheless this route remains very tax-efficient, and those who have the advantage of it should preserve their advantage for as long as possible.

If maintenance to or for a child attracts tax relief under the transitional provisions care needs to be taken if there is any likelihood maintenance will still be payable to the child after he attains the age of 21. The transitional arrangements for maintenance payments for years after 1988-89 in FA 1988 s 38 only apply so long as the child is under 21. Once the child is over 21 FA 1988 s 38 has no application, but that does not preclude the application of other transitional provisions in FA 1988 s 36(3) and (4). These provisions state that if an annual payment was due to be paid under an obligation made prior to 15th March 1988 tax relief will continue until the obligation to make the payment ceases, provided the obligation is not subsequently varied. In relation to maintenance for a child who reaches 21 the practical effect is that the parent who is paying the maintenance continues to get tax relief for payments after the child attains the age 21, and the maintenance is taxable income of the recipient child if the payment is due under a direct to child court order, or of the mother if it is payable to her for the maintenance of the child. If the payment is due direct to a child under a court order tax relief to the payer should be at his highest marginal rate of tax, and not restricted to the basic rate, as under Revenue practice this type of court order is not a settlement within ICTA 1988 s 683, and the same should apply if the maintenance is payable under a court order to a parent for the maintenance of a child. If maintenance is payable under a written agreement to a mother for the maintenance of a child then it is a settlement within the anti-avoidance provisions[3], and is technically not within the exemption for maintenance payments in ICTA 1988 s 683(3) as it is for the maintenance of a child rather than the recipient spouse. The payer's tax relief may therefore be restricted to relief at the basic rate although, in the past, the Revenue are not thought to have taken this point.

It must be emphasised that, if tax relief for maintenance for children continues after their twenty-first birthday by virtue of the transitional provisions in FA 1988 s 36(3) and (4), the maintenance is not paid gross. The provisions requiring payment of maintenance gross are in FA 1988 s 38, and this section has no application to maintenance for children over 21. Accordingly the maintenance is treated in the same way as any other

1 FA 1988 s 38(4).
2 FA 1988 s 38(6). Only one deduction is available against both the spouse's own maintenance and maintenance she is receiving for a child.
3 *Harvey v Sivyer* (1985) 58 TC 569.

annual payment, such as a payment due under a deed of covenant, which is continuing to attract tax relief because the obligation to make the payment was entered into before 15th March 1988. Accordingly ICTA 1988 ss 348 and 349 apply to the payment and the payer is entitled or required to withhold income tax at the basic rate on paying the maintenance. If he fails to do so he risks losing his basic rate tax relief. Conversely, the recipient is taxable on the gross maintenance, but has paid basic rate tax on it by withholding at source.

It must also be emphasised that tax relief for a child after he attains 21 will only be available for maintenance orders or agreements if the order or agreement was made or varied before 15th March 1988 and has not been varied since that date. Variation orders or agreements made on or after 15th March 1988 only qualify for continued transitional relief if they satisfy the requirements of FA 1988 s 36(5), one of which is that any child to or for whom maintenance is payable under the variation order must be under 21. The total loss of tax relief when a child reaches 21 is therefore a factor which has to be taken into account when consideration is given to varying a pre-15th March 1988 maintenance order for a child. Obviously there will only be a problem if there is a realistic possibility that the child will still need maintenance after 21.

7.13 School fees

If one parent is required by a maintenance order or agreement first made on or after 15th March 1988 to pay school fees for a child the amount paid will be tax free income of the recipient child or parent, and will only attract a tax deduction for the payer in the unusual circumstances where the other parent is not receiving maintenance for herself, and maintenance for the child, apart from the school fees, does not exceed the maximum maintenance deduction available under the new rules of an amount equivalent to the married couple's allowance, £1,720 for 1990-91. If this is the case then the agreement or order should require payment of school fees to be paid to the other parent for the education and maintenance of the child, and the amount paid will then qualify for a tax deduction up to the maximum of £1,720[1]. The amount ordered should be an amount equivalent to the school fees, and any reference to tax should be omitted[2]. The occasions when this combination of circumstances arise are likely to be exceptional, and in practice there are now normally no tax reasons for dealing with school fees in a maintenance order or agreement, although there may still be family law reasons for doing so.

The real problem with school fees orders concerns those orders which were originally made before 15th March 1988, whether or not they have been varied subsequently, and which continue to attract tax relief under the transitional provisions. Under the pre 1988 law, provided a parent was ordered by a court to pay additional maintenance equal to school fees to his child, the amount ordered was fully tax deductible to the parent and

---

1 ICTA 1988 s 347B.
2 See the views of the Principal Registry of the Family Division on school fees, (1989) 19 Fam Law 295.

taxable income of the child. For the arrangements to be effective for tax purposes it was essential that the parent paying the maintenance should not be contractually liable to the school for payment of the fees, as the payment of the school fees would not then be an annual payment *from* one person *to* another person, the prerequisite for tax relief. In practice it was normally sufficient for the parent with care and control of the child, normally the mother, to take over contractual liability to the school for the school fees, and the father to be ordered in a court order[1] to pay the school fees to the child. He then paid the amount ordered to the mother and she used it to pay the fees. However, if it was desired that the father should pay the school direct without loss of tax relief, this could be achieved applying a *Practice Direction* issued by the Senior Registrar of the Family Division in June 1983 with the concurrence of the Inland Revenue[2]. In addition to a court order obliging the father to pay school fees as maintenance to his child, the child was required to enter into a written contract with a school under which the school agreed to educate the child and to act as agent for the child in collecting the fees from the father. Because of all these complications, in practice it only made sense to become involved in school fees arrangements if the father was a higher rate taxpayer, when worthwhile tax savings could be made.

The 1983 Practice Direction was found to be defective in that the precedent of a court order which it provided directed that payment of school fees should continue until the child shall attain the age of 17 years or for so long as the child continues to receive full time education or further order. The Revenue interpreted this wording as meaning that the order terminated on the earliest of the three events to happen, and consequently no further tax relief was available once the child reached 17 even if he was still at school. To rectify this a further *Practice Direction* was issued in June 1987[3] which enabled court orders made under the original practice direction to be corrected at minimal cost by the addition of the words 'whichever is the later' after the three determining events, if that was the result the original order was intended to produce. Even if the correction is made on or after 15th March 1988 and amounts to a variation rather than a correction, there will be no adverse tax consequences at least until the child is 21, as variations of pre-15th March 1988 orders remain under the old system even if made after that date. If the order is still continuing after the child is 21 it will be necessary to argue that any correction made on or after 15th March 1988 under the 1987 Practice Direction was merely a correction and not a variation, as variation orders for children cease to be effective for income tax purposes once the child reaches 21 whereas an unvaried order does not[4].

School fees orders reached their zenith with the House of Lords decision in *Sherdley v Sherdley*[5]. In divorce proceedings a father obtained custody care and control of his three minor children. He had a gross income of £50,000 and was paying £8,000 pa in school fees for the education of his

1 A court order was essential to avoid ICTA 1988 s 663.
2 [1983] 2 All ER 679.
3 [1987] 2 All ER 1084.
4 See **7.12** above.
5 [1987] STC 217.

children. It was estimated that there would be a tax saving of £4,726 if tax relief could be claimed for the payment of the school fees. Accordingly the father applied for a court order against himself requiring him to pay maintenance equivalent to the school fees to his children. It was envisaged that the children would then make separate contracts with the school for their education. Both the High Court and the Court of Appeal refused to make the order sought. The majority of the Court of Appeal refused on the ground that it would be wrong to make the order where the sole reason for it was to enable the father to gain a reduction in his tax liability particularly as, in Lord Donaldson MR's view, the contracts that the children were going to have to make with the school were effectively shams. However the House of Lords allowed the father's appeal and made the orders sought, saying that not to make the orders would discriminate unfairly against a custodial parent. The Law Lords were prepared to accept the artificiality of the children's contracts if these were acceptable to the Revenue. The House of Lords heard this case after the development of the new approach of the courts to tax avoidance schemes in such cases as *Ramsay (WT) Ltd v IRC*[1], *IRC v Burmah Oil Ltd*[2], and *Furniss v Dawson*[3]. Although strictly a family law case rather than a tax case, in that the Inland Revenue were not involved, *Sherdley v Sherdley* illustrates that the courts still retain and give effect to a concept of acceptable tax avoidance and unacceptable tax avoidance[4], as, if ever steps were inserted into a transaction which had no commercial purpose other than the avoidance of tax (the *Furniss v Dawson* test), they were here.

Prior to 1989-90 basic rate tax relief for maintenance payments which were variable amounts, such as school fees, was given under ICTA 1988 s 348 by entitling the payer of maintenance to withhold income tax at the basic rate on making the payment. Higher rate relief on the gross amount was given either through an adjustment in the payer's notice of coding or in an assessment. Conversely the recipient, normally the child, was taxable on the gross maintenance but was treated as having paid basic rate tax on it by withholding at source. As the full amount of school fees had to be paid to the school it became standard practice to draft the order as a net of tax amount, and the draft order issued with the 1983 Practice Direction required the payer to pay '... an amount equivalent to such sum as *after deduction of income tax at the basic rate* equals the school fees.' Under the transitional provisions for maintenance arrangements made before 15th March 1988 the payer of maintenance will continue to get tax relief for payments under a school fees order, but subject to the overriding limit that the total maintenance payments for which he can obtain a tax deduction in 1989-90 or a later year cannot exceed the total maintenance deduction he was entitled to for 1988-89. The amount on which the recipient is taxable is similarly capped.

Of much greater significance for school fees orders than the capping of maintenance at its 1988-89 levels was the change in the method of payment of maintenance from payment net of basic rate tax to payment gross as

1　(1981) 54 TC 101.
2　(1981) 54 TC 200.
3　(1984) 55 TC 324.
4　See *In re Weston's Settlements* [1969] 1 Ch 223 at 245, per Lord Denning MR.

from 1989-90. Applying the natural interpretation of a standard school fees order, this change requires the father to pay not the actual school fees, as he had hitherto, but that amount grossed up at the basic rate of income tax. Subject to the overall limit of his 1988-89 maintenance payments, he will get basic and higher rate tax relief for the full amount paid in a notice of coding or an assessment, but some time may elapse before the relief is given. Conversely the child remains taxable on the gross amount of the school fees, but has now not paid any of his tax liability by withholding at source. The child is therefore now likely to receive a tax demand from the Revenue, and he will need extra money from his father to pay it. In a note in (1988) 121 Taxation 318 HW Fisher & Co report that the Inland Revenue Claims Branch had advised them that, if there was an arrangement under which school fees are payable direct to the school, the additional amount representing the tax should be paid directly to the child.

Example

Under a court order made prior to 15th March 1988 a father was ordered to pay such sum as, after deduction of income tax at the basic rate, equals the school fees. For 1990-91 the school fees are £1,200 due on 1st May 1990, £1,500 due on 1st September 1990, and £1,800 due on 1st January 1991. The payments the father is obliged to make are therefore:

	£ Gross	£ Tax	£ Net
1 May 1990	1,600	400	1,200
1 Sept 1990	2,000	500	1,500
1 Jan 1991	2,400	600	1,800
	6,000	1,500	4,500

If the order requires payment of the school fees direct to the school, on 1st May 1990 the father will pay £1,200 to the school and £400 to the child, with corresponding payments on 1st September 1990 and 1st January 1991. For 1990-91 £6,000 will be added to any other maintenance payments the father makes under pre-15th March 1988 court orders or agreements, and he will be entitled to claim a tax deduction of the lower of total maintenance due for 1990-91 and paid, or total maintenance due for 1988-89 and paid. The child will be taxable on the lower of the maintenance plus £6,000 fees to which he was entitled in 1990-91 or the total maintenance, including the grossed up amount of any school fees, to which he was entitled in 1988-89.

The implications for school fees orders of a change in the method of paying maintenance from net to gross appear not to have been fully thought out before the change was made. In response to one of a series of questions posed by the Senior Registrar of the Family Division[1] requesting clarification of the Revenue's interpretation of school fees orders made under the 1983 Practice Direction the Revenue stated:

'There are two possible interpretations applicable from April 1989. Either: (a) the obligation becomes one to pay the net amount of school fees, or (b) the obligation is to pay the grossed up sum to the child — by paying the school fees to the school and the balance to the child. The latter may be considered to be the more natural reading of the order; it being a formula

1   Reported at (1989) 19 Fam Law 294 and (1989) 123 Taxation 117.

to calculate the gross amount of maintenance due. The Inland Revenue does not consider that it is for it to give a definitive ruling on the amount such an order requires to be paid. The Inland Revenue will interpret the order in whichever way the parties agree. For example, if the order is agreed from 1989-90 to require payment of the grossed up sum, the payer will get tax relief accordingly, and the payee will be assessed on that sum. It is assumed that the terms of the original order will either have been agreed or have been decided by the court. In both cases, the object will have been clear. Account may have to be taken of the effect of reimbursement of part of the tax on the school fees on the amount specified in the order for general maintenance. It should be possible in most cases for parties to agree which interpretation produces the figures closest to the net sums which were anticipated to flow from the original order. It is not possible to state by Practice Direction which interpretation is correct; only a judicial decision can decide the point.'

Whichever interpretation the parties decide to adopt does not alter the fact that all maintenance, including school fees maintenance, is now paid and received gross. If the parties agree that a school fees order only obliges a parent to pay the net school fees, they will also have to agree on how the child is to be provided with funds to pay any tax liability he may have on this net amount.

The capping of the maximum deduction for maintenance under pre-15th March 1988 orders at 1988-89 levels poses another problem for school fees orders. The maximum amount for which tax relief is available remains constant, whereas school fees will rise inexorably over the years. Increasingly a parent subject to a standard school fees order will be obliged to pay more in school fees than he can claim a tax deduction for. This problem is compounded if an obligation to pay the school fees grossed up at the basic rate of income tax is accepted as the more natural interpretation of a standard school fees order.

Example

Since 1986 a father has been ordered under a school fees order drafted in the terms of the 1983 Practice Direction to pay as additional maintenance to his child such a sum as, after deduction of income tax at the basic rate, equals the school fees. In 1988-89 the actual school fees were £4,000. The father therefore paid £4,000 to the school, or to the mother as the child's agent, and was entitled to tax relief on the grossed up amount, ie £4,000 × 100/75 = £5,333.33. Basic rate relief was obtained by withholding at source; higher rate relief was obtained in an assessment. The child was taxable on £5,333.33 on which he had paid £1,333.33 tax by withholding at source. If in 1990-91 school fees have increased to £6,000, but other maintenance has remained constant, the father is obliged to pay £6,000 to the school and £2,000 to the child, a gross payment of £8,000. However he will only get tax relief on £5,333, and the child will only be taxable on the same amount. The additional amount over £1,333.33 that the child is receiving to pay his capped tax liability is therefore a windfall.

As the Inland Revenue have indicated in their reply to the Senior Registrar of the Family Division, quoted above, that they are prepared to take a pragmatic approach to school fees orders, one possible solution to the problem is for the father to continue to pay the net school fees to the school, but only to pay £1,333.33 to the child. As the father will have paid to the child as school fees and tax more than the gross amount on which he is claiming tax relief for 1990-91, there should be no objection to a tax deduction of £5,333.

An alternative solution is to consider varying the school fees order to require the school fees to be paid to the mother for the maintenance and education of the child, rather than directly to the child as was normal with a standard school fees order. Even if a variation order is obtained after 15th March 1988 it is effective under the transitional provisions. FA 1988 s 36(4)(d) applies to an order or agreement made on or after 15th March 1988 which replaces, varies or supplements an order made before that date provided the variation order complies with FA 1988 s 36(5). FA 1988 s 36(5) includes as a qualifying order a variation order requiring payments to be made to any person for the benefit, maintenance or education of a person under 21 if the order replaced or varied provided for payments to be made for the benefit, maintenance or education of the same person[1]. The variation order envisaged satisfies these requirements. Some support for this interpretation can be derived from the Revenue's answer to another question posed by the Senior Registrar of the Family Division[2]:

> 'Can the total amount of tax relief due under the "pegging" provisions be swapped between payees? For example: in 1988-89 a husband/father is ordered to pay a wife and three children each £5,000 pa, so that he would be entitled to the full tax relief on a total of £20,000 in this year and subsequent years. When the children cease to be entitled to maintenance, assume that the wife's order is increased to £20,000 pa. Will the husband still receive tax relief on the full amount of the order even though the wife's entitlement in 1988-89 was only £5,000 pa?
>
> Yes, but new recipients cannot be added — see s 36(5).'

If it is effective, the variation order has very beneficial income tax consequences. The school fees become income of the mother for tax purposes rather than income of the child[3]. The father's tax relief is not affected because under FA 1988 s 38(3) all tax deductible maintenance payments are *aggregated* both in computing maintenance paid in the current year and the overall limit for relief of maintenance paid in 1988-89. But under FA 1988 s 38(4) each recipient of maintenance is taxed *separately*, so that the maintenance on which a mother is taxable in a later year cannot exceed the maintenance on which she was taxable in 1988-89. The effect of the variation is therefore that the payer gets a tax deduction for the school fees but the recipient does not get taxed on them, assuming her own maintenance has not decreased since 1988-89. If the variation order is made the payer will cease to be entitled to any tax relief for maintenance payments made under the school fees order when the child reaches 21.

7.14 Maintenance for children in higher education

This section is concerned solely with maintenance payable to or for a child under a court order or agreement made before 15th March 1988, whether or not subsequently varied, which is continuing to attract tax relief under

---

1   FA 1988 s 36(5)(b).
2   (1989) 19 Fam Law 294 and (1989) 123 Taxation 117, Q 7.
3   *Stevens v Tirard* (1940) 23 TC 321; *Morley-Clarke v Jones* (1984) 59 TC 567, High Court.

the transitional provisions. Maintenance first awarded on or after 15 March 1988 is not taxable income of the recipient, and should be ignored in computing any means tested grant to which the child may be entitled if he is in higher education[1]. Under the transitional provisions it was normally beneficial to direct in a court order maintenance to be paid to a child, as this enabled maximum advantage to be taken of the child's personal allowance. If the child enters higher education this advantage may disappear as the maintenance will then count as part of the child's resources and, subject to a small de minimus limit[2], will reduce any means tested grant. In these circumstances it may be preferable to vary the maintenance order to require the maintenance to be paid to the child's custodial parent, assumed to be the mother, for the education of the child, rather than directly to the child. Until the child reaches 21 the father's tax relief will be unaffected as, under the transitional provisions, he gets tax relief on the lower of the total maintenance payments for which he was entitled to relief in 1988-89 or the total payments made in a later year. The maintenance under the varied order will become income of the mother, but she can only be taxed on the lower of the maintenance on which she was taxable in 1988-89 or the maintenance to which she is entitled in a later year and, if she has not remarried, she is entitled to a deduction equivalent to the married couple's allowance from this amount. If a maintenance order is varied in this way tax relief for the maintenance will cease when the child becomes 21, and the maintenance will also then cease to be taxable income of the mother. If the father is not worried about tax relief for the maintenance, an alternative solution is for the father and child to agree to terminate the maintenance order to the child and for the father to continue paying maintenance voluntarily. The maintenance will then not be income of the child either for income tax or for grant purposes.

Provisions dealing with the computation of grant for 1989-90 are contained in the Education (Mandatory Awards) Regulations 1989[3], but the regulations are generally replaced and renewed annually in the summer with only minor amendments. Under the regulations a child's grant is computed by deducting from the maximum available grant the child's own resources (ignoring for 1989-90 the first £565) and any parental contribution. Maintenance payments required to be made to the child directly appear to be part of his resources and therefore, to the extent that they exceed the *de minimus* threshold, directly reduce his available grant[4]. Maintenance payments to a parent for the maintenance of a child are income of the recipient parent for grant purposes and are not income of the child[5]. Where parents are separated the LEA may assess whichever parent they deem appropriate for parental contribution[6]. In practice it seems that they normally assess the

---

1 Although the Education (Mandatory Awards) Regulations 1989, SI 1989 No 1458, do not appear to have been amended to make this point clear.
2 £565 for 1989-90.
3 SI 1989 No 1458.
4 If the need arises it may be possible to argue that they come within the wording of SI 1989 No 1458 Sch 3 para 5(5), and so count as the income of the parent assessable to parental contribution and not as income of the child.
5 Education (Mandatory Awards) Regulations 1989, SI 1989 No 1458, Sch 3 para 5(5) with para 1(1)(c).
6 Ibid Sch 3 para 5(7).

custodial parent. If they agree to assess the mother as custodial parent and her income, including the maintenance, is below the threshold for parental contribution (£10,600 for 1989-90[1]), or not significantly above it, the child will receive a higher grant than if the maintenance was paid direct to him.

Against this higher grant has to be offset any additional income tax that may be payable on the maintenance by the mother, although an additional charge will only arise if the mother's other maintenance has decreased since 1988-89. Prior to 15th March 1988 it used to be possible to offset this additional charge if the mother entered into a deed of covenant in favour of the child to pay the gross amount of the maintenance to him, as payments under deed of covenant to a child over 18 by a parent who was being assessed for means tested grant were effective for income tax purposes but were ignored for grant purposes. With the abolition of tax relief for deeds of covenant made on or after 15th March 1988 this is no longer possible, but parents of children entering higher education in September 1988 or later, or who were under 18 on 15th March 1988, have been compensated by a 25% reduction in their parental contribution[2].

7.15 Secured maintenance

An unsecured maintenance order only helps the recipient so long as she is confident that the payer will satisfy his obligations under it. In a bitter divorce this confidence may be lacking. Therefore under the Matrimonial Causes Act 1973 a court is empowered to make an order for secured periodical payments for a spouse[3] and for a child of the family[4]. Exactly what may be ordered under a secured periodical payments order is somewhat obscure. Originally the order was not an order to pay maintenance and secure the payment. It was an order to secure[5]. As Hill J said in *Shearn v Shearn*[6]:

> 'The two orders [secured and unsecured maintenance] are essentially different. The order under s 190 [Supreme Court of Judicature (Consolidation) Act 1925] is not an order to make periodical payments and secure the payments: it is an order to secure and nothing else. Under it the only obligation of the husband is to provide the security; having done that he is under no further liability. He enters into no covenant to pay and never becomes a debtor in respect of the payments. The wife has the benefit of the security and must look to it alone; if it ceases to yield the expected income she cannot call upon the husband to make good the deficiency.'

A typical secured maintenance order would therefore require a husband to transfer income-producing assets such as shares to independent trustees to secure stated maintenance, so that the wife received her income from the trust, any excess income being paid to the husband[7]. The drafting of

1   Ibid Sch 3 para 4(1).
2   Ibid Sch 3 para 4(2).
3   MCA 1973 s 23(1)(e).
4   MCA 1973 s 23(1)(e), and see also s 23(2), (4) and s 27(6)(a)(b).
5   *Medley v Medley* (1882) 7 PD 122; *Smith v Smith* [1923] P 191; *Shearn v Shearn* [1931] P 1; *Barker v Barker* [1952] P 184.
6   [1931] P 1 at 4.
7   See eg *Hooper v Hooper* [1919] P 153, although there were variations, eg *Smith v Smith* [1923] P 191; *Hodges v Hodges* [1963] P 201 at 212.

a secured maintenance order was potentially complicated, so the court was given power to refer the matter to conveyancing counsel, a power still preserved in the Matrimonial Causes Act 1973 s 30(4).

The real problem with secured periodical payments is whether a court now has jurisdiction to order a person to pay periodical payments, and then order the payments to be secured on a non-income producing asset, such as the former matrimonial home. Although there were dicta in the early case of *Harrison v Harrison*[1] that might suggest that secured maintenance can simply be charged on property, it would seem to be part of the ratio of *Shearn v Shearn* and *Barker v Barker* that the court has no jurisdiction to order a person to pay maintenance and then charge that order on property in the way in which repayment of a mortgage loan is normally charged. Yet even before the Matrimonial Proceedings and Property Act 1970 courts were beginning to make such orders[2], and this development met with the approval of the Law Commission who commented[3]:

> '... we think it would be desirable that secured payments for a payee's wife should be awarded more readily. At present they are rarely, if ever awarded unless the husband had free investments in addition to the home and its contents and the like. We see no reason why in suitable cases the home should not be used to secure payments to the wife.'

This approach has been followed in the later cases of *Parker v Parker*[4] and *Flatt v Flatt*[5], although in *Powys v Powys*[6] Brandon J emphasised that the distinction between securing money and paying it should still be maintained. Nevertheless it may be that courts are now increasingly willing to secure payments on non-income producing assets.

For legal purposes, in addition to providing some insurance that periodical payments awarded will actually be paid, secured periodical payments have a number of advantages over unsecured periodical payments. Whereas unsecured periodical payments, whether for a spouse or for a child, terminate on the death of the payer, secured periodical payments for both spouses[7] and children[8] can extend beyond the death of the payer. Secondly, a secured periodical payments order is technically property of the recipient spouse[9] and can therefore continue even if the spouse who has to provide the security goes bankrupt. Conversely, at least in theory, if the recipient spouse becomes bankrupt the secured payments pass to her trustee in bankruptcy, whereas if she is only in receipt of unsecured payments, these are treated as a personal allowance and do not pass to her trustee in bankruptcy[10].

Whatever the legal advantages of a secured maintenance order, it now causes considerable tax problems, both for income tax and capital gains

1   (1888) 13 PD 180 at 187, per Fry LJ.
2   See *Aggett v Aggett* [1962] 1 All ER 190; *Foard v Foard* [1967] 2 All ER 660.
3   Report No 25 (1969) on financial provision in matrimonial proceedings, para 11.
4   [1972] Fam 116.
5   (1973) 118 Sol Jo 183.
6   [1971] P 340.
7   MCA 1973 s 28(1)(b).
8   MCA 1973 s 29(4):
9   *Harrison v Harrison* (1888) 13 PD 180.
10 *Watkins v Watkins* [1896] P 222.

tax. In the following discussion of these problems it is assumed that the order follows the standard pattern of requiring a husband to transfer income producing assets such as shares to trustees, the income to be used to pay maintenance for a separated or former wife or a child. The husband remains entitled to any surplus income, and he is also entitled to the return of the trust assets once the obligation to pay maintenance ceases. As different principles may apply, secured maintenance for a spouse and for a child are considered separately.

Where a secured maintenance trust is created in favour of a wife it will arguably constitute a settlement within ICTA 1988 s 660(3) and s 681(4) even though it is created by a court order. In *Yates v Starkey*[1] the Court of Appeal held that an order of a court to a father to pay maintenance to his wife in trust for his minor child was a settlement even though ordered by a court, because of the specific use of the words 'in trust for'. However it should be noted that Hodson LJ specifically made the point that the order before the court was not a secured maintenance payments order but a requirement to pay maintenance to a wife in trust for a child[2], so it is still open to argument should the need arise that a secured maintenance payments order is not a settlement within the meaning of the anti-avoidance provisions. Nevertheless any tax planning should proceed on the assumption that the order is within the provisions.

As the husband is entitled to a return of the trust assets when the obligation to pay maintenance ceases, he has retained an interest in the settlement. Accordingly all the trust income is prima facie taxable as income of the husband under ICTA 1988 s 647A assuming the trust is created on or after 14th March 1989[3]. However ICTA 1988 s 674A(1)(c) excludes from charge income arising under a settlement made by one party to a marriage by way of provision for the other after dissolution or annulment of the marriage, or while they are separated, provided the income is payable to or applicable for the benefit of the other spouse. Secured maintenance should therefore not give rise to an income tax charge under ICTA 1988 s 674A irrespective of the date of creation of the settlement. Apart from ICTA 1988 s 674A the only other relevant provision is ICTA 1988 s 673. This deems the income from settlements in which the settlor retains an interest to be income of the settlor to the extent that it is not distributed, but as the intention of a secured maintenance trust is to distribute the income, this section is unlikely to have any unintended adverse income tax consequences.

If a secured maintenance order is made on or after 15th March 1988[4] the income tax effect of the order is that income distributed to the wife as maintenance is her income and she is taxable on the full amount under Sch D Case III. Any surplus income is taxable income of the husband. The practical effect of this is to preserve the pre-15th March 1988 system of taxing maintenance for secured maintenance orders for spouses even if the trust is created after this date. The recipient spouse is not exempt

1 (1951) 32 TC 38.
2 (1951) 32 TC 38 at 51.
3 ICTA 1988 s 674A(5)(a). ICTA 1988 s 674A(5)(b) which applies the section to all settlements in favour of spouses, whenever created, does not apply to settlements on a former spouse after decree absolute of divorce, and under MCA 1973 s 23(5) a secured maintenance order cannot take effect until after decree absolute.
4 The date the new system of taxing maintenance payments took effect.

from tax on the maintenance because ICTA 1988 s 347A(2) only applies to 'any annual payment *made by an individual*'. Under a secured maintenance trust the maintenance is paid by trustees, not by an individual. However, since the husband is not being taxed on the income the trustees pay to his former wife, he is effectively getting tax relief for the payments. If a secured maintenance order was made before 15th March 1988 the wife remains taxable under Sch D Case III on the gross maintenance she receives. The amount taxable is not limited to the amount on which she was taxable in 1988-89, and she is not entitled to a deduction equivalent to the married couple's allowance against any of the secured maintenance. Both these privileges are conferred by FA 1988 s 38, which only applies to payments made by an individual[1]. However the husband continues to avoid tax on the total amount paid to his wife, and is similarly not restricted to a maximum exclusion from his income of the maintenance paid for 1988-89.

Husbands are likely to be happy with these income tax consequences; wives less so. If it is desired to set up a secured maintenance trust after 15th March 1988 the income from which is tax free to the wife and not deductible to the husband (apart from the maximum maintenance deduction for the year), and the capital gains tax hurdles discussed later in this section can be surmounted, it may be sensible to employ a tax planning device which has been in use for some years in connection with secured maintenance for children. The technique as it relates to children is outlined in *Potter & Monroe's Tax Planning with Precedents* (10th edn, 1987), p 40[2]. Applying it to maintenance for a wife, a husband is required under a standard maintenance agreement or order to pay maintenance to his wife. Additionally he is required to transfer income producing assets into trust under the terms of which the income is to be paid to the husband so long as he continues to pay the maintenance. But if the wife satisfies the trustees that the husband has defaulted with maintenance payments, the trustees are obliged to use the trust income to pay the wife up to the amount of her maintenance order. So long as the maintenance is paid it will be tax free to the wife, and the husband will be entitled to a tax deduction of a maximum of the married couple's allowance. The husband will remain taxable on the trust income.

If secured maintenance has been ordered to be paid to a child under 18 under an order made before 15th March 1988 it may be sensible to assume, following *Yates v Starkey*[3], that the order constitutes a settlement within the income tax anti-avoidance provisions, although the contrary view remains open to argument. Under ICTA 1988 s 663 income from the trust will therefore remain taxable as the income of the father and not of the child. The father will receive no tax relief, and the child's personal allowance will be wasted, and it was to avoid these disadvantages that the *Potter & Monroe* scheme outlined above was devised. Although it remains possible to vary the original secured maintenance order to a maintenance order payable direct to a child and remain within the transitional provisions set out in FA 1988 s 36(4) and (5), it needs to remembered that the maximum

1   FA 1988 s 38(1)(b).
2   The 11th Edn, 1989, does not contain the precedent.
3   (1951) 32 TC 38.

maintenance deduction that a father can now obtain is limited to the tax relief to which he was entitled in 1988-89, so there is little point in obtaining a variation order unless other maintenance payments have been reduced. If a secured maintenance order for a minor child is made on or after 15th March 1988, and is held to be a settlement, the income is taxable as the father's and not the child's. However this simply reflects the new rules for maintenance, which are that maintenance to a child is neither taxable income of a child nor tax deductible to the father, so that *Potter & Monroe*-type orders for secured maintenance for children offer no tax advantages under the new system. There would be considerable tax advantages in a *Potter & Monroe* order if a court could be persuaded that the facts of *Yates v Starkey* are distinguishable from a secured maintenance order, and that a secured maintenance order is not a settlement within the anti-avoidance provisions. The maintenance paid out of the secured maintenance trust would then effectively be tax deductible to the father and taxable income of the child. However it is anticipated that a court would take some persuading before it would agree to this interpretation.

Secured maintenance orders also pose considerable capital gains tax problems. Indeed with the withdrawal of gifts hold-over relief the capital gains problems may in many cases now be so great as to render the creation of secured maintenance trusts impractical. The transfer of assets into the trust appears to constitute the creation of a settlement as, while the trust continues, the transferor cannot claim to be absolutely entitled as against the trustees to the trust assets, and so within the protection of CGTA 1979 s 46(1). The transferor and the trustees are connected persons[1], and therefore deemed to be parties to a bargain otherwise than at arm's length[2], so that the assets are deemed to have been disposed of at their market value at the date of transfer[3]. With the withdrawal of gifts hold-over relief for transfers on or after 13th March 1989 there does not now seem any way in which any resultant capital gains tax liability can be deferred unless the assets are business assets qualifying for hold-over relief under CGTA 1979 s 126[4]. For inheritance tax the transfer into trust is either an exempt transfer under ITA 1984 s 11 (exemption for maintenance settlements) or a potentially exempt transfer tax because an individual will be beneficially entitled to the trust income. Either way the CGT hold-over relief in CGTA 1979 s 147A for transfers that are chargeable transfers for inheritance tax will not apply.

As the transferor is entitled to the return of the trust assets on the cessation of his obligation to pay maintenance, he retains an interest in the settlement. Consequently any gains realised by the trustees on the disposal of trust assets while the trust continues will be chargeable gains of the settlor taxable at his top marginal rate of income tax[5], although he will be entitled to recover this tax from the trustees[6].

When the obligation to pay secured maintenance ceases and the assets revert to the settlor, the reversion will not give rise to a charge to inheritance tax, at least if the settlor is still alive[7]. Consequently no gifts roll-over

---

1   CGTA 1979 s 63(3).
2   CGTA 1979 s 62(2).
3   CGTA 1979 s 29A(1)(a).
4   See **3.10** above.
5   FA 1988 Sch 10 para 2, and see **3.6** above.
6   FA 1988 Sch 10 para 5.
7   ITA 1984 s 53(3) or s 54(1).

relief is available for capital gains tax. For capital gains tax there would appear to be a charge under CGTA 1979 s 54(1), unless the reason for the reversion is the death of the person entitled to the maintenance. CGTA 1979 s 54(1) provides that, where property is settled property, and a person becomes absolutely entitled to it, the trustees are deemed to have disposed of the trust assets for a consideration equal to their market value and immediately reacquired them in their capacity as trustees within CGTA 1979 s 46(1). The effect is to produce a chargeable disposal. Since the settlor has retained an interest in the settlement any chargeable gains will be taxed as his gains at his top marginal rate of income tax[1]. As gifts hold-over relief was withdrawn without any transitional provisions for trusts which had been established prior to 13th March 1989, these principles also apply to a secured maintenance trust which terminates after this date even if it was created before it.

If the reason for the termination of the secured maintenance trust is the death of the person entitled to the maintenance, and the settlor is still alive, the settlor reacquires the assets at a value which results in neither gain nor loss to the trustees[2]. If the settlor is dead, the person entitled to the assets acquires them at their market value on the termination of the secured maintenance trust[3], but the trustees are chargeable on any gain which was originally held over under FA 1980 s 79[4].

For inheritance tax purposes a secured maintenance order appears to create a settlement, as ITA 1984 s 43(2)(c) defines settlement to include a disposition of property as a result of which property is: 'charged or burdened (otherwise than for full consideration in money or money's worth paid for his own use or benefit to the person making the disposition) with the payment of any annuity or other periodical payment for a life or any other limited or terminable period.' On a divorce settlement it may be argued that the transferor has received full consideration for the transfer, although it is difficult to see how the consideration has been 'paid' to him. Assuming a settlement is created, the transfer into the trust should cause no inheritance tax problems as the exemption in ITA s 11 (maintenance settlements) will apply, and there will be no tax charge if the trust ceases before the death of the settlor, because of the reverter to settlor exemption in ITA ss 53(3) or 54(1). As has been seen in the preceding paragraphs, it is this lack of inheritance tax problems that now causes all the problems for capital gains tax[5]. However if secured maintenance is ordered for a wife or child and the trust is subsisting at the death of the settlor, there would seem to be a potential inheritance tax charge on the the settlor on the value of his reversion, as ITA 1984 s 48(1)(b) precludes it from being excluded property. There is a potential additional charge on the whole property on the termination of the wife's or child's interest in possession, as the death of the settlor will preclude the reverter to settlor exemption applying but, provided the interests terminate during the life of the wife or child and the trust assets then revert to an individual, the transfer will be a potentially

1   FA 1988 Sch 10 para 2.
2   CGTA 1979 s 56(1)(b).
3   CGTA 1979 s 56(1).
4   CGTA 1979 s 56A(1) and (2).
5   If there is an immediate inheritance tax charge gifts roll-over relief is available for CGT by virtue of CGTA 1979 s 147A.

exempt transfer[1] so that no tax will be payable unless the wife or child die within seven years of the cessation of the secured maintenance trust.

1 ITA 1984 s 3A(7) with s 52.

CHAPTER 8

Marriage breakdown — the matrimonial home and other capital provision

8.1 Mortgage interest relief following matrimonial breakdown

Prior to 6th April 1988 a taxpayer was entitled to tax relief on interest paid on a loan used to acquire an interest in a house which he used as his only or main residence or a house which was occupied by a former or separated spouse of his or by a dependent relative. Only one £30,000 loan limit was available to cover loans on both the taxpayer's own main residence and a residence occupied by a former or separated spouse[1]. The continued payment of mortgage interest on the former matrimonial home by the spouse who had left it was therefore not a practical long term proposition even under the pre-6th April 1988 system, but the relief for houses occupied by a separated spouse at least ensured that there was no loss of tax relief during the period immediately following a marriage breakdown and before the spouse who had left the matrimonial home acquired a new house.

FA 1988 s 44(1) changed the position dramatically by amending ICTA 1988 s 355(1)(a) and s 357(2)(a) to stop a taxpayer from claiming tax relief on interest paid on or after 6th April 1988 on a loan to acquire a house occupied by a former or separated spouse or a dependent relative. The new provision is not retrospective, and continued tax relief is available on a loan taken out before 6th April 1988 provided the payment of interest immediately before 6th April 1988 qualified for relief *only because* the house was occupied by a former or separated spouse or dependent relative[2]. If there was no payment of interest before 6th April 1988 the first payment within 12 months after that date, or such longer period as the Revenue may allow, must qualify for relief only because the house was so occupied, and the house must not have been used for any other purpose in the intervening period[3]. Thus the transitional provisions do not apply to a spouse who leaves the matrimonial home following a marriage breakdown on or after 6th April 1988 even if the relevant loan had been taken out long before 6th April 1988. The payment of interest immediately before 6th April 1988 will have qualified for relief because the taxpayer was then occupying the house as his main residence, not because it was occupied by a separated spouse.

There are no provisions equivalent to the 'bridging loan' provisions in ICTA 1988 s 354(5) to extend tax relief for a limited period after a taxpayer has left the matrimonial home, and no concessional relief has yet been announced by the Revenue. Thus if a husband is paying the mortgage

---

1   ICTA 1988 s 357(1).
2   FA 1988 s 44(2) and (3)(a).
3   FA 1988 s 44(3)(b).

on a matrimonial home which he owns and the marriage breaks down following which he permanently leaves the house, he is not entitled to tax relief on the first payment of interest due after he has permanently left the house or on any subsequent payment of interest. Under ESC A27 mortgage interest relief is allowed during an absence from a main residence for up to four years if the absence is due to employment and up to one year if the absence is for any other purpose, but it is a precondition to the application of both these concessions that the absence is temporary and that the taxpayer should be intending to return to the house after his absence. A spouse who has left the matrimonial home following marriage breakdown will find it difficult to satisfy these requirements although, if the need arises and the facts justify it, it can always be argued that the departing spouse intended the absence to be temporary because he was hoping for a reconciliation. Similarly the bridging loan provisions in ICTA 1988 s 354(5) and (6) allow tax relief on two loans up to £30,000 if the taxpayer is selling one house and acquiring another, but it is a pre-condition to this relief that the intention should be to sell the first house. This will not normally be the case in relation to the former matrimonial home.

The problem is aggravated if the spouse who leaves the matrimonial home is paying mortgage interest and getting tax relief under MIRAS by withholding at source. Once he has left the matrimonial home any subsequent payments of mortgage interest cease to be relevant loan interest, and MIRAS relief is no longer available[1]. However it may be some time before the lender and the Revenue become aware of this. If interest payments cease to qualify as relevant loan interest the borrower is obliged to notify the lender of that fact[2], but this is unlikely to be uppermost in the thoughts of someone who has just had to leave his home because his marriage has broken down. Nevertheless failure to notify the lender, or to take other steps to ensure that the interest payments continue to qualify for MIRAS relief, could possibly result in a claim by the Revenue at a later date to recapture tax relief incorrectly given under MIRAS. Until the borrower does give the appropriate notice to the lender, the lender is protected if he continues to apply MIRAS[3], but the Revenue are entitled to recover any excess tax relief given to the borrower by direct assessment on the borrower[4].

In practice it is suspected that some concessionary relief will be given for a transitional period, as otherwise spouses leaving a matrimonial home following a marriage breakdown are in an almost impossible position if they have to continue paying mortgage interest on it. The best short term solution is for the spouse remaining in the matrimonial home, henceforth assumed to be the wife, to take over paying the mortgage, and to pay the lender out of her own bank or building society account. If she has inadequate funds to make the payments, her husband can provide her with the amount needed. Theoretically, to be entitled to tax relief on the payments the wife must show that she is paying interest on a loan (which does not necessarily have to have been made to her) to acquire an estate or interest in land

1   ICTA 1988 s 370(1) and (2).
2   ICTA 1988 s 375(1).
3   ICTA 1988 s 375(2).
4   ICTA 1988 s 375(3).

which she is occupying as her main residence[1]. If the wife has no ownership of the land this condition is technically not satisfied. But in relation to a husband and wife living together the Revenue have stated in Statement of Practice A34[2] that:

> 'In the case of husband and wife living together, relief will be allowed for interest paid by either spouse notwithstanding that the relevant property rights in the house or land in question are owned wholly or partly by the other.'

Although this is stated to apply only while spouses are living together, it appears to be the practice to extend it to the period between separation and divorce, as the Revenue leaflet IR 30 'Income Tax — Separation and Divorce'[3] states:

> 'Following a separation, you may be able to claim relief even if you do not own the home you shared before the separation. But you must live in it *and* pay the interest. If husband and wife each pay a part of the interest, the relief is divided between them. It is particularly important for the wife to tell her tax office if she pays mortgage interest following a separation. After a divorce the normal rules for relief apply.'

Thus far there has been no indication that the change to independent taxation will result in the withdrawal of these principles, although the concession may have to extend to giving the wife a sharer's limit even though technically she is not legally liable to make payments under the loan[4].

It is not a precondition for relief under MIRAS that the person claiming the relief should have taxable income in excess of the interest on which relief is being claimed[5]. This is an intentional part of the MIRAS arrangements, as it enabled the old option mortgage provisions to be repealed[6]. Under these provisions, which applied in years when mortgage interest was paid gross, a person whose interest payments were greater than his taxable income after personal allowances could elect to make lower interest payments but not claim tax relief for them. Accordingly payments of mortgage interest under MIRAS by a wife who is remaining in the matrimonial home after separation are payments of relevant loan interest even if she has little or no taxable income and can only make the payments out of tax-free maintenance that she is receiving from her husband.

8.2 Mortgage interest relief after separation — the long-term solution

When arrangements for the payment of mortgage interest on the former matrimonial home are considered for the longer term it is essential from a tax planning perspective that the spouse remaining in the matrimonial

1   ICTA 1988 s 354(1).
2   Originally issued as a press release on 11th June 1970.
3   November 1987 p 6.
4   Under ICTA 1988 s 356C(8) references to a spouse in the new mortgage interest provisions do not include references to a separated spouse.
5   ICTA 1988 s 369(4).
6   FA 1982 s 27.

home should take over the mortgage payments, as this is the only way in which tax relief on the mortgage, up to a maximum loan of £30,000, can continue to be claimed. After divorce if the spouse remaining in the the house is to be entitled to tax relief, she must own at least some interest in the house, as otherwise she cannot satisfy the requirements of ICTA 1988 s 354. Ideally she should own the whole of the interest in the land that the mortgage loan is being used to acquire, but in practice part ownership of the house may be sufficient. The spouse remaining in the matrimonial home should also enter into a legal obligation to the lender to repay the mortgage. Some lenders may only be prepared to agree to this if the spouse who has left agrees to act as guarantor. Once this is done tax relief under MIRAS at the basic rate will be available even if the payer has a low taxable income. If a husband who has left the matrimonial home has to increase maintenance payments to enable his former wife to pay the mortgage the maintenance need only be increased by the net mortgage payments due under MIRAS, thus effectively ensuring that the husband continues to get tax relief for mortgage interest payments on the former matrimonial home. The maintenance payments have no significant income tax implications as they are not taxable income of the wife and, apart from the first £1,720[1], are not tax deductible to the husband. The husband will be able to claim tax relief on a new loan up to £30,000 to purchase a house in which he is to reside following the marriage breakdown, whether or not he continues to pay interest on a loan to purchase the former matrimonial home. As interest paid on the latter loan no longer qualifies for tax relief it no longer enters into cumulation.

8.3 Mortgage interest relief after separation — transitional provisions

As explained in **8.1** above, the repeal in FA 1988 s 44(1) of provisions entitling a taxpayer to mortgage interest relief on a house occupied by a former or separated spouse does not apply if the taxpayer had permanently left the matrimonial home before 6th April 1988, so that the only reason the payments qualified for relief was because the house was occupied by a former or separated spouse. Under the law prior to the 1988 Finance Act changes the effect of this was to apply a maximum loan limit of £30,000 to the aggregate of the loan on the former matrimonial home and any subsequent loan the taxpayer took out to purchase a house for himself. The £30,000 loan limit was applied to the loans in the order they were created for the purposes of determining the interest eligible for relief.

The introduction of a 'per residence' basis for mortgage tax relief in the Finance Act 1988 rather than a 'per person' basis appears to have had a beneficial knock-on effect for tax relief which continues to be available on a former matrimonial home under the transitional provisions. Provided the loan on the former matrimonial home was taken out *before* a loan to purchase the taxpayer's main residence the two loans no longer have to be aggregated, so that a £30,000 loan limit is available for a loan on the former matrimonial home, and an additional £30,000 loan limit is

---

1 The maximum deduction for 1990-91.

available on a loan to purchase the taxpayer's main residence. The reasoning is that under ICTA 1988 s 356C(7) interest which is eligible for tax relief only because a house is occupied by a dependent relative or a former or separated spouse does not come within the new residence provisions for mortgage interest in ICTA 1988 ss 356A and 356B, and therefore does not have to be cumulated under the somewhat obscure provisions of ICTA 1988 s 356D(6). However any new loan taken out by a taxpayer who has left the matrimonial home comes within the residence basis in ICTA 1988 s 356A as applied by s 356C(1), and this is so even if the new loan was taken out before 1st August 1988 unless a person other than the taxpayer's spouse also had a loan on the property and was residing in it[1]. Relief for interest on a loan to purchase the former matrimonial home continues to be given under ICTA 1988 s 357 and, as there are no prior qualifying loans, the full £30,000 loan limit is available.

On the other hand if the loan to purchase the taxpayer's main residence was taken out before the loan to purchase the house occupied by a dependent relative or former or separated spouse, the maximum loan limit of £30,000 available on the latter loan has to be reduced by the amount of the earlier loan even if that earlier loan is now subject to the residence basis of tax relief[2]. The practical effect is that a single loan limit of £30,000 is available for both loans.

Evidence that the Revenue interpret the transitional provisions for mortgage interest relief on the former matrimonial home in the way described in the preceding paragraphs is provided by 'Notes of Guidance' issued by the Inland Revenue MIRAS Central Unit, the relevant paragraphs of which are set out in full in **2.16:4** above, as the same interpretation also applies to mortgage interest relief for a house occupied by a dependent relative.

8.4 Mortgage interest relief and lump sum orders

One possible financial provision order following a marriage breakdown is for complete ownership of the matrimonial home to be transferred to the spouse who is remaining there, with the spouse who is departing being compensated by the payment of a lump sum. Apart from the practical advantages of ensuring the maximum economic independence of the spouses from each other after divorce[3], such an order is beneficial for capital gains tax, because it ensures that there is no chargeable gain either on the disposal of the husband's interest in the former matrimonial home or on the eventual sale of the house by the wife[4], and the transfer into the wife's name has no stamp duty implications even if the value of the interest transferred exceeds £30,000[5].

The spouse remaining in the matrimonial home will often not have sufficient cash available to pay the lump sum, and will need to borrow from a bank or building society on the security of a mortgage. Indeed

1   ICTA 1988 s 356C(2).
2   ICTA 1988 s 357(1).
3   Thus complying with the statutory requirements in MCA 1973 s 25A(1).
4   See **8.5** below.
5   See **8.13** below.

in many cases this type of lump sum order will only be viable if the spouse who has to pay the lump sum is in employment, and so can pay the monthly mortgage instalments out of her earnings. To ensure that the spouse gets tax relief on the loan it is essential to make clear in the court order, financial agreement, or surrounding correspondence that the lump sum is required to be paid to enable the spouse who is remaining in the matrimonial home to acquire the interest in the home of the spouse who is departing, and is not simply an ordinary lump sum order made under the court's powers in MCA 1973 s 23(1)(c). Under ICTA 1988 s 354 tax relief is available for interest paid on money borrowed to acquire an estate or interest in land which is to be the borrower's only or main residence; tax relief is not available on money borrowed to pay lump sums.

In agreeing the amount of any lump sum that is to be paid attention should be given to the anti-avoidance provision in ICTA 1988 s 355(5)(a) and (d). S 355(5)(a) denies tax relief where the buyer and seller are husband and wife, but s 355(5)(i) restricts this to a husband and wife who are living together, and so it should not normally cause any problems for transfers following a marriage breakdown. ICTA 1988 s 355(5)(d) denies tax relief if a purchaser is directly or indirectly purchasing from a person who is connected with him and the price paid substantially exceeds the value of what is acquired. A husband and wife remain connected persons until the decree absolute of divorce[1]. If a lump sum is to be paid to acquire an interest in the former matrimonial home and the payer wishes to claim tax relief on money borrowed to pay it, it is therefore essential to ensure either that the lump sum is not excessive in relation to the interest that is acquired, or that the transaction is implemented after decree absolute of divorce[2].

8.5 Capital gains tax and transfers of an interest in the matrimonial home

The effect of capital gains tax on the ownership of the family home, including the application of the principal private residence exemption to husband and wife, has been considered in detail in **3.7** above, and this section of the book therefore concentrates on the capital gains tax problems which may arise if there is a marriage breakdown and one spouse leaves the matrimonial home. If the spouse who leaves, for ease of explanation assumed to be the husband, owns a beneficial interest in the matrimonial home and transfers that interest to his wife within 24 months of leaving, the whole of any gain on the disposal remains exempt[3] assuming that, apart from the last 24 months and permitted absences, the house was occupied by the husband as his main residence since the date of acquisition, or since 31st March 1982 if later. If the transfer takes place more than 24 months after the husband has left the matrimonial home he would, in the absence of a concession, be liable to capital gains tax on the gain attributable to

1   ICTA 1988 s 839 as applied by ICTA 1988 355(5).
2   Financial provision ordered by a court normally is only implemented after decree absolute, MCA 1973 s 23(5).
3   CGTA 1979 s 102(1).

his period of absence, less the last 24 months. Accordingly extra-statutory concession D6 provides that in these circumstances the husband will be deemed to be in occupation provided:

(1) the matrimonial home remains the principal private residence of the other spouse; and

(2) that during the period of absence the husband does not acquire a residence on which he seeks to claim principal private residence exemption.

The limited nature of the concession should be noted. In particular it only covers a transfer of an interest in the home from one spouse to another spouse, as opposed to a sale to a third party, and it presupposes that the departing spouse does not buy a new main residence on which he seeks to claim principal private residence exemption. It is therefore important to consider at an early stage how the matrimonial home is to be dealt with in the divorce property settlement, possible complications over mortgage interest relief providing an added incentive.

8.6 *Mesher* orders

Where there are young children for whom a home must be preserved, one possible order is that the matrimonial home should be transferred into the joint names of the spouses, held on trust for sale, the sale to be postponed until the youngest child reaches 18, with the wife and children being permitted to reside there in the meantime. The ultimate proceeds of sale are to be divided between the husband and wife in stated proportions. This type of order has become known as a *Mesher* order after the case in which it originated, *Mesher v Mesher*[1]. A *Mesher* order has the attraction of preserving some capital for the husband and protecting it against inflation while providing a home for the wife and children. It was a popular order in the early 1970s[2], but it has the major disadvantage that a sale of the property is forced when the children reach 18, and the wife's share of the proceeds may be insufficient to rehouse her. This disadvantage is compounded by the lack of any statutory power to enable a court to vary a *Mesher* order once it has been made[3], although it does have jurisdiction to advance the date of sale[4]. For these reasons the continued use of *Mesher* orders has been deprecated by some courts[5], although they can still be made on appropriate facts[6]. The tax discussion that follows should therefore not be taken as a recommendation in favour of such orders, but the standard *Mesher* order provides a good illustration of the tax implications of the rearrangement of property interests in the matrimonial home following

1 (1973) Times, 13th February, now fully reported sub nom *Mesher v Mesher and Hall* [1980] 1 All ER 126.
2 For further cases where such orders were made see eg *Chamberlain v Chamberlain* [1974] 1 All ER 33; *Allen v Allen* [1974] 3 All ER 385.
3 *Carson v Carson* [1983] 1 All ER 478.
4 *Thompson v Thompson* [1986] Fam 38.
5 See eg *Martin v Martin* [1978] Fam 12; *Hanlon v Hanlon* [1978] 2 All ER 889; *Carson v Carson* [1983] 1 All ER 478; *Harvey v Harvey* [1982] Fam 83.
6 *Drinkwater v Drinkwater* [1984] FLR 627.

a marriage breakdown, particularly if the original acquisition of the house was prior to 31st March 1982, so that the rebasing provisions apply.

If a *Mesher* order is made then for capital gains tax purposes, as both spouses are absolutely entitled to the house and there is no element of succession, there is no settlement[1]. It is not thought that the compulsory postponement of sale makes any difference[2]. Each spouse will therefore be treated as dealing with their own interest[3]. The husband's initial transfer to his former wife will be a part disposal, with the original cost of the house, or its 31st March 1982 market value if the house was acquired before this date but the matrimonial settlement is on or after 6th April 1988, being apportioned between the part disposed of and the part retained under the rules set out in CGTA 1979 s 35. Indexation allowance from March 1982, or the date of acquisition if later, is then applied to the cost apportioned to the part transferred from the husband to the wife. Any gain of the husband resulting from the part disposal is likely to be exempt from capital gains tax by virtue of the principal private residence exemption in CGTA 1979 s 102(1) as extended, if necessary, by ESC D6.

On the eventual sale of the house the wife's share of any gain will normally be exempt from CGT as she has been in occupation throughout her period of ownership, and is therefore entitled to the principal private residence exemption[4]. The husband will, however, be chargeable on the gain attributable to his retained share, computed as follows:

		£
	Husband's share of sale proceeds	a
Less	original cost, or 31 March 1982 value, of interest retained	(b)
	Unindexed gain	c
Less	indexation allowance	(d)
	Indexed gain	e

A portion of this gain will be exempt from tax because of the application of the principal private residence exemption to the period the husband was in actual occupation of the matrimonial home, plus his deemed occupation for the final two years of ownership. If actual occupation ceased prior to 31st March 1982 the exemption for actual occupation is nil, but the taxpayer remains entitled to the deemed occupation of the final two years provided he occupied the former matrimonial home as his main residence at some time during his period of ownership[5].

Example

In May 1975 a matrimonial home was acquired solely by H at a cost of £15,000. In May 1980 the spouses separated, H leaving the matrimonial home. In June 1981 H transferred the house into the joint names of himself and W on trust for sale, the sale to be postponed until their youngest child reached 18, with H being entitled to two thirds of the net proceeds of sale and W being entitled to one third. The market value of the house in June 1981 was £30,000, and

1 CGTA 1979 s 46(2); *Booth v Ellard* (1980) 53 TC 393; *Harthan v Mason* (1979) 53 TC 272.
2 *Harthan v Mason*, supra.
3 CGTA 1979 s 46(1).
4 CGTA 1979 s 102(1).
5 CGTA 1979 ss 101(1) and 102(2).

its market value on 31st March 1982 was £33,000. In June 1989 the house was sold for £117,000[1].

On the transfer of the one third interest in the house in June 1981 H made a part disposal computed as follows:

			£
	1/3rd market value		10,000
Less	allowable cost £15,000 ×	$\dfrac{£10,000}{£10,000 + £20,000}$	(5,000)
	Gain		5,000

This gain is exempt from tax by virtue of the principal private residence exemption[2].

On the eventual sale of the house in June 1989 W's gain is exempt under the principal private residence exemption, but H will incur a chargeable gain computed as follows:

			£
	Sales proceeds	2/3 × £117,000	78,000
Less	31 March 1982 market value	2/3 × £ 33,000[3]	(22,000)
	Unindexed gain		56,000
Less	indexation allowance	£22,000 × 0.453	(9,966)
	Indexed gain		46,034
Less	PPR exemption	$\dfrac{0 + 24^4 \times £46,034}{87}$	(12,699)
	Chargeable gain		33,335

In the above example the date on which the one third interest to the wife was transferred has intentionally been chosen as a date prior to 31st March 1982 to illustrate a problem that has arisen in relation to the valuation of assets owned in co-ownership on 31st March 1982 following the rebasing of capital gains tax to that date by FA 1988. On 31st March 1982 the husband owned a two thirds interest and the wife owned a one third interest in the former matrimonial home. If there is a disposal on or after 6th April 1988 of an asset which was owned on 31st March 1982 the acquisition value is computed on the assumption that the asset was sold by the person now making the disposal, and immediately reacquired by him at its market value at that date[5]. Unlike the transitional provisions which applied when capital gains tax was first introduced in 1965, there is no option under the new rebasing provisions to compute the total gain on the disposal of an asset, and then time apportion that total gain to obtain the gain attributable to the period after 31st March 1982.

There is some evidence that the Revenue valuations department take the view that, if a taxpayer only had part ownership of an asset on 31st March 1982, what has to be valued is that part share on the assumption that only that part share was disposed of and reacquired on 31st March 1982. This

1   The facts have some similarity to the example 'Simon' in **3.7**, qv.
2   CGTA 1979 s 102.
3   See the discussion in the next paragraph for problems in determining the 31st March 1982 market value.
4   The last 24 months of ownership divided by the number of months from March 1982 to June 1989, the month of disposal.
5   FA 1988 s 96(2).

method of valuation will inevitably produce a lower 31st March 1982 market value than a valuation on the assumption that the whole asset was sold on 31st March 1982, with each co-owner being entitled to their proportionate share of the total proceeds. Thus in the above example, if the value of H's two thirds share on 31st March 1982 has to be valued on the assumption that he was only disposing of his own share, it will be materially less than £22,000. Since indexation allowance is computed on the 31st March 1982 market value, assuming it is greater than original cost, this reduced valuation will also reduce the indexation allowance available, so that a taxpayer will end up being taxed on a much greater gain since 31st March 1982 than he has in fact realised. It will probably require a court decision to determine the correct method of valuation for assets disposed of on or after 6th April 1988 which were held in co-ownership both at the date of disposal and on 31st March 1982. But until there is legal authority to the contrary, it is suggested that a taxpayer should resist any attempt by the Revenue on facts similar to those in the above example to value each taxpayer's share on a basis other than a proportion of the total market value of the asset on 31st March 1982. Any other basis ignores the fact that *all* the co-owners are deemed to have disposed of their shares on 31st March 1982, and if they had done that to a single purchaser the amount they would have received would have been the open market value of their house, not the aggregate of the value of their respective shares.

For inheritance tax purposes the creation of a trust for sale with the sale being postponed, as required by a normal *Mesher* order, should not of itself constitute a settlement as defined in ITA 1984 s 43(2). Accordingly the death of one spouse will be treated as a disposition of that spouse's share in the house, and the deceased spouse will be liable to inheritance tax on the value so transferred.

8.7 'Occupation rents'

In recognition of the potential problem which will be caused to a wife by a *Mesher* order if her share of the ultimate sales proceeds is too low to purchase another house, the courts started to develop the concept of the 'occupation rent'. Such an order was similar to a *Mesher* order except that there was no forced sale when the children reached 18. The wife was free to remain in the former matrimonial home as long as she wanted, but once the children had grown up she was obliged to pay an occupation rent to her former husband to compensate him for the fact that he was being kept out of his share of the proceeds of sale of the house[1]. Although the court has called these payments 'occupation rents' it has recognised that they may not actually be rent[2]. Nevertheless such 'occupation rent' orders could cause potential tax problems, as they could result in the rent being assessable on the recipient under Sch A with no tax deduction being available for the payer. If it is desired to make this type of order it is suggested that the order should be formulated so as to require the wife to pay maintenance to her former husband, and that all references to rent should

1 See *Harvey v Harvey* [1982] Fam 83 and *Brown v Brown* (1981) 3 FLR 161.
2 *Harvey v Harvey* [1982] Fam 83 at 89 per Purchas J.

be omitted from the order. If such a maintenance order is first made on or after 15th March 1988 any maintenance received will not be taxable income of the husband. If the husband has not remarried the wife will be entitled to claim a tax deduction of an amount equivalent to the married couple's allowance for the year, or the maintenance paid, whichever is the less.

8.8 Deferred charges

A further alternative to a *Mesher* order is a deferred charge. Full legal ownership of the matrimonial home is transferred to the spouse remaining there, assumed to be the wife, but the house is then charged with payment to the husband at some future date of a sum of money. The charge may either be for a fixed amount, eg £10,000, or more commonly a variable amount, eg one third of the net equity in the house on the date the charge is payable. A typical example of the latter is provided by *Knibb v Knibb*[1] where the matrimonial home was vested in the wife subject to a charge in favour of her husband of 40% of its value on the ultimate disposal of the house. Often the order will state that the charge should be realisable on the death or remarriage of the wife, on her voluntary removal from the house, or when the youngest child reaches 18. Hayes and Battersby point out[2] two advantages of such an order. First, if the husband has a mortgage on the matrimonial home which the wife is going to take over, lenders appear more willing to release him from his personal covenant to repay the mortgage if he ceases to have any ownership of the matrimonial home. This will, in turn, make it easier to for him to obtain a new mortgage for any home he may need to purchase for himself. Secondly, a wife who has complete legal ownership of the former matrimonial home may feel more secure than if ownership is shared, even if the house is subject to a charge. However a deferred charge has land law problems[3]. It also has capital gains tax problems.

In the discussion that follows it is assumed that, as part of a financial settlement following a marriage breakdown, a husband has been obliged to transfer complete ownership of the matrimonial home to his wife, but the house is charged with payment of one third of the value of the net equity at the payment date, the charge to be paid in ten years time. For capital gains tax any beneficial ownership transferred from the husband to the wife is a chargeable disposal at the time of the order, but any gain accruing to the husband should be exempt from tax under the principal private residence exemption in CGTA 1979 s 102 as extended, if necessary, by ESC D6.

The husband's capital gains tax position when the charge is realised after ten years is more problematic, and depends to some extent on an analysis of the legal effect of a deferred charge order. On one analysis it is no different from a *Mesher* order, in that the husband has disposed of

1   [1987] Fam Law 346.
2   In 'Property adjustments: further thoughts on charge orders' [1986] Fam Law 213.
3   See Hayes & Battersby 'Property adjustment: order or disorder in the former matrimonial home' [1985] Fam Law 213.

a two thirds beneficial interest in the house at the time of the order but has retained a one third beneficial interest which will be realised in ten years time. If this is the correct analysis the husband will have a chargeable gain when the charge is realised computed as for a *Mesher* order, and as discussed in detail in **8.6** above. In particular the husband will be deemed to be in occupation of the house for the last two years of his ownership of his one third interest for the purposes of computing his principal private residence exemption.

However a better analysis may be that the husband has completely disposed of his ownership of the matrimonial home to his wife in exchange for a new asset, the deferred charge. Any gain on the matrimonial home is then realised in full at the time of the court order, but will be exempt from tax by virtue of the principal private residence exemption. The problem concerns the tax treatment of the deferred charge, and in particular whether a chargeable gain will arise when the charge is realised and, if so, how the gain should be computed. Incorporeal property, which includes a deferred charge, is a chargeable asset for capital gains tax[1], and any charge is ignored when computing the gain on an asset which is charged[2]. The realisation of the charge will constitute a disposal for CGT[3]. However under CGTA 1979 s 134(1) it is enacted that no chargeable gain shall accrue to the original creditor, or his personal representatives, on the disposal of a debt, other than a debt on a security. If s 134(1) applies to the realisation of a deferred charge the effect will be to eliminate from capital gains tax any gain the husband could otherwise be treated as having made on the disposal of his charge.

The meaning of 'a debt on a security' was considered by the House of Lords in *Aberdeen Construction Group Ltd v IRC*[4] and *WT Ramsay Ltd v IRC*[5]. While finding the meaning of the phrase obscure, they held that it was not synonymous with a secured debt[6]. Rather it envisaged a security that is marketable. This accords with the Revenue's own view of the meaning of a debt on a security, as as in a press release issued on 11th June 1970[7] they state:

'The definition of "security" in CGTA 1979, s 82(3)(b) which applies also for the purpose of CGTA 1979, s 134(1) is regarded as exhaustive so that the debt must be a loan stock or a similar security of a government, public or local authority or company. The view is also taken that the reference to loan "stock" implies in general a class of debt the holdings in which are transferable by purchase and sale and the words "whether secured or unsecured" in the definition make the existence of a charge immaterial.'

Consequently a deferred charge is not taxable as a debt on a security, and is prima facie exempt from tax as a debt.

The meaning of 'debt' in s 134(1) was considered by the House of Lords in *Marren v Ingles*[8] and by the High court in *Marson v Marriage*[9]. In

1 CGTA 1979 s 19(1)(a).
2 CGTA 1979 s 23(3).
3 CGTA 1979 s 20 as interpreted in *Marren v Ingles* (1980) 54 TC 76.
4 (1978) 52 TC 281.
5 (1981) 54 TC 101.
6 *WT Ramsay Ltd v IRC* (1981) 54 TC 101 at 193, per Lord Fraser.
7 See [1989-90] CCH Income Tax Statutes vol I pp 3,123.
8 (1980) 54 TC 76.
9 (1979) 54 TC 59.

Marren v Ingles the taxpayer sold shares in a company for a fixed sum plus the right, in circumstances which might never occur, to receive a percentage of the value of the shares when they were resold by the purchaser. In *Marson v Marriage* land was sold subject to a condition, inter alia, that in the event of the purchaser becoming liable to transfer its interest in the land or any part thereof by way of nationalisation or compulsory acquisition or otherwise, the vendor would be entitled to half the net sum received. In *Marren v Ingles* the taxpayer received additional payments when the shares were resold; in *Marson v Marriage* he received an additional payment in discharge of the obligation to pay the deferred charge. In both cases the Revenue assessed the additional receipts to capital gains tax. In both cases the taxpayer claimed that the asset from which he had derived a capital sum was a debt within CGTA 1979 s 134(1), and any gain was therefore exempt from tax. The courts held that an asset was not a debt for the purposes of s 134(1) where it was a *possible* liability to pay an *unidentifiable* sum at an *unascertainable* date[1].

Unlike the debts considered in *Marren v Ingles* and *Marson v Marriage*, only the amount of the variable secured charge under consideration is uncertain, since the liability to pay it is certain, as also is the date on which it is payable. Some deferred charges have both the date of payment and the amount uncertain, as where a former matrimonial home is charged with payment to the husband of one third of the net equity in the house when the wife sells it, or on her death, whichever is the earlier. A variable secured charge is therefore not on all fours with the contingent obligations under consideration in *Marren v Ingles* and *Marson v Marriage*, and it may be that these two cases can be distinguished. Clearly an adviser for a taxpayer must argue that they are distinguishable, and that a variable secured charge is a debt within CGTA 1979 s 134(1), so that any money received on the realisation of the charge is exempt from capital gains tax. If this view proves to be correct, a deferred charge has significant tax advantages over a *Mesher* order, to which it is similar in substance, as it is clear that the eventual sale of a house subject to a *Mesher* order will give rise to a capital gains tax liability for the non-resident spouse[2]. However one of the main purposes in creating a variable deferred charge is to provide the spouse who is being kept out of his capital in the former matrimonial home with an appreciating asset, and there seems little reason in principle why this asset should not be a chargeable asset for capital gains tax. A future court may therefore identify the uncertain amount payable as the crucial feature in *Marren v Ingles* and *Marson v Marriage* which prevented the deferred entitlements from being exempt debts within CGTA 1979 s 134, and that accordingly variable deferred charges are within the ratio of the two cases and are chargeable assets for capital gains tax. Until this issue is authoritatively resolved it is recommended that professional advisers should at least advise a person entitled to the benefit of a variable deferred charge of the possibility that capital gains tax may be payable when the charge is realised.

If a variable deferred charge is a chargeable asset, on realisation of the

---

1 *Marren v Ingles* (1980) 54 TC 76 at 100 per Lord Fraser who regarded the cumulative effect of the three factors underlined as important.
2 See **8.6** above.

charge the husband will have a chargeable gain of the amount he receives, less the market value of the debt when it was created, plus indexation allowance. This cost base is easier to state than it may be to compute. As Lord Fraser commented in *Marren v Ingles*[1]:

'The value of that right on 15 September 1970 [the date of creation of the right to receive the deferred consideration] has not yet been assessed; indeed, there is a suggestion that it may be impossible to assess, and nothing that I say is intended to indicate any opinion on the valuation of the right as at 15 September 1970.'

There may be less difficulty where, as with a deferred charge, the ultimate realisation of the asset is certain. The relevant question is: at the date of its creation, what could the right to receive one third of the net value of the matrimonial home in ten years' time have been sold for? The whole of the gain, after deducting indexation allowance arising on the realisation of the deferred charge will be chargeable to capital gains tax. Unlike the position under a *Mesher* order, a husband will not be entitled to claim principal private residence exemption under CGTA 1979 s 102(2) for the last two years of his ownership.

Example

In 1976 Michael purchased a home for himself and his wife Jenny for £13,000. In June 1988, following a divorce, complete ownership of the house was vested in Jenny, but charged with payment of one third of the net equity in the house at the date or realisation, the charge to be realised when their youngest child, now aged 4, reached 18, or when Jenny remarried, or sold the house, whichever should be the earlier. The market value of the house in June 1988 was £85,000. In June 2002 the youngest child attains 18 without Jenny having remarried or the house having been sold. The market value of the house is then £201,000, and the indexation factor from June 1988 to June 2002 is 0.652.

The transfer of ownership of the house from Michael to Jenny in June 1988 will be exempt from CGT by virtue of the principal private residence exemption extended, if necessary, by ESC D6. Similarly when Jenny sells the house any gain that she makes will also be exempt under the principal private residence exemption. But the realisation of Michael's charge in June 2002 will give rise to a chargeable gain computed as follows:

		£
	1/3rd market value at June 2002	67,000
Less	acquisition value of the deferred charge, say	(25,000)
	Unindexed gain	42,000
Less	indexation allowance £25,000 × 0.652	(16,300)
	Chargeable gain	25,700

If the deferred charge is for a fixed amount, eg £10,000, it should constitute a debt within CGTA 1979 s 134(1). Consequently any gain on the disposal of the husband's interest in the house will be wholly realised at the time it is transferred to his wife, when it will be covered by the principal private residence exemption, and there will be no further CGT charge when the deferred charge is ultimately realised. This interpretation is assisted by

1   (1980) 54 TC 76 at 98.

CGTA 1979 s 40(2) which enacts that any gain on the disposal of an asset is to be computed initially without regard to any postponement of the right to receive the consideration. In *Marson v Marriage*[1] it was held that this subsection presupposed a future consideration of an ascertainable amount, and therefore had no application to a deferred consideration of an uncertain amount. Conversely the subsection should apply to a deferred charge for a fixed amount[2].

8.9 Transfer of a house not the matrimonial home after separation

In years following separation but before divorce a husband and wife remain connected persons for capital gains tax[3]. One consequence of this is that assets transferred between them in years after the separation are deemed to take place at open market value[4]. Thus in *Aspden v Hildesley*[5] the court held that where, in a year after separation but before divorce, a husband transferred a house which was not his principal private residence to his wife, he realised a chargeable gain of the difference between the market value of the house at the time of transfer and its cost. Although husband and wife cease to be connected persons after decree absolute of divorce, it is still considered that if an asset is transferred for no consideration after divorce from one spouse to another there is a disposal at open market value by the transferor spouse. This is because CGTA 1979 s 29A(1)(b) provides that market value is to be the consideration for capital gains tax if an asset is disposed of wholly or partly for a consideration which cannot be valued, which is likely to apply to many financial settlements following a marriage breakdown.

Prior to 13th March 1989 it was possible to argue that gifts roll-over relief under FA 1980 s 79 was available to roll over any gain made by the transferor and reduce the acquisition value of the transferee spouse by the same amount. Provided the transferee occupied the house as her main residence throughout her period of ownership, any gain she made on the eventual disposal of the house, including the gain which had been rolled over, was exempt from tax under the principal private residence exemption in CGTA 1979 s 102. The withdrawal of gifts roll-over relief by FA 1989 s 124(1) closed this attractive tax avoidance loophole for disposals on or after 13th March 1989. Under CGTA 1979 s 7A capital gains tax payable on the disposal of land 'by way of gift' may be deferred over a period of ten years. However it will be difficult to argue that a transfer of property as part of a financial settlement following a marriage breakdown is a gift; the arguments in favour of roll-over relief being available were based on more technical reasons[6]. Indeed the Revenue are known to take the view that property settlements following a marriage breakdown are in consideration of the satisfaction by the transferor of his legal obligation

1 (1979) 54 TC 59.
2 (1979) 54 TC 59 at 73 and 74.
3 CGTA 1979 s 63(2), and see **3.9** above.
4 CGTA 1979 s 29A(1).
5 (1981) 55 TC 609.
6 See the discussion in **3.10** above.

to maintain his former or separated wife. Accordingly a claim to defer CGT in these circumstances is unlikely to be accepted by the Revenue.

8.10 Exchange of interests in property after marriage breakdown

During a marriage it may happen that the spouses acquire joint ownership of more than one house, for example a main residence and a holiday home. If the marriage breaks down they may decide that the husband should have complete ownership of one residence and the wife should have ownership of the other residence. This type of arrangement potentially gives rise to considerable capital gains tax implications, as technically each spouse has made a disposal of their share in the house of which full ownership is being transferred to the other spouse[1]. However concessionary relief may be available under ESC D26 to enable each spouse to take over the other's cost base and date of acquisition so that there will be no CGT charge on the exchange of interests, but the gain on the disposal of each of the houses will be computed on the basis that the spouse who now has complete ownership of the house always had complete ownership of it.

Extra-statutory concession D26 is a complex concession. Explaining the reason for its introduction in 1984, Mr John Moore told Parliament[2] that representations had been received over a long period that some relief should be given to alleviate the hardship which otherwise arose where there was an exchange of interests by people who had joint beneficial ownership of land, and that he had therefore authorised the Revenue to issue a concession to enable a capital gains tax charge to be deferred until the disposal of the interest acquired as a result of the exchange. However as a result of the way the concession is worded there will only be a total deferral if the value of the interests exchanged are equal. If a beneficial share in one property is more valuable than a beneficial share in the other property one of the parties will have a non-deferrable capital gain. The material part of the concession reads:

'Where interests in land which is in the joint beneficial ownership of two or more persons are exchanged after 19 December 1984, and

either a holding of land is held jointly and as a result of the exchange each joint owner becomes sole owner of part of the land formerly owned jointly,

or a number of separate holdings are held jointly and as a result of the exchange each joint owner becomes sole owner of one or more holdings,

relief along the lines of sections 111A and 111B, CGTA 1979 (roll-over relief on compulsory acquisition of land) may be claimed, to alleviate the charges to capital gains tax which would otherwise arise.

If the consideration received or deemed to be received for the interest relinquished is less than or equal to the consideration given or deemed to be given for the interest acquired, relief will be allowed on the lines of that provided by section 111A(2) and (5), CGTA 1979; where it is greater relief will be allowed on the lines of section 111A(3) and (5). For this purpose the interest relinquished will be treated as the "old land" and the interest acquired as the "new land". "Land" includes any interest in or right over

---

1   See [1984] STI 793.
2   [1984] STI 793.

land and "holding of land" includes an estate or interest in a holding of land and is to be construed in accordance with section 108(3), CGTA 1979.

Relief will not be allowed to the extent that the "new land" is, or becomes, a dwelling house or part of a dwelling house within the meaning of sections 101 to 105, CGTA 1979; however where individuals who are joint beneficial owners of dwelling houses which are their respective residences become sole owners of those houses in consequence of an exchange of interest, concessionary relief may be claimed as if by virtue of sections 101 and 102, CGTA 1979 each gain accruing on the disposals of each dwelling house immediately after that exchange would be exempt. Each individual must undertake to accept for capital gains tax purposes that he is deemed to have acquired the other's interest in the dwelling house at the original base cost and the original date on which that joint interest was acquired.'[1].

It is clear that the first paragraph of the concession does not apply when interests in jointly-owned residences are partitioned following a marriage breakdown, as the 'new land' in each case constitutes a dwelling house irrespective of whether it becomes a main residence. It is less clear whether the concession in the last part of the final paragraph applies, but the implications are most easily seen through an example.

Example

In June 1983 Matthew and Joan purchased Blackacres for £30,000 as beneficial joint tenants for use as their matrimonial home. In May 1985 they purchased Whiteacres for £16,000 as beneficial joint tenants for use as a holiday home. In July 1990, following a marriage breakdown, they agree that Joan should acquire absolute ownership of Blackacres and Matthew should have absolute ownership of Whiteacres. Blackacres then has a market value of £110,000, and Whiteacres has a market value of £50,000. Applying the strict law, and ignoring indexation allowance for simplicity, the capital gains tax position following the exchange of interests appears to be:

(1) *Blackacres:* Matthew has made a chargeable gain computed as follows:

		£
	½ market value at the time of disposal	55,000
Less	acquisition value	(15,000)
	Gain	40,000

This gain is however exempt from CGT by virtue of the principal private residence exemption in CGTA 1979 s 102. Joan's acquisition value of her complete share in the house is now £70,000 (£15,000 + £55,000), and indexation allowance on any disposal will have to be computed from June 1983 on £15,000 and from July 1990 on £55,000. However this will cause no practical problems if Joan continues to occupy the house as her main residence.

---

1 ESC D26 was reissued in September 1988 to include an exchange of milk or potato quotas; see [1988] STI 693, but the latter part of the concession is not relevant for present purposes.

(2) *Whiteacres:* Joan has made a chargeable gain computed as follows:

		£
	½ market value at the time of disposal	25,000
Less	acquisition value	(8,000)
	Gain	17,000

As Whiteacres does not qualify for principal private residence exemption Joan will have a non-deferrable gain of £17,000 less indexation relief on £8,000. Matthew's acquisition value of Blackacres will be £33,000 (£25,000 + £8,000).

If the concession in the second paragraph of ESC D26 applies Joan is deemed to have acquired Blackacres for £30,000 in June 1983, and Matthew is deemed to have acquired Whiteacres for £16,000 in May 1985. Although there will be no immediate chargeable gain for either spouse, Matthew will eventually have a massive chargeable gain on the disposal of Whiteacres, whereas Joan escapes CGT altogether as she is treated as owning Blackacres since June 1983 but it has been her main residence throughout her period of ownership. Matthew may therefore not agree to the application of ESC D26 even if the Revenue would be prepared to accept it.

To see to see how the first paragraph of ESC D26 operates, assume that the facts of the above example remain the same, except that Blackacres and Whiteacres are not dwelling houses. The first problem is to work out what consideration Matthew has received for the disposal of his half share of Blackacres to Joan, and what consideration he has paid for the acquisition of her half share in Whiteacres. If the transfer is between separation and divorce it is deemed to take place at market value because spouses remain connected persons until divorce[1]. Even if the transfers take place after divorce it is arguable that they still take place at market value because they are part of an overall settlement following a marriage breakdown the consideration for which cannot be valued, and hence market value is deemed to be the transfer value for capital gains tax by virtue of CGTA 1979 s 29A(1)(b). On this basis Matthew has received £55,000 for his half share in Blackacres and has paid £25,000 for Joan's half share in Whiteacres. Conversely Joan has received £25,000 for her half share in Whiteacres and paid £55,000 for Matthew's half share of Blackacres. Matthew's deferred gain under the concession is therefore computed applying CGTA 1979 s 111A(3) and (5), and Joan's deferred gain will be computed applying CGTA 1979 s 111A(2) and (5).

---

1 CGTA 1979 s 63(2) with s 29A(1)(a).

(1)   *Matthew's gain on the disposal of ½ share in Blackacres*

		£
	½ market value at the time of disposal	55,000
Less	acquisition value	(15,000)
	Gain	40,000
Less	roll-over relief (s 111A(3)(a))	(10,000)
	Unexpended consideration (£55,000 − £25,000)	30,000

Matthew therefore has a non-deferrable chargeable gain on the disposal of his half share in Blackacres of £30,000, and a deferrable gain of £10,000. This is because under CGTA 1979 s 111A(3) the amount he received for his half share in Blackacres exceeded by £30,000 the amount he paid for Joan's share in Whiteacres, and he is deemed to have retained and not reinvested this amount of his total gain of £40,000. He therefore has an immediate charge to capital gains tax. Matthew's acquisition value for Whiteacres then becomes[1]:

		£	£
	Original acquisition value		8,000
Plus	price paid for Joan's share	25,000	
	less roll-over relief	(10,000)	15,000
	Acquisition value of Whiteacres		23,000

(2)   *Joan's gain on the disposal of ½ share in Whiteacres*
As Joan is deemed to have reinvested in the purchase of a half share in Blackacres more than she received from the disposal of her interest in Whiteacres she is deemed to have disposed of her half share in Whiteacres at neither a gain nor a loss[2]. The consideration which she is paying for Matthew's half share in Blackacres (£55,000) is then reduced by the consideration she received for her share in Whiteacres (£25,000)[3] to give a net consideration of £30,000. Consequently the acquisition value for her ownership of Blackacres becomes:

		£
	Original acquisition value	15,000
Plus	net price of acquiring Matthew's ½ share	30,000
	Revised acquisition value	45,000

8.11   Capital gains tax — transfers of assets after separation

Detailed consideration has been given in earlier sections of this chapter to the tax implications of transfers of interests in the matrimonial home. The remainder of this chapter is therefore mainly concerned with assets other than the matrimonial home. Under the new system of independent taxation husband and wife are taxed separately throughout their marriage on their capital gains, and capital losses of one spouse may only be set against that spouse's gains. Each spouse's net chargeable gains are charged to CGT at that spouse's marginal rate of income tax. However, as explained in chapter 4 above, a married couple who are living together still have

1   CGTA 1979 s 111A(3)(b).
2   CGTA 1979 s 111A(2)(a).
3   CGTA 1979 s 111A(2)(b).

one major advantage over a couple living together who are not married — the ability to transfer assets from one to the other at no gain or loss[1]. This effectively enables losses of one spouse to be offset against gains of the other, enables both spouses to take maximum advantage of their £5,000 annual exemption, and ensures that chargeable gains in excess of the exemption can be realised by the spouse with the lowest marginal rate of income tax. These privileges disappear if a marriage breaks down, and thus the capital gains tax implications of marriage breakdown, although less significant under independent taxation than the previous system, still exist.

For capital gains tax the crucial year is the year of separation and not the year of divorce. Transfers of assets between spouses while they are living together, and throughout the year of separation, take place on a no gain/ no loss basis with the transferee taking over the transferor's cost base plus indexation allowance and, if the asset was acquired prior to 6th April 1965, his date of acquisition[2]. It should be noted that, because of the wording of CGTA 1979 s 44(1), it appears that the relief for inter-spousal transfers continues throughout the year of separation, irrespective of whether the asset is transferred before or after the actual date of separation. Thus if assets subject to CGT are transferred between spouses before the end of the tax year in which the spouses separate, there will be no tax charge. However the recipient spouse will ultimately be taxed on the gain arising over the total period of ownership, or from 31st March 1982 if later, unless the disposal is on death. Where the recipient spouse is likely to dispose of the asset before death, and any gain would be a chargeable gain, it may be preferable to transfer assets in the year after separation so that each spouse will bear any CGT attributable to their own period of ownership.

In years following separation, but before divorce, a husband and wife remain connected persons for capital gains tax[3]. One consequence of this is that transfers between them are deemed to be at market value and any actual consideration is ignored[4]. For transfers prior to 13th March 1989 this deeming provision in CGTA 1979 s 63(2) made it possible to argue that gifts roll-over relief under FA 1980 s 79 could be claimed for transfers made as part of a financial settlement following marriage breakdown provided the assets were actually transferred prior to decree absolute. The abolition of gifts roll-over relief by FA 1989 s 124 for transfers of assets other than business assets and transfers into discretionary and accumulation and maintenance trusts now renders this argument of limited use.

A husband and wife cease to be connected persons after decree absolute of divorce, and most financial settlements do not take place until after this date[5]. Nevertheless it is considered that a transfer of assets as part of a divorce settlement on one spouse by the other which takes place after decree absolute will still be deemed for capital gains tax to be a disposal of the assets at their market value at the time of transfer. This is because

1 CGTA 1979 s 44(1).
2 CGTA 1979 s 44(1) with Sch 5 para 17.
3 CGTA 1979 s 63(2).
4 CGTA 1979 s 29A(1)(a), and see *Aspden v Hildesley* (1981) 55 TC 609, discussed in **8.9** above.
5 MCA 1973 s 24(3), although it is possible for spouses to implement an earlier date by agreement.

it is normally impossible to value the consideration, if any, which the recipient has given for the assets transferred to her, and CGTA 1979 s 29A(1)(b) deems the market value to be the transfer value if an asset is transferred for a consideration which cannot be valued.

8.12 Inheritance tax and property settlements following marriage breakdown

With the abolition, subject to some exceptions, of the inter-vivos gifts element of capital transfer tax by FA 1986, when the tax was renamed inheritance tax, separation and divorce are now less likely to pose particular inheritance tax problems. Transfers of assets to an individual or into a fixed interest trust or an accumulation and maintenance trust will, at a minimum, be potentially exempt transfers[1], so that no inheritance tax will be payable if the transferor survives for at least seven years. However liability to inheritance tax will still be relevant if the transferor dies within seven years, or the transfer is to a discretionary trust.

A transfer of assets from one spouse to another is exempt from inheritance tax if the transfer is made prior to the decree absolute of divorce[2]. If a transfer satisfies this requirement it is irrelevant whether the transferor survives seven years. If the transferor spouse is domiciled in the UK and the recipient spouse is not domiciled in the UK the exemption is limited to £55,000[3]. Although property transfers as part of a divorce settlement normally do not take effect until after decree absolute, there is no objection to making the transfers in anticipation of the decree if it is particularly desired to take advantage of the exemption for inter-spousal transfers.

Apart from the exemption for transfers between spouses, two other exemptions are relevant to a transfer of property to a spouse following a marriage breakdown. If either exemption applies the transfer is an exempt transfer, and it is therefore irrelevant whether the transferor survives seven years. ITA 1984 s 10(1) provides that a disposition will not be a transfer of value if it is not intended to confer gratuitous benefit and is made at arm's length between people unconnected with each other, or was part of a transaction which might be expected to be so made. In August 1975 the Senior Registrar of the Family Division of the High Court issued a statement with the agreement of the Inland Revenue that this exemption will normally be regarded as covering transfers of property pursuant to orders of the divorce court. The statement reads[4]:

> 'Transfers of money or property pursuant to an order of the court in consequence of a decree of divorce or nullity of marriage will in general be exempt from capital transfer tax [now inheritance tax] as transactions at arm's length which are not intended to confer any gratuitous benefit.
> If, exceptionally, such a benefit is intended it is the duty of the transferor to deliver a capital transfer tax account to the Controller ED Office [now Capital Taxes Office, Minford House, Rockley Road, London W14 0DF].'

1   ITA 1984 s 3A.
2   ITA 1984 s 18(1).
3   ITA 1984 s 18(2).
4   New Law Journal, 28th August 1975 p 241.

The statement only applies to transfers made under court orders and, in practice, the Inland Revenue are likely to scrutinise consent orders more closely than contested orders. It is in sufficiently wide terms to cover transfers both to spouses and to children, but it may be dangerous to rely on it in relation to transfers to children.

ITA 1984 s 11(1) provides that:

'A disposition is not a transfer of value if it is made by one party to a marriage in favour of the other party or of a child of either party and is —

(a)   for the maintenance of the other party, or
(b)   for the maintenance, education or training of the child for a period ending not later than the year in which he attains the age of eighteen or, after attaining that age, ceases to undergo full-time education or training.'

'Marriage' in relation to a disposition on the dissolution or annulment of a marriage, and in relation to a disposition varying such a disposition, includes a former marriage.

This exemption covers all payments under ordinary maintenance agreements, and it is probable that maintenance would be widely construed and would include transfers of property provided the transfer was to maintain the spouse (for example, a transfer of the matrimonial home). However it will rarely be possible to bring transfers to children within the section because of the requirement that the transfer must cease at eighteen, or on the termination of education if later. S 11(5) envisages that transfers may be made which partly satisfy and partly fail to satisfy the provisions. In such circumstances the disposition is to be treated as two separate dispositions and the gratuitous disposition will be liable to IT. Where the transfer involves the creation of a settlement it is understood to be the Inland Revenue's view that an apportionment of the trust fund under s 11(5) is only possible if the disposition of an identifiable part of the fund completely satisfies the subsection. S 11(5) does not permit separation of the beneficial interests in the property comprised in the settlement. The exact scope of s 11(5) has yet to be tested in the courts[1].

If it is desired to make substantial transfers of property to children as part of a financial settlement following marriage breakdown, it will be difficult to satisfy the Inland Revenue that they are not gratuitous, particularly in the light of the current policy of the courts to such transfers. The courts have held that, although they have jurisdiction to order property settlements in favour of a child, a father should not normally be required to settle property on, or transfer property to, a normal healthy child[2]. His obligation to a child is solely an obligation to maintain, and not an obligation to set up in life. However, if a father is failing to discharge this obligation it is proper to order him to pay a lump sum for the maintenance of the child, and the order should be a secured order if possible[3].

It will also be impossible to take advantage of the relief for maintenance arrangements in ITA 1984 s 11 unless the assets transferred are to be spent

1   See *G v G* (1976) 6 Fam Law 8.
2   *Chamberlain v Chamberlain* [1974] 1 All ER 33 at 38; *Lord Lilford v Glynn* [1979] 1 All ER 441; *Draskovic v Draskovic* (1980) 11 Fam Law 87.
3   *Griffiths v Griffiths* [1984] Fam 70.

for the child's maintenance or are to return to the parent when, at the latest, the child ceases full-time education. However in a case such as *Griffiths v Griffiths*[1], where a father was ordered to pay a lump sum of £2,750 to the mother for the benefit of the children partly in lieu of maintenance, it should be possible to argue that the payment is not a chargeable transfer either because it is not intended to confer a gratuitous benefit, and is therefore exempt under ITA 1984 s 10, or because it is exempt under s 11 as provision by way of maintenance. In any event small amounts should cause few problems because they will be exempt if the transferor survives seven years and, even if he does not, the annual IT exemption of £3,000 (plus any unused £3,000 exemption from the previous year) can be deducted from the transfer to the extent that it has not otherwise been used.

Therefore if an outright transfer of capital assets to children is desired, it may be preferable to take advantage of the provisions governing accumulation and maintenance settlements under ITA 1984 s 71[2]. The initial transfer into the trust is a potentially exempt transfer[3], so that there will only be an IT charge if the transferor dies within seven years of the transfer. Even then, if the transferor's death is more than three years after the transfer, tapering relief will reduce any IT otherwise payable[4]. The assets in the trust will not be subject to the ten year anniversary charge[5] and there will be no exit charge provided the reason for the distribution is because the beneficiary has attained the requisite age[6]. However distributions while the trust is continuing, and while the child is under 18, will be taxed as income of the transferor, except to the extent that they exceed the total income of the settlement, whether retained or distributed[7].

8.13 Stamp duty on financial settlements following marriage breakdown

Stamp duty is charged on dutiable documents, not on transactions. All dispositions of property on divorce or separation by written instrument or court order are conveyances or transfers for the purposes of stamp duty[8]. If stamp duty is chargeable it may either be charged on an ad valorem basis or at a nominal 50p. The ad valorem rate on documents which constitute transfers on sale of assets other than shares and marketable securities is 1% of the value transferred. The duty on sales of shares and marketable securities is ½%[9]. Limited relief applies for transfers of property other than stocks and shares and certain leased land. Instruments transferring such property with a total value up to £30,000 which contain a certificate

1   [1984] Fam 70.
2   Discussed fully in **6.2:3** above.
3   ITA 1984 s 3A(1)(a).
4   ITA 1984 s 7(4).
5   ITA 1984 s 58(1)(b), 64.
6   ITA 1984 s 71(4).
7   ICTA 1988 s 664(2)(b), (3).
8   Stamp Act 1891 ss 54 and 62.
9   It was announced in the March 1990 Budget that the ½% stamp duty on share transfers will be abolished when the TAURUS system of paperless share transfers takes effect, probably towards the end of 1991.

to that effect complying with FA 1958 s 34(4) are exempt from duty[1]. Once the £30,000 limit is exceeded 1% duty is payable on the full value transferred, with no relief for the first £30,000.

Until the Finance Act 1985 documents transferring property by way of inter-vivos gifts were liable to stamp duty on the same basis as sales, but ad valorem duty on inter-vivos gifts was abolished for instruments executed on or after 26th March 1985, or instruments executed on or after 19th March 1985 which were stamped on or after 26th March 1985. Such instruments became liable to a 50p fixed duty as a 'conveyance or transfer of any other kind'. FA 1985 s 87(2) authorised total exemption from duty to be enacted by regulation provided the exempt document contained an appropriate certificate. Regulations have since been made[2] and apply to instruments executed on or after 1st May 1987. Voluntary dispositions for no consideration which contain a certificate in writing to that effect signed by the grantor, his solicitor, or duly authorised agent, are exempt from all duty. They are also exempt from any requirement to have the document adjudicated[3]. Instruments which do not contain the appropriate certificate remain liable to a 50p duty, and are not properly stamped unless they are adjudicated[4]. Transfers of property consequent on a divorce or separation should either be exempt from duty (or subject only to nominal duty) under these provisions or under the relief for sales discussed in the next paragraph.

Some transfers on divorce and separation may technically constitute sales. For example it might be argued that, if a separated wife is required to pay a lump sum to her husband in return for the transfer to her of his interest in the matrimonial home, this is a sale for stamp duty purposes. Similarly if an asset, such as the former matrimonial home, is transferred from one spouse to the other with the recipient spouse assuming liability to pay the outstanding mortgage, the Revenue regard this as a sale for stamp duty purposes[5]. FA 1985 s 83 provides relief for transfers on divorce and separation which would otherwise be stampable as sales. It applies to instruments executed on or after 26th March 1985[6] and substitutes a nominal 50p duty. Adjudication is not required. Instruments executed on or after 1st May 1987, and which contain an appropriate certificate, are completely exempt from duty[7]. FA 1985 s 83 applies to an instrument under which property is transferred from one party to a marriage to the other provided the instrument is executed in pursuance of a court order made on granting, or after granting, a decree of divorce, judicial separation, or nullity. Thus if this exemption is needed, the spouses will at some stage have to proceed to at least judicial separation. A mere agreement to separate will not be sufficient.

1   FA 1963 s 55(1).
2   The Stamp Duty (Exempt Instruments) Regulations 1987 SI 1987 No 516.
3   FA 1985 s 82(9).
4   FA 1985 s 82(5).
5   See SP 6/90, [1990] STI 414, fully discussed in **4.4** above.
6   Fa 1985 s 83(3).
7   Schedule to the Stamp Duty (Exempt Instruments) Regulations 1987, para H.

CHAPTER 9

The poll tax, foreign aspects, and future developments

9.1 The poll tax

The legislation dealing with the poll tax, or community charge, is contained in the Local Government Finance Act 1988 as supplemented by various statutory instruments, of which the most important is the Community Charges (Administration and Enforcement) Regulations 1989[1]. The Act imposes three main taxes, the personal community charge, the standard community charge, and non-domestic rates. If property, such as a hostel, is normally occupied by a transient population, the owner of the property may be subject to a collective community charge.

Poll tax is chargeable on a daily basis[2] and is dependent on an appropriate entry in the community charges register[3]. If there is no entry in the community charges register a taxpayer cannot be assessed to the tax, even if he is in fact subject to it. Conversely, subject to one exception, if a taxpayer is shown on the community charges register as subject to the tax, he has to pay it until the entry in the register is amended, even if he is no longer subject to it. The one exception is that if a taxpayer is shown as subject to the personal community charge on the same day in the register of two or more local authorities, he need only pay the charge which was first registered provided that at least one of the entries is under appeal[4]. As community charge is assessable on a daily basis the community charges register is a 'rolling register' so that people becoming liable to the charge for the first time in the middle of the financial year, for example because they have just moved into the area, will be registered as subject to the charge only from the date they become liable to it. Conversely, people who cease to be resident in a local authority area are entitled to have their names removed from the register as from the date they ceased to be resident there. Community charge is levied by the charging authority on the basis of the register, and the charging authority is not concerned with the accuracy of the register, which is the responsibility of the registration officer.

A person is subject to a charging authority's personal community charge if on any day he is over 18, has his sole or main residence in the authority's area at any time on the day, and is not an exempt individual[5]. A person who is in full-time education in England or Wales is deemed to have his sole or main residence on each day of the course in the place he is resident

---

1 SI 1989 No 438.
2 LGFA 1988 s 2(1).
3 LGFA 1988 ss 12(1) and 14(1).
4 Community Charges (Administration and Enforcement) Regulations 1989, reg 19(3)-(5).
5 LGFA 1988 s 2(1).

for the purpose of undertaking the course[1].

A person is subject to an authority's standard community charge if on any day he has a *legal* estate[2] in property which is domestic property situated in the local authority's area and which is not the sole or main residence of any individual[3]. If the freehold of the property is subject to a lease of six months or more the charge falls on the lessee rather than the freeholder, and the same applies if a sub-lease has been carved out of a head lease[4]. The standard community charge is mainly aimed at second homes. Local authorities have some discretion as to the rate they charge, and it may range from zero to twice the personal community charge for the area in which the property is situated[5]. To avoid the charge it should only be necessary to ensure that someone occupies the house as their main residence, and lodgers may gain a new found attraction.

In one set of circumstances considered earlier in the book the income tax treatment of a residence may differ materially from its community charge treatment. Suppose that a family resides outside London, but the husband's main place of business is in London, and he owns a flat there where he resides throughout the working week. At weekends and holidays he returns to the family home. For mortgage interest relief purposes the residence purchased first is deemed to be the only or main residence of both husband and wife, and the residence purchased second is deemed to be the only or main residence of neither of them[6]. For community charge purposes it will be in the husband's interests to argue that the London flat is his main residence. If this argument succeeds he will pay the personal community charge levied by the London borough in which the flat is situated, and his wife will pay a personal community charge for the district in which the family home is located. If the argument fails both spouses will pay personal community charges for the district in which the family home is located, and the husband will additionally have to pay a standard community charge of up to double the personal community charge for the London flat. In these circumstances the attractions of taking a lodger into the London flat may become irresistible.

In the absence of a relieving provision a double charge to the standard community charge could arise where the legal title to domestic property not occupied as a main residence was in joint names. This was not the intention, and the Community Charges (Administration and Enforcement) Regulations 1989 reg 59(2)(a)[7] therefore provides that there is only to be one standard community charge if a house is owned by co-owners, and the charge is to be a joint and several liability of the co-owners[8]. There are to be separate charges if the property is in co-ownership for part only of the financial year. There is no problem if there is only beneficial, rather than legal, co-ownership, as where the legal title to a house is in one person's name but another person has contributed to the purchase price so as to

1   LGFA 1988 s 2(5).
2   LGFA 1988 s 4(2).
3   LGFA 1988 s 3(1).
4   LGFA 1988 ss 3(2)(4) and 4(3).
5   LGFA 1988 s 40(1)(9).
6   ICTA 1988 s 356B(5).
7   Made under the authority of LGFA 1988 s 19.
8   CC(A & E) Regs 1989, reg 59(2)(d).

acquire an equitable interest in it. In these circumstances only the legal owner is chargeable, although there may still be a joint and several liability to pay the charge if the equitable co-owners are a married couple or cohabitees[1].

The personal community charge is the amount set in advance by the local authority for the financial year. The charge is normally levied and collected by the district council, but its charge will include a precept from the county council, and may also include a charge from a community council. It is important to appreciate that the charges levied at the start of the financial year are only estimated assessments which have to be made on certain assumptions laid down in the Community Charges (Administration and Enforcement) Regulations 1989, reg 15(3). These assumptions are:

> '(a)   that the person will be subject to the community charge to which the notice relates on every day after the issue of the notice;
> (b)   if he is shown on the register as undertaking a full-time course of education on the day the notice is issued, that he will undertake such a course on every day after the issue of the notice;
> (c)   if the notice is issued with respect to a standard community charge, that the property by virtue of which he is shown in the register as subject to the charge will on every day after the issue of the notice be in the class specified in regulation 62 in which it is shown in the register as falling on the day the notice is issued;
> (d)   ...'

These assumptions are not appealable[2]. However if later in the financial year it transpires that an assumption was unwarranted because a change has subsequently been made in the charges register, the initial estimated assessment has to be revised to the true liability for the year[3]. For the personal community charge the amount is[4]:

$$\frac{A \times B}{C}$$

where A is the community charge for the year, B is the number of days in the financial year the taxpayer is shown in the register as liable to the charge, and C is the total number of days in the financial year. Students are liable to 20% of the amount so computed provided they were in full-time education throughout the period they are subject to the charge[5]. If they are only full time students for part of the period their liability has to be computed applying the formula[6]—

$$\frac{P \times A}{C} + \left(\frac{Q \times A}{C} \times \frac{1}{5} \right)$$

where A is the community charge for the year, C is the total number of days in the financial year, P is the number of days the student is liable

1   Under LGFA 1988 s 16; see below.
2   CC(A & E) Regs 1989, reg 25.
3   CC(A & E) Regs 1989, Sch 1 paras 6 and 7.
4   LGFA 1988 s 12.
5   LGFA 1988 s 13(2).
6   LGFA 1988 s 13(3).

to the charge, but is not in full-time education, and Q is the number of days he is liable to the charge and is in full-time education. The regulations envisage that several reassessments may need to be made during the financial year[1]!

An initial estimated assessment to both the personal community charge and the standard community charge is payable in 10 instalments[2], or by such other method as the local authority may agree[3]. The instalments must run for 10 consecutive months but, subject to this, may be for any 10 month period in the financial year at the authority's option provided the demand notice is issued at least 14 days before the first instalment is due[4]. The day on which each instalment is to be paid is also to be specified by the authority[5]. If an assessment is issued late in the financial year the number of instalments in which it can be paid is reduced. If a taxpayer fails to pay an instalment on the due date the local authority must serve a notice on him specifying the arrears of instalments and requiring them to be paid[6]. If the taxpayer pays the arrears within 7 days, together with any further instalments due in that period, that is the end of the matter and the taxpayer continues to be entitled to pay the remainder of his liability by instalments[7]. But if he fails to pay the outstanding liabilities within 7 days the whole of the outstanding balance immediately becomes payable[8].

9.2 Poll tax liabilities — spouses and cohabitees

Normally only the individual subject to the charge is liable to pay a personal or standard community charge. However if a person is married to a spouse aged 18 or over the liability to pay the tax becomes a joint and several liability of both the taxpayer and the spouse. A spouse is defined as follows by LGFA 1988 s 16(9):

> 'For the purposes of this section people are married to each other if they are a man and a woman —
> (a)   who are married to each other and are members of the same household, or
> (b)   who are not married to each other but are living together as husband and wife.'

People are not married to each other on a particular day unless they are married to each other at the end of it[9].

Spouses are therefore only jointly and severally liable for each other's liabilities if they are living together, and this brings the poll tax concepts into line with income tax concepts. To this extent poll tax differs from rates, as in certain circumstances a husband who had separated from his wife and left the matrimonial home could nevertheless remain liable to

1   CC(A & E) Regs 1989, Sch 1 para 8.
2   CC(A & E) Regs 1989, Sch 1 paras 1-4.
3   CC(A & E) Regs 1989, reg 17(3) and (4).
4   CC(A & E) Regs 1989, Sch 1 para 4.
5   CC(A & E) Regs 1989, Sch 1 para 1(3).
6   CC(A & E) Regs 1989, reg 20(1).
7   CC(A & E) Regs 1989, reg 20(2).
8   CC(A & E) Regs 1989, reg 20(2).
9   LGFA 1988 s 16(10).

pay the rates on it[1]. If a couple are only married and living together for part of the financial year the total poll tax liability of each of them for the year is apportioned between the period they were married and living together and the period they were not, and joint and several liability only applies to poll tax due for the former period[2]. The definition in LGFA s 16(9) makes it clear that cohabitees are subject to joint and several liability, but it is unusual in that it actually deems them to be married.

Apart from legal co-owners subject to the standard charge and the collective charge, the imposition of joint and several liability on spouses and cohabitees for their respective charges is the only exception to the principle that liability is personal to the taxpayer who has been charged with the tax. Consequently a parent is not liable for the unpaid poll tax liability of his child, and a child is not liable for the unpaid poll tax liability of his parent.

The consequence of spouses being jointly and severally liable for their poll tax payments is that each becomes liable to pay the whole of their own and their spouse's liability. In practice, as will be seen when we look at the enforcement provisions, it is not intended to enforce this against a spouse who has no separate resources, and initially separate bills will be sent to each spouse liable to pay the charge. If one spouse does pay a poll tax liability of the other then if, and only if, the reason the payment was made was the wilful refusal or culpable neglect of the chargeable spouse to pay, the spouse making the payment to the local authority is entitled to recover it from the chargeable spouse[3]. Thus there is no right of recovery if one spouse pays the poll tax liability of the other because the chargeable spouse has inadequate resources. Joint and several liability is extended to liability for payment of instalments of poll tax by the Community Charges (Administration and Enforcement) Regulations 1989 reg 22 in provisions which mirror the main provisions in LGFA 1988 s 16. However a spouse only becomes liable to pay an instalment due from a chargeable spouse if a notice requiring payment is served on him by the charging authority stating the amount due, and the notice must allow at least 14 days for payment[4]. If a spouse pays instalments following service of a notice by a local authority and subsequently it becomes apparent that a rebate is due, the rebate is to be paid to that spouse up to the amount of any payments made by that spouse[5].

9.3 Poll tax — enforcement procedures

If poll tax instalments remain unpaid the first obligation of the local authority is to serve a reminder notice on the taxpayer requiring payment of the outstanding instalments within 7 days[6]. If that fails to produce results

1 See eg *Routhan v Arun District Council* [1981] 3 All ER 752; *R v Harrow Magistrates' Court ex p London Borough of Harrow* (1983) 81 LGR 514; *Moore v Durham City Council* [1987] RVR 129; cf *Doncaster Metropolitan Borough Council v Lockwood* [1987] Fam Law 241.
2 LGFA 1988 s 16(4)-(6).
3 LGFA 1988 s 16(7).
4 CC(A & E) Regs 1989, reg 23.
5 CC(A & E) Regs 1989, reg 23.
6 CC(A & E) Regs 1989, reg 20(1).

and the taxpayer has a spouse or cohabitee the next option of the local authority is to serve a notice on the spouse or cohabitee requiring payment of the taxpayer's outstanding instalments[1]. There is no obligation on the authority to exercise this option if it decides it is undesirable to do so, as where it is satisfied that the spouse has no independent resources. If, whether or not the option of requiring payment from a spouse is exercised, payments are still not received, the local authority will have to exercise its enforcement powers. Before the local authority can exercise any of these powers it is required to apply to the magistrates' court for a 'liability order'[2]. It is a precondition to such an application that the authority must first serve on the chargeable person a reminder notice[3]. However no further reminder notice is necessary if a reminder notice has already been served under reg 20(1) to collect arrears of instalments and the liability order is sought to collect those unpaid instalments[4]. If the chargeable person is married or cohabiting the local authority may also apply for a liability order against the spouse or cohabitee provided that a notice under reg 23 requiring payment has been served on the spouse or cohabitee and that a reminder notice has also been served[5]. A liability order may be obtained against the chargeable person alone or against the chargeable person and his spouse. It may not be made against the spouse alone[6].

A liability notice is obtained by a complaint to a justice of the peace requesting the issue of a summons directed to the person charged to appear before the magistrates' court to show cause why the sum claimed has not been paid[7]. The court must make a liability order if it is satisfied that the sum claimed has become payable by the defendant and has not been paid[8]. The liability order is to be for the amount claimed plus costs[9].

Once the local authority has obtained a liability order a battery of enforcement powers becomes available to it if the taxpayer then fails to pay the amount shown as due in the liability order. The options are:

(1) an attachment of earnings order;
(2) deduction from income support;
(3) distress;
(4) a charging order;
(5) imprisonment for up to 3 months (only as a last resort, and if distress has been tried and failed);
(6) bankruptcy.

Provided a liability order has been issued against both the chargeable person and his spouse, an attachment of earnings order, distress, or a charging order may be made against either the chargeable person or his spouse[10]. But once one of those three options has been commenced against

1 CC(A & E) Regs 1989, reg 23.
2 CC(A & E) Regs 1989, reg 29.
3 CC(A & E) Regs 1989, reg 28(1).
4 CC(A & E) Regs 1989, reg 28(3).
5 CC(A & E) Regs 1989, reg 48(2).
6 CC(A & E) Regs 1989, reg 48(2).
7 CC(A & E) Regs 1989, reg 29(2).
8 CC(A & E) Regs 1989, reg 29(5).
9 CC(A & E) Regs 1989, reg 29(5).
10 CC(A & E) Regs 1989, reg 48(4).

a person subject to a liability order no other remedy may be implemented until the initial option has been exhausted[1]. The rules for an application for imprisonment are a little more complex. All the other remedies may be implemented by the local authority without further reference to the court after obtaining a liability order. Imprisonment, as might be expected, requires a further court order. No application for commital to prison may be made unless distress has been levied against the chargeable person but insufficient goods have been realised to pay the outstanding poll tax and costs[2]. If an order for commital to prison of a spouse is sought, distress must have been unsuccessfully levied against both the chargeable person and the spouse[3]. On an application for commital to prison the court must, in the debtor's presence, inquire whether the failure to pay which led to the liability order being made against him/her was due to his or her wilful refusal or culpable neglect[4]. If, and only if, this is the case a magistrates' court can impose a maximum term of imprisonment of up to 3 months[5]. An order of imprisonment is automatically discharged if the arrears outstanding are paid, and the court has a discretion to defer the implementation of a term of imprisonment[6]. As there can be no imprisonment for inability to pay, there should be no question of a spouse without funds being imprisoned because a spouse with funds has failed to pay their joint poll tax liabilities, and in any event the plethora of enforcement remedies available to a local authority apart from imprisonment should ensure that it is a remedy which only has to be exercised in the most exceptional cases. The main problem with poll tax is not likely to be the enforcement of liabilities once the liability has been established and the taxpayer tracked down; the main problem is likely to be to keep track of taxpayers and to maintain a reasonably up-to-date poll tax register.

9.4 Poll tax appeals

All poll tax assessments sent out at the start of the financial year are estimated assessments based on the assumption that a taxpayer's status at the time the estimated assessment is issued will remain unchanged for the whole of the financial year. No appeal may be made of the ground that this assumption is wrong because, for example, the taxpayer will cease to be resident in the local authority's area during the year, or will cease to be in full-time education during the year[7]. Incorrect estimated assessments of this type can only be altered once the change of status has occurred, and the taxpayer remains liable to pay the estimated assessments until the appropriate amendment is made in the community charges register. Subject to this restriction, appeals are governed by LGFA 1988 ss 23 and 24. An appeal may be made to a valuation and community charge tribunal on

1   CC(A & E) Regs 1989, regs 46(2) and 48(9).
2   CC(A & E) Regs 1989, reg 41(1).
3   CC(A & E) Regs 1989, regs 41(1) and 48(5) and (7).
4   CC(A & E) Regs 1989, reg 41(2).
5   CC(A & E) Regs 1989, reg 41(3).
6   CC(A & E) Regs 1989, reg 41(3)-(6).
7   CC(A & E) Regs 1989, reg 25.

any of the grounds set out in LGFA 1988 s 23(2) of which the most important are:

(a) the fact that a person is, or is not, entered in the community charges register as subject to a community charge,

(b) the contents of an entry in the register are wrong,

(c) any estimated assessment is wrong,

(d) the imposition of a penalty,

(e) the designation of a building as subject to a collective community charge, or the refusal to remove the designation.

It is a precondition to any appeal that the taxpayer first serves a written notice on either the charging authority or the registration officer, depending on the matter being appealed against[1]. The notice must state both the matter about which the appellant is aggrieved and reason for his grievance[2]. The charging authority or the registration officer then has two months to respond either accepting the complaint and making an appropriate adjustment or rejecting it. If the complaint is rejected a reason for the rejection must be given[3]. If the complainant is still unhappy, or he has received no response at all within the two-month period allowed, he may then appeal to the valuation and community charges tribunal[4]. The fact that a notice of grievance has been served, or an appeal is under way, does not normally relieve the appellant from paying instalments of poll tax to which he has been assessed and which fall due during the period the appeal is under consideration. However if an appeal is being made because the taxpayer has been assessed to personal community charge for the same day or days by two different authorities, he need only pay the charge of the authority which was the first to register him for liability[5]. If the taxpayer's name is removed from the register during the financial year, whether as a result of an appeal or otherwise, because he has ceased to be subject to a community charge, he is immediately freed from the obligation to pay any instalments of poll tax due after the date of removal, even though it may take the authority some time to issue an adjusted assessment for the year[6].

9.5 Overseas aspects — residence of spouses

The residence status of a husband and wife has always been determined separately as, prior to 1990-91, a husband and wife were deemed to be living apart for income tax purposes if one of them was and one of them was not resident in the United Kingdom, or if both of them were resident in the United Kingdom but one of them was absent from the country for the whole of the tax year[7]. If ICTA 1988 s 282(3) applied the income tax liabilities of both spouses were computed separately, but the aggregate of their tax liabilities was not to be greater than it would have been if they

1 LGFA 1988 s 24(1).
2 LGFA 1988 s 24(3).
3 LGFA 1988 s 24(5)(b).
4 LGFA 1988 s 24(1) and (4).
5 CC(A & E) Regs 1989, reg 19(3)-(5).
6 CC(A & E) Regs 1989, Sch 1 para 6.
7 ICTA 1988 s 282(3).

had been assessed as a married couple living together[1]. Following the introduction of independent taxation these provisions have been repealed as superfluous[2], so that the residence status of each spouse is now only relevant to compute that spouse's taxable income, and there is no restriction on the maximum tax liability.

As a matter of general principle an individual who is not resident in the United Kingdom remains liable to UK income tax on UK source income, but is exempt from tax on foreign source income whether or not it is remitted to the UK. Non-residents are not normally entitled to any personal allowances[3], but an exception is made for an individual who[4]:

'(a) is a Commonwealth citizen or a citizen of the Republic of Ireland; or

(b) is a person who is or who has been employed in the service of the Crown, or who is employed in the service of any missionary society or in the service of any territory under Her Majesty's protection; or

(c) is resident in the Isle of Man or the Channel Islands; or

(d) has previously resided within the United Kingdom, and is resident abroad for the sake of his or her health, or the health of a member of his or her family resident with him or her; or

(e) is a widow whose late husband [or a widower whose late wife,][5] was in the service of the Crown.'

Prior to 1990-91 an individual who satisfied one of these conditions was entitled to a proportion of his personal allowances. The proportion was arrived at by a complicated calculation which required that a taxpayer's UK income tax liability should not be less than[6]:

$$\text{Income tax on world wide income} \quad \times \quad \frac{\text{UK source total income}}{\text{World wide total income}}$$

As from 1990-91 this restriction has been repealed[7], so that a UK or Commonwealth citizen, or other qualifying individual, is now entitled to full personal allowances to set against his UK source income irrespective of the amount of his foreign source income. Thus if a taxpayer is a UK citizen who is a married man living with his wife and who is non-resident because he is working abroad, he will now be entitled to the personal allowance of £3,005 and the married couple's allowance of £1,720. These allowances could prove very useful if, for example, he has let his UK home during his absence and so remains liable to UK income tax on the rental profit. If a husband resident abroad has insufficient UK source income to absorb both his personal allowance and his married couple's allowance any unused personal allowance may be transferred to his wife, assuming she is entitled to claim personal allowances. However the transitional relief in ICTA 1988 s 257D which may enable a husband with a low income to transfer unused personal allowance to his wife[8] cannot be claimed if the husband is non-resident[9].

1 ICTA 1988 s 282(3).
2 FA 1988 Sch 3 para 11.
3 ICTA 1988 s 278(1).
4 ICTA 1988 s 278(2).
5 Amendment inserted by FA 1988 s 31(2) with effect from 1990-91.
6 ICTA 1988 s 278(3).
7 By FA 1988 s 31(4).
8 See **1.7** above.
9 ICTA 1988 s 278(2A).

Under ICTA 1988 s 232 a non-resident individual who is entitled to claim personal allowances under ICTA 1988 s 278(2) is also entitled to any tax credit attaching to a distribution of income by a UK company, although this will often be affected by provisions in a tax treaty between the UK and the country in which the taxpayer is now resident. Under ESC B13 if a non-resident receives UK source interest without deduction of income tax no action is taken to pursue his liability to tax on the interest except to the extent that it can be recovered by set-off in a claim to relief in respect of taxed income from UK sources. With many UK non-residents now retaining the right to claim their full personal allowances against their UK source income, the occasions when this recovery by set-off applies may increase.

The principle that a husband and wife were treated as living apart if one of them was resident and the other was not also applied for capital gains tax purposes[1], with complications for inter spousal transfers well illustrated by *Gubay v Kington*[2]. The withdrawal of the provision from 1990-91 for income tax also applies for capital gains tax[3], so that transfers between husband and wife who are in fact living together take place on a no gain/no loss basis by virtue of CGTA 1979 s 44(1) irrespective of the residence status of the spouses. In limited circumstances this change may give scope for tax planning. UK capital gains tax is imposed on gains realised on the disposal of chargeable assets by an individual who is resident or ordinarily resident in the UK[4]. In general there is no source rule for capital gains tax, so that there is no CGT liability on the disposal of assets situated in the UK by an individual who is neither resident nor ordinarily resident here[5]. If a UK individual goes abroad for the purposes of foreign employment it is normal Inland Revenue practice to treat him as both not resident and not ordinarily resident in the UK from the day following the day of departure to the day before the date of return provided his contract of foreign employment covers a period including a complete tax year, and he does not return to the UK for more than six months in any tax year or an average of at least three months a year during his absence[6]. It is sensible tax planning for an individual who satisfies these conditions to sell any UK source assets which are showing substantial unrealised capital gains, and to re-purchase them under a bed and breakfast transaction if it is desired to retain them. If one spouse is non-resident, and so able to take advantage of this relief, but the other spouse is resident and thus liable to CGT, tax savings can be made if the resident spouse first transfers the assets to the non-resident spouse under a no gain/no loss transfer within CGTA 1979 s 44, and the non-resident spouse later sells the assets. To avoid a possible challenge under the new anti-avoidance doctrine in *WT Ramsay*

1 CGTA 1979 s 155(2).
2 (1984) 57 TC 601, and see **3.5** above for a full discussion.
3 CGTA 1979 s 155(2) provides that references to a husband and wife living together shall be construed in accordance with ICTA 1988 s 282, the amended version of which applies from 1990-91.
4 CGTA 1979 s 2(1).
5 There is a charge if the assets are part of a busines being carried on through a branch or agency in the UK.
6 Revenue booklet 'Residents and Non-residents — Liability to Tax in the United Kingdom', IR 20, 1986, para 18.

Ltd v IRC[1] and *Furniss v Dawson*[2], it is desirable that there should be as long a gap as possible between the inter-spousal transfer and the eventual sale, that no sale should have been agreed at the time the assets are transferred between the spouses, and that the non-resident spouse should not be under any legal obligation to hand the sale proceeds over to the resident spouse.

9.6 Overseas aspects — domicile

A person's domicile can also have a significant impact on his liability to UK taxation. As a matter of general principle a person who is resident in the United Kingdom but is not domiciled here is liable to UK income tax on his UK source income plus foreign source income remitted to the UK[3]. Foreign source income retained abroad is exempt from income tax. A person who is resident or ordinarily resident in the UK but is not domiciled here is liable to capital gains tax on gains arising from the disposal of assets situated in the UK plus gains from the disposal of assets situated abroad which are remitted to the UK[4]. Liability to inheritance tax is primarily based on an individual's domicile. An individual who is domiciled in the UK is liable to inheritance tax on his world-wide assets; an individual who is not domiciled in the UK is only liable to inheritance tax on his UK source assets[5]. While transfers of assets between spouses are normally exempt transfers for inheritance tax purposes[6], there is an exception when the transferor spouse is domiciled in the UK and the recipient spouse is not domiciled. The maximum exempt transfer is limited to £55,000[7] but, if the transfer is an inter-vivos transfer, any excess over the £55,000 limit will be a potentially exempt transfer[8], so that there will be no charge if the transferor survives for at least seven years[9].

The concept of domicile is separate from the concept of citizenship, and is the civil law jurisdiction which an individual regards, or is deemed to regard, as his permanent home. Civil law jurisdictions are not the same as political entities, so that each State of the United States constitutes a separate domicile, and England and Wales, Scotland, and Northern Ireland are all separate domiciles within the United Kingdom. Unlike residence, an individual can only have one country of domicile at any one time. At birth an individual acquires a domicile of origin. A legitimate child takes as his domicile of origin the domicile of his father at the time of his birth. An investigation of the domicile of the father may therefore be necessary to determine the domicile of a child[10]. An illegitimate or posthumous child takes the domicile of his mother at the time of his birth as his domicile of origin. An individual's domicile for tax purposes is his domicile of origin

---

1   (1981) 54 TC 101.
2   (1984) 55 TC 324.
3   ICTA 1988 s 65(4) and (5).
4   CGTA 1979 s 14.
5   ITA 1984 s 6(1).
6   ITA 1984 s 18(1).
7   ITA 1984 s 18(1).
8   ITA 1984 s 3A(2).
9   ITA 1984 s 3A(4).
10 See eg *Douglas v Douglas* (1871) LR 12 Eq 617.

unless it can be established that he has acquired either a domicile of dependency or a domicile of choice.

A domicile of dependency is a domicile assigned by law to an individual regarded as incapable of having an independent domicile, and it now applies mainly to children. In general a child's domicile of dependency follows that of the parent who gave him his domicile of origin, and will alter as that parent's domicile alters. Prior to 1974 a legitimate child automatically took as a domicile of dependency the domicile of his father and retained that domicile even when his parents divorced, the child continued to reside with his mother, and the mother acquired a different domicile from that of the father. However the Domicile and Matrimonial Proceedings Act 1973 s 4 now provides that where the parents are alive and living apart the child's domicile of dependence is to be that of his mother if (*a*) his home is with her and not with his father, or (*b*) the child has acquired his mother's domicile under (*a*) and has not since then had a domicile with his father. A child's domicile of dependency lasts until he attains the age of 16 or marries under that age[1]. If a child has a domicile of dependency immediately prior to attaining 16, he retains that domicile as a domicile of choice[2] until either a new domicile of choice has been acquired or the domicile of dependency being abandoned without a new domicile of choice being acquired, in which case the child's domicile of origin will revive.

Prior to 1974 on marriage a woman acquired her husband's domicile as a domicile of dependency. She retained this domicile even if she subsequently separated from him and acquired what would otherwise have been a different domicile, although domicile of dependency did cease on divorce or death of the husband. However as from 1st January 1974 domicile of dependency for married women was abolished, and a married woman's domicile is to be determined as if she was capable of having an independent domicile[3]. Women who were married prior to 1st January 1974, and so had acquired their husband's domicile as a domicile of dependency, are deemed to retain that domicile, as a domicile of choice if it is not their domicile of origin, unless and until it is changed by the acquisition or revival of another domicile[4].

To escape the shackles of a domicile of choice it is necessary to show (*a*) an intention to cease to reside in the domicile of choice and (*b*) the cessation of residence in the domicile of choice[5]. The legal test for abandonment of a deemed domicile of choice acquired under the DMPA 1973 is no less stringent than the test for abandonment of a domicile of choice acquired through personal choice. This issue was tested in the High Court in *IRC v Duchess of Portland*[6]. The taxpayer had a domicile of origin in Quebec and had always been a Canadian citizen. In 1948 she married the Duke of Portland, and so acquired an English domicile of dependency. On 1st January 1974, following the enactment of the DMPA 1973, this English domicile of dependency was converted into an English domicile of choice. The taxpayer always maintained strong links with

1 DMPA 1973 s 3, although this section does not extend to Scotland.
2 *Gulbenkian v Gulbenkian* [1937] 4 All ER 618.
3 DMPA 1973 s 1(1).
4 DMPA 1973 s 1(2).
5 *Udny v Udny* (1869) LR 1 Sc & Div 441; *IRC v Duchess of Portland* (1981) 54 TC 648.
6 (1981) 54 TC 648.

Quebec. She owned a house there, returned there every year to visit her parents, and intended to live permanently in Quebec if her husband pre-deceased her. She had agreed with her husband that they would live in Quebec when he retired. In July 1974 she made her annual visit to Quebec. The taxpayer claimed that, at least as from July 1974, her Canadian domicile of origin had revived, and that she was accordingly no longer liable to UK income tax on her foreign source income which she retained abroad. The Special Commissioners upheld her claim on the ground that (a) she intended to abandon England as a domicile of choice and (b) her departure from England in July 1974 was sufficient actual abandonment, even though it was not a permanent absence. The High Court reversed this decision. Nourse J held that the summer visit to Canada did not constitute the cessation of residence in England, and accordingly the second requirement of the actual cessation of residence was not satisfied. It was agreed on all sides, following *IRC v Bullock*[1] discussed below, that had the taxpayer's marriage occurred on or after 1st January 1974 she would have retained her Quebec domicile of origin, and would not have acquired a domicile of choice in England because of her lack of intention to reside there permanently.

Every individual who is not subject to a domicile of dependency is capable of acquiring a domicile of choice. To establish the acquisition of a domicile of choice it must be proved *both* that the individual has become resident in a country other than his domicile of origin *and* that he intends to make that country his country of permanent residence. This latter requirement can be extremely difficult to prove, particularly where it is the Revenue authorities who are trying to assert it and the taxpayer is trying to resist it. Thus a taxpayer may be resident in a country for many years but still not have acquired a domicile of choice in that country because he has never intended to make it his permanent home. Good illustrations are provided by *Buswell v IRC*[2] and *IRC v Bullock*[3]. In the latter case the taxpayer had a domicile of origin in Nova Scotia, Canada, but came to England in 1932 to join the RAF. He continued to regard himself as Canadian and intended to return to Canada on completing his military service. However in 1948 he married an English wife who, after visiting Canada, made it clear that she was not prepared to live there. The taxpayer reluctantly accepted this and a matrimonial home was bought in England. He continued to hope that she would change her mind and firmly intended to return to Canada should she pre-decease him. In 1966 the taxpayer made a will subject to Nova Scotia law in which he declared that he remained domiciled in Nova Scotia to which he intended to return after his wife's death. He retained his Canadian citizenship. On these facts the Court of Appeal held that the Inland Revenue had failed to establish the necessary intent to reside in the United Kingdom to prove the acquisition of a domicile of choice. The taxpayer's intention to return to Canada was more than a vague hope or aspiration. He accordingly retained his Canadian domicile of origin despite the fact that he had resided in the United Kingdom for forty years and would in all probability continue to reside here for many more years. The contrast between this case and *IRC v Duchess of Portland* has already been mentioned.

1 (1976) 51 TC 522.
2 (1974) 49 TC 334.
3 (1976) 51 TC 522.

Because considerable tax advantages accrue from non-domiciled status, attempts have been made from time to time to impose by statute a UK domicile for tax purposes. Currently the only surviving provisions relate to inheritance tax. A person who permanently leaves the UK and who was domiciled here on or after 10th December 1974 is deemed for inheritance tax purposes to retain his UK domicile for three years after he actually acquires a different domicile[1]. There is therefore a minimum waiting period of three years after departure from the UK before inheritance tax-free disposals of foreign assets may be made, but the actual waiting period may be much longer, as the three-year waiting period only begins to run from the date of acquisition of the foreign domicile, which may be much later than the date of arrival in a foreign country. An individual who was resident in the United Kingdom on or after 10th December 1974 and in not less than seventeen out of the twenty years of assessment ending with the year in which the relevant transfer was made is deemed to be domiciled in the UK for inheritance tax[2]. The Law Commission have made proposals for a more extensive review of the law of domicile[3], and in July 1988 the Revenue issued a consultative document 'Residence in the United Kingdom — The scope of UK taxation for individuals.' No concrete proposals have emerged from either document, and there is no suggestion that any legislative change is imminent. As the special statutory provisions only apply for inheritance tax purposes, an individual who has been resident in the United Kingdom for many years but who still intends to live permanently in another country may well be domiciled in the UK for inheritance tax but not domiciled here for income tax and capital gains tax.

Once a domicile of choice has been acquired it can only be abandoned if the individual *both* ceases to reside there *and* intends to cease to reside there permanently. Authority for these tests, and an illustration of the practical difficulties in satisfying it, are provided by *IRC v Duchess of Portland*[4], discussed above[5]. If a domicile of choice is abandoned the domicile of origin will revive unless a new domicile of choice has been acquired.

9.7 Tax planning under independent taxation for a non-domiciled spouse

Under independent taxation there is scope for tax planning if both spouses are resident in the UK but one is domiciled here for income tax and capital gains tax purposes and the other is not. As the income and gains from foreign source assets are exempt from UK income tax and capital gains tax if they are beneficially owned by a person who is not domiciled in the UK provided they are retained abroad, it is sensible tax planning to

1 ITA 1984 s 267(1)(a), (3).
2 ITA 1984 s 267(1)(b), (3).
3 Law Com Report No 168, 1987, Cm 200, 'Private International Law, The Law of Domicile', preceded by Working Paper No 88 'Private International Law, The Law of Domicile', 1985.
4 (1981) 54 TC 648.
5 See also *Buswell v IRC* (1974) 49 TC 334; *Re Lloyd Evans* [1947] Ch 695; *Fielden v IRC* (1965) 42 TC 501.

ensure that all foreign source assets are owned by the non-domiciled spouse. If there is to be an overall tax saving as a result of this arrangement it is clearly also important to take into account the tax treatment of the income and gains from the foreign source assets in the country in which they arise, as there is little point in escaping the manacles of UK tax only to discover that higher rates of tax are imposed on the income and gains by another country. If assets currently owned by a spouse domiciled in the UK are gifted to a non-domiciled spouse to take advantage of this relief, the transfer will effectively be exempt from capital gains tax by virtue of the relief for inter spousal transfers in CGTA 1979 s 44 provided the spouses are living together. However if the transfer value exceeds £55,000 and the non-domiciled spouse is not deemed to be domiciled in the UK for inheritance tax under ITA 1984 s 18(2) the excess over £55,000 will be a potentially exempt transfer for inheritance tax purposes rather than an exempt transfer, although this will only pose a problem if the transferor spouse fails to live for seven years after the transfer. If the recipient spouse is not domiciled in the UK for inheritance tax as well as for income tax and capital gains tax, a further advantage of transferring foreign source assets into her name is that they will cease to be liable to inheritance tax. For all these arrangements to work it is essential that the transfers should be absolute gifts of assets with no strings attached. If any form of settlement is used there is considerable risk that it will be caught by an anti-avoidance provision. It is therefore important that the marriage should be stable.

9.8 Maintenance arrangements — foreign court orders and agreements

For income tax purposes the source of maintenance income is the maintenance agreement or court order, and the country of source is the country in which the agreement or order is given legal effect. The country of residence of the payer and the country from which maintenance is actually paid are both irrelevant[1]. Thus where the payee is resident in the UK and the payments are made under foreign order, they are assessable under Sch D case V[2]. However the Finance Act 1988 had as significant an effect for overseas maintenance orders as it did for UK orders. If a foreign maintenance order or agreement is first made or entered into on or after 15th March 1988, a recipient of maintenance payable under it is exempt from income tax on it even if she is resident in the UK, and this applies whether the recipient is a spouse or a child[3]. Conversely, with one possible exception, the payments are not tax deductible to the payer even if he is resident in the UK and the payments are made out of income liable to UK income tax. The legislation authorising a maintenance deduction of up to the married couple's allowance, £1,720 for 1990-91, excludes payments due under a foreign order or agreement[4]. The exception arises where the payer has foreign emoluments out of which he pays the foreign source maintenance, in which

---

1   *IRC v Anderstròm* (1927) 13 TC 482.
2   *IRC v Anderstròm*, above; *Chamney v Lewis* (1932) 17 TC 318.
3   ICTA 1988 s 347A(4).
4   ICTA 1988 s 347B(1).

case the maintenance payments may qualify for a maximum deduction of £1,720. This exception is discussed in more detail below.

If maintenance payments are due under a foreign order or agreement first made before 15th March 1988 and the recipient is resident in the UK, the recipient remains liable to income tax under Sch D Case V on the maintenance, but subject to a number of modifications designed to bring the tax treatment of foreign maintenance orders into line with the tax treatment of UK maintenance orders. First, the amount of maintenance on which the recipient can be taxed is capped at its 1988-89 level, so that for 1990-91 a recipient is taxable on the lower of the maintenance to which she is entitled in 1990-91 or to which she was entitled in 1988-89[1], and this applies whether the recipient is a spouse or a child. Secondly, if foreign source maintenance is payable to a former or separated spouse who has not remarried, or to such a spouse for the maintenance of a child of the family, the spouse may claim a deduction of £1,720 from any maintenance otherwise assessable under Sch D Case V[2].

The payer of maintenance under a foreign order or agreement first made before 15th March 1988 must pay the maintenance gross[3], and is in general not entitled to any tax relief on the payments[4]. However, because of the way in which FA 1988 s 38 is worded, relief may be available where in 1988-89 an individual was paying maintenance under both a UK order and a foreign order and the person entitled to maintenance under the foreign order is now resident in the UK. As payments under the foreign order did not qualify for tax relief in 1988-89, the payer's maintenance cap is determined by the maintenance payments he made under the UK order in 1988-89. But if the payments under the UK order have since ceased, there is nothing in FA 1988 s 38 to prevent payment due under a foreign court order or agreement from qualifying for a tax deduction provided the other requirements of FA 1988 s 38(1) are satisfied. One requirement of particular relevance is that the recipient of maintenance must be chargeable to UK tax on it under Sch D Case V.

Limited relief may also be available if the taxpayer has 'foreign emoluments' assessable under Sch E case I or II. 'Foreign emoluments' are emoluments of an individual not domiciled in the UK from an employer who is not resident in the UK[5]. A taxpayer may claim a deduction from his gross foreign emoluments for payments made out of the emoluments in circumstances corresponding to those in which the payments would have reduced his liability to income tax under UK law, although the granting of the claim is within the Revenue's discretion[6]. In practice this will include payments due under foreign orders or agreements made before 15th March 1988 up to a maximum of the maintenance paid in 1988-89. Dealing with such a claim in a booklet which has recently been withdrawn[7], 'The Taxation of Foreign Earnings and Foreign Pensions: Finance Act 1977', IR 25, the

---

1   FA 1988 s 38(1)(c), (2)(b), (4), (8).
2   FA 1988 s 38(2)(b), (4), (5).
3   *Keiner v Keiner* (1952) 34 TC 346.
4   *Bingham v IRC* (1955) 36 TC 254.
5   ICTA 1988 s 192(1).
6   ICTA 1988 s 192(3).
7   See [1990] STI 188. The withdrawal should not affect the validity of the statement cited.

Revenue stated:

> 'It is a condition of such a claim that the payments are made out of the foreign emoluments which are charged to United Kingdom tax. Moreover the Board, in exercise of their discretion to allow such claims, will in practice require the claimant to show that he has not sufficient overseas income (on which United Kingdom tax is not chargeable) to enable him to make the payments without having recourse to the foreign emoluments.'

9.9 Maintenance arrangements — foreign aspects of UK orders and agreements

If maintenance is due under a UK order or agreement first made on or after 15th March 1988 the recipient is exempt from income tax on maintenance paid under it whether she is resident in the UK or resident abroad[1]. If the recipient is a former or separated spouse who has not remarried the payer is entitled to a tax deduction of an amount equivalent to the married couple's allowance or the amount of maintenance paid, whichever is the less[2].

The position is more complicated if the maintenance order or agreement was made before 15th March 1988. As it is due under a UK source order or agreement the payer, irrespective of his residence status, remains entitled to a tax deduction from any income chargeable to UK income tax of the maintenance for which he was entitled to tax relief in 1988-89 or the maintenance paid in the current tax year, whichever is the less[3]. Under ESC A-12 if the payer is resident abroad and under the law of the foreign country he is required to withhold foreign income tax on paying maintenance due under a UK order or agreement, the recipient may claim a foreign tax credit of the amount withheld against any UK income tax liability she may have on the maintenance.

Conversely, as the maintenance is UK source income it remains assessable income of the recipient under Sch D Case III, but on an actual year basis[4], even if she becomes non-resident[5]. However a number of reliefs may assist. First, if the recipient is a divorced or separated spouse who has not remarried she may claim a deduction equivalent to the married couple's allowance from any assessable maintenance[6]. Secondly, if the recipient is a Commonwealth citizen, or a citizen of the Republic of Ireland, she is now entitled to her full personal allowances against any income liable to UK income tax[7]. Thus if a separated or divorced wife who is a Commonwealth citizen is resident abroad and has a qualifying child resident with her, she may claim the personal allowance (£3,005 for 1990-91) and the additional personal allowance (£1,720 for 1990-91). Thirdly, a provision in a double tax treaty may exempt maintenance due under a UK order or agreement from UK income tax if the recipient is non-resident. A few treaties (eg

1   ICTA 1988 s 347A(1).
2   ICTA 1988 s 347B(2)(3).
3   FA 1988 s 38(3)(4).
4   FA 1988 s 38(8).
5   FA 1988 s 38(4).
6   FA 1988 s 38(5).
7   ICTA 1988 s 278(2).

UK/Canada, UK/USA) provide that alimony is to be taxed only in the country in which the payee is resident. A considerable number of treaties, even if silent on alimony, provide that income not otherwise dealt with in the treaty is to be taxed only in the country in which the recipient is resident. The fact that maintenance may escape UK income tax by virtue of a double tax treaty does not affect the payer's entitlement to tax relief on the payments.

9.10 Independent taxation — future developments

As the earlier chapters of this book have indicated, the United Kingdom has not yet moved to a tax system under which the tax treatment of the income and assets of individuals is the same whether or not they are married to each other. However the balance of taxation has swung against cohabitation and, if anything, is now in favour of marriage. Virtually all the tax disadvantages of marriage have been removed. Spouses now have their incomes and gains taxed as if they were unmarried rather than have them aggregated, and cohabitees no longer have the ability to claim double mortgage interest relief, or double additional personal allowance if they have two or more children. Indeed a married couple without children are now significantly better off than their unmarried counterpart. The husband is entitled to claim married couple's allowance, and assets can be freely transferred from one spouse to the other with no capital gains tax or inheritance tax penalty.

Of these concessions in favour of marriage perhaps the most anomalous is the married couple's allowance. This was retained mainly to ensure that married men did not suffer a significant drop in their take home pay following the introduction of independent taxation, but in an era of legislation against discrimination on the grounds of sex, it is difficult to see why it can only be deducted from a wife's income if her husband has insufficient taxable income against which to offset it, and even then only on a claim to transfer the unused allowance being made by the husband. It is also difficult to see why marriage, as such, should qualify a couple for higher tax allowances than if they remained unmarried. When responses were made to the Government's 1980 Green Paper *The Taxation of Husband and Wife*[1] there seemed to be some consensus that the married man's allowance should be abolished as part of any reform of the taxation of married couples[2]. The Child Poverty Action Group and the National Council for Civil Liberties both considered that the tax saved through the abolition of the married man's allowance should be used to increase child benefit. If capacity to pay is to be one criterion of a good tax system it is not difficult to advance a case that taxpayers with dependent children should receive greater tax allowances than taxpayers without children, as the capacity of a couple without children to pay income tax is clearly greater than a couple with children where both have the same joint total income.

1 Cmnd 8093.
2 See eg the Meade Committee Report pp 381, 182; *Social Priorities in Taxation* from the Child Poverty Action Group, October 1981; and the National Council for Civil Liberties Guide to Income Tax and Sexual Discrimination.

It may therefore be that in the future the additional personal allowance will be separated from the married couple's allowance and made available to families with children, whether married, cohabiting, or single parent, leaving the married couple's allowance to be phased out. Not the least of the attractions of the additional personal allowance is that, if two or more people are entitled to claim the allowance in respect of the same child, they are free to agree how it should be apportioned between them. This contrasts favourably with the married couple's allowance, which can only be deducted from a wife's income if the husband has insufficient income, and then only if the husband agrees.

A further change of emphasis along the same lines would be a recognition that, apart from married couple's allowance or additional personal allowance, no relief is given through the tax system for families with children; that such relief used to be given in the form of child tax allowances; and that the reason for abolishing child tax allowances and family allowances was to produce an integrated system of child benefit which could be paid in cash to the mother, rather than have the benefit going to the father as was often the effect of child tax allowances. It is therefore a mistake to view child benefit as part of the social security system and preferable to view it as a tax rebate to families with children in much the same way as MIRAS operates as a tax rebate to families with mortgages. Indeed it is much easier to make a case for the abolition over a period of time of mortgage interest relief, except for first time buyers, than it is to make a case for the abolition of child benefit. Child benefit is paid to those with no taxable income (as is MIRAS tax relief), but it is a flat rate benefit so that those with high incomes receive the same benefit as those with low incomes, and are thus less well off than if relief for children was given in the form of child tax allowances. One possible future reform is therefore a recognition that child benefit is in substance a tax relief and should be shown in the national accounts as a reduction from income tax receipts, rather than a social security payment, and that it should be maintained for all taxpayers with dependent children irrespective of their incomes and, in common with personal allowances, should be indexed in line with inflation.

Index